Reflections on the Dawn of Consciousness

REFLECTIONS ON THE DAWN OF CONSCIOUSNESS

JULIAN JAYNES'S BICAMERAL MIND THEORY REVISITED

Edited by

Marcel Kuijsten

Julian Jaynes Society

Publishers Cataloging-in-Publication Data

Kuijsten, Marcel

Reflections on the Dawn of Consciousness: Julian Jaynes's Bicameral Mind
Theory Revisited

Includes bibliographical references and index.

1. Consciousness. 2. Consciousness—History. 3. Psychology.

ISBN-13: 978-0-9790744-0-0
ISBN-10: 0-9790744-0-1

Library of Congress Control Number: 2006936708

Printed in the United States of America

First Edition

Cover design by Marcel Kuijsten.
Cover photograph by Glen Allison/Getty Images.
Back cover photograph by George Dunbar.
Back cover illustration by Julian Jaynes (see Chapter 12).

Julian Jaynes Society
Henderson, NV
www.julianjaynes.org

CONTRIBUTORS

MICHAEL CARR retired from teaching at Otaru University of Commerce in Japan and established a translation company (www.carrconsultants.net) in Hawaii. He has published extensively on Chinese and Japanese linguistics and lexicography, including the *New Japanese-English Character Dictionary*.

SCOTT GREER is Associate Professor and Chair of the Department of Psychology at the University of Prince Edward Island. He is also Editor for the Canadian Psychological Association journal, the *History and Philosophy of Psychology Bulletin*, and is coordinator for the annual Julian Jaynes Conference on Consciousness. Dr. Greer has published over a dozen articles on the history and theory of psychology, with particular emphasis on the history of self research and psychoanalysis.

JOHN HAMILTON retired as Director of Psychology from Gracewood Hospital, the original Georgia facility for the mentally and physically handicapped. Presently he works with Katherine Sturm, therapist, in a research and education project specializing in interpersonal relationships.

JULIAN JAYNES (1920–1997) is author of the influential and controversial book *The Origin of Consciousness in the Breakdown of the Bicameral Mind*. He taught psychology at Princeton University from 1966 to 1990, lectured widely, and published numerous academic articles.

MARCEL KUIJSTEN is Founder and Executive Director of the Julian Jaynes Society. He received his bachelor's degrees in Psychology and English from California State University and his MBA from the University of Nevada, Las Vegas.

JOHN LIMBER is an Associate Professor in the Department of Psychology at the University of New Hampshire where he teaches and investigates topics relating to language, consciousness, and the evolution of primates.

BRIAN J. MCVEIGH teaches in the East Asian Studies Department at the University of Arizona. He has written seven books and researched nationalism, bureaucracy, historical psycholinguistics, education, gender, religion, and linkages between psychology and material culture.

MICHAEL A. PERSINGER is Professor of Behavioral Neuroscience in the Biomolecular Sciences Program at Laurentian University. During the past 40 years he has been investigating the relationship between brain structure and behavior by exposing rodents and human beings to weak, physiologically-patterned magnetic fields. He has published more than 200 technical articles in refereed journals and written six books.

JAN SLEUTELS is Assistant Professor of Philosophy at Leiden University. His teaching and research interests range from metaphysics to philosophy of mind and cognitive science. He is currently working on a large project in media philosophy.

DAVID C. STOVE (1927–1994) taught philosophy at the University of Sydney from 1960 to 1987. He published books on the philosophy of science and on Darwinism as well as numerous academic and controversial articles. His views were atheist and conservative, his style biting.

JUNE F. TOWER and her husband, Walter Tower, were neighbors and friends of Julian Jaynes and his family.

WILLIAM R. WOODWARD took his master's in psychology with Julian Jaynes at Princeton in 1967–1969. His Ph.D. comes from Yale in history of science and medicine. He has published articles on scientific biographies of many psychologists and co-edited four books. He teaches international, ethnic, and political psychology from an historical perspective.

FOREWORD

THE UNDERSTANDING OF OURSELVES and the universe in which we exist has progressed by conceptual increments from the intuitive subjective experiences of specific people. There was Copernicus who removed the human from the center of the universe and Darwin who replaced the explanation of mankind's special creation with a biological process of evolution. Julian Jaynes's theories for the nature of self-awareness, introspection, and consciousness have replaced the assumption of their almost ethereal uniqueness with explanations that could initiate the next change in paradigm for human thought.

During his profound intellectual career Julian Jaynes inferred that the sense of self awareness emerged about four millennia ago when the experiences from the right hemisphere, attributed to external agents such as gods and deities, intercalated with the linguistic properties of left hemispheric function. Language, consciousness, and the sense of self may have emerged as synergistic products of culture. The consequences of these insights are infinite possibilities.

In this book, Marcel Kuijsten and his colleagues have integrated a quintessential collection of original thoughts concerning Jaynes's concepts as well as some of Jaynes's original essays. I have rarely read a manuscript that so eloquently and elegantly examines a complex and pervasive phenomenon. The contributors of this volume have integrated the concepts of psychology, anthropology, archaeology, theology, philosophy, the history of science, and modern neuroscience with such clarity it should be considered an essential text for any student of human experience.

When I first read Jaynes's *The Origin of Consciousness in the Breakdown of the Bicameral Mind*, I understood its essence and that we, as a species, were only a few years away from a technology that might verify his concepts. In the last 15 years a methodology has been developed, thanks to computer software, that has allowed us to stimulate the right hemisphere of the human cerebrum with weak, physiologically-patterned magnetic fields and to facilitate the type of interhemispheric intercalation that Jaynes would have predicted. The sensed presence and the feeling of a "sentient being" can be evoked now in this manner within the laboratory, by experiment, as easily as other psychological phenomena.

Perhaps the greatest lesson we should learn from Jaynes's thoughts and the reception of his ideas by his "peers" is that reflexive rejection of novel concepts is the antithesis to discovery. Science is the pursuit of the unknown and open-mindedness to contentious concepts — not contrived social consensus and grant support for what one should study — is the optimal environment for discovery. I remember very well one of the comments by an anonymous referee when I referenced Jaynes's book for an article ("The Feeling of a Presence and Verbal Meaningfulness in Context of Temporal Lobe Function") Kate Makarec and I had submitted to *Brain and Cognition* (1992). The referee had suggested "remove [the] Jaynes reference, his ideas are no longer relevant." However, I kept the reference because his ideas are very relevant.

Less than a decade later there was experimental support for the right hemispheric involvement of "intrusive" experiences into awareness. Although imaging technology has shown us that the cerebral volume in which "mind space" exists is configurational and complex, the results strongly support Jaynes's essential thesis. But perhaps the most compelling congruence with Jaynes's insights is genetics. Within the last five years science has found that single point mutations on genes can produce permanent changes in speech production. There is now evidence that point mutations, whose mechanisms must still be discerned, can diffuse within decades throughout entire populations.

There have been approximately 15 million changes in our species' genome since our common ancestor with the chimpanzee. There are human accelerated regions in the genome with genes known to be involved in transcriptional regulation and neuro-development. They are expressed within brain structures that would have allowed precisely the types of phenomena that Jaynes predicted had occurred around 3,500 years ago. Related genes, attributed to religious beliefs, are found on the same chromosome (for example, chromosome 10) as propensities for specific forms of epilepsy (partial, with auditory features) and schizophrenia. From what we now know about antibody titres and viral infections, the concept of a relatively swift and pervasive change in the microstructure and function of all human brains is no longer that improbable.

The concepts covered as well as the extrapolations inferred within the chapters of this book herald the questions and the problems with which our consciousness will be confronted within the next century. If religious beliefs are residuals from the bicameral mind, will they hinder the natural evolution of human existence? With the growing electromagnetic matrix of communication systems, within which all of our brains are immersed, will there be an expansion of consciousness with unexpected properties and possibilities? Julian Jaynes opened the door to a revolution of thought about the essence of ourselves. This text allows the reader to be prepared to walk through the doorway.

Michael A. Persinger
October 2006

PREFACE

A S FOUNDER AND EXECUTIVE Director of the Julian Jaynes Society, I receive a steady flow of inquiries and new members that serve as a constant reminder of the continued, worldwide interest in Julian Jaynes and his important ideas.

This project is the culmination of a series of events that started with Jaynes's death in 1997. Up to that point, I, like many others, had remained hopeful that Jaynes's promised second volume, *The Consequences of Consciousness*, would still materialize. After news of his death, my hopes began to diminish. It was at that point that I started the Julian Jaynes Society and began a quest for the unpublished manuscript, with the hopes of having it published posthumously. Inquiries were made by myself and others with the Princeton University Psychology Library, Jaynes's literary executor Professor Marcia Johnson (then at Princeton, now at Yale), Jaynes's publisher Houghton-Mifflin, Jaynes's associates and closest living relatives, and finally the Archives of the History of American Psychology, where many of Jaynes's papers now reside. Disappointingly, no one seemed to have any knowledge of an unpublished manuscript. Several years passed and I reluctantly came to the conclusion that a near-finished version of *The Consequences of Consciousness* did not exist. However, some writing toward the book was completed; primarily drafts of three chapters left out of the first volume (see Chapter 1). Hopefully these chapters will be made available in the near future.

With little hope that more than a few chapters of unpublished material by Jaynes were in existence, a need for new material by other authors became evident. At that point I began preliminary work on a follow up to Jaynes's book. However, I soon realized it would be a major, time-intensive effort involving extensive library research and would take many years to complete. I also knew readers were eager for new material on the bicameral mind and, wanting to get something published in a shorter time frame, the idea for an edited volume arose. I was already acquainted with several authors that had written on Jaynes, I took up contact with others that had an interest in Jaynes's work going back decades, and along the way I discovered new authors as well. My initial requests for contributed chapters were met with great enthusiasm, and by the spring of 2005 the current project was underway.

Although it is briefly summarized in various chapters, this book presumes an understanding of Jaynes's theory. If you are not already familiar with Jaynes's ideas, or if you just need a refresher, I suggest you start by reading his lecture "Consciousness and the Voices of the Mind," which provides a good overview of the theory. This article can be downloaded from the Julian Jaynes Society website (www.julianjaynes.org) in the "Articles by Julian Jaynes" section. Of course, there is no substitute for reading Jaynes's book, *The Origin of Consciousness in the Breakdown of the Bicameral Mind*, in its entirety. As of this writing, it is still in print and widely available, and, if you have not already done so, I would strongly encourage you to read it before or concurrently with the present volume. I would also like to encourage you to visit the Julian Jaynes Society companion website for this book (www.julianjaynes.org/book) which contains supplementary material and a discussion forum where you can discuss the topics in this book with the authors and other readers.

Marcel Kuijsten
September 2006

CONTENTS

Let us expand, live much, and be many things, and not shirk the complexity of the world or of ourselves.

— Julian Jaynes

Reflections on the Dawn of Consciousness

Introduction

MARCEL KUIJSTEN

All great truths begin as blasphemies.

— George Bernard Shaw

IT HAS NOW BEEN 30 years since Julian Jaynes first published *The Origin of Consciousness in the Breakdown of the Bicameral Mind*. In it he presented his theory that consciousness was a learned process based on complex metaphorical language, developed after the advent of writing to handle the growing complexities of large societies and trade between differing cultures. Jaynes asserts that prior to the development of consciousness around the end of the 2nd millennium B.C., humans operated under a previous mentality called the bicameral mind, referring to the brain's two hemispheres. When faced with a difficult decision or fight or flight situation, bicameral man experienced an auditory hallucination directing his action, much as modern schizophrenics do today. These hallucinations, the means by which the right hemisphere conveyed stored up experience in the form of behavioral commands to the left hemisphere, were interpreted as the voices of chiefs, rulers, or the gods. To support his theory, Jaynes draws evidence from a wide range of fields, including neuroscience, psychology, archeology, ancient history, and the analysis of ancient texts.[1]

Initially, Jaynes's bicameral mind theory was met with several enthusiastic reviews and a few criticisms. But over the decades that followed, there have been few in-depth discussions, either positive or negative. Why has there not been more academic discussion? Of course critics would argue it is because Jaynes was wrong. But I think this answer is too simplistic.

While there are probably many reasons, William Woodward noted that "one is tempted to reserve judgment on such a daring thesis as this, realizing that it demands an impossibly broad range of knowledge to endorse or refute."[2] The majority of research today focuses on incremental advances in highly specialized fields of study. The complexity of the theory — its broad, multidisciplinary approach — makes it challenging for any one individual to properly evaluate.

Scientists are inherently skeptical (and rightly so) of any theory that proposes sweeping changes to our view of history. Most academics would not want to risk their credibility by advocating the theory only to discover Jaynes had it wrong in an area outside their expertise. Few would risk being considered naïve for advocating a bold theory in the event that it is later disproved. And so it has gone on for decades, with academics and lay people alike the world over maintaining a quiet interest in Jaynes's theory while patiently waiting for someone to come along to either support or disprove it.

I often hear the question, "Why isn't Jaynes a household name like Darwin or Freud?" I think this has more to do with the fact that the world has changed than with the validity of his ideas. Darwin and Freud came before movies, television, major league sports, and an exponential growth in the number of scientists and academic journals. Contemporary scientists are rarely well known outside of academia. Einstein was probably the last truly famous scientist; Carl Sagan was well known by the general public, but as a spokesperson for science, not for his scientific work.

Jaynes's ideas remain as relevant today as when they were first published. We are no closer to solving the problem of consciousness than we were 30 years ago, and Jaynes's thinking remains ahead of much of the contemporary literature on the topic. Jaynes's ideas have recently received renewed attention due to both an increased interest in the topic of consciousness and studies using advanced brain imaging techniques showing support for some of his early predictions.[3]

Objections to Jaynes's Theory

The issue of the complexity of Jaynes's theory and its multi-disciplinary nature is one possible reason for the absence of greater formal discussion on the topic. But perhaps the most common reason for the rejection of Jaynes's theory is due to a misunderstanding (or complete lack of awareness) of Jaynes's definition of consciousness; there have been countless times I've heard someone offer a strong opinion on Jaynes only to discover they've never read his book.

The notion that ancient civilizations were populated by unconscious people generates a knee-jerk response that the theory is "preposterous," primarily because of the deeply ingrained but mistaken notion that consciousness is necessary for the majority of higher mental processes (and even basic sensory perception), coupled with the tremendous difficulty in compre-hending a mental state without an internal dialogue for anyone that has one. Thus there is a widespread lack of understanding of Jaynes's more precise definition of consciousness. Put simply, critics reject the notion of pre-conscious civilizations prior to 1200 B.C. based on *their* definition of consciousness, not Jaynes's.[4]

Definitions of consciousness have become diluted to the point where there are as many interpretations of its meaning as there are of the word "god." While Jaynes goes to great lengths to carefully describe his operational definition of consciousness,[5] many either still misunderstood it or in many cases prejudged his ideas without reading his discussion of the term. When Jaynes describes early civilizations as being populated by people who have not yet developed consciousness, he is not implying these were civilizations of "zombies" in the popular sense of the term. A clear understanding of Jaynes's definition of consciousness dispels this notion. When Jaynes compares the bicameral mentality to the state of somnambulism, this is meant only to illustrate the lack of a sense of self, a lack of introspection and internal dialogue, and an inability to think about time in a linear fashion. Bicameral man was intelligent, had language, was highly social, and could think and problem-solve; only these processes took place in the absence of an introspectable internal mind space.

The problem over the definition of consciousness persists today, with many articles and books written on the topic of consciousness all describing different things. For example, neurologists often use the term to describe simply a waking, alert state, i.e., not being anesthetized, comatose, or knocked unconscious. For this Jaynes uses the more precise term "reactivity." Clinical psychologist Robert Kretz, in his doctoral dissertation on the bicameral mind, opted to avoid confusion over the term by replacing it with the phrase "modern self awareness."[6] Anthropologist Brian McVeigh devoted an article to the problem, commenting that "students of mind use terms — such as consciousness, cognition, awareness, thinking, experience, and subjectivity — rather loosely, often interchangeably, and at times without working definitions."[7]

Jaynes recognized this problem as well, commenting that perhaps if he had given the book the title, "The Origin of Conscious Experience in the Breakdown of the Bicameral Mind," it might not have met with such resistance. However, he preferred to "remain with consciousness as Locke and Descartes and most other people — including behaviorists — would define it: as what is introspectable."[8] Those that use the term consciousness when discussing cognition, awareness, or sensory perception should opt for more precise language.

In a recent lecture at the Julian Jaynes Conference on Consciousness,[9] Brian McVeigh discussed the problem of multiple definitions of consciousness, as well as related barriers to understanding Jaynes's theory, such as the assumption that cognition is primarily conscious, the equating of consciousness with perception, and in general a lack of amazement at the very existence of consciousness, with consciousness often being taken for granted.

Beyond the confusion surrounding the definition of consciousness, McVeigh described additional obstacles to understanding Jaynes's theory, such as the fact that, in its effort to become a "hard science," mainstream psychology generally ignores anomalous psychological behavior such as hypnosis, spiritualist mediums, automatic writing, glossolalia, spirit possession, and poetic and religious frenzy — issues central to understanding Jaynes's ideas. McVeigh also discussed the tendency in academia to ignore history as a source of evidence and insight for appreciating the "psychic diversity and psychic plasticity of the human condition."[10]

Finally, the role of hallucinations in Jaynes's theory causes some to dismiss it out of hand. Without examining Jaynes's evidence, hallucinations seem too alien an experience for some to accept that they once played such a major role in human mentality. While other reasons undoubtedly exist — for example, the implications of Jaynes's theory for religion — these are probably the most important.

The Politics of Academia

In addition to objections to the theory, the politics of academia also present an obstacle to the acceptance of Jaynes's ideas for several reasons. First, areas of research that do not generate grants and publications are largely ignored by professors seeking tenure at large universities. Also, a certain amount of dogmatism exists in mainstream psychology, and topics that cannot be explained are brushed aside as nonexistent or unimportant. Thus, while this is slowly beginning to change, the study of consciousness has in general not been viewed as an area of viable research.[11]

Furthermore, due to the explosion of scientific research in the last 50 years, most scientists are, out of necessity, highly specialized. Careers are built conducting cutting edge research in narrow fields of investigation. It is difficult to advance in academia without this level of intense specialization, and as a result, broad, multidisciplinary theories are not encouraged and when they do appear, they are often overlooked. For example, Egyptologists typically are unfamiliar with clinical psychology and psychologists and psychiatrists rarely analyze ancient historical figures or religious texts.[12] Yet this type of broad approach is essential to understanding Jaynes's theory, which draws on a range of disciplines. The lack of discussion of Jaynes's ideas in academic psychology may in turn lead clinicians to question its overall validity, even though they have in general been the most interested in his theory because of their direct experience with clinical populations.[13]

Although Jaynes was in academia, he remained somewhat of an outsider throughout his career. Jaynes lectured part-time at Princeton University and never pursued a tenure track position. Yet this is perhaps what allowed him the freedom and flexibility to devote so much of his time to his own work and the development of his ideas, rather than having to focus on obtaining research grants and publishing articles in scholarly journals on a consistent basis.

The History of Ideas

Lack of mainstream academic publications regarding the bicameral mind theory does not equate with well-reasoned arguments against it. While there have been some criticisms and alternate interpretations, none, I think, invalidate the theory and all fail to offer alternate, more convincing hypotheses for many of the phenomena Jaynes describes.[14] Many of the issues central to understanding Jaynes's theory remained unexplained. For example, why are auditory hallucinations found on a continuum throughout society? Why do hallucinations often command or direct behavior? If consciousness is not a relatively recent, learned process, how is it that through hypnosis and "spirit possession" it can so easily be altered? Why are gods and idols ubiquitous throughout the ancient world? What can better account for the emergence of oracles and divination? In criticisms of Jaynes's theory these questions are not addressed, and attempts to explain them by others remain largely unsatisfactory.

There is a long history of scientific ideas that were first ignored or rejected but that later turned out to be correct. While an entire book could be written on the subject of resistance to new ideas and related topics such as the nature of belief systems and the process of opinion formation, I will mention just a few examples.[15] Arguably the most famous example is Copernicus, who, in the mid-1500s, proposed the heliocentric or "Sun centered" model of the solar system (actually first proposed by Aristarchus in 270 B.C.). Up to that time the generally accepted view, put forth by Ptolemy in the 2nd century A.D., was that the Earth stood fixed and motionless at the center of the universe, and the Sun, stars, and planets revolved around the Earth. With a few exceptions, Copernicus's model received little attention by his contemporaries and was not widely known by those outside of astronomy — in part due to fear of persecution by the Church. It was not until it was promoted by Galileo nearly 75 years later that the idea slowly began to gain acceptance. Gregor Mendel, now considered the "Father of Genetics," published a report on heredity in 1865 that had no impact on the scientific community, but finally received the attention it deserved in 1900 — 16 years after his death.[16]

While Charles Darwin's theory of evolution was immediately accepted by many scholars, nearly 150 years later it is still either unaccepted or widely misunderstood by a majority of people. Sigmund Freud's *The Interpretation of Dreams* only sold a few hundred copies in the first several years after it was published and initially had very little impact, but later became highly influential to the field of psychology. The theory of continental drift proposed by Alfred Wegener in 1915 was not initially accepted because scientists could not conceive of a method by which the massive continents could move, even though similar fossils were found in South America and Africa and any child could look at a map of the world and see that the two continents fit roughly together. It was not until 1965 that the idea gained acceptance when Canadian geophysicist J. Tuzo Wilson combined the continental drift and seafloor spreading hypotheses to propose the theory of plate tectonics.

Despite the lack of academic debate, Jaynes's bicameral mind theory continues to generate discussion 30 years after its publication. Interest in the topic of consciousness has grown steadily over the past two decades and with it has come a renewed interest in Jaynes's ideas: Jaynes continues to be cited in books on a variety of subjects, neurological research relevant to Jaynes's bicameral mind was the topic of a doctoral dissertation by clinical psychologist Robert Kretz, Danish science writer Tor Nørretranders devoted a chapter to Jaynes's theory in his book on consciousness, and British psychotherapist Heward Wilkinson has written on the significance of Jaynes's ideas to therapy. In addition, new neurological evidence for the involvement of the right hemisphere in hallucinations has renewed interest in Jaynes's theory in scientific publications.[17] Jaynes's book continues to sell steadily, and the Julian Jaynes Conference on Consciousness was recently organized by psychology professor Scott Greer at the University of Prince Edward Island to discuss both Jaynes's theory and the topic of consciousness in general. Jaynes's ideas have tremendous significance for the understanding of our history, our contemporary culture, and our ongoing conscious evolution. Perhaps through continued discussion the importance of Jaynes's theory will eventually be recognized by the wider academic community.

NOTES TO THE INTRODUCTION

1. For a more in-depth explanation of Jaynes's theory see "Consciousness and the Voices of the Mind," which can be downloaded from the Julian Jaynes Society (www.julianjaynes.org) in the "Articles by Julian Jaynes" section.
2. Woodward, 1979.
3. New evidence for Jaynes's theory is the topic of Chapter 4.
4. For further discussion of this see Chapter 6.
5. See Jaynes, 1976, pp. 21–66.
6. Kretz, 2000.
7. McVeigh, 1993.
8. Jaynes, 1986.
9. More information on Jaynes-related conferences and events can be found at www.julianjaynes.org.
10. McVeigh, 2006.
11. There is a great deal of pressure toward conformity in psychology beginning with students. Undergraduates planning to go on to graduate school gain experience and improve their chances for acceptance by assisting with the research of a professor at their university. When I was applying to doctoral programs in neuroscience, it was suggested by a well intentioned professor that I remove the reference to Jaynes as one of my interests from my letters of introduction. This unfortunately was good advice, as in order to be accepted to a graduate program, typically a professor has to decide you are a good match to work in his or her lab, which means sharing their research interests. The focus often is not on finding someone with diverse interests or original ideas but on selecting someone that will be a productive lab assistant. Graduate students work in their professor's lab and publish articles related to their professor's research, often in the same area they studied as an undergraduate. Branching off into new areas or attempting to publish original research is difficult and (while there are exceptions) usually not encouraged.
12. There are a few exceptions, such as Flemish psychologist Dr. Herman Somers, who studies the psychopathology of Biblical prophets and the prophet Mohammed, and the partnership of psychiatrist Jerome Kroll and historian Bernard Bachrach, who study the psychology of medieval religious figures.
13. Jaynes, 1986.

14. For recent critical discussions of Jaynes's theory, see Johnson, 2003 and Leudar and Thomas, 2000. Both arguments, I think, contain major flaws, which I will address in a future article.
15. For examples in this section, see Watson, 2005.
16. Henig, 2001.
17. Kretz, 2000; Nørretranders, 1999; Wilkinson, 1999; Olin, 1999; Sher, 2000. For a more complete list of related books and articles please see www.julianjaynes.org.

REFERENCES

Dennett, D. 1986. "Julian Jaynes's Software Archeology." *Canadian Psychology*, 27, 2, 149–154.

Henig, R.M. 2001. *The Monk in the Garden: The Lost and Found Genius of Gregor Mendel, the Father of Genetics*. Mariner Books.

Jaynes, J. 1976. *The Origin of Consciousness in the Breakdown of the Bicameral Mind*. Boston: Houghton-Mifflin.

Jaynes, J. 1986. "Consciousness and the Voices of the Mind." *Canadian Psychology*, 27, 2, 128.

Johnson, D.M. 2003. *How History Made the Mind: The Cultural Origins of Objective Thinking*. Open Court Publishing Company.

Kretz, R.K. 2000. "The Evolution of Self-awareness: Advances in Neurological Understandings Since Julian Jaynes's 'Bicameral Mind.'" *Dissertation Abstracts International: Section B: The Sciences & Engineering*, 60, 12-B, 6413.

Leudar, I. and P. Thomas. 2000. *Voices of Reason, Voices of Insanity: Studies of Verbal Hallucinations*. Florence, KY: Taylor & Francis/Routledge.

McVeigh, B. 1993. "Beyond Confusion: Culture, Cognition, and Consciousness." *Cross Culture*, 11.

McVeigh, B. 2006. "Overcoming Intellectual Barriers to Understanding Jaynes' Theory." Paper presented at the *Julian Jaynes Conference on Consciousness*, University of Prince Edward Island, August 4–5.

Nørretranders, T. 1999. *The User Illusion: Cutting Consciousness Down to Size*. Penguin Books.

Olin, R. 1999. "Auditory Hallucinations and the Bicameral Mind." *Lancet*, 354, 9173, 166.

Sher, L. 2000. "Neuroimaging, Auditory Hallucinations, and the Bicameral Mind." *Journal of Psychiatry & Neuroscience*, 25, 3, 239–40.

Watson, P. 2005. *Ideas: A History of Thought and Invention, from Fire to Freud*. HarperCollins.

Woodward, W. 1979. "Review of *The Origin of Consciousness*." *Isis*, June, 70, 293.

PART I

Julian Jaynes

CHAPTER 1

Julian Jaynes

Introducing His Life and Thought

WILLIAM R. WOODWARD
&
JUNE F. TOWER

I N THE EARLY 1840s the railroad from Boston made its way eight miles west to forever change the way of life of the small farming community at West Newton. Healthful countryside now lay less than an hour's journey from Boston. Adding to this natural attraction, educator Horace Mann brought the progressive State Normal School for Girls and its Model School for Children to West Newton in 1844. Soon fellow educators joined him as did other forward thinkers and their families. Abolition was a popular cause and a wide variety of new ideas found an audience in the growing enlightened community. Those of a liberal theological persuasion, not satisfied with the long established Congregational Church, began their own meetings and in 1848 organized the First Unitarian Society in Newton.

By the mid-1880s, when members of the Jaynes family first arrived in the now prosperous suburb of West Newton, the population had grown to over 3,000. The intellectual fervor had mellowed but not gone away. Woods and farmlands were gradually being replaced by the comfortable homes and large estates of prosperous Boston businessmen and professionals. Most of the new residents, as well as the old, were of old New England stock, thrifty of habit, honest and forthright, and tending to be Congregational or Unitarian in belief.

Despite some alterations in lifestyles and architectural fashions and the beginnings of ethnic diversity, the turn of the century and the four decades to follow saw little change in habit. Life in West Newton marched onward much as it had before. And so it was when Julian Jaynes was born there on February 27, 1920, in a large green shingled house at 76 Prince Street near the top of the hill overlooking the busy village center and the railroad that had long since crossed the continent.

New England Ancestry

Julian's family came from a world of serious purpose and moral principle rooted in the ways of their Puritan forefathers, yet they looked forward with liberating theology and with happy acceptance of the prosperity and comforts that had come their way. His maternal grandfather, George Bullard, grew up on a prosperous farm southwest of Boston where Sunday mornings were spent at the Congregational Church and Sunday afternoons were spent quietly reading the Bible. Christmas, in Puritan style, was not celebrated at all. His maternal grandmother, Nina Jenks, came from a more liberal family of Universalists from the neighboring town where they met in high school in the 1870s. A decade later, after their marriage and arrival in West Newton, George and Nina Bullard joined the First Unitarian Society in Newton now led by a recent Harvard Divinity School graduate, the Rev. Julian Clifford Jaynes. His roots, too, lay in New England, although he had been born on a pre-Civil War plantation in northern Virginia that was bought by his Connecticut-bred father so that he might buy slaves and free them.

From his family background and childhood, the young Julian Jaynes, like every child, took what he needed and built upon it. The resulting combination of freedom of belief and principled action would underpin almost everything he undertook, letting his mind soar forward without the constraints of religious fears and superstitions, but sometimes allowing his staunch courage and adherence to principle to serve to his detriment.

Julian's father, the Rev. Julian Clifford Jaynes, at 66 years old, had been minister of the First Unitarian Society of Newton for 35 years when Julian was born. Clara Bullard Jaynes, 30 years younger, was the Rev. Jaynes's second wife, a cultured, active woman with literary and musical interests who played the bells in the church's tower. She had traveled with her well-to-do parents in Europe, thanks to her father's success in the iron and steel business and his banking and railroad interests. Julian, the middle child, grew up with an older sister, Helen, and a younger brother, Robert.

Sadness entered their lives early on when the Rev. Jaynes died of a heart attack in June 1922, while the family was aboard a train ferry en route to Prince Edward Island, Canada, and their summer home overlooking the sea at Keppoch near Charlottetown. (At the time, the train went onto the ferry at the New Brunswick terminal, crossed the Straits of Northumberland, disembarked at Borden, Prince Edward Island, and then continued on to Charlottetown. There is a model of it in the Maritime Museum in Halifax, Nova Scotia.) Clara Jaynes was left to raise three small children by herself. She chose to keep her Keppoch home, which her husband had bought for her. They continued to spend their summers at Keppoch. Eventually Clara Jaynes lived there year-round. She died in Charlottetown in 1980 in her 96th year.

Unitarian Childhood

In West Newton, Julian grew up in the big family home where he was born, a house that the congregation had built for the Rev. Jaynes in 1895. Julian once told an interviewer: "What some would think a disadvantage, growing up in a fatherless home, didn't seem so at the time. There was a single parent and a father was spiritually present, so to speak, and he didn't have any faults because he wasn't there to show them."[1] His father's possessions stayed in the house, along with stories to go with them. On the third floor, the Rev. Jaynes's study contained 48 volumes of his sermons that his son Julian delved into for many years.

Beyond the family home, Julian found further reminders of his father's life in the handsome stone church that the Rev. Jaynes had been instrumental in building in 1905. The carvings and stained glass windows he had chosen celebrated important people and events in Christianity's long road to reform. Julian learned their stories but when asked if he was planning to follow in his father's footsteps he answered "no."[2]

In 1922, the newly widowed Clara Jaynes published a fitting memorial to her departed husband, a book of his sermons selected from the volumes in his study that she titled *Magic Wells*. Clara chose to open the book with a sermon about the woman of Samaria. It began with a Scripture reading from John 4:15: "The woman saith unto him, Sir, give me this water, that I thirst not, neither come hither to draw." The Rev. Jaynes had spoken these words:

> No more weary trudging to Jacob's well! No more climbing up on the hot pathway to the cottage door! Something for nothing! Blessing without effort. The magician's world at last, where to wish is to have and to ask is to receive! And so she eagerly cries, "Give me to drink of this water, that I thirst no more, neither come hither to draw!" And this woman's pathetic appeal is with us to-day. Nay, we have heard it through all the history of the past, breaking in now and then with its sad refrain, upon the marching music of the world, like plaintive echoes from the far-away Eden of indolence and ease.[3]

Unitarians worship the god within us all and in nature in their churches called "societies." Explained the Rev. Jaynes: "Consider the principle in its application to what we call the practical affairs of life." He went on, "The god of luck is dead. But opportunity is alive."[4]

> On and on we go — more burdens, more temptations, more crosses! And through it all, what? A poor, worn-out, mutilated life? No! But an ever increasing capacity — wider visions, stronger powers, tenderer sympathies, better knowledge of ourselves, better knowledge of what life means, a quickening in the thrill and stir of holy war, and moments of spiritual exaltation, moments of divine peace, moments of conscious victory that are worth more than a million years among the flowers and sweetmeats of the dreamed-of Paradise.[5]

It is likely Julian, the reflective, sensitive, dreamer of a son, who lost his father at age two, read and reread this opening sermon in his father's book of sermons as arranged by his mother. He must have admired the cadence of his father's speech, indeed he may have read these sermons aloud, then fancied that he heard his father's voice. As he grew older, he would have pondered the meaning of "wider visions, stronger powers." Humankind is evolving, as he learned in high school biology and college philosophy, "better knowledge of ourselves, better knowledge of what life means." Forget original sin, his father had implied by scoffing at "more temptations, more crosses." Behold instead "moments of conscious victory that are worth more than a million years among the flowers and sweet-meats of the dreamed-of Paradises." Julian carried this message with him through life.

As a very bright, sensitive, and inquisitive boy, Julian did well in school but sometimes found himself a bit out of step with his classmates. He received a fine education at his West Newton elementary and junior high schools and later at Newton High School where he enjoyed writing and history, but found mathematics to be his favorite subject. He also learned piano and tennis, commenting much later on their implications for consciousness: "And anyone who plays tennis at my indifferent level knows the exasperation of having his service suddenly 'go to pieces' and of serving consecutive double faults! The more doubles, the more conscious one becomes of one's motions (and of one's disposition!) and the worse things get. ... The present writer improvises on the piano, and his best playing is when he is not conscious of the performance side as he invents new themes or developments, but only when he is somnambulistic about it and is conscious of his playing only as if he were another person."[6]

Peripatetic College Years

Julian graduated from Newton High School in the spring of 1937 and went off to the University of Virginia that fall. He wrote home telling his mother that the second term was "much harder," that he had earned 97 in mathematics and a 92 in biology; "on the other hand, my English is better, my French is coming up."[7] He also gave an accounting of his expenditures and assured her that he could get along on $450 until the fall semester. By May, he was weighing a degree with honors at the University of Virginia against Harvard, which he called "the best university in a dirty city." He liked the fact that Virginia had a tutor system patterned after Oxford:

> No exams except for a long very difficult, comprehensive exam at the end of his senior year; all he does is read, read, read, read, and after that read some more; but it is not a grind, for you study only those topics you wish to; you are assigned to a tutor, who is a full-fledged

professor. (Mr. Shepparson is one of these.) With this
tutor, you discuss weekly your reading.[8]

In fact, he transferred to Harvard College but again only for a
year. In late summer 1939, with his father's Unitarian principles
(and perhaps his voice) resonating in his consciousness, Julian
went to Newton City Hall and asked to be put on a list of
conscientious objectors in case America should go to war.

A few days later he left for Montreal at a time when Canada
had just gone to war. Finances had become a problem — his
maternal grandfather's death and the great depression had
sapped the family of its affluence. A scholarship to McGill
University won out over being a day student at Harvard. The
common denominator of his undergraduate education became
philosophy. He grew particularly fond of Professor George Brett
at McGill. From him he adopted a perspective on the entire
history of thought. However, Brett's *History of Psychology* was too
scholastic, too rooted in traditional Catholic theology. Tripartite
souls, rationalism, and empirical psychology did not strike a
chord in Julian, though they circled around the problem of
consciousness. He found his two years at McGill challenging
and rewarding, even though he had not found answers to his
questions about consciousness in either philosophy or psychology. He graduated in the spring of 1941 with a bachelor's
degree in psychology.

Next he enrolled in graduate school in psychology at the
University of Toronto to learn more about the brain. Here he
wrote his mother that he was "up to my neck in work." He
consoled her regarding her regrets about her daughter, Helen:

> You brought up three children alone — the best way
> you knew how. I wish I could have you read some of
> the case histories of families we have here in the psyc.
> dept. so you could compare your methods to those of

others. I think you would feel better. ... Such would show you the true roles that parents play in a child's development, how the parents control only a small part of the child's environment, and how such personalities as Helen's are entirely unexplainable in terms of any environmental influences. When you say you still hope for a change in Helen, I may disagree with you but your faith is your business, not mine. But when you say that you are to blame for what Helen is, then, as a psychologist I say you are absolutely wrong.[9]

Clara apparently felt responsible for Helen's bouts with mental illness. Jaynes at 22 here espoused the view that personality develops largely through maturation of inborn dispositions, consistent with his later embrace of instinct theory.

Conscientious Objection as Principled Resistance

In the summer of 1942, following college and a year of graduate school, and with the U.S. now part of the Allied Forces, Jaynes registered for the draft and received his conscientious objector status. He owned the ninth printing (July 1, 1942) of the pamphlet, *The Conscientious Objector under the Selective Training and Service Act of 1940*, whose National Service Board for Religious Objectors contained a Consultative Council with 27 denominations, including the "Unitarian Pacifist Fellowship." He was sent to a Civilian Service work camp near Thornton, New Hampshire. Three months later he wrote to the Attorney General of the United States that

On September 3rd, 1942, I entered Civilian Public Service Camp #32, having previously been classified IV-E. I am now leaving camp. In so doing I am violating the Selective Training and Service Act of 1940 as amended, refusing allegiance to a law which I cannot conscientiously comply with, and acknowledging the compromise I have made. ... Speaking as a pacifist, there are two main reasons behind my position:

(1) The Selective Training and Service Act of 1940 is an integral part of the war effort; to conform to it is to conform to war policy of the government. ...

(2) The principle of nationalistic conscription is a totalitarian measure and a type of government; to acquiesce in it is to approve of the principle and the sort of government which it establishes. ...

Is conforming to the government's war measures a pacifist protest against war? Can we work within the logic of an evil system for its destruction? Jesus did not think so; neither did Debs [Eugene Debs, the labor leader 1855–1926, five-time Socialist candidate for President], nor Gandhi in India. Nor do I.[10]

He apparently walked away from the camp and was soon arrested. While awaiting trial at home in West Newton, he wrote a letter to *The Boston Globe* in which he mentioned that Jesus preached love as "the only successful way," and that Gandhi is "regarded as a prophet by 300 million men" and is called a "traitor" when he "applies the moral principles of Jesus to international struggle."[11] Jaynes was a man of principle, some might say impulsively and even recklessly so. He seemed to draw energy from jousting windmills, somewhat like Miguel De Cervantes's hero Don Quixote de la Mancha.

Prison Life and Family Support

At his trial in New Hampshire the judge found no sympathy for Jaynes's cause and sentenced him to four years at the U.S. Penitentiary at Lewisburg, Pennsylvania, a medium security facility that housed many other conscientious objectors among its population. War resistance was not a popular choice in 1942 and prison a concept far removed from Jaynes's family experience, but his family accepted that Julian had done what he felt he must and tried to be supportive. Distance, prison rules, and wartime fuel shortages limited visits but letters kept them in touch.

His sister Helen, 18 months older than Julian, had attended Smith College but left before graduating. She now had found wartime work with a Boston defense contractor. Later she would marry but soon divorce. Though musically and artistically talented, her ongoing mental illness, later worsened by alcoholism, kept her from any sustained happiness or success. At the end of her life other physical ills overtook her as well and she died at 52 in the fall of 1970.

Robert, his younger brother, shared Julian's pacifist views but chose not to carry them to extremes. He was drafted into the Army as a non-combatant and spent most of his wartime service as an aerial photographer. After the war he returned to college at Miami University in Ohio, graduated in 1947, attended the London School of Economics and later Yale, where he received a master's degree in sociology in 1950. He married, worked for the CIA as a cryptographer for five years, and finally with his wife, Millie, moved to southwestern New Hampshire and a new career working with handicapped people as a counselor and head of the Keene district office of vocational rehabilitation. He suffered a debilitating stroke in 1992 but continued to find pleasure in his rural New Hampshire life and summers on Prince Edward Island. His death came three months before Julian's in 1997.

Jaynes's mother spent her wartime summers in Prince Edward Island but now ran her large home there as an inn where she and her small staff could house several guests and serve meals to quite a few more. It was an attractive place by the sea and she a charming hostess. Her guests returned again and again. At home in West Newton she rented rooms, which helped with her expenses and contributed to alleviating the wartime housing shortage. Finally she rented the whole large house to a family and settled into a small apartment on Beacon Hill in Boston for the duration of the war.

Helen and Robert wrote to Julian at Lewisburg to tell of their activities, people they met, and Bob's wartime experiences. His mother sent encouragement and news of her busy life, and mailed packages as often as she was allowed.

In return Jaynes reported on prison life, often with deliberately cheerful letters:

> With the spring, quite a few birds have come to this part of Pennsylvania — in all 3 of the prisons I have been in, I have found many bird enthusiasts. I guess they are an unconscious symbol of freedom to prisoners. The other day, one of my friends here came back from work excited — for his three years here, he had been watching for a particular species he had seen once before, and today he succeeded.[12]

At other times, the frustrations of prison life were very evident: "It seems that no longer can one have books or magazine subscriptions paid for by someone on the outside — as you subscribed to *Time* and the *Book Review* for me. Everything has to be bought through the commissary now."[13]

Jaynes considered himself fortunate to be assigned to work in the prison hospital where he might learn something and have some contact with the scientific world he hoped to enter. In his free time he happily volunteered to help in the Protestant chapel where he could enjoy playing the organ and plan the music for Sunday services. Alone in his cell he read, studied, and wrote with the puzzle of consciousness never far from his mind. In a tape of recorded reminiscences from 1984, he tells us "It will be 40 years at least since I was there, where so much of my life was determined, since that event out in stockade one spring, when I remember picking up a worm in the grass. There was so little grass there in the stockade and I remember vowing that I would devote my life to finding out the difference between the insensate earth, the sensitive worm, and my thinking self."[14]

A few days before his release he wrote to his mother:

> No doubt you have received the package I sent home by express. It contains some journals, a book, and my notes, various and sundry, accumulated over three years.
>
> It is going to be very odd coming out of prison — I have become so accustomed to life here, falling into a quiet and uneventful routine between my work and my cell, month after month, year after year, hardly noticing the seasons as they came and went outside my window. In spite of the frustration, there was a certain peace about it which was conducive to thought. And thinking is something I would rather do than anything else.[15]

On May 30, 1946, he was discharged from Lewisburg, a year in advance of his sentence, "based on commutation for good conduct." At 26, he would enroll next in psychology at Yale University, hoping that in animal behavior he would find clues to the beginnings of consciousness.

Graduate School in Experimental Psychology

Over the next three years, 1946 to 1949, Jaynes lived, breathed, and thought experimental research on animals. Legend has it that he slept in a large heating duct underneath Yale University, where he put himself on a work schedule independent of the sun and stars. Like graduate students then and now, he earned his keep as a "research assistant." He was mentored ultimately by Frank Beach and, in the spring of 1949, completed a dissertation on the maternal behavior of animals of different species. "Only by encouraging and supporting a larger number of comparative investigations can psychology justify its claim to being a true science of behavior," Beach had written. "To put the question bluntly: Are we building a general science of behavior or merely a science of rat learning?"[16] In the heyday of behaviorists Clark Hull at Yale, E.C. Tolman at Berkeley, and B.F. Skinner at Harvard, these remarks constituted a head-on challenge to a prominent direction in psychology. Instead of rodents, Beach especially urged scientists to study instinctive behavior in a wider spectrum of subhuman species. Jaynes took up the challenge that Beach set out and expanded it beyond experimental psychology and ethology to the entire history of observations about animals and humans. Beach had skillfully integrated a broad knowledge of invertebrates, hormones, and sexual behavior with psychology.[17] Jaynes would go further to integrate vertebrates and invertebrates with historical, theological, and archeological evidence into a bold theory of consciousness.

Jaynes's master's degree was awarded by Yale in the spring of 1948 and he was scheduled to receive his Ph.D. in the following year; however Jaynes did not actually receive his Ph.D. in 1949. He told me (WRW) that the Ph.D. is a license that can produce conformity and reduce originality. He also mentioned that he thought the $25 fee required by Yale was unjustified because he had earned the Ph.D. He told June Tower and her husband, and other West Newton friends, that a senior faculty member had disagreed with him on some point and he refused the degree rather than change something he knew to be right. There were other stories as well. In matters of educational credentials, a principle was at stake. A principle goes beyond the person because it stands for the people and posterity, to paraphrase three-time presidential candidate William Jennings Bryant. The principle that institutions can corrupt independent thought, be it the military or the university, resonated deep in his Unitarian character.

Interlude in Theater Abroad

Having finished his work at Yale without finding an answer to his questions about the beginnings of consciousness, without his Ph.D. for entrance into the academic world, and deeply saddened by the manic-depressive illness of Martha Dimock, the woman he loved, Jaynes boarded a ship at the end of the summer to sail to Great Britain, where away from all he had known he could ponder the next turn in his self-commitment to the puzzle of consciousness while leading a very different life. In October 1949, he settled in Salisbury, England, where he performed and wrote theater pieces through 1953. He wrote for an English audience, submitting his scripts to stage companies. His thespian life and numerous plays deserve a separate chapter. For example, "The Liar" is a farce about Dominic the male liar and Verity the truth-seeking maiden in a tempestuous sequence of deceptions. Finally, "[f]ace to face in their true selves, Dominic and Verity agree they do love each other, and that in a world where deception is inevitable, truth in human relationships is only in the love binding them together" (Act V Synopsis).

Another play titled "Night is My Kingdom" revolves around Edward, King of England, who is faced with a challenge by powerful lords, Harold and his brother Tostig. "The king no more understands their heroic patriotism and code of honor, than do they understand his sentimental love for all mankind and his religious view of life. ... The play ends with the funeral of King Edward and the coronation of Harold in 1066" (from the Synopsis). Other titles are "The Lover," "The Hater," "The Holy Grail," "Thomas Masaryk: A Tragedy in Two Acts," and "The Battle of Bluebird Lane." All are farces conveying the ironies of human frailties, perhaps caricatured best by "The Lover," in which a Mr. Scrutable suspects his wife of unfaithfulness, and Mrs. Scrutable then suspects him of same, and it takes place "in the city of Camelot in the legendary present."

Early Career in Experimental Learning and Ethology

Jaynes returned to Yale from 1954 to 1960 as an Instructor and Lecturer. He published with Beach, first his dissertation on the effects of early experience in animals, then three studies on maternal retrieving in rats, and three more on neural mediation of mating in male cats.[18] He also published four of five parts of his dissertation: "Imprinting: The Interaction of Learned and Innate Behavior."[19] This was reprinted in a Bobbs-Merrill series,[20] establishing his reputation by age 40 in the field of ethology, the study of animals in their natural habitats. The experimental field of animal learning in which he had studied in the late 1940s and early 1950s produced endless variations on learning in the laboratory. At that time Jaynes joined the new ethology movement in questioning learning as studied under artificial laboratory conditions from the perspective of inherited, unlearned instincts in natural environments. Thus his early work, guided by Frank Beach, addressed imprinting in neonate chicks in their first few days of life. Jaynes discovered that imprinting improved with speed of the artificial stimulus, size (green cardboard cubes of 4, 7, and 10 inches on a side), and practice. He followed with particular interest the emotional changes of the chicks, ranging from distress to contentment, hypothesizing that they "may act as a kind of autoreinforcement in the acquisition of filial responses."[21] This work belongs at the crossroads of European field ethology and the North American experimental learning research, and it hints at his ongoing interest in consciousness.

E.G. Boring as Mentor in History of Comparative Psychology

Jaynes's return to his field of animal learning had not brought useful answers to his questions about consciousness. Discouraged once more, he left by ship for England, arriving in Southampton on October 28, 1960. Again he lived in Salisbury for a three year interlude, during which he kept busy acting and writing plays.

The trip back landed in Quebec on October 29, a 13-day journey. Julian always loved to be on the ocean. Early in 1963, at age 42, had come a letter from Edwin G. Boring at Harvard University, long retired at age 77. Boring confided, "It is Frank Beach who puts me up to writing you. ... Frank is uncertain about the address he has given me."[22] To the invitation to write 120 pages on the history of comparative psychology for a Basic Books series, Jaynes answered:

> The tentativeness of my yes consists only of my financial position. To write the volume, I would wish to return to the U.S. where most of my notes and papers are on file. And I shall be sending out a few feelers to friends looking for some half-time work to pay my living expenses with an office and a bit of lab space in some academic setting.[23]

As the historian of comparative psychology Donald Dewsbury remarked, "on completing research in his laboratory, one remained a member of the Beach family."[24] This comment referred to the closeness that developed among the students of Beach.

Jaynes returned to the United States in late October 1963, ready to resume academic life and research. Beach had written to Boring, but neither was able to find Julian a job. In January 1964, Byron Campbell, a former graduate student friend at Yale, arranged a research associate position and work space at Princeton University, which became Jaynes's academic home for the next three decades.

Meanwhile, Scribner's wanted Boring for a series of autobiographies, and Julian's advice to Boring rang true for himself:

> What should a man do? He should choose the work he puts to his hand by some rule of uniqueness, of what he, of all lives in the world and he alone, can best do. ...

But even among psychologists you have a candor that astonishes, a warmth uniquely joined with a devoted, rugged honesty; you are the only one I know who represents the unfortunately disappearing idea that a psychologist enters his profession almost like taking a religion, making himself a part of his own subject matter and baring his soul to the cruelty of objectivity. Can you name me anyone except yourself who fits these words I am rambling on with?[25]

The autobiography never came to pass, but the relationship with Boring continued. Boring wrote:

I am feeling quite gay over Arthur [Rosenthal]'s having acquired you for the Comparative series (with me as a medium, of course). It is working out as the more perfect choice than I could even have anticipated. My bet is that this series will get realized and get started, and that it will make a dent in the courses in comparative psychology. Yours, Gary. Edwin G. Boring.[26]

The next year Boring initially critiqued, then praised Jaynes's essay on "The Roots of Science," remarking that "its main theme is scorn of the unity of science," and quoting Julian's line: "And where was psychology in all this? Anxiously toad-eating with the positivists." Boring went on: "I looked up 'toadeating' in the OED [Oxford English Dictionary] and found it with a hyphen: 'toad-eater: the attendant of a charlatan, employed to eat or pretend to eat toads (held to be poisonous) to enable his master to exhibit his skill in expelling poison.'"[27] Jaynes had suggested that psychologists were guilty of aping the physical scientists in their frantic rush to construct a scientific discipline.

In letters at a pace of two a month, they went on to discuss many topics, among them functionalism. Julian wrote:

I have always been troubled about functionalism ...
What interested me in your letter was that you referred
to a closely-knit in-group built around Dewey and
Angell that had great enthusiasm and great influence. I
find it difficult to be able to find such an influence in
studies in animals. Long before them there were studies
being done that could just as well be called Functionalist, and long after them as well. And I therefore have
always found it difficult to refer to them as a school —
in the same way that we can refer to Titchenerism or
Gestalt or Behaviorism as a school.[28]

Jaynes was using Boring as a foil for his far broader "functional" view of the origins of instinctive behavior, recounting the
history of observations about animals. The term "origin of consciousness" had not yet entered into their correspondence.

Jaynes did indeed begin to write a history of comparative psychology, even as he and Boring maintained a lively correspondence about other matters until the latter's death in 1968. The
chapter drafts (with titles partly his own and partly taken from
the headings of fragments) include:

In the Beginning: Early Civilizations, Notes on Early Man
  and his Relation to Animals, Insert for the Development of
  Animal Icons into Gods
Errors of Aegean Psychobiologists and the Ionian Revolution
Pythagorus and the Origins of Dualism
The Aristotelian Corpus
Roman Compilers: Pliny, Seneca, Origen, Galen
Medievalism: Arabian Comparative Psychology, Man in
  Nature, Bestiaries and the Norman Renaissance
Renaissance: Mechanism, Newness in 16th and 17th Century
  Science, Trembly and LaMettrie
Eighteenth Century Naturalists
Romanes and Darwin

These fragments, amounting to perhaps 500 manuscript pages, redundant and full of fits and starts, with blanks left for facts to be looked up, erupted into a comet-like burst in 1968. That was the summer in which Julian gave a week of lectures at the National Science Foundation "Summer Institute in the History of Psychology" at the University of New Hampshire. He reshaped the above material, filling in the gaps and extending the scope into the 20th century. He left behind a full outline. The theoretical lines emerged much more sharply in these 21 chapters. They are worth listing here, with regrets that space does not allow for the paragraph of subheadings for each one:

I.   In the Beginning
II.   The Ionian Revolution
III.   Origins of Dualism
IV.   The Aristotelian Corpus
V.   Roman Sects and Compilers
VI.   The Medieval Dream and the Light of Islam
VII.   The Sicilian Renaissance
VIII.   The Sixteenth Century Catalogues Nature
IX.   The Seventeenth Century Studies Motion
X.   The Wide Wake of Descartes
XI.   The Idea of Evolution Springs out of the Nature-Nurture Controversy
XII.   Eighteenth Century Naturalism
XIII.   The Evolution of Evolution
XIV.   The Nineteenth Century Founds its Sciences
XV.   The Neural Basis of Behavior in the 19th Century [Flourens, Marshall Hall, J. Müller, Carpenter, Pflüger-Lotze controversy, Fritsch & Hitzig]
XVI.   Objectivism Springs from Study of Invertebrates [Sechenov, Loeb, Beer, Bethe, Uexkull]
XVII.   The Study of Learning [Lloyd Morgan, Thorndike, Hall, Hobhouse, Twitmeyer, Pavlov]
XVIII. The Evolution of Mind [Hobhouse, Köhler, Yerkes,

Uexküll, Washburn]
XIX. Behaviorism and Learning Theory [Watson, Yerkes,
      Meyer, Weiss, Holt, Watsonianity, Lashley,
      Schneirla, Tolman, Hull, Guthrie, Crozier, Skinner]
XX.   The Rise and Fall of Instincts [Fabre, Whitman and
      Craig, McDougall, Woodworth, Warden, Heinroth,
      Lorenz, Tinbergen, Lehrman attack]
XXI. Twentieth Century Psychoneurology [Franz, Stone
      and Beach, Cannon-Bard, Papez, Hess, Olds-Milner
      discovery]

Although publication of this enormous panorama would be desirable, let us immediately add that we have not found chapters XIV to XXI in his archival papers and it is doubtful that they were ever written. Chapters I–XIV are very rough collections of fragments, transcribed by the Princeton Psychology Department secretary from a Dictaphone machine. The latter chapters apparently derived from his lecture notes. Would that we had a tape of those lectures in Durham, New Hampshire. As his only graduate student during 1967–1969, I (WRW) had the task of preparing the slides to illustrate his talk. The slides ranged from antiquity to the magnificent evolutionary charts of Romanes on the evolution of mind from lower animals.

On his way to the National Science Foundation (NSF) Summer Institute, Jaynes had stopped to visit his friend Gary Boring. It was a sad time shortly before Boring's death on July 1, 1968. Jaynes later wrote a long obituary, which appeared in the *Journal of the History of the Behavioral Sciences* in April 1969 and reflected the depth of his fatherly identification with him. Jaynes also would organize a session at the American Psychological Association "In Memory of E.G. Boring" for September 1969. Besides Jaynes, other speakers who reflected on Boring's "outsize personality" were Henry Murray, Harry Helson, Saul Rosenzweig, and Gardner Murphy, plus the presidential address by George Miller.[29]

At this time Jaynes also wrote an important article on the history of ethology, submitted on Sept. 7, 1968, and revised on February 7, 1969. "Comparative psychology," he argued, arrived with Pierre Flourens's book *La Psychologie Comparée* (1864), which was followed by five important tracts on animal instincts in the 1870s — by G.J. Romanes, D.A. Spalding, J. Lubbock, H.C. McCook, and G.H. Schneider, and textbooks by Henri Joly, J. Tissot, T. Vignoli, and Alfred Espinas. "Ethology" came from Alfred Giard's writings in the 1870s, which emulated Lamarck's emphasis on environment in evolution, according to his student George Bohn (1910, 1911). The field of ethology finally sprang up in the 1960s, invoking the earlier observations of Konrad Lorenz (1935) and Niko Tinbergen (1940), and reflecting "this polarization of thought between laboratory analysis and naturalistic observation."[30]

Although his work in ethology and the history of psychology played an important part in Jaynes's pursuit of the origin of consciousness, his main focus was about to turn elsewhere. The NSF Summer Institute served as the finale of his work in the history of animal psychology. His lectures there gave momentum to a new coterie of historians of psychology, whose researches in turn gave synergy to Jaynes in the years to come. However, his own direction suddenly shifted and deepened.

A New Theory of Consciousness and its Historical Origin

Jaynes took advantage of the excitement of life at Princeton, becoming a participant in a full range of campus activities and controversies. But, as always, his long search for answers to the problem of the origin of man's consciousness came first.

His part-time position as research associate and lecturer allowed time for his own work and for his involvements at Princeton and beyond. Time to do his own work was far more important to Jaynes than financial reward. He lived frugally, spent most of his waking hours in his office, and retired to his single room to sleep. He was free to arrange his time however he chose. His usual habit was to work until about 10 p.m. and then go out to socialize with friends, but when his work demanded more of his time he might work far into the night and leave tapes for the department secretary to transcribe before he arrived back in his office late morning. When he did emerge from his office, Jaynes was good company: witty, often charming and charismatic, and full of interesting facts and ideas. Although Jaynes's late evenings of social drinking were happy and welcome occasions, they led to a dependency that he had to struggle to control. Long continuous hours of work in his office helped in this regard as did numerous cups of tea and a great deal of self-discipline, especially when it was time for him to present his work. Later in life, Jaynes successfully gave up the small cigars he had so enjoyed, but he never parted with the solace of drinks at the end of the day.

Toward the end of the late 1960s, his friends and students began to hear interesting facts and ideas about a new theory he was working on, not the overlying concept but rather whatever evidence he was investigating at the time: split-brain research, big-eyed idols, hypnosis, language, children's imaginary playmates — and usually only intriguing and isolated parts of these. But soon there would be an opportunity to present these thoughts as a cohesive whole.

By the deadline of the American Psychological Association's (APA) call for papers in January 1969, Robert MacLeod in psychology at Cornell University had invited him to give a talk on his new theory at the annual meeting in September 1969.[31] This would be the first public presentation of what Julian titled "A New Theory of Consciousness."

Jaynes had a busy and productive year in 1969 as he worked on the material for his APA talk and fulfilled other commitments and responsibilities. At Easter time he wrote and directed a play about the crucifixion of Christ that he titled "Journey to

Golgotha." It was presented at the Princeton University Chapel on Good Friday, April 4th and again on the 5th. His friend, EveLynn McGuiness, then a graduate student at nearby Rutgers University, assisted in the production and felt that it may have had some influence on his developing theory.[32]

At this time, too, his mother was readying to move from their longtime West Newton home to full-time residency in Prince Edward Island. Soon after the production ended, Jaynes left for Canada to see that things were ready for her at the Keppoch house. He told June Tower that he stopped for the night at Fredericton, New Brunswick, and as he looked out of his hotel window watching the ice break up on the St. John River, his theory at last came together for him. But how or why, we do not know.

In June he resigned his position as Master of Woodrow Wilson College, a residence and eating facility for students who had not joined Princeton's traditional eating clubs. In his four years as master, Jaynes had enjoyed exchanging ideas, debate, and camaraderie with the students in his charge. He rehearsed many of his theoretical ideas during dinner table conversations and felt a rapport with these serious students.

In this year of transition there was also a beginning. At Princeton in early summer 1969, Jaynes, as one of the founders, hosted the first meeting of the International Society for the History of the Behavioral Sciences, soon to be called the Cheiron Society. I (WRW), as a second year graduate student teaching at nearby Trenton State College, met with the organizing committee, Mary Henle and John J. Sullivan at Princeton, and assisted with the preparations. Jaynes agreed with the other founders that the organization should remain informal and open to graduate students, that it should be international, and that it should include the social as well as the behavioral sciences. He proposed that its symbol should be Cheiron, a deity of health with the head of a man and the body of a horse. Jaynes looked forward to subsequent annual meetings of the group and attended as often as he could.

Jaynes gave three invited lectures in 1969 — at the State University of New York in the "Frontiers of Social Science" series, the Smithsonian Institution "Symposium on Man and Beast," and the one that was most important to him at the American Psychological Association meeting in Washington, D.C.

Over the spring and summer months Jaynes typed and scribbled a 50-plus-page manuscript that gives the main ideas of his future book. He called it "A New Theory of Consciousness": "consciousness is indeed like an emergency repairman that goes only where he is needed ... in most other behavior as well, the role of consciousness has been much overestimated." He wrote "A New Introduction" in 12 pages, then "Misconceptions of Consciousness" in 12 pages, with subheadings "Its Extensiveness," "As a Copy of Experience," and "The Seat of Reason." Then came a handwritten third section, "Consciousness as an Analogue of the Behavioral World," in which he penned a line made famous in his book: "Subjective conscious mind is an analog of what is called the real world. It is built up with a lexical field whose terms are all metaphors or analogs of behavior in the physical world. ... Like mathematics, it is an operator rather than a thing or repository." A fourth piece of manuscript is typed in six pages and called "The Origin of Consciousness in History." He would later expand it into Book II of *The Origin*. It began:

> From these considerations it is not far to the statement that the conscious mind is the invention of man. If so, it is impossible that the conscious mind could have been invented without language, without the holding action of words whose publicly monitored sounds do not merely signal behavior as in animals, but symbolize it in stable relationships, and so allow for metaphors. If so, conscious mentality must have occurred after language had developed to an advanced degree, which would mean after the first cities, and after the beginnings of civilization.

Impossible you say! Human history without consciousness? Why everything in civilization is dependent upon it for its very functioning! Not at all. The reason I was at such pains to begin with certain misconceptions about consciousness was to prepare you for this point.

Finally came 14 pages with the headings "The Religion of the Greeks," "The Relationship of the Hero to the Gods," and "The Bicameral Mind." Here was the embryo of "Book II. The Witness of History."

The American Psychological Association meeting was the first time that Jaynes had publicly presented his ideas on the origin of consciousness. It did not attract a large audience and some of those present were quite baffled by what he had to say. The reception of his lecture was a bit disappointing, but soon he would be asked to speak elsewhere and his energies were turned to the expansion of his emerging theory.

He presented his talk on the origin of consciousness widely, as word of his slightly outrageous but tantalizing theory had spread. By 1975 he wrote:

I have been something of an itinerant lecturer, various parts of this work having been given at colloquia and lectures at various places, including Harvard, Johns Hopkins, Cornell, Columbia, Rutgers, York, Dalhousie, Florida State, Northwestern, the New School, the Universities of Pennsylvania, New Hampshire, and Massachusetts at Amherst and Boston Harbor, Payne-Whitney Clinic, Wellesley, SUNY at Geneseo, Plattsburgh, Oswego and Brockport, as AAAS Lecturer at Franklin and Marshall, the William Allinson White Institute, two radio broadcasts at the University of Michigan, and as a series of lectures at Hunter, Hope College, and in my capacity as Scholar-in-Residence at Skidmore, Lake Forest, and at the University of Prince Edward Island.[33]

Some of the ideas for the book appeared in a paper delivered at Cornell University on June 3, 1972: "The Origin of Consciousness." After telling what consciousness is not, he posed the question: "What is it?" He answered that:

> Its reality is of the same order as mathematics. It allows us to short-cut behavioral processes and arrive at more adequate decisions. Like mathematics, it is an operator (cf. Functionalism – WRW), rather than a thing or a repository. And it is intimately bound up with volition and decision.

The words we use for "mind-space" are metaphors of actual space: e.g., "we 'see' solutions to problems." He introduced the features of consciousness: spatialization, excerption, the analog 'I', the metaphor 'me', and narratization. Then he confronted the anti-evolutionary implications of his emphasis on language:

> Now if conscious mind is a spatial analog of the world and mental acts are analogs of bodily acts, and it is all generated by metaphor on the basis of language, a rather startling deduction can be made as to the origin of consciousness. It is one that is completely contradictory to the evolutionary solutions which I at one time and most of you have believed for this problem. For if consciousness is based on language, then it follows that only humans are conscious, and that we became so at some historical epoch after language was evolved.

He continued by acknowledging that "this is an extremely serious statement. Certainly it directs us to the earliest writings of mankind to see if we can find any hints as to when this important invention of consciousness might have occurred." As in his later book, he reviewed first the *Iliad* as an oral composition between

1200 and 850 B.C., in which *nous* ("mind") meant merely "recognition," and *psyche* ("soul") meant "life." Astonishingly, "it is a behaviorist world inhabited by noble automatons who know not what they do." The gods who instructed people were auditory hallucinations "as distinctly heard by the Iliadic heroes as voices are heard by schizophrenic patients today." He called this phenomenon the bicameral mind, and he asserted that it is found in prior civilizations in Egypt, the Hittites, later in India and then China, and then much later in early civilizations in Mesoamerica and the Andean Highlands — "A consistent picture of divinely managed societies based on auditory hallucinations."

In the Introduction of his book four years later, Jaynes would reveal the expanded train of his thought: the problem of consciousness, "the difference between what others see of us and our sense of our inner selves." "Consciousness, then, emerges as something genuinely new ... this antireductionist doctrine," replaces "behaviorism as program if not truth ... with its gleaming stainless-steel promise of reducing all conduct to a handful of reflexes and conditional responses." Chapter 1 on "The Consciousness of Consciousness" discusses what consciousness is not. It is "a much smaller part of our mental life than we are conscious of." Playing the piano is an example of how little we are conscious.[34]

He traces the dawn of civilization to the transition at Natufian, a Mesolithic culture in present day Israel, where hunters lived in caves and open-air settlements, such as that at Eynan north of the Sea of Galilee. Each town contained about 50 mud-roofed huts arranged in a circle, meaning a population of about 200. No longer were 20 or so on the hunt, but now a community survived through agriculture. These towns date from 9000 B.C. The surprising thing about these people is that they are "signal bound," he speculates, listening to and obeying the hallucinated voices of their god. He reproduces the sketch of the skull and bones of the dead king from the excavations of 1959: "the king's tomb as the god's house continues through the millennia as a feature of many civilizations, particularly in Egypt."[35]

Since Julian rarely dated his manuscripts, we shall probably never know the order of composition. His Chapter 6 in Book I on "The Origin of Civilization" cites literature from 1960 to 1968, with the single exception of his own article on language in the late Pleistocene in 1976. In Chapter 2 of Book 2 on "Literate Bicameral Theocracies," he cites nothing newer than 1971. His "theory of idols" brought to bear the evidence of eyes in statues, the eye index, whereby the ratio of eye to head is close to 20 percent, whereas in real life it is less than 10 percent. He found large eyes in idols, for example, in Iran and Mesopotamia, in Egypt, in Tlatilco near Mexico City, and in the Incas of South America, but curiously not in the Mayans. Citing the importance of eye-to-eye contact in primates, Jaynes interpreted the large eyes as evidence that idols, viewed as gods, were a source of hallucinated voices in preliterate bicameral societies.[36]

Book II, Chapter 3, addresses the "Causes of Consciousness" in the breakdown of the bicameral mind. In an argument akin to the fall from grace in the garden of Eden, Jaynes argues that the "social control" by the gods gave way in Assyria, in the Hittite and Mycenaean empires, and in the exodus of the Israelites from Egypt — all around 1200 B.C. Markets, rule by cruelty, the breakdown of the authority of the gods, and the origins of narratization in epics all happened around the same time.[37] Deceit originated in the analog *I* — for without consciousness long-term treachery was not possible.

Publishing His Book

By the early 1970s Jaynes felt his theory was nearly ready for publication and he looked about for a publisher. He wanted it to be a trade book published by a major firm that might carry it for a number of years. After considering his options Jaynes sent off his manuscript to Basic Books, Houghton Mifflin, Harcourt Brace Jovanovich, Prentice Hall, and McGraw-Hill. And letters came in return. In 1972, for example, editor Judith Greissman at Harcourt Brace Jovanovich, Inc., conveyed comments from readers: psychologists Ernest Hilgard and Isidor Chein, and "the anthropologist." She wrote to Julian that "It's pretty rare to have a manuscript labeled 'highly original and fascinating' and 'original, creative, often brilliant, etc.' — especially from tough critics — but, then, those superlatives come as no surprise to us. ... We are looking forward to seeing you within a few days."[38] Two years later, publisher Thomas H. Quinn at the Scholarly Books Division of McGraw-Hill Book Company returned three reviews to Jaynes and remarked that "the criticism seems too intelligent and serious to ignore."[39]

While he had heard from the other publishers nothing had come from Houghton Mifflin Company in Boston since their receipt of his manuscript. When he next visited in West Newton he told his friends of this disappointment. Thinking it strange that there had been no reply, Walter Tower called Austin Olney — the editor-in-chief of Houghton Mifflin's Trade Division — to inquire. Indeed the manuscript had been misplaced, left in a drawer by a suddenly departing editor. Fortunately, Olney liked the book and thought it might be a long-term steady seller.

On December 9, 1974, Randy Warner, a female editor for Houghton Mifflin, wrote:

> Dear Prof. Jaynes,
> Herewith those portions of your MSS which I have been reading these past months. I confess the actual time I have spent with these chapters has been scant. I've fussed and worried quite a bit, but constructive work I think, has not amounted to much! ... Overall intriguing! The pace for the most part is brisk ... the "tone" throughout is a very effective almost familiar one

which I find most agreeable and appropriate. It has very much the feeling of a series of lectures, rather than a hermetically sealed, isolated opus. I think it should be read as such and the almost informality of it counted upon as access for readers. I do recognize a conflicting view, though, that would recommend a more formal, more "written" approach. ... I hope you are well, and that my few comments will be of some value, and that the MSS will soon be on its way to an eagerly awaiting HMCo! Yours sincerely, Randy Warner

Houghton Mifflin would be his publisher and he was to enjoy a close working relationship with his editors. Everything about the publishing process was important and interesting to Jaynes. He chose the typeface and the idea for the stark black-on-white dust jacket was also his.

Although 1976 is listed as the publication date of *The Origin of Consciousness in the Breakdown of the Bicameral Mind*, the book did not actually appear on bookstore shelves until mid-January 1977. On Sunday, January 16, Walter and June Tower hosted a publication party at their home in West Newton to celebrate the occasion. Jaynes's guest list included those who had helped in the publication at Houghton Mifflin Company, longtime West Newton friends and neighbors, and Boston area colleagues in psychology. Also present was one copy of the book. The atmosphere was festive and fun, but Jaynes knew that relationships with his colleagues would never be quite the same again.

Meanwhile, amid the prepublication activity of 1976 something quite unexpected happened. Friends had prevailed upon Yale to grant his Ph.D. Other friends urged Jaynes to accept it. As requested, he submitted his four published papers titled "Imprinting: The Interaction of Learned and Innate Behavior" with the unpublished final study "V. On the Essential Nature of the Stimulus Object."[40] Jaynes returned to Yale for commencement in the spring of 1977 and graciously accepted his Ph.D.

Soon other positive things would happen as well. After the publication of *The Origin of Consciousness in the Breakdown of the Bicameral Mind* came a time of reward and excitement. Sales of the new book quickly mounted and the first printing sold out before the next could replace it. Reviews by well-known critics like Christopher Lehmann-Haupt in the *New York Times* on February 9, 1977, Marshall McLuhan in the *Toronto Globe and Mail* on June 18, 1977, and others nationwide helped spur sales beyond expectations. Articles about Jaynes as well as his book began to appear. On March 14, 1977, John Leo's article "The Lost Voices of the Gods" appeared in *Time* magazine. Later in the year Sam Keen wrote an article by the same name for *Psychology Today* and for *Quest* Richard Rhodes wrote, "Alone in the Country of the Mind: The Origin of Julian Jaynes" in early 1978. Many others would follow. Invitations to speak increased. In 1978 *The Origin of Consciousness* was named runner-up for the National Book Award for non-fiction. And, as foreseen by Houghton Mifflin's Trade Division editor-in-chief, sales would continue at a steady pace. After 30 years Jaynes's book remains in print.

Fragments about "The Consequences of Consciousness"

What about the promised second volume? Jaynes was indeed thinking about and working on a second volume; in fact, some of it was originally slated to be included in *The Origin of Consciousness*. We noticed this when we packed up the manuscripts for the Archives of the History of American Psychology in Akron, Ohio, and wrote them a note of explanation. The numbering of chapters was otherwise inconsistent. Houghton Mifflin Company had thought the book too long. Keeping "Book III. The Consequences of Consciousness" for a new volume was their idea. Jaynes agreed, and cut, rearranged, and rewrote.

If we compare the table of contents from the original manuscript with that of the published book we can see what happened.

Book III. The Consequences of Consciousness
1. Vestiges of Bicamerality in Modern Times
   (containing divination, possession, idols)
2. Schizophrenia
3. Dreams (exists in a 38-page manuscript)
4. The Mind of the Child
5. The Mind of the Tribe

By comparison, the final book had:

Book II. The Witness of History
4. A Change of Mind in Mesopotamia
   (added divination)
Book III. Vestiges of the Bicameral Mind in the Modern World
1. The Quest for Authorization (added idols)
2. Of Prophets and Possession
   (added possession and demonization)
3. Of Poetry and Music (new)
4. Hypnosis (new)
5. Schizophrenia (retained)
6. The Auguries of Science (new)

So Jaynes divided "Chapter 1: Vestiges of the Bicameral Mind in Modern Times" into three sections. The section on divination went into "Book II, Chapter 4: A Change of Mind in Mesopotamia."[41] The second section on idols went into "Book III, Chapter 1: The Quest for Authorization."[42] The third section on possession and demonization went into "Book III, Chapter 2: Of Prophets and Possession."[43] His new opening chapter of "Book III, Chapter 1: The Quest for Authorization" thus added idols to his material on oracles. His new Chapter 2 became as stated. Then he dropped the sections:

1. Dreams
2. The Mind of the Child

3. The Mind of the Tribe
4. The Moral Imperative

He kept "Chapter 2: Schizophrenia" but relocated it to Chapter 5. And he penned a brief concluding "Chapter 6: The Auguries of Science."[44] He had completed "Chapter 4: The Mind of the Child" and he left behind both this outline and a fragmentary manuscript of it:

The problem stated and its difficulties
Seeing children through conscious categories
Evidence of bicamerality in young children
Are imaginary playmates hallucinated?
Hallucinations in childhood
The four year old child
The child's concept of mind
The parental teaching of consciousness
The effect of the development of consciousness on memory
The ontogeny of guilt
Children of antiquity
Incipient bicameral dreams of childhood
The shift to conscious dreams
Language in the child's development

An expansion of this fertile exposition of the growth of consciousness in the maturation of the child would likely have appeared in his second volume, *The Consequences of Consciousness*. In addition, he would have included an updated version of his unpublished "Chapter 5: The Mind of the Tribe." In it Julian extrapolated beyond his study of selected civilizations in Book II, Chapter 2 on Mesopotamia and Egypt (originally titled "The Holy Theocracies of Mesopotamia and Egypt"), Chapter 3 on Sumer, Mesopotamia, Assyria and the Hittites, Mycenae, Chapter 4 on Assyrians (originally titled "The Military Consciousness of Assyria"), Chapter 5 on Greece, and Chapter 6 on the Hebrews.

He wrote:

> Our attention so far in this book has been directed at
> the greatest civilizations only and particularly our own.
> But the true and total picture is more complex — as is
> always the case in historical perception where simplicity
> is ever leading us into a false clarity. For all over the
> more easily habitable zones of the earth, particularly
> where sudden agriculture was possible, we should
> imagine from time to time over the last ten millennia
> the periodic existence of other smaller agricultural civi-
> lizations, presumably bicameral. Whether such group-
> ings were due to migration or diffusion from the greater
> bicameral civilizations or developed spontaneously as
> occurred in 9000 B.C. in the Near East is a question
> that cannot always be answered. But that such civiliza-
> tions did exist is demonstrable almost everywhere that
> archeology has looked for their remains.

His "Afterword" appeared in the 1990 edition of *The Origin*.
It reveals very briefly where he might have wanted to expand his
thinking: "The Cognitive Explosion, The Self, From Affect to
Emotion, From Fear to Anxiety, From Shame to Guilt, and
From Mating to 'Sex.'"[45]

In the second edition of *The Origin* in 1982, he wrote in the
preface: "Originally, I had planned Books IV and V to complete
the central positions of the theory. These will now become a
separate volume, whose working title is *The Consequences of
Consciousness*, not yet scheduled for publication." Unfortunately,
we have not found manuscripts for all of these chapters. Some
may have only existed in the form of notes and tapes, as this was
Jaynes's mode of writing. Moves, storages, sortings, and raccoons
all took their toll on his possessions. Apparently, Jaynes's
thoughts on the consequences of consciousness will have to be

pieced together from a few chapter manuscripts, a few taped lectures, and scattered notes and publications.

Through the years after the publication of *The Origin of Consciousness*, as Jaynes continued to work on his second volume, he began to wish that some of the material about the consequences of consciousness could have been included in the first book. Houghton Mifflin was waiting to publish *The Consequences of Consciousness* and Jaynes, as we have seen, had already thought through, outlined, and written much of what would be included. He was adding more and more as the months passed. However, he realized that it would be difficult to make *The Consequences of Consciousness* stand on its own as a successful book when, truly, no matter how many and important were the consequences, this second volume could only be a support for the theory proposed in *The Origin* and not something of equal weight. He was troubled by this, and though he knew that *Consequences* would have its own appeal, answer more questions, and help to explain his theory, he could not bring to fruition a book that to his perfectionist eyes was not quite resolved.

Jaynes's theory and book had been his lifelong work and it was sometimes hard for him to see beyond this concentrated world. Similarly, he felt he had not truly succeeded because there were people who disagreed with him whom he felt had not really read his book or understood it. He was right about people not reading the whole book, or understanding it, and his reaction was quite valid. Perhaps he succumbed to an emotional reaction, as opposed to what his more logical side would have enjoyed — that is, a good debate and vibrant exchange of thought.

Later Writings: Language Embedded In Cultures

In the years following the publication of his book, Jaynes continued on with his life's work, adding new evidence to support and expand his theory. Thus material from his book was merged with new discoveries and interests and consequences of consciousness with its origins.

Jaynes spoke at colleges and universities as well as at conferences and symposia centered on some aspect of his work. He especially enjoyed speaking as a visiting scholar presenting his theory one evening and the consequences the next, with time to meet with smaller groups during the day.

He presented his ideas at a conference on "Consciousness and Therapy" and at several on imagination, healing, and the brain. In 1983, he gave the keynote address at a conference on "Language: Crucible of Consciousness."

His writings tell us of other applications of his theory. Jaynes wrote an invited commentary called "Paleolithic Cave Paintings as Eidetic Images" for *Behavioral and Brain Sciences* and in *Art/World* appeared "The Meaning of King Tut," "Dragons of the Shang Dynasty: The Hidden Faces," "The Ghost of a Flea: Visions of William Blake," and "Art and the Right Hemisphere."[46]

In 1977, he wrote about memory in an article titled, "The Remembrance of Things (Far) Past," stating:

> When we remember, we are allowed into an enchanted other world where the past is present and time is reversible. How is this possible? It is like a space of unhappening events, of associations and experience through which we can move about in any direction. ... It is of course a metaphorical space, really, a something made to be like actual space, a mind-space generated by the metaphoric associations of the language we use to describe mental acts, until we have an analog 'I' that can move about in that space of memory even as the physical self can travel about the actual world. ... It has not always been so. I believe that conscious memory only began around 1000 B.C. — a mere hundred

generations ago. Before that time men moved about in an intellectual darkness through a more confined world with a different mentality, an unconscious bicameral mind in which decisions and rememberings were not conscious, but heard from another part of the brain as auditory hallucinations called gods. There was no conscious remembering then. Achilles did not live in a frame of past happenings and future possibilities as do we. He had no lifetime stretching between birth and death as do we.

A fragment of about seven pages, titled "The Other World of Our Lives," reveals Jaynes's critical acceptance and rejection of neobehaviorism, the tradition in which he had been trained at Yale graduate school:

This means that memory as we know it is only 3,000 years old. The confusion we feel in reading such a statement is directly due to the ineptness of modern psychology in its treatment of the subject. The confusion is of two kinds of time. ... Modern psychology confuses time and again memory with learning which is as distinct [as] painting from music. Learning is the repetition of a new response to stimuli until it is automatic. Memory is the present recreation of past events or knowledge. Learning is governed by reward. Memory has nothing to do with reward. Learning occurs in almost all animals. Memory only in ourselves.

We see that Jaynes in the 1970s epitomized the shift away from behavior to the study of cognitive process — dubbed the cognitive revolution.

In a commentary from 1978 on three papers by animal psychologists Donald Griffith, David Premack, and Sue Savage-

Rumbaugh, Jaynes complains:

> Although it is not explicit, all three papers seem to say that because animal behavior can be made to simulate aspects of human behavior, therefore such animals are similar to human conscious functioning. It is the same argument used with that other method of cognitive processes, computer intelligence. But — to use a wildly dissimilar and probably inaccurate example — because Mickey Mouse looks and behaves so humanly on a screen does not mean that a celluloid film is conscious; it means he is made to look conscious.

The power of Jaynes's theory underlies this comment. It was language embedded in cultures that had heralded the advent of consciousness. And within languages of many varieties, it was metaphor that conveyed consciousness by spatializing the physical world. To demonstrate such a linguistic change required historical evidence such as he had accumulated in his book. It also forced the conscientious evolutionist to admit that the time scale was much too fast for physical or even cultural evolution to operate. The shift to subjective consciousness occurred in the period 1200 to 600 B.C. as a result of historical events such as the death of many Mediterranean civilizations due to the eruption of the volcano of Thera north of Crete, ensuing "mass migrations and invasions" and "a policy of frightfulness" by the king of Assyria ca. 1100 B.C.[47]

He was much in demand as a lecturer and confident in his role as promulgator of a new scientific and historical theory. At Emory University in 1978, for example, he reviewed the term "pre-conscious hypotheses" just prior to Solon. He asked his audience to read the book of Amos and compare it to the book of Ecclesiastes: Amos directly hearing the words of God, relates them to scribes; Ecclesiastes with a notion of an inner mental life and spatialized time. He thanked the Department of Religion for inviting him and promised the members of his seminar to begin with an Old Testament reading, Psalm 42: "As the hart pants after the water brook ... my mind thirsts for gods, living gods, when shall I come face to face with God." From the New Testament he read from John 4, where Jesus is drinking water: "Whosoever drinketh of the water that I shall give him shall be in him as a well of water, springing up with everlasting life." "My contrast here is between the 42nd Psalm, which is no different from the psalms in Assyria at the time of the breakdown of the bicameral mind," lectured Jaynes. "The New Testament recalls waters and wells in nomadic life, reminiscent of self-fulfillment quenching thirst. It is about the woman of Samaria. Jesus is really trying to reform Judaism." The well inside you is like consciousness, he explained. It is a metaphor. Thirst is the metaphier. Whoever has sex will want it again, whereas whoever has love will have everlasting life. He recommended *The Growth of the Greek Historical Spirit* by Chester Starr from which he had drawn examples.

Jaynes wanted to show that historical time became a preoccupation in this period, and he interpreted it as "spatialized time" becoming historical time. He pointed out that this is exemplified in three places in the 6th century B.C. From Egypt came the story of Pharaoh Psammetichos, who asked the question "What is the oldest language?" To answer this he had twins raised by a shepherd whose tongue had been cut out. The first word they spoke would indicate the oldest language: it was "bekos" — not an Egyptian word but a Phrygian (a language spoken in Asia Minor at that time) word for bread. The second story comes from the beginnings of the Old Testament and Deuteronomy, the magnificent legend of the Hebrews and the Exodus.

The third story concerned the origin of the earth as an orb from which grew plants and animals that came onto land and became men. This was the Anaximandrean theory of evolution,

passed through Lucretius to the 18th century, to Lamarck and
Erasmus Darwin, Alfred Russel Wallace and Charles Darwin.
Of significance in each example is the emergence of the notion of
time, and of time as space. He acknowledged Henri Bergson on
flowing time, a book he had read in his teens. "We are not
distinguishing between memory, and spatialized time." Knowing
someone's telephone number, or a dog responding to his name, is
simply a "knowing that." These are mere habits. "It is a very
different thing when we have our memories in spatialized time,
and go back in time and say, 'yes that happened here.'"

In the spring of 1981 he had been invited to give a Sunday
sermon at the First Unitarian Society in Newton and chose "The
Magic Wells of Consciousness," again focusing on the woman of
Samaria as his father had once done, but with the younger Jaynes
relating the metaphoric content to his theory of consciousness.
On January 27, 1985, he was invited back to speak at the 100th
anniversary of his father's ordination. He told of his father's
interesting life and then read the sermon that his father had
preached 100 years before, "A Religion of Selfhood," which a
century later seemed surprisingly up to date.

Teaching Undergraduates about Consciousness

Beginning in the spring of 1979 through at least 1992, Jaynes
taught a seminar on "The Psychology of Consciousness" to
classes of a dozen or more students. He may have given it since
1970; the senior author (WRW) can attest that he was still teaching the history of animal psychology to undergraduates in the fall
of 1967. He assigned students his book, 50 to 100 pages at a
time for a month, then went on for six more weeks to develop his
theory. He also assigned two 15-page papers, to be chosen from a
list of topics under four categories: library research studies, historical studies, theoretical studies, or empirical studies. His syl-
labus also listed outside readings to accompany each text assignment. We want to give detailed attention to this course because it

sheds light on the direction of his thinking as he worked on his sequel to *The Origin*.

The initial section of the course, "The Nature of Consciousness, Its Features and Modes," covered the beginning of his own book (Introduction–I.2). He recommended as additional readings Richard Nisbett and Timothy Wilson on "verbal reports," the introductions to chapters by Gordon Globus, et al. in *Consciousness and the Brain*, and William James's "Stream of Thought" chapter. Then came a second week devoted to "The Bicameral Mind, its Neurology and Evolution"; his *The Origin* (I.3–II.3) was assigned, with recommended readings by J.E. Bogen, "The Other Side of the Brain," Posey and Losch on auditory hallucinations, David Galin on left and right cerebral specialization, Ruth Ley on emotion and the right hemisphere, and Jaynes himself on language in the late Pleistocene. Students also viewed a film, "Left Brain-Right Brain." So far, he was deepening his lateralization thesis: that the gods spoke to mankind through the right hemisphere.[48]

In the third week, he took up "Mind from 9000 B.C. to 1000 A.D." with assignments from *The Origin* (II.4–III.3), Jaynes's "On Tutankhamun," and "Amos" and "Ecclesiastes" in the Bible. Here he was bolstering the evidence for the bicameral mind in antiquity. The fourth week on "Alterations of Consciousness in Hypnosis and Schizophrenia" assigned *The Origin* (III.4–III.5) and E.R. Hilgard's chapter on hypnosis in *Divided Consciousness*, which describes the contemporary clinical evidence of automatic action in divided consciousness. Four recommended readings included Ernst Bleuler's *Elementia Praecox, or The Group of Schizophrenias*, E.R. Dodds's *Greeks and the Irrational*, Martin Orne's "Nature of Hypnosis," Theodore Barber on hypnosis, and finally Nick Spanos's, "Hypnotic Behavior," with commentaries in *Brain and Behavioral Science*. Much of this material had appeared since *The Origin*, showing that Julian kept up with recent literature.[49]

The remaining six weeks spelled out his new material: "Time, Lives and Memories," "Feelings, Selves, and Will," "Consciousness in Dreams and Literature," "Consciousness Therapy," "Consciousness in the Child," and "The Mentality of Tribes." In the first new section, "Time, Lives and Memories," we see Jaynes trying to develop the sense of time in ancient textual scholarship, while bolstering it with empirical studies of amnesia or the loss of the time sense. The sense of time, in other words, connects with memory in the post-bicameral conscious self. Students were assigned Jaynes's own one-page manuscript, "Remembrance of Things (Far) Past," Gorman and Wessman's "Images, Values, and Concepts of Time in Psychological Research," Hilgard's "Amnesia and Repression," and Starr's book on *The Awakening of the Greek Historical Spirit*. His recommended readings again combine classical scholarship with contemporary theory and research in cognitive psychology, a field that was booming in the 1970s and 1980s: Dodds on *The Greeks and the Irrational*, Bower's "analysis of a mnemonic device," J.T. Fraser's *The Voices of Time*, Endel Tulving's "Episodic and Semantic Memory," and Frances Yates's *The Art of Memory*.[50]

Then came "Feelings, Selves, and Will," featuring the assignment of "the chapter on emotion from any introductory text," two *Behavioral and Brain Science* comments by Jaynes — "A Two-Tiered Theory of Emotions" and "Sensory Pain and Conscious Pain." Then he had students read Michael Lewis, "The Origins of Self" and John Benton, "Consciousness of Self and Perceptions of Individuality" in *Renaissance and Renewal of the Twelfth Century*. His recommended readings varied from John Lyons's literary study of the 18th century, *The Invention of Self*, to William James's chapter on "The Consciousness of Self," and Robert Wicklund's "Objective Self-Awareness." Evidently, the historical emergence of the self was based for Jaynes in a two-level theory of consciousness, one automatic and one reflective, that continued to develop in the Middle Ages. He reviewed this in his "Afterword" in 1990.[51]

Next he extended his theory in the direction of "Consciousness in Dreams and Literature." He assigned Freud's *Interpretation of Dreams*, Chapter 1, and Erich Kahler's *The Inward Turn of Narrative*. Along with three empirical studies of dreams, he assigned two literary authors who had applied his theory: Judith Weissman, "Vision, Madness and Morality in Nineteenth Century British Poetry," and Edward Proffitt, "Romanticism, Bicamerality, and the Evolution of the Brain." Jaynes was open to any realm of knowledge that shed light on consciousness.[52]

Then he followed with "Consciousness Therapy" with assignments of Anees Sheikh, Katharina Richardson, and L. Martin Moleski, "Psychosomatics and Mental Imagery," Jordan, "Mental Imagery and Psychotherapy: European Approaches," and Lerner, "Cognitive Therapy." Clearly, he believed that the manipulation of consciousness through any cognitive method helped to strengthen his theory. The recommended readings included Donald Meichenbaum, *Cognitive Behavior Modification*, Cautela and McCullough, "Covert Conditioning," in *The Power of the Human Imagination*, Alan Kazdin, "Covert Modeling," and Berghausen and Sachs, "Hypnotic Treatment of Hallucinations and Disordered Impulse Control."[53]

"Consciousness in the Child" depended upon readings from Jerome Singer, "Some Theoretical Implications," in his book on *The Child's World of Make-Believe* and Vygotsky's "The Genetic Roots of Thought and Speech" in *Thought and Language*. Recommended readings comprised Charles Brainerd, "The Stage Question in Cognitive-Developmental Theory," Arthur Applebee, *The Child's Concept of Story*, and John Flavell and Henry Wellman's "Metamemory."[54]

Finally, he introduced "The Mentality of Tribes," with anthropological readings from Lucien Levy-Bruhl, *Primitive Mentality*, and Ernest Gellner, "The Savage and the Modern Mind." Recommended were Edward Evans-Pritchard's, *Theories of Primitive Religion,* Christopher Hallpike's "Is There a Primitive Mentality?," Paul Heelas and Andrew Lock, *Indigenous Psychologies: The Anthropology of the Self,* and Maurice Leenhardt, *Do Kamo: Person and Myth in the Melanesian World.* It is remarkable that anthropological sources played such a minor role in his history of consciousness, but his interest in its mechanisms and anthropology's interest in cultures may be the reason. Or it may be that he did not want to undermine his own originality.[55]

Consolidating His Revisions of the Theory: Four Hypotheses

In 1983, Jaynes gave an invited address at the University of New Hampshire. He was invited to talk about his book, but he offered to talk about his future book in the question period. He situated his talk in "the problem of consciousness and its evolution." This evolution was material. "How can you get all this internal experience out of that?" The notion of studying learning came from studying the threshold of consciousness: "If learning was the association of ideas ... this was consciousness." He called this the "error" of his early career in psychology. He had thought learning was going to turn into consciousness. Here he noted that he was then very confused, and "in my confusion, I turned to the history of psychology for the purpose of trying to sort out this problem."[56]

For the most part, Jaynes found his work pleasurable and rewarding, but he sometimes felt discouraged. On a tape made during a long trip which took him to California and back, we listen to his words on the return flight from St. Louis to Newark, the last leg of his trip:

> It was an interesting time but always there is this foreign quality of people in my own field who simply are not ready for what it is I have to say. And I have to say that it really isn't pleasant and I think I'm going to stop

doing these lectures even though the income from them
I need. But there's something wearing about them, as if
I should have to try to interest anyone.[57]

However, positive things were in the air as well, and Jaynes
went on working and his lectures continued. His audience
broadened internationally with publication of his book in Italian
in 1984, Spanish in 1987, German in 1988, and French in 1994.
Further invitations followed, to Europe and Mexico. When possible, he chose to enjoy long train journeys and Atlantic crossings
on the Queen Elizabeth II over air travel. En route he often visited ancient sites and museums but also found time to see old
friends from his theater days in England.

In 1979, he had been awarded an honorary Ph.D. by Rhode
Island College and another came his way from Elizabethtown
College in 1985. In 1984, Jaynes was invited to give the plenary
lecture to the Wittgenstein Symposium in Kirchburg, Austria,
and he titled his talk "Four Hypotheses on the Origin of Mind."
Although by now Jaynes was trying to relax his busy pace, he
gave six major lectures in 1985 and nine in 1986.

At Harvard on the second day of a conference on Jaynes's
work — which included commentary by Daniel Dennett,
Willard Van Orman Quine, and others prominent in their own
fields — Jaynes gave an overview of the "consequences of consciousness." Here he seems to have been developing the feeling
side of consciousness in its evolution during the 1st millennium
B.C. He reminded his audience of the historical origins of shame
in human and animal experience:

Think of primary school, toilet accidents. Think how
painful it was. ... If you say to a dog, "bad dog," he
wonders what he did wrong. He puts his tail between
his legs and crawls off. It is such a biological part of us
that we are ashamed to admit it. ... Guilt is the consciousness of shame over time.[58]

For Jaynes, the Bible remains our best source on ideas of sin. He lectured that "sin is an awful word for it," but "the whole Hebrew Bible is talking about the importance of guilt." He asked rhetorically "how do you get rid of guilt?" and then answered that "it is very interesting to remember what Paul makes of the crucifixion of Jesus: Jesus was taking away the sins of the world."

After shame and guilt, he went on to the consequences of consciousness in "mating and sex, which is one of the interesting things to us." Theoretically, that is. Julian hastened to point out that "if you go back to the bicameral world, all the art is extremely chaste. ... Then if you go to the Greek world that begins around 700 B.C., it is anything but. You have never seen anything so dirty. ... There were brothels at this time. It happens in the Etruscans. You find these very gross sexual scenes. So I am saying that sex is a very different thing than it was before." What is the significance of all this lewdness appearing in human history? "You can imagine what your own sex life would be if you could not fantasize about it. This is consciousness coming in and influencing our behavior, and our physiology. Here we have consciousness, and guilt, and sex, and anxiety."[59]

Jaynes wrote of this again in the "Afterword" to the 1990 edition of his book. He urged that there was no single red thread to his argument. Rather, it consisted of four main hypotheses, any one of which might be shown to be wrong without the others collapsing. He reviewed each in turn:

1. Consciousness is based on language and it goes beyond sense perception. To Bertrand Russell's example of logical atomism, "I see a table," Jaynes replied, "I suggest Russell was not being conscious of the table, but of the argument he was writing about." "He should have found a more ethologically valid example ... such as ... How can I afford alimony for another Lady Russell?" He concluded, "such examples are consciousness in action."[60]

2. As for the bicameral mind, his second main hypothesis, he invoked new evidence that a third of all people experience auditory hallucinations. Congenital quadriplegics understand language and hear voices of gods, without ever having moved or spoken.[61] In short, we continue to show artifacts of bicamerality.

3. In the hypothesis of dating, he adds a weak form of the theory, dating consciousness from 12,000 B.C., assuming that both mentalities developed together and then the bicameral one was "sloughed off." The stronger form of the dating argument, the one he presented in the book, was that consciousness arose around 1200 B.C.

4. Finally, his double brain hypothesis about hallucinations occurring in the right hemisphere and "heard" by the left, could now be tested, he suggested, using cerebral glucography with positron emission tomography (PET) scans. Jaynes cited a study showing more glucose uptake occurred in the right hemisphere when a patient was hearing voices.[62]

Full Circle: Retiring To Prince Edward Island, the Family Home

Though lecture fees and royalties from his book had brought a sense of security and a few pleasures to his life, Jaynes continued to live frugally in his single room at Princeton, and to keep his late morning to mid (or sometimes late) evening working pattern every day of the week, with an occasional invitation, movie, or Princeton event providing an excuse for a break.

Away from Princeton, Jaynes enjoyed long trips to speaking engagements and his migrations to and from his home in Prince Edward Island. The three-day trip to Keppoch was made in a large comfortable car, the last of which was a middle-aged light blue Mercury Grand Marquis that could hold great quantities of his belongings. On his way he usually stopped for a visit in West Newton, often for a party with friends, perhaps a visit to his father's church (as he had befriended each successive minister), walks around his old neighborhood, and a drive into Boston to see his publisher or dentist. He enjoyed being in these familiar surroundings, but after his mother sold their long-time West Newton family home in 1969, the house by the sea at Keppoch became his only true home.

Jaynes loved Prince Edward Island. Here was the summer escape of his childhood, a happy place far more carefree than West Newton, a place where, as a child, he could run freely to the beach and sea and later enjoy long hikes through the countryside. It was a home to which he often returned. Here he visited his mother in her last years and found a quiet place to work in his study in a small barn near the house. He was interested in the history of the island and its current affairs and took a special interest in the development of the University of Prince Edward Island.

Always a very private person, Jaynes was uncomfortable with frivolity and small talk. Under the self-assurance of the deep-baritone delivery of his lectures lay a sensitive, even shy, and very introspective nature that, as in his childhood, often kept him a bit apart from his peers. His values often seemed of the 19th century yet his mind seemed to surge far into the 21st. In retrospect he regretted the zeal of his youthful protests but maintained his independent spirit nonetheless. Alone late in life he was also rather sorry that he had not married but, as the women who had entered his life all knew, his work came first and his well entrenched lifestyle was far from compatible with domesticity.

Jaynes's last years at Princeton were difficult. Remodeling plans eliminated his comfortable office and left him with two small ones that just did not seem to quite work out. His health continued to fail and he very much felt his advance into old age. In the spring of 1995, when he was 75, Jaynes retired to his home by the sea at Keppoch where he lived alone surrounded by memories and mementos. A very able housekeeper, Wilma Weeks, kept his practical affairs in order and cooked his meals.

She and other Prince Edward Island friends kept him busy with invitations, some help with the house, and in planting a garden. Jaynes kept up his interest in the outside world with magazines, newspapers, television, and radio. He enjoyed visits from old friends but seldom could summon the energy or interest to answer his mail or to look into his boxes of papers and possessions that had been sent there from Princeton. In the coldest months of the year he moved to a Charlottetown hotel and, though he found it quite acceptable, looked forward to each spring in Keppoch.

In October 1997, he suffered a major stroke and was hospitalized. Julian Jaynes died in Charlottetown on November 21, 1997 at the age of 77. As he had wished, a memorial service was held for him in the spring of 1998 at the First Unitarian Society in Newton, his father's West Newton church.

NOTES TO CHAPTER 1

1. Rhodes, 1978.
2. Jaynes to J. Tower, ca. 1980.
3. J.C. Jaynes, 1922, p. 4.
4. Ibid., pp. 9, 12.
5. Ibid., pp. 16–17.
6. Jaynes, 1976a, p. 26.
7. Jaynes to C.B. Jaynes, February 6, 1938.
8. Jaynes to C.B. Jaynes, May 16, 1938.
9. Jaynes to C.B. Jaynes, April 27, 1942.
10. Jaynes to Biddle, December 14, 1942.
11. Jaynes to the *Boston Globe* Editor, 1943.
12. Jaynes to C.B. Jaynes, April 12, 1944.
13. Jaynes to C.B. Jaynes, April 25, 1944.
14. Jaynes, Lewisburg tape, 1984.
15. Jaynes to C.B. Jaynes, May 21, 1946.
16. Beach, 1950, pp. 123, 121.
17. Dewsbury, 2000.
18. F.A. Beach and J. Jaynes, 1954; F.A. Beach and J. Jaynes, 1956a, b, c; F.A. Beach, J. Jaynes, and A. Zitrin, 1956a, b.
19. Jaynes, 1956, 1957, 1958a, 1958b.
20. F.A. Beach and J. Jaynes, 1960.

21. Jaynes, 1956.
22. Boring to Jaynes, February 21, 1963.
23. Jaynes to Boring, March 3, 1963.
24. Dewsbury, 2000.
25. Jaynes to Boring, October 28, 1965.
26. Boring to Jaynes, November 15, 1965.
27. Boring to Jaynes, March 31, 1966.
28. Jaynes to Boring, May 23, 1966.
29. Capshew, 1999, p. 262.
30. Jaynes, 1969, p. 605.
31. Jaynes, 1976a, 1982, Preface.
32. McGuinness, phone interview by W.R. Woodward, 2000.
33. Jaynes, unpublished Preface, 1975.
34. Jaynes, 1976a, pp. 2, 10, 15, 23.
35. Ibid., p. 143.
36. Ibid., pp. 169–173.
37. Ibid., p. 217.
38. Greismann to Jaynes, July 27, 1972.
39. Quinn to Jaynes, April 4, 1974.
40. Jaynes, 1956, 1957, 1958a, 1958b; Jaynes, 1977a.
41. Jaynes, 1976a, pp. 236–246.
42. Ibid., pp. 332–338.
43. Ibid., pp. 344–360.
44. Ibid., pp. 433–446.
45. Jaynes, 1990, pp. 456–469.
46. Jaynes, 1979a, 1979b, 1980, 1981a, 1981b.
47. Jaynes, 1976a. pp. 209, 214.
48. Nisbett and Wilson, 1977; Globus, et al., 1976; James, 1890; Bogen, 1973; Posey and Losch, 1983; Galin, 1974; Ley, 1981; Jaynes, 1976b.
49. Jaynes, 1979; Hilgard, 1977; Bleuler, 1950; Dodds, 1951; Orne, 1959; Barber, 1969; Spanos, 1986.
50. Jaynes, 1977b; Gorman and Wessman, 1979; Hilgard, 1977; Starr, 1968; Dodds, 1951; Bower, 1970; Fraser, 1968; Tulving, 1972; Yates, 1966.
51. Jaynes, 1982, 1985; Lewis, 1979; Benton, 1927; Lyons, 1978; James, 1890; Wicklund, 1979.
52. Freud, 1950/1900; Kahler, 1973; Weissmann, 1979; Proffitt, 1978.
53. Sheikh, Richardson, and Moleski, 1979; Jordan, 1979; Lerner, 1983; Meichenbaum, 1977; Cautela and McCullough, 1978; Kazdin, 1978; Berghausen and Sachs, 1986.
54. Singer, 1973; Vygotsky, 1964; Brainerd, 1978; Applebee, 1978; Flavell and Wellman, 1977.

55. Levy-Bruhl, 1973; Gellner, 1973; Evans-Pritchard, 1965; Hallpike, 1976; Lock and Heelas, 1981; Leenhardt, 1971.
56. Jaynes, University of New Hampshire tape, 1983.
57. Jaynes, Lewisburg tape, 1984.
58. Jaynes, Harvard lecture, 1988.
59. Ibid.
60. Jaynes, 1990, p. 448, citing Russell, 1921, 1927.
61. Hamilton, 1985 (reprinted as Chapter 5 of this volume).
62. Jaynes, 1990, pp. 455–456, citing M. S. Buchsbaum, et al., 1982.

UNPUBLISHED SOURCES

Greismann, J. to J. Jaynes. July 27, 1972.
Jaynes, J. Preface. Unpublished manuscript.
Jaynes, J. Talcott Mountain Science Center. Videotape.
Jaynes, J. 1969. "A New Theory of Consciousness." Invited address at the American Psychological Association.
Jaynes, J. to F. Biddle. December 14, 1942.
Jaynes, J. to E.G. Boring (1963–1969). Archives for the History of Psychology at Akron.
Jaynes, J. to C.B. Jaynes. February 6, 1938.
Jaynes, J. to C.B. Jaynes. May 16, 1938.
Jaynes, J. to C.B. Jaynes. April 27, 1942.
Jaynes, J. to C.B. Jaynes. April 12, 1944.
Jaynes, J. to C.B. Jaynes. April 25, 1944.
Jaynes, J. 1978. "The Consequences of Consciousness." Emory University. Audiotape. May 23.
Jaynes, J. 1983. University of New Hampshire lecture. Audiotape recorded by June Tower. April 28.
Jaynes, J. 1984. Lewisburg Audiotape.
Jaynes, J. 1985. 100th Anniversary of his Father's Ordination. First Unitarian Society in West Newton. Audiotape recorded by E.G. Dyett.
Jaynes, J. 1988. Harvard University lecture. Audiotape recorded by June Tower.
McGuinness, E. 2000. Glendale, CA. Interview by telephone with William R. Woodward. June 21.
Quinn, T. to J. Jaynes. April 4, 1974.

REFERENCES

Applebee, A.N. 1978. *The Child's Concept of Story: Ages Two to Seventeen*. Chicago: University of Chicago Press.

Barber, T.X. 1969. *Hypnosis: A Scientific Approach*. N.Y.: Van Nostrand Reinhold.

Baumeister, R.F. 1986. *Identity: Cultural Changes in the Struggle for Self*. N.Y.: Oxford University Press.

Beach, F.A. 1950. "The Snark was a Boojum." *The American Psychologist*, 5, 115–124.

Beach, F.A. and J. Jaynes. 1954. "Effects of Early Experience upon the Behavior of Animals." *Psychological Bulletin*, 51, 239–263.

Beach, F.A. and J. Jaynes. 1956a. "Studies of Maternal Retrieving in Rats: I: Recognition of Young." *Journal of Mammology*, 37, 177–180.

Beach, F.A. and J. Jaynes. 1956b. "Studies of Maternal Retrieving in Rats: II: Effects of Practice and Previous Parturitions." *American Naturalist*, 90, 103–109.

Beach, F.A. and J. Jaynes. 1956c. "Studies of Maternal Retrieving in Rats: III: Sensory Cues Involved in the Lactating Female's Response to Her Young." *Behavior*, 10, 104–125.

Beach, F.A., J. Jaynes, and A. Zitrin. 1956a. "Neural Mediation of Mating in Male Cats: I. Effects of Unilateral and Bilateral Removal of the Neocortex." *Journal of Comparative Physiological Psychology*, 49, 4, 321–7.

Beach, F.A., J. Jaynes, and A. Zitrin. 1956b. "Neural Mediation of Mating in Male Cats. III. Contributions of Occipital, Parietal and Temporal Cortex." *Journal of Comparative Neurology*, 105, 1, 111–25.

Beach, F.A. and J. Jaynes. 1960. "Effects of Early Experience upon the Behavior of Animals." Bobbs-Merrill Reprints.

Benton, J.F. 1927. "Consciousness of Self and Personality." In *The Renaissance of the Twelfth Century*. Cambridge: Harvard

Berghausen, P.E. and L.B. Sachs. 1986. "Hypnotic Treatment of Hallucinations and Disordered Impulse Control." *Imagination, Cognition and Personality*, 5, 311–319.

Bible, Amos and Ecclesiastes.

Bleuler, R. 1950. *Dementia Praecox or the Group of Schizophrenias*. N.Y.: International Universities Press.

Bogen, J.E. 1973. "The Other Side of the Brain." In Ornstein, R.E. *The Nature of Human Consciousness*. San Francisco: W.H. Freeman.

Bohn, G. 1910. *Alfred Giard et Son Oeuvre*. Paris: Mercure de France.

Bohn, G. 1911. *La Nouvelle Psychologie Animale*. Paris: Alcon.

Brainerd, C.J. 1978. "The Stage Question in Cognitive Developmental Theory and Commentary." *Behavioral and Brain Sciences*, 1, 173–214.

Buchsbaum, M.S, D.H. Ingvar, R. Kessler, R.N. Waters, J. Cappelletti, D.P.

van Kammen, et al. 1982. "Cerebral Glucography with Positron Tomography: Use in Normal Subjects and in Patients with Schizophrenia." *Archives of General Psychiatry*, 39, 251–259.

Carr, M. 1983. "Sidelights on *Xin* 'Heart, Mind' in the *Shijing*." Abstract in *Proceedings of the 31ˢᵗ CISHAAN*, Tokyo and Kyoto, 824–825.

Cautela, J., and L. McCullough. 1978. "Covert Conditioning." In J.L. Singer and K.S. Pope (eds.), *The Power of Human Imagination: New Methods in Psychotherapy*. N.Y.: Plenum Press.

Crick, F. and G. Mitchison. 1983. "The Function of Dreams." *Nature*, July 14.

Dennett, D. 1986. "Julian Jaynes's Software Archeology." *Canadian Psychology*, 27, 149–154.

Dewsbury, D. 2000. "Frank A. Beach, Master Teacher." *In Portraits of Pioneers in Psychology*, 4. Hillsdale, N. J.: Erlbaum.

Dodds, E.R. 1951. *The Greeks and the Irrational*. Berkeley, CA: University of California Press.

Evans-Pritchard, E.E. 1965. "Essays on Thinking in Western and Non-Western Society." In *Theories of Primitive Religion*. Oxford: Clarendon Press.

Flavell, J. H. and H.M. Wellman. 1977. "Metamemory." In R.V. Kail and J.W. Hagen (eds.), *Perspectives on the Development of Memory and Cognition*. Hillsdale, N.J.: Erlbaum.

Foulkes, D. 1985. *Dreaming: A Cognitive-Psychological Analysis*. Hillsdale, N.J.: L. Erlbaum Associates.

Fraser, J.T. 1968. *The Voices of Time: A Cooperative Survey of Man's Views of Time*. N.Y.: G. Braziller.

Freud, S. 1950/1900. *The Interpretation of Dreams*. N.Y.: Modern Library. Chapter 1.

Galin, D. 1974. "Implications for Psychiatry of Left and Right Cerebral Specialization." *Archives of General Psychiatry*, 31, 572–583.

Gazzaniga, M.S. 1973. "The Split Brain in Man." In R.E. Ornstein. *The Nature of Human Consciousness*. San Francisco: W. H. Freeman.

Gellner, E. 1973. "The Savage and the Modern Mind." In R. Horton and R.H. Finnegan (eds.), *Modes of Thought*. London: Faber.

Globus, G.G., G. Maxwell, I. Savodnik and E.M. Dewan. 1976. *Consciousness and the Brain: A Scientific and Philosophical Inquiry*. N.Y.: Plenum.

Gorman, B.S. and A.E. Wessman. 1979. "Images, Values, and Concepts of Time in Psychological Research." In B.S. Gorman and A.E. Wessman (eds.), *The Personal Experience of Time*. N.Y.: Plenum.

Gower, G.H. 1970. "Analysis of a Mnemonic Device." *American Scientist*, 496–510.

Hall, C.S. and G. Lindzey. 1978. "Self Theories." In *Theories of Personality*. 3ʳᵈ edition. N.Y.: Wiley.

Hallpike, C.R. 1976. "Is There a Primitive Mentality?" *Man*, 2, 253–270.

Hamilton, J. 1985. "Auditory Hallucinations in Nonverbal Quadriplegics." *Psychiatry*, 48, 382–392.

Hilgard, E.R. 1977. "Amnesia and Repression." In *Divided Consciousness: Multiple Controls in Human Thought and Action*. N.Y.: Wiley.

Hobson, J.A. and R.W. McCarley. 1977. "The Brain as a Dream State Generator: An Activation Synthesis Hypothesis of the Dream Process." *American Journal of Psychiatry*, 134, 1335–48.

Hooke, S.H. 1963. *Babylonian and Assyrian Religion*. Norman, OK: University of Oklahoma Press.

Iverson, E.G. 1985. "Bluff." *Analog*, 105, 90–114.

James, W. 1950. "The Consciousness of Self"; "Will." In *Principles of Psychology*. N. Y.: Dover, 2 Vols.

Jaynes, J.C. 1922. *Magic Wells: Sermons by Julian Clifford Jaynes*. Boston: Press of Geo. H. Ellis Co.

Jaynes, J. 1956. "Imprinting: The Interaction of Learned and Innate Behavior: I. Development and Generalization." *Journal of Comparative and Physiological Psychology*, 49, 201–206.

Jaynes, J. 1957. "Imprinting: The Interaction of Learned and Innate Behavior: II. The Critical Period." *Journal of Comparative and Physiological Psychology*, 50, 6–10.

Jaynes, J. 1958a. "Imprinting: The Interaction of Learned and Innate Behavior: III. Practice Effects on Performance, Retention, and Fear." *Journal of Comparative and Physiological Psychology*, 51, 234–237.

Jaynes, J. 1958b. "Imprinting: The Interaction of Learned and Innate Behavior: IV. Generalization and Emergent Discrimination." *JCPP*, 51, 238–242.

Jaynes, J. 1966. "The Routes of Science." *American Scientist*. 94–102.

Jaynes, J. 1969. "The Historical Origins of 'Ethology' and 'Comparative Psychology.'" *Animal Behavior*, 17, 601–606.

Jaynes, J. 1969. "Edwin Garrigues Boring, 1886–1968." *Journal of the History of the Behavioral Sciences*, 5, 99–112.

Jaynes, J. 1973. "The Origin of Consciousness." In D. Krech and H. Levin (eds.). *A Symposium in Honor of Robert MacLeod*. Ithaca: Cornell Department of Psychology.

Jaynes, J. 1976a. *The Origin of Consciousness in the Breakdown of the Bicameral Mind*. Boston: Houghton Mifflin. Reprinted in 1982 with a new Preface and in 1990 with a new Afterword.

Jaynes, J. 1976b. "The Evolution of Language in the Late Pleistocene." In S. Harnad, H.D. Steklis and J. Lancaster (eds.), "Origins and Evolution of Language and Speech." *Annals of the New York Academy of Science*, 280, 312–325.

Jaynes, J. 1977a. "Imprinting: The Interaction of Learned and Innate Behavior: V. On the Essential Nature of the Stimulus Object." Unpublished.

Jaynes, J. 1977b. "Remembrance of Things (Far) Past." *Quest*, 77, 1, November–December.

Jaynes, J. 1978. "In A Manner of Speaking: Commentary on Cognition and Consciousness in Non-Human Species." *Behavioral and Brain Sciences*, 1, 578–579.

Jaynes, J. 1979a. "Paleolithic Cave Paintings as Eidetic Images." *Behavioral and Brain Sciences*, 2, 605–607.

Jaynes, J. 1979b. "The Meaning of King Tut: A Review of the Tutankhamun Exhibition from the Perspective of Bicameral Theory." *Princeton Alumni Weekly*, June 25, 1979. Reprinted in *University Magazine*, 1979, No. 80, 12–13.

Jaynes, J. 1980. "Dragons of the Shang Dynasty: The Hidden Faces." *Art/World*, 4, No. 9, May 21, 5.

Jaynes, J. 1981a. "Ghost of a Flea: Visions of William Blake." *Art/World*, 5, 1, 1–6.

Jaynes, J. 1981b. "Art and the Right Hemisphere." *Art/World*, 5, 10, 3–6.

Jaynes, J. 1982. "A Two-Tiered Theory of Emotions." *Behavioral and Brain Sciences*, 5, 379–380.

Jaynes, J. 1985. "Sensory pain and Conscious Pain." *Behavioral and Brain Sciences*, 8, 61–63.

Jaynes, J.C. 1907. "Unitarianism in Newton." In H. Taylor and M.R. Royden (eds.), *The Mirror of Past and Present* (pp. 67–69). Newton, MA.: Newton Federation of Women's Clubs.

Jordan, C.S. 1979. "Mental Imagery and Psychotherapy: European Approaches." In A.A. Sheikh and J.T. Shaffer (eds.), *The Potential of Fantasy and Imagination*. Brandon House.

Kahler, E. 1973. *The Inward Turn of Narrative*. Princeton, N. J.: Princeton University Press.

Kazdin, A. 1978. "Covert Modeling." In J.L. Singer and K.S. Pope (eds). *The Power of Human Imagination: New Methods in Psychotherapy*. N.Y.: Plenum.

Leenhardt, M. 1971. *Do Kamo: Person and Myth in the Melanesian World*. N.Y.: Arno Press. Rpt. 1979. Chicago: University of Chicago Press.

Lerner, S. 1983. "Cognitive Therapy." *Carrier Foundation Letter* #92, October.

Levy-Bruhl, L. 1973. *Primitive Mentality*. N. Y.: Macmillan.

Lewis, M. 1979. "The Origins of Self." In M. Lewis and J. Brooks-Gunn (eds.). *Social Cognition and the Acquisition of Self*. N. Y.: Plenum Press.

Ley, R.G. 1979. "Cerebral Asymetrics, Emotional Experience, and Imagery: Implications for Psychotherapy." In A.A. Sheikh and J.T. Shaffer (eds.), *The Potential of Fantasy and Imagination*. N.Y.: Brandon House.

Ley, R.G. and M.P. Bryden. 1981. "Consciousness, Emotion, and the Right Hemisphere." In G. Underwood and S. Stevens (eds.), *Aspects of Consciousness*. N. Y.: Academic Press.

Lock, A. and P. Heelas. 1981. *Indigenous Psychologies: The Anthropology of the Self*.

N.Y.: Academic Press.

Lorenz, K. 1935. "Der Kumpan in der Umwelt des Vogels." *Journal der Ornithologie* (Leipzig) 83, 137–213; 289–413.

Lyons, J.O. 1978. *The Invention of the Self: The Hinge of Consciousness in the Eighteenth Century*. Carbondale: Southern Illinois University Press.

Meichenbaum, D. 1977. *Cognitive Behavior Modification*. N. Y.: Plenum Press.

Orne, M. 1959. "Nature of Hypnosis: Artifact and Essence." *Journal of Abnormal and Social Psychology*, 58, 277–299.

Ornstein, R.E. 1973. *The Nature of Human Consciousness*. San Francisco: W. H. Freeman.

Posey, T.B. and M.E. Losch. 1983. "Auditory Hallucinations of Hearing Voices in 375 Normal Subjects." *Imagination, Cognition, and Personality*, 3, 99–114.

Prescott, J. 1936. *The Story of Newton Massachusetts. Its Natural Beauty, Attractive homes and Historical Associations*. Newton, MA.: Newtonville Library Association.

Proffitt, E. 1978. "Romanticism, Bicamerality, and the Evolution of the Brain." *The Wordsworth Circle*, 9, 98–105.

Rhodes, R. 1978. "Alone in the Country of the Mind." *Quest*, 2, 71–78.

Russell, B. 1921. *Analysis of Mind*. London: Allen and Unwin.

Russell, B. 1927. *Philosophy*. N.Y.: Norton.

Sheikh, A.A., P. Richardson, and L.M. Moleski. 1979. "Psychosomatics and Mental Imagery." In A.A. Sheikh and J.T. Shaffer (eds.), *The Potential of Fantasy and Imagination*. N.Y.: Brandon House.

Singer, J. 1973. "Some Theoretical Implications." In J. Singer, *The Child's World of Make-Believe*. N.Y.: Academic Press.

Spanos, N. 1986. "Hypnotic Behavior and Commentaries." *Behavioral and Brain Sciences*, 9, 449–502.

Starr, C. 1968. *The Awakening of the Greek Historical Spirit*. N. Y.: Knopf.

Tinbergen, N. 1940. "Die Übersprungsbewegung." *Zeitschrift für Tierpsychologie*, 4, 1–40.

Tulving, E. 1972. "Episodic and Semantic Memory." In E. Tulving and W. Donaldson (eds.), *Organization of Memory*. N.Y.: Academic Press.

Vygotsky, L.S. 1964. "The Genetic Roots of Thought and Speech." In L.S. Vygotsky, *Thought and Language*. Cambridge, MA: MIT Press.

Weissman, J. 1979. "Vision, Madness, and Morality: Poetry and the Theory of the Bicameral Mind." *Georgia Review*, 33, 118–148.

Wicklund, R.A. 1979. "Objective Self-Awareness." *American Scientist*, 67, 287–193.

Yates, F.A. 1966. *The Art of Memory*. Chicago: University of Chicago.

PART II

Voices of the Mind

CHAPTER 2

The Ghost of a Flea

Visions of William Blake

JULIAN JAYNES

DID WILLIAM BLAKE really see visions? And were these the origins of some of his drawings and paintings with their anatomical style, allegorical shadowless frontality, and overwhelming invention?

One night about 1819, he suddenly interrupted his company by exclaiming, "Good God! Here's Edward III ... I have hitherto seen his profile only. He now turns his pale face towards me ... And if you say another word, he'll vanish. Be quiet while I take a sketch of him."

At another time he haughtily rebuked a visitor, "But I see him, Sir, there he is, his name is Lot — you may read of him in the Scripture. He is sitting for his portrait."

Ghost of a Flea

The most curious and therefore unfortunately the most celebrated instance was described by his friend Varley: "He told me he had seen a wonderful thing — the ghost of a flea! 'And did

---

you make a drawing of him?' I inquired, 'No indeed,' said he, 'I wish I had, but I shall if he appears again!' He looked earnestly into the corner of the room, and then said, 'here he is — reach me my things — I shall keep my eye on him! ... I felt convinced by his mode of proceeding, that he had a real image before him, for he left off, and began on another part of the paper to make a separate drawing of the mouth of the Flea, which the spirit having opened, he was prevented from proceeding with the first sketch, til he had closed it."

Such invisible sitters talked to Blake as they posed, explaining their lives. These included Voltaire, various angels, Moses, Caesar, Milton; and even the above flea who told him that "fleas were inhabited by the souls of such men as were by nature bloodthirsty to excess."

Was Blake making all this up? Lying to fit himself into the excessive ideas of the new antirational Romanticism of his time? Or at least wildly exaggerating for his own belief in himself? Or simply humoring his simpleton guests who wanted to believe him a seer in the ancient sense?

Smiling Indulgence

Many modern scholars with a standardized idea of greatness have thought so and glossed over such instances with a smiling indulgence of Blake's poetic license. They have done so to defend Blake against the cruel accusations of insanity in the public press that followed his first and only exhibition. (He was so hurt that he shrank back into the obscurity of a small circle of disciples for the rest of his life.) After all, if Blake was telling the truth about himself in 'seeing' his visions and 'hearing' his voices, perhaps he really was mad. And they have felt it their duty to protect their subject from such supposed derogation.

But the data on Blake's life will not support such kindly meant skepticism. Not at all.

Always in Paradise

Blake was not devious, certainly not so devious as to maintain any such deception so strongly, so vividly, and for so long. As his devoted wife who helped him almost all day long once complained, "I have very little of Mr. Blake's company, he is always in Paradise." While he called these voices and visions his "imaginations" and knew they somehow came from his own head (because his culture constantly told him so), so did other sensations of the external world. They were external because they were internal: the distinction was artificial. The real reality was not the barren numbered world of Newton and Locke but the world of his hallucinatory imagination. And it was this capacity to hallucinate the realities behind the world that was the salvation of mankind. He said of this capacity that "all men partake of it — but it is lost by not being cultivated." And he taught it to his wife so that she too could see the visions.

Memory and reason in Blake's definitions of them were wrong, diseases to be cured, shackles to be cast off. Only intellect leaping into imagination out of their entanglement is the true path, a path which Milton in Blake's epic of that name is made to undergo. Milton and every would-be creator has to travel through the warring intersection of Urizen (Reason) and Luvah (Passion) through the Satan space of all mental contraries, until the self becomes permeated by all contending forces, until all the "Contrarities" become "Positives," and one sees the world not just from without like a black pebble, but from within, concavely, truly in Blake's sense of truly. This is the place of Urthona, of cleansed doors of perception, of what I am here calling hallucination and Blake called Imagination. It is, I suggest, a mental struggle that is able to unlock the effortless creativity of the bicameral mind. That is Milton's great track in Blake's poem.

The Grandest Poem

Even this poem and all its philosophy was hallucinated. He called *Milton* "the grandest poem that this world contains" and said so humbly since he was just its secretary. "I have written this poem from immediate Dictation, twelve or sometimes thirty lines at a time, without premeditation and even against my will."

Of course this claim could be seen (and has been) as the result of a desire on Blake's part to imitate Milton's own claimed process of poetic inspiration. But when put with so many other instances, particularly with his daily hallucinations of his beloved brother after his death about which he certainly would not be misleading, and with the manner of his own death (see any biography), together with what we now know about the capacities of the mind, we can be sure that Blake was telling how it really was with him.

Still to some, all this is difficult to accept literally. But I would like to suggest that with the notion of the bicameral mind, the realization that all of us to a greater or less extent, have locked away within us an ancient mentality based on hallucinations of the speech and visions of gods, that with this new understanding of the origins of mind, we can for the first time be comfortable with the genuine Blake who 'heard' his poetry and 'saw' his paintings.

Blake was not insane. Schizophrenic insanity, being a partial relapse to the bicameral mind, is indeed usually accompanied by 'voices' and 'visions' of a religious nature. But it is also accompanied by panic, distress, an inability to be coherent in conversation, to know who and where one is, to manage one's own affairs, to sustain ordinary human relationships. And Blake was the opposite of these.

He was indeed what one of his friends called him, "a new kind of man," one who had both consciousness and a bicameral mind, and probably unique in modern art history.

CHAPTER 3

Verbal Hallucinations
and Pre-Conscious Mentality

JULIAN JAYNES

T HERE IS WIDE agreement that verbal hallucinations are the
most preeminent symptom in the psychopathology of schizophrenia, even though the phenomenon does not apparently occur
in every case. Some psychiatrists, indeed, think that schizophrenic episodes *always* begin with such hallucinations, but this
is very difficult to establish, just as it is very difficult to study
hallucinations in schizophrenics at all. Very often a patient will
deny hearing voices for any or several of three reasons: either at
the command of his hallucination, or because he fears some
treatment such as electro-shock, or because he does not want his
voices probed into. In this chapter, I shall first present some of
the data we have found in our studies and then suggest a
theoretical framework into which they can be placed.

Our first study, naturally enough, was of hospitalized schizophrenics in a New York psychiatric ward. It was done by my
student Michael Rosenberg. A tape recorder was sometimes used
but usually not because of its obtrusiveness. Mr. Rosenberg had

Presented at a conference at the Harvard University Department of Psychology,
October, 1989. First published in M. Spitzer and B.A. Maher (eds.), 1990,
Philosophy and Psychopathology, New York: Springer-Verlag. © 1990 Springer-
Verlag. Reprinted with permission.

in his mind a list of questions which was loosely followed. After each interview, he reconstructed what had been said into a paragraph. Here is a typical example:

VIOLA: The voices appeared somewhat suddenly and gradually got more and more intense. At first there were only angels. These would tell me good things. For instance, "Viola, you're a good person." But then sometimes diabolical voices appeared and would say things like "You're lying." These diabolical voices would tell me that I was bad and should die. They told me that I was going to hell. When these voices spoke, I could see fire and I definitely felt burning on my body from this fire. The angels were often my sisters talking to me. The diabolical voices were the devil talking and he was trying to pull me down into hell, but I resisted.

In answers to questions, the patient said she had been very religious as a child and that her grandmother had had a church in the basement. The voices sounded as if they were coming from behind her. She said they never sounded like her mother, father, or son. She thought they started because she was trying to communicate with "the soul of my son's father." The angels did not like this and the devil tried to take advantage of this opportunity.

I use this as an illustration because it shows certain characteristics common to the hallucinations of hospitalized patients: The suddenness of onset, the deeply religious nature of the experience, the self-contradictory nature of the messages, and their critical emphasis either positive or negative. All these factors are I think very familiar to most of you.

Now the question here is why? Why the religious quality? Why the admonitory nature of the voices?

Let me give some other examples of verbal hallucinations in these hospital patients.

JEREMY (A 25-year-old black man who had started taking drugs when he was 9, well groomed, somewhat sedated): I kept on turning around, but there was never any one there. ... In a 'crack house' a couple of weeks ago, the voices started screaming really loudly and I just flipped. The police came and took me to the hospital. The voices almost always occurred several at a time being both male and female. I didn't ever recognize any of them as being friends or relatives. When I was taking a lot of drugs, the voices would be nice and tell me how good a person I really am inside. However, whenever I stopped taking the drugs, the voices would change very quickly. They became evil and would tell me to do some very bad things. They were always very specific in their commands. For instance, they would tell me "go rob that store," "go mug that lady," ... the voices wouldn't leave me alone until I had done what they had told me to do. I couldn't ever shut the voices down and they just got louder and louder until I couldn't deal with them. Then I would do what they wanted.

It is interesting to note the relationship of the hallucinations to drugs and therefore to brain chemistry. This case also illustrates the sex differences in hallucinations, that males hear more commands to commit some act than do females.

MERCEDES (Hispanic female in her mid-twenties, disheveled, responds only after being offered a cigarette): If the thinking thoughts stop, then I will die. They have taken over my mind and control it, you understand? I am able to communicate with you, but they are telling me things and explaining some information to me. They usually come from behind me but I know they're in my mind. They go on all day. They're talking right now. At night they let me sleep, but start talking to me in the morning again. They say all different kinds of things to me. Sometimes nice things, sometimes bad things, sometimes just repeating whatever I say. They tell me about other people, before I even meet them. The voices didn't tell me about you. But now they're talking about you and listening. They won't let me tell you what they're saying.

TOBAS (20 years old, neatly dressed, from the Dominican Republic, about to be moved to a more permanent ward for schizophrenics): I felt the Lord in me. This is when the voices began. At first they were only whispers, but then louder, but still soft. It was Jesus speaking to me. He would tell me what to do and ask me questions. Jesus would speak to me alone and no one else. Then I became a backslider. The Devil started talking to me. (He was unable to imitate the voice of The Devil.) The Devil told me bad things. He told me to kill myself. The Devil just wouldn't leave me alone because I was a backslider.

ANGEL (An Hispanic male in his mid-twenties, well groomed, quite willing to talk, carrying a Spanish comic book): About three weeks ago the voices started and I would look around to see if anyone was there but there never was. At first they were almost funny. There would be a poster advertising a movie and the voices would say "Angel, look at that poster over there saying such and such." I would look and the posters always said what the voices had said they would. After a while though the voices started getting louder and talking more often. They would just say really bad things over and over. They would tell me that I am a bad person and I'm going to die. When I couldn't take them anymore, I tried blinding myself by looking at the sun, but this didn't work. At around 3:00 in the morning I went to the church to find a preacher, but the church was locked. I started to walk up and down Broadway. The voices just kept talking and talking day and night. I don't know why I went to the church, since I had never been very religious, but I guess that I thought the preacher might be able to explain where the voices were coming from. When he wasn't there, I just didn't know what to do anymore. After a couple of days the police picked me up and brought me to the hospital. With the medicine, the voices have stopped, but I'm not better yet. (Angel was then afraid to say anything more about the voices "because he could not control these voices and they did not let him control his own mind.")

In general, most of our hospital interviewees were Hispanic. Eighty percent at some time heard multiple voices. Most of the voices were male and were frightening to 63% of the subjects. Twenty-two percent of the hospital subjects could not understand some of the time what the voices were saying. Of some pertinence to hypotheses of the relation of schizophrenia to laterality is the finding that 56% of our hospitalized subjects were left handed or ambidextrous.

Hallucinations in the "Homeless"

We next turned to a rather haphazard selection of so called "homeless" people in New York City, particularly along Broadway and in the huge Port Authority Bus Station. Interviews were casually begun by Mr. Rosenberg and might continue over coffee or a pizza. The subject of hearing voices was casually introduced into the conversation. In contrast with the hospitalized patients, they seemed not at all anxious in talking about the voices, even eager at times and very cooperative. Also of interest was the phenomenon of hearing multiple voices all speaking at once. Obviously some of these subjects had at one time been hospitalized and some were on medication. The voices were again admonitory and usually religious, often telling the person what to do, which in most of these subjects is resisted. Here are some examples.

GABRIEL (A poorly dressed 32-year-old Puerto Rican man outside the Port Authority): Yeah, I hear voices sometimes. I'll tell you about them if you give me money. O.K., I'll tell you anyway. Man, it's a really scary experience. Really frightening. They can tell you anything. No, I don't ever do any drugs. I don't know whose voices they are. They just talk; sometimes in other languages. Yeah, sometimes Spanish. They are hard to understand. They can say a lot of different things. They can tell you bad things to do; so you just do them. For instance, "hit that man, spit on her." Sometimes you just say out loud what they told you like "she's ugly." You can't control or stop them. They can go on and off all day long lasting about a minute.

BREHMAN (A 32-year-old black man sitting on the ground leaning against a wall on 43rd Street and 8th Avenue; well groomed for someone whom is living on the streets): I don't hear any imaginary voices. I hear real voices. I was in a fight last March in Atlanta. When the doctor stitched me up he implanted some kind of monitoring device so that they can keep track of me and communicate with me. Now whenever I'm in the city I see people on the street or anywhere and they can start yelling at me. See, there are a lot of evil people in cities. There are some good people, but the bad ones in the city start yelling at me through this monitoring device. In the country nobody's voice yells at me through the device. It can get real bad, especially at night. You see these people could get on the same frequency as you and start yelling at you. They don't leave you alone. Yeah, sometimes they say nice things but almost never. They come at you five, six at a time. … When they yell at me now, I yell back real loud at them and they shut up after a while.

BRUNO (A bearded white man in his thirties living in a hotel for homeless men, met on Broadway at 96th Street while sitting on a bench talking to some 'winos'; he seemed open, honest, and happy, and was very excited and anxious to discuss his voices): I hear voices a lot. It's perfectly normal, but you can't tell the doctors or they give you medicine that makes you sick. … But I just hear the voices and don't do what they say to do. That's normal, right? A couple of minutes ago I was on a bus and the voices told me to get off the bus. They're usually men talking. They can say your thoughts. Sometimes they say "Bruno, you're a good guy," but at the same time there are other louder voices saying "Bruno, you're a real bad person." ... The voices come from in my head. Actually from in my right ear. ... I don't do anything bad they tell me to do. They told me yesterday to "hit an old lady," but I didn't because I knew it was only a voice in my mind.

THE ECHOLAILIC (a 25-year-old black man in the Port Authority bus terminal whose hands were shaking, perhaps from having been on psychotropic medications for too long; when asked about voices, he responded in short, stuttered speech): I hear voices talking to me a lot. They yell at me and bother me. I don't know who they are or what they say, but they annoy me. They started, I don't know, yesterday? They go on and off a lot. "What's it about? What's it about? What's it about? (At this point, he became echolalic, repeating everything and no longer looked as disturbed as before. Then he suddenly stopped repeating what the interviewer had said and spoke about food and what he might eat later.)

THE STREET MAN (A black man in the corner of the Port Authority, relatively kempt above 35): Voices? I hear all the voices. But they don't tell me nothing I don't already know. You see, I know everything. My thoughts are always ahead of everything. What voices do you want to know about? Cosmologian, terrestrian, solarian, universalian...? You see, it's the psychology. Yes, listen, when everything started the earth was made and God did it. I know all that. Jesus knows it. I already know everything even if they're yelling. I know what's wrong and what's right. You see, I'm always trying to catch up with my reality. I don't even try anymore. It's always so far ahead of everything. I can't even keep up with it. ... No one can ever know me or understand it.

MR. JOHNSON (A 42-year-old black man in the Bowery with a wooden cross hanging from some beads around his neck): I used to want to be better, but I'm too old to be cured. The problem began because I just was too smart. Jesus would talk to me and he took my brain away because I was too smart. Hitler would tell me nice things sometimes (he used Hitler and Jesus interchangeably). There were other voices too. They would yell at me and tell me to do bad things. They wouldn't leave me alone. I've been having these voices for a long, long time. After a while, you just get use to 'em. I'm a very, very religious man, but I don't go to church. I pray to God all the time in my own way … I don't think the voices are ever going to stop. The ones that yell are mainly men.

THOMAS (A 43-year-old white man in ragged clothing on the third floor of the bus terminal playing around with a small broken television set and its antenna; he offered to sell it for twenty dollars; when the subject of voices came up, he became very serious, almost paternal): Listen! Don't you pay any attention to those voices. They're bad. They'll get you into trouble. Just ignore them and after a while they won't bother you as much. I was in the hospital for a long time because of those fucking voices. Those little bastards would just start yelling at you. Listen to me! Start ignoring them now before they get too bad. … The voices can talk to you through the television. That's how they first started. It's really frightening because you think the TV's talking to you. I'm not going to sell you this TV if you hear voices. It might scare you too much.[1]

These examples are fairly typical of those homeless people who do hear voices. Although we made no effort to make an estimate of what percent of the people wandering the streets of New York are hallucinating, it seemed that almost half of those approached did so. Most of these street subjects were black. 72% of positive cases at sometime had heard multiple voices. Almost all voices were male. As with hospital subjects, most of them were afraid of their hallucinations and about the same percentage (21%) could not understand what the voices were saying some of the time. But in contrast to the hospital patients, only 21% of the homeless were either left handed or ambidextrous, although that is still more than double the frequency in the general population.

All this material is quite familiar to most of you and would obviously come under the heading of psychopathology. But what follows is more controversial.

Hallucinations in Normal Students

We next turned to study verbal hallucinations in a normal population. The subjects were 74 Princeton students taken from the student telephone directory by a strict and careful randomization procedure. Each of the subjects filled out a carefully worded questionnaire in private and anonymously. None of the students so contacted refused to participate. Again, the study was done by Michael Rosenberg.[2] 27.8% replied yes to the statement "I am positive that I have heard a voice at some point when no one had spoken to me." 12.5% clearly recall hearing a dead relative's voice. 3% had heard God's voice, 78% could still hear a song after it had stopped, and 67% replied "yes" to the statement "I've heard my name being called when no one has called me." The important figure here I think is the first, namely, that roughly 28% of all Princeton University undergraduates have experienced at least one auditory hallucination.

Many of the descriptions they provided of verbal hallucinations were similar to those of psychiatric patients. The voices they heard were parents, relatives, friends, dead relatives, or God. Some had only heard one voice speaking while others had heard more than one voice. Both male and female voices were heard. Some were slow deep voices while others spoke quickly. The great difference is that these hallucinations of normal students were of much less intensity and frequency than those of psychiatric patients.

These results are consistent with those found previously by Posey and Losch[3] in a questionnaire given to 375 college students. I suggest that it is now clearly established that about 1/3 of the normal population hear verbal hallucinations at some time, and that such hallucinations do not therefore indicate pathology as biological psychiatrists have been taught to believe.

Hallucinated Playmates in Children

The spectrum of incidence of auditory hallucinations not only has to include normal non-schizophrenic adults but also children. Those who have studied the phenomena of "imaginary playmates" (which should read hallucinated playmates) are convinced that such children hear the 'voices' of their to-us-unseen friends in their conversations with them.[4] In my own research, I have found that about half of women students at a religious college had had such hallucinated playmates, and half of those clearly remembered the pitch and quality of the voices.

One of these women is of special interest. She came from a very poor family in which both parents had to work, leaving the girl in the care of a schizophrenic grandmother who was hallucinating voices in various rooms of the house. The girl developed hallucinated playmates, different ones for different rooms. Her mother, realizing the situation, quit her job, sent the grandmother to a mental hospital, and tried to train the child out of such hallucinations — which was successful in part. But the girl, now grown up, still has her hallucinated playmates who are also grown up like her, and appear in times of stress and try to tell her what to do. Their voices were clearly 'heard' and not imagined. She did not impress me as being psychotic. She was concerned as to whether her hallucinated playmates were innate or learned, I imagine because she was going to be married and was not going to have children if it was possible that they would go through what she has gone through.

And I will report here the case that happened just the other day to a friend of mine. A precocious 3½-year-old boy had an hallucinated playmate named Henry. He was visiting his grand-father with his parents. While playing with some toy dinosaurs on the living room coffee table, he suddenly looked startled, jumped up and ran over to a ventilating grill on the floor and cried out into it, "Go back Henry! Don't come any further! You'd get stuck. Go back down to the cellar!" He then returned to his dinosaurs as if nothing had happened. I mention this case as another demonstration that it is not an imagined voice in the conscious sense of imagination but a true hallucination. This small vignette will remind some of you of hallucinating patients in the hospital who are convinced that the voice emanates from someone stuck in the ventilating system.

Verbal Hallucinations in a Nonverbal Population

A group that I would like to mention has been discovered only recently.[5] These are cerebral palsied spastic-athetoid nonverbal congenital quadriplegics who have never spoken in their lives. They must be fed, bathed, toileted, and moved by others, and they are often regarded by the nursing staff as "vegetables." Surprisingly, some of them are fully capable of understanding speech at a normal level — even though they have never learned how to speak. Using finger, lip, or eye movements, communication can be established with a known technique, something like the game of "20 questions," in which the patient can indicate yes or no.[6]

When asked privately through this technique about the possibility of hearing voices, most of these patients "gave startled expressions followed by excited 'yes' signals." The voices were usually the same sex as the patient, sounding like a relative, but identified as God. They spoke as from outside the patient, usually from the upper left (when hearing the voice the patient's eyes shifted to the left as if involuntarily), told the patient what to do and what was right, and made the patient miserable when disobeyed. Usually the voices were helpful, telling the patients to cooperate with any training program that was initiated. The patients felt they could not communicate with the voices. The data were checked for possible Clever Hans effects by having a second questioner who did not know the earlier results. This work has recently been carefully extended, demonstrating that these speechless subjects can present the content of their own phenomenal field accurately and that investigators' interpretations are accurate.[7] Unfortunately, CAT scans on these patients were not available.

Other Observations

The variety of verbal hallucinations is remarkable. I have in my files unsolicited letters from many correspondents who wish to tell me about their hallucinations. One of the most unusual was from a transsexual who as a boy suffered considerable sexual molestation and then as an adult, after a spell of Scientology, became "overwhelmed" with voices until his sex change operation when they abated. Others had been shipwrecked sailors during the war who conversed with an audible God for hours in the water until they were saved. A woman in her car heard a voice from the left car window telling her to write her funeral, and when she got out paper and pen "the words poured visually into my head." She had never had a similar experience. Another was a deeply religious man who one summer, following an interest in spiritualism, heard at least 20 divine voices extremely similar to the voices heard by Schreber described in his famous autobiography. While he was hospitalized at the demand of his family, he never received medication or therapy or lost his objectivity, and was sorry when the voices went away. If you have a tendency to say this was a schizophrenic episode with spontaneous remission, I wonder what you would say about Emanuel Swedenborg, the brilliant early 19th century scientist who heard voices he identified as everyone from Socrates to Jesus, and whose verbal hallucinations founded the Swedenborgian religion. Or his one time follower William Blake, whose poems were heard from believed-in angels all about him. It is to be noted through this material the important relation to belief in those voices and particularly religious belief.

Why are verbal hallucinations so common in such disparate groups, both normal and pathological? Why are hallucinations so often admonitory, 73% commands in men and more often criticisms in women? Why are they often religious in nature? Why do criminal psychotics commonly feel they must obey their voices?

Hallucinations in Ancient Civilizations

As a way of trying to answer these questions, let us look back into the earliest history of civilizations for evidence of verbal hallucinations. The earliest text of any size that we can translate with relative assurance is the *Iliad*. I would point out two characteristics. First, verbal as well as visual hallucinations are everywhere in this poem. The voices are, of course, called gods and they manage and control the actions and emotions of this bloody story. The gods or verbal hallucinations begin the Trojan War, determine its strategy and its end.

A second characteristic of the *Iliad* is that in its older layers there is no introspective consciousness. Nor are there words in the original text for conscious operations, such as think, feel, experience, imagine, remember, regret, etc.[8] The hallucinated voices or gods *were* human volition. The springs of action were not in conscious decision making or introspective musings of what will follow from one specific act versus another. We should always be vigilant in realizing that consciousness is not the same as cognition or perception as common street knowledge assumes, but something added to them, something learned through language and its power of metaphors and analogies.[9]

The older parts of the *Iliad*, then, display a pre-conscious mentality, one in which verbal hallucinations called gods are absolutely central. This mentality I have called in other work the bicameral mind — a rather inexact metaphor to a bicameral legislature of an upper and lower house. Such bicameral individuals moved through their lives on the basis of habit — just as we do, but when any novel occurrence or situation came along, a choice-point as we might say, in came an hallucinated voice telling the person what to do, precisely the point at which consciousness in modern times would be choosing our own behavior.

What triggered these hallucinations? I suggest it was even the slight stress of making a decision in a novel circumstance, whereas in ourselves in modern times the stress threshold for such triggering of a verbal hallucination is much higher. The reason they are so prevalent in all cultures today, in the hospital patients and homeless I have talked about, in children and speechless quadriplegics, is because they were once the genetic basis of this ancient mentality, and the genes for this potentiality are with us today. Verbal hallucinations, we think, evolved along with the evolution of language during the late Pleistocene[10] as the response part of the brain register of all admonitory information. Its survival value at first was simply to direct an individual in various long-term tasks, which cued their occurrence. By 9000 B.C., such voices were called what we call gods.[11] The bicameral mind produced a new kind of social control that allowed agricultural civilizations to begin. Historical speculation, yes, but touching data points in archaeological evidence all along the way.

Let me broadly summarize a huge amount of data by several assertions at this point. Civilization, by which we mean human beings living together in large groups, begins in various sites in Mesopotamia, spreads into Anatolia (modern Turkey), westward into Egypt, then into Africa, from Anatolia into Greece and Southern Russia, then India, Thailand, and China, and then independently in a series of civilizations in Mesoamerica and the Andean highlands, and *all* these early civilizations show some kind of evidence of being bicameral or organized by hallucinations called gods (which is the same thing), be it the presence of idols, or depictions in murals, reliefs, or seals, or, where there was a written language, actual descriptions of such interactions between men and their hallucinated gods — not entirely unlike the descriptions of modern hallucinators earlier in this chapter.

Some Ancient and Modern Parallels

Now let me briefly draw your attention to a few instances of the similarity of some modern phenomena that I have already mentioned and ancient bicameral ones. One is the business of idols. This is an important topic that no psychologist has studied. Idols are material effigies that provoked and sustained verbal hallucinations in ancient times. They are everywhere in all ancient civilizations. It is as if they make the voices plausible. We can remember here the little boy running to his hallucinated friend under the floor grating where the voice seemed to be coming from. Or "Thomas" with his broken television in the Port Authority Bus Station. I have seen on city streets what I regarded as homeless men making imaginary telephone calls at a pay booth, never putting in a coin, and flubbing the fingers over the dial without ever dialing, and then conversing at length with what I assume is a verbal hallucination. In another instance, something which probably some of you have observed, a patient in the hospital was sitting in a chair intently watching a blank television screen, and saying in amazement, "But how does President Reagan know so much about me?" Note the hierarchical underpinnings of this. Almost always verbal hallucinations are of somebody above the person in a hierarchical relationship just as it was in bicameral times. It may seem strange to regard a ventilation grating, or a broken television, or a silent telephone as an idol, but such is their function.

A second note I would add concerns hallucinated playmates, in particular the case I have mentioned of the woman whose playmates grew up with her and tried to tell her what to do in times of stress. Hallucinated playmates appear to occur in almost 50% of children, although many are forgotten or suppressed. We can at least imagine that something parallel happened in bicameral times where all children, encouraged and supported with expectancies by the cultural values of the society, developed hallucinated playmates that grew up with them and became their personal god, their *ili* in Mesopotamia and the *ka* in Egypt.

I think it can easily be inferred that human beings with such a mentality of hearing hallucinations had to exist in a special kind of society so that the hallucinations would agree. It would be one rigidly ordered in strict hierarchies with strict expectancies organized into the mind so that the social fabric was preserved. And such was definitely the case. The texts clearly show that bicameral theocracies were all hierarchical, submerged in ritual, with a god, often an idol or robed statue as throughout Mesopotamia at its head from whom hallucinations seemed to come, or else, more rarely, with a human who was divine (that is, heard in hallucination by those just below him in the hierarchy) being head of state as in Egypt. The *Iliad* with its loose organization of hero-warriors may seem to be an exception, but archaeological evidence from the period of the Trojan War show idols were common, and Linear B describes a strictly hierarchical society. For the evidence of all this, I have to refer you to my earlier work.[12]

The Breakdown of Hallucinations
and the Beginning of Consciousness

Such theocracies with their strict hierarchies require stability, require children to be brought up with similar expectancies. When there is social unrest, particularly when people are forced to migrate and leave their stability-inducing temples and idols, the voices heard by the individuals of a society no longer agree and the bicameral mind no longer can function. The Exodus and the ensuing turmoil in Canaan was just such an event. The whole of the Hebrew Testament can be read as the slow inevitable breakdown of this hallucinatory mentality and its replacement by wisdom. In Mesopotamia one of the chief causes of the breakdown of the bicameral mind was overpopulation because of its huge success in running agricultural city-states. And there too, the 2nd millennium B.C. towards its end is seeing more and more wars and invasions. Social chaos was most certainly exacerbated by the great eruption of Thera (sometimes called by its Christian name Santorini) that devastated the Near Eastern world and began several centuries of migration and invasion. And the success of writing in relaying the commands of the gods weakened the power of auditory hallucinations. With the social underpinnings of the bicameral mind gone, with people no longer hearing their voices, what could people do?

In this chapter I have not gone into the nature of consciousness and why it is reasonable to suppose that consciousness is not a biological given evolved in some mystical fashion somewhere back in animal evolution, but is a specifically human ability built upon the basis of the power of language to form metaphors and analogies just at this time. This can most clearly be seen in the earliest Greek literature. Beginning with the Linear B Tablets, going through the *Iliad* and then the *Odyssey*, through the lyric and elegiac poets of the next two centuries to Solon in 600 B.C., provides the clearest description of the breakdown of the bicameral mind and the development of the vocabulary of consciousness on the basis of metaphor. Such words as *thumos*, *phrenes*, *kardia*, *psyche* change from external objective referents to internal mental functions.[13] And this process is going on elsewhere at the same time. I have gone into this in much more depth elsewhere.[14] In the Hebrew world, I would ask you to compare the oldest pure book, Amos, an almost bicameral man, with the most recent, Ecclesiastes of about 200 B.C.[15]

So in this chapter we have started off with several contemporary studies of verbal hallucinations which sometimes may be regarded as psychopathology and sometimes not. Then we looked back into history and found that the ancient literatures show the phenomenon to be practically universal and every day. Schizophrenia then is a partial relapse to the bicameral mind, but only partial, because the person has learned consciousness in childhood, and is desperately trying to hang on to it. I think the evidence warrants the conclusion that the evolutionary origin of the phenomena of verbal hallucinations seen so clearly in schizophrenia is in this ancient preconscious mentality I have called the bicameral mind.

Summary

Verbal hallucinations were studied in a variety of groups. In a sample of hospitalized schizophrenics and a sample of homeless people on the streets of New York City, such voices were often multiple, critical in women, but more often commands in men, and commonly religious. In a carefully randomized sample of normal college students, a questionnaire study revealed that almost a third had "clearly heard a voice when no one had spoken to me." The voices were identified as parents, friends, dead relatives, or God. From a study of "imaginary playmates," it was concluded that verbal hallucinations were occurring here also. And a non-verbal group of congenital quadriplegics, who had never spoken but with whom communication could be established, heard voices they identified as God, such voices being usually helpful.

Parallels were then drawn between modern verbal hallucinations and what is revealed in ancient texts. Ancient civilizations seem to have been governed by such hallucinations called gods, a mentality known as the bicameral mind. It was concluded that the reason verbal hallucinations are found so extensively, in every modern culture, in normal students, schizophrenics, children, and vividly reported in the texts of antiquity is that such hallucinations are an innate propensity, genetically evolved as the basis of an ancient preconscious mentality.

NOTES TO CHAPTER 3

1. When the interviewer tried to correct Thomas's misunderstanding by saying that he didn't hear voices but was a student at Princeton University doing research with Professor Jaynes, Thomas immediately cut in, "That's just the kind of thing they tell you! I said don't listen to them."
2. Rosenberg, 1988.
3. Posey and Losch, 1983.
4. Harvey, 1918; Pines, 1978.
5. Hamilton, 1985.
6. See Moore, 1972.
7. Sappington, et al., 1988.
8. Modern translations are notorious for naïvely projecting modern consciousness into the text.
9. I apologize for what must seem contentious and provocative in its brevity. I go into these matters fully in Jaynes 1976a, Chapter 1.1, and Jaynes, 1986, particularly pages 140–142.
10. Jaynes, 1976b.
11. This theory is thus one that explains the origin of gods and therefore religion.
12. Jaynes, 1976a.
13. See Snell, 1953; Adkins, 1970.
14. Jaynes, 1976a.
15. By "pure" I mean books of the Bible that for the most part are not mixtures from various sources as is most of the Old Testament. Prophets such as Amos were transitional persons retaining enough bicamerality to relay the words of gods to others with an authenticity that convinced.

REFERENCES

Adkins, A.D.H. 1970. *From the Many to the One*. Ithaca: Cornell University Press.

Hamilton, J. 1985. "Auditory Hallucinations in Nonverbal Quadriplegics." *Psychiatry*, 48, 382–392.

Harvey, N.A. 1918. *Imaginary Playmates*. Ipsilanti: State Normal College.

Jaynes, J. 1976a. *The Origin of Consciousness in the Breakdown of the Bicameral Mind*. Boston: Houghton Mifflin. (German translation by K. Neff. 1988. *Der Ursprung des Bewusstseins durch den Zusammenbruch der Bicameralen Psyche*. Rowohit, Reinbeck).

Jaynes, J. 1976b. "The Evolution of Language in the Late Pleistocene." *Annals of the New York Academy of Sciences*, 280, 312–325.

Jaynes, J. 1986. "Consciousness and the Voices of the Mind." *Canadian Psychology*, 27, 128–186.

Moore, M.V. 1972. "Binary Communication for the Severely Handicapped." *Archives of Physical Medicine and Rehabilitation*, 53, 532–533.

Pines, M. 1978. "Invisible Playmates." *Psychology Today*, 12, 38–42.

Posey, T.B. and M.E. Losch. 1983. "Auditory Hallucinations of Hearing Voices in 375 Normal Subjects." *Imagination, Cognition, and Personality*, 2, 99–113.

Rosenberg, M.E. 1988. "Auditory Hallucinations in Princeton University Undergraduates." Senior thesis at Princeton University on file in the Mudd Library.

Sappington, J., S. Reedy, R. Welch, and J. Hamilton. 1989. "Validity of Messages from Quadriplegic Persons with Cerebral Palsy." *American Journal on Mental Retardation*, 94, 49–52.

Snell, B. 1953. *The Discovery of Mind*. Cambridge: Harvard University Press.

CHAPTER 4

Consciousness, Hallucinations, and the Bicameral Mind

Three Decades of New Research

MARCEL KUIJSTEN

I N *THE ORIGIN of Consciousness in the Breakdown of the Bicameral Mind*, Julian Jaynes proposes four main hypotheses: that consciousness is based on language; that preceding the development of consciousness there was a different mentality based on verbal hallucinations called the bicameral mind; that the development of consciousness dates to around the end of the 2nd millennium B.C.; and that the bicameral mind is based on a double-brain neurological model. In the 30 years since the publication of Jaynes's book, a substantial amount of research has emerged that provides new evidence supporting these hypotheses. Much of this research has been produced by neuroscientists, psychologists, and psychiatrists unfamiliar with Jaynes's work. This chapter outlines developments in our understanding of consciousness, hallucinations, schizophrenia, and neuroscience over the past three decades that relate to Jaynes's four hypotheses, as well as examines the significance of the theory to religion and mental health.

This chapter is a substantially revised and expanded version of an interview with John Soderlund that appeared in *New Therapist* (July/August 2004, Vol. 32). Thanks to Brian McVeigh and John Schedel for their comments and suggestions.

HYPOTHESIS ONE:
CONSCIOUSNESS BASED ON LANGUAGE

According to Jaynes, consciousness is based on metaphorical language: "Consciousness is not all language, but is generated by it and is accessed by it."[1] At the time, this was a controversial idea, as many theorists placed the development of consciousness far back in human evolution. In the following discussion it is not my intention to provide a convincing argument that consciousness is based on language, but rather to demonstrate that the idea has gained a great deal of acceptance among a wide variety of scholars over the past 30 years.

A growing number of researchers now recognize the important role of language in consciousness, often referred to as the "language-dependency hypothesis." Neurology professor Antonio Damasio explains that according to this hypothesis, consciousness "follows language mastery and thus cannot occur in organisms that lack that mastery. When Julian Jaynes presents his engaging thesis about the evolution of consciousness, he is referring to consciousness post-language. ... When thinkers as diverse as Daniel Dennett, Humberto Maturana, and Francisco Varela speak about consciousness, they usually refer to consciousness as a post-language phenomenon."[2]

The association of language with consciousness is not new. As noted by psychologist Merlin Donald, "Darwin believed that what he called 'complex trains of thought' were totally dependent on language, just as mathematical thought depends on appropriate notation. The belief that advanced forms of thought, and higher forms of consciousness, were completely dependent on language was widely held in the late nineteenth century."[3] Discussing the development of language and its impact on thought Donald states, "Once the mind starts to construct a verbally encoded mental 'world' of its own, the products of this operation — thoughts and words — cannot be dissociated from one another."[4]

University of Chicago professor Howard Margolis makes a similar argument. On language as a means of both thought and communication, he states:

> Given language, we can describe to ourselves what seemed to occur during the mulling that led to a judgment, produce a rehearsable version of the reaching-a-judgment process, and commit that to long-term memory by in fact rehearsing it. And the same capacity for describing internal imagery, or reconstructing it, but now "out loud" rather than only as a private rehearsal, serves the social function of persuasion. Language, intelligence, and sociality are mutually symbiotic, and Darwinian selection would reinforce that.[5]

In his textbook on evolutionary psychology, University of California Santa Cruz professor Bruce Bridgeman explores the relationship of language to thought and consciousness, concluding that much of our thinking is intertwined with language: what evolved as a communication system is used for planning and to link ideas in our own mind. He also points out the interesting fact that studies of split-brain patients — who have had the connection between the two brain hemispheres severed to control severe epilepsy — are completely aware of directions or stimuli presented to their left hemisphere, yet lack any conscious awareness of those presented to their right hemisphere. While the right hemisphere information is outside of their awareness, they can understand it and can act on it. When they do, the actions initiated by their right hemisphere feel to the patient as though someone else is performing activities in their body. As language ability in right-handed people is located in the left hemisphere, this illustrates an interesting way in which consciousness and language seem to be related: patients only have conscious awareness of things presented to their dominant hemisphere for language.[6]

In *Thinking Without Words*, philosopher José Luis Bermúdez discusses differences between linguistic and non-linguistic thought, arguing that there are significant limitations on the cognitive abilities of animals without language. Higher forms of thought require a suitable vehicle by which they can be held in the mind. According to Bermúdez, only language provides that vehicle: "Thoughts can only be the object of further thoughts when they have linguistic vehicles."[7]

Philosopher Daniel Dennett notes that "language infects and inflects our thought at every level."[8] When asked, "What do you believe is true even though you cannot prove it?" Dennett states the case more strongly:

> I believe, but cannot yet prove, that acquiring a human language (an oral or sign language) is a *necessary precondition* for consciousness — in the strong sense of there being a subject, an I, a 'something it is like something to be.' It would follow that non-human animals and pre-linguistic children, although they can be sensitive, alert, responsive to pain and suffering, and cognitively competent in many remarkable ways — including ways that exceed normal adult human competence — are not really conscious (in this strong sense): there is no organized *subject* (yet) to be the enjoyer or sufferer, no *owner* of the *experiences* as contrasted with a mere cerebral *locus* of *effects* [emphasis in original].[9]

Dennett's comments are strikingly similar to (and undoubtedly influenced by) Jaynes's. University of Washington neurobiologist William Calvin agrees with Dennett's emphasis on acquiring language as a precondition for consciousness. To support this notion, Calvin quotes a story from the neurologist Oliver Sacks. In his book, *Seeing Voices*, Sacks describes an 11-year-old boy named Joseph, who was believed to be mentally retarded but turned out only to be deaf. Following a year of sign language instruction, Sacks interviewed the boy, relating the following:

> Joseph saw, distinguished, categorized, used; he had no problems with perceptual categorization or generalization, but he could not, it seemed, go much beyond this, hold abstract ideas in mind, reflect, play, plan. He seemed completely literal — unable to juggle images or hypotheses or possibilities, unable to enter an imaginative or figurative realm. ... He seemed, like an animal, or an infant, to be stuck in the present, to be confined to literal and immediate perception....[10]

Sacks's description of the seemingly non-conscious Joseph — a modern person who only acquired basic language skills after the critical period for language development had passed — is remarkably similar to Jaynes's characterization of the mentality of individuals living in ancient societies before the development of consciousness.

Note that Jaynes is not associating consciousness with *speech*. For example, the quadriplegics described by John Hamilton in Chapter 5 could not speak, but were intelligent and had learned language. Physically impaired and brain-injured patients incapable of speech are of course conscious — although unable to speak, they have still learned language and thus developed an internal mind-space and the ability to introspect.

Jaynes, like Dennett, argues that children are not conscious prior to their use of metaphorical language (i.e., they do not possess an internal mind-space, abstract thinking, or a linear concept of time). Although different terminology is used, research in the cognitive development of children by Jean Piaget and Dorothy Singer generally supports this idea.[11]

While others disagree with the language dependency hypothesis, support for this first aspect of Jaynes's theory is clearly
growing. While Jaynes was not the first to identify the association
between language and consciousness, he was the first to propose
the notion that consciousness is a learned process made possible
by metaphorical language. In Chapter 6, John Limber provides a
more in-depth discussion of the role of language in consciousness, including similarities between Russian psychologist Lev
Vygotsky's ideas and Jaynes's.

HYPOTHESIS TWO: THE BICAMERAL MIND

Jaynes's second hypothesis is that preceding the development
of consciousness, a different mentality existed based on verbal
hallucinations called the bicameral mind.[12] Before we discuss the
new evidence for this hypothesis, some lingering misconceptions
about the definition of hallucinations should be addressed. In
some cases people confuse auditory verbal hallucinations, which
are experienced as coming from outside of oneself as if spoken by
another person, with our "inner voice," which may be more
closely related to our internal dialogue. When Jaynes discusses
voices he frequently uses the term hallucinations and is almost
always referring to the former: "Mental voices that are heard
with the same experiential quality as externally produced
voices"[13] — not an inner voice or conscience. Jaynes draws clear
parallels between the auditory verbal hallucinations of modern
schizophrenics and those that governed ancient civilizations.[14]

When asked about the relationship of one's conscience to the
bicameral mind, Jaynes remarked that "the idea of conscience
today is like a faint and wayward echo of it." He goes on to say
that as a boy when his mother told him to listen to the voice
inside him to help him tell the difference between right and
wrong, nothing happened. He concluded that "either I was too
wicked to have a conscience or too good to need one."[15]

Jaynes theorizes that prior to the development of a conscious mind-space, individuals were guided in stressful situations by auditory hallucinations that were interpreted as the commands of their chief, king, ancestors, or "the gods." Some of Jaynes's reviewers had difficulty accepting the substantial role of hallucinations in the bicameral decision-making process. Daniel Dennett considered hallucinations to be an optional aspect of the theory that should be dispensed with, and David Stove commented that the experience of hallucinations seems too rare to play such an important role.[16] These criticisms were perhaps justified given the state of research on hallucinations in the normal population at the time. If Jaynes is correct that hallucinations played such a critical role in the past, we might expect to find a greater prevalence of hallucinations in the general population even today. Writing in the early 1970s, Jaynes was able to find only a few obscure surveys that showed a higher than expected occurrence of hallucinations in the normal population, but predicted they were far more common than was generally believed.

Over the past 30 years, discoveries in three areas support the hypothesis that hallucinations played a major role in a past mentality: hallucinations are more widespread throughout society than was previously known, hallucinations are often triggered by stress, and hallucinations frequently command behavior. We will examine each of these in turn.

Hallucinations in Normals

After the publication of Jaynes's book, interest in hallucinations among the normal population grew steadily. Inspired by Jaynes's work, in 1983 psychologist Thomas Posey and then-graduate student Mary Losch published a study on auditory hallucinations in the normal population, reporting that roughly 70 percent of those sampled had experienced some type of brief auditory hallucination during wakefulness (hallucinations are known to be more common when one is just waking up or falling asleep — these were not included in that number). In 1985, clinical psychologist John Hamilton, also inspired by Jaynes, published the fascinating study, "Auditory Hallucinations in Nonverbal Quadriplegics," describing hallucinations in a non-verbal population after a method of communication was devised (see Chapter 5).

Jaynes also continued to research hallucinations. In "Verbal Hallucinations and Pre-Conscious Mentality," he describes hal-lucinations in a variety of populations (see Chapter 3). In "The Ghost of a Flea: Visions of William Blake," Jaynes discusses the auditory and visual hallucinations of the poet and artist, which served as the inspiration for Blake's work (see Chapter 2).

By the 1990s there was an explosion of interest in the topic. And in this area, at least, Jaynes couldn't have been more right: study after study showed a higher than expected percentage of normal (i.e., non-psychotic) people reporting hallucinations. A variety of researchers have now documented hallucinations in children, college students, women, the elderly, low-income urban populations and various ethnic groups, evangelical Christians, high altitude climbers, and those who have had a so-called "near-death experience."[17] Based on these findings, a growing number of clinicians — most notably Dutch psychology professor Marius Romme and his co-author Sondra Escher — now advocate a continuum model for hallucinations, promoting the idea that hallucinations are found throughout society and are not in all cases indicative of mental illness.[18]

Taken together, this body of research establishes beyond question that hallucinations are far more common throughout society than was previously believed, although these findings have yet to become widely known. Until recently, the stigma of hallucinations has kept this fact hidden, as the association of hallucinations with mental illness often deters individuals from disclosing their experiences.

Over the years I've talked to quite a few "normal" (non-psychotic) people that have shared their hallucinatory experiences with me once they felt it was safe to do so. The experiences range from simply hearing one's name called when just waking up or falling asleep, to one woman (a lecturer in psychology) that regularly heard a voice that would criticize and insult her. She called it "the black crow on her shoulder" (interestingly the left shoulder, as the left ear is connected to the right hemisphere — the significance of this will be discussed below under Hypothesis Four). Another woman (an author and linguist) experienced hallucinatory voices that were so pronounced and disorienting that at first she wondered if the fillings in her teeth were somehow picking up a radio station.

The current prevalence of hallucinations, present on a continuum throughout societies worldwide, provides strong support for Jaynes's second hypothesis: hallucinations today are a vestige of an earlier mentality, where, in the absence of consciousness, they played an essential role in decision-making.

Hallucinations and Stress

Further evidence for the bicameral mind comes from research that shows hallucinations are often instigated by stress. In bicameral societies, Jaynes argues that hallucinations were often triggered by stressful, confusing, or "fight or flight" situations. On the topic of modern hallucinatory triggers, Spanish psychologist Salvador Perona Garcelán writes:

> The starting point of the hallucinatory process occurs when the individual faces different vital situations he cannot cope with and which he interprets as threatening his physical or psychological integrity. As a result, the individual feels overcome by the situation and highly stressed. These situations concern a vast number of ex-

periences ranging from traumas to social conflict (for example, very emotional environments) including also inner conflicts such as the experience of unwanted private events in the form of thoughts, images or memories the individual appraises as intrusive and annoying, as well as the experience of very intense emotional and physiological states.[19]

A growing body of research shows this to be the case. One study documents acute transient stress-induced hallucinations in soldiers, while another discusses auditory and visual hallucinations as being frequent in combat veterans with chronic post-traumatic stress disorder. Hallucinations have been associated with stress resulting from chemical-factory explosions, mining accidents, hostage situations, combat exposure, sustained military operations, and loss of a spouse. Researchers have found that "by systematically reducing the anxiety associated with particularly stressful situations, there is a corresponding reduction in hallucinatory activity."[20]

The majority of the research on the association of stress with hallucinations has appeared after Jaynes's book was published. If Jaynes is correct that the stress of decision-making triggered hallucinations in bicameral individuals, new research on the association of stress and hallucinations provides further support for his theory.

Command Hallucinations

While the discovery of the pervasiveness of hallucinatory experiences throughout society and the correlation of hallucinations with stress provide strong supporting evidence for Jaynes's second hypothesis, recent research studying "command hallucinations" in schizophrenics is even more compelling. In a stunning parallel with Jaynes's descriptions of the role of hallucinations in bicameral societies, psychiatrists have discovered that the verbal hallucinations experienced by schizophrenic patients often consist of behavioral commands. One study reported that more than half of schizophrenic patients with auditory hallucinations experienced hallucinatory commands, in some cases urging them to commit violent acts. In another study, one-third of those surveyed reported having command hallucinations specifically to harm others, and a significant number complied with the commands. Another study reports a 21-year-old Chinese factory worker who, after some probing, disclosed to doctors that he had been hearing commanding voices for the past year. Responding to command hallucinations, 21-year-old Marc Sappington of Kansas City killed four people in 2001, hacking one of them into pieces, which he then devoured. According to Sappington — who police described as bright and articulate — the voices took over his behavior and instructed his murderous actions. Command hallucinations are not restricted to those suffering from schizophrenia. Japanese psychiatrists describe three elderly, non-schizophrenics that experienced hallucinations directing their behavior.[21]

German psychiatry professor Ralf Erkwoh and his team attempted to determine predictors for obeying or resisting command hallucinations. In an article titled "Command Hallucinations: Who Obeys and Who Resists When?" they report three psychopathological characteristics as being significant in predicting whether schizophrenic patients follow the commands of their hallucinations: whether the voice is known to the patient, emotional involvement during the hallucinations, and perceiving the voice as real.[22] These predictors make sense in light of Jaynes's theory: in bicameral societies the voices of the gods were unquestioningly real, universally accepted, and served an integral role in social cohesion. It is likely that continued research in this relatively new area will reveal a greater prevalence of command hallucinations in those that hear voices than was previously known. The fact that hallucinations often command or direct behavior further supports Jaynes's hypothesis that modern hallucinations are a vestige of an earlier mentality where behavior was guided by commanding hallucinations in novel situations.

Research on auditory hallucinations has revealed that the content of the voices often revolves around the person's behavior: criticizing it, commenting on it, commanding it, and describing it. Why might this be the case? The greater frequency of hallucinations throughout society is now well established, yet questions regarding why they are common, why they often consist of behavioral commands, and why they are often brought on by stressful situations remain unanswered. Psychological and psychiatric research on hallucinations primarily focuses on treatment and articles addressing theoretical questions such as origins and causes offer little more than speculation.

The past three decades of research on hallucinations provide strong support for Jaynes's hypothesis that hallucinations once served an important role in a previous mentality known as the bicameral mind by directing behavior in times of stress and decision-making. Jaynes's bicameral mind theory provides an explanation for why hallucinations would be commanding in nature and triggered by stress. Other theories on hallucinations, such as the misattribution of internal thoughts, fail to address these issues. Given this new body of evidence, the bicameral mind theory merits renewed attention by those interested in the origin, treatment, and neurological basis of hallucinations.

HYPOTHESIS THREE:
THE DATING OF CONSCIOUSNESS

Jaynes's third hypothesis is dating the development of consciousness to around 1200 B.C. in areas such as Mesopotamia and Egypt (however, in other areas — such as South America —

evidence suggests this transition occurred much later).[23] Jaynes arrived at this date based in part on the analysis of ancient texts such as the *Iliad* and the *Odyssey*, and the early books of the Bible, which show the gradual emergence of mental language and abstract thinking. In addition, Jaynes documents evidence that around this time period people stop hallucinating and, as a result, seek new ways to obtain guidance from the gods, giving birth to a range of new phenomena such as oracles, divination, and prayer. While the dating of the emergence of consciousness in human history is the most difficult of the four hypotheses to address, there is some new research and discussion that is relevant.

The Beginnings of Art

Most scholars date the dawn of modern consciousness much earlier, around 30,000 years ago. It is around this time period when such things as more complex tool technology, beads and personal adornment, and cave art found in Europe first appear. Although generally accepted, citing these developments as evidence for the emergence of the modern mind relies on a great deal of speculation. Jaynes counters that cave art can be accomplished without consciousness, just as easily as one can ride a bicycle without consciousness.[24] In an article published in 1979 titled "Paleolithic Cave Paintings As Eidetic Images," Jaynes argues for viewing cave art not as similar to modern art but as eidetic imagery. He outlines four reasons favoring this idea:

1. The cave paintings cannot be art in our sense of being meant for public display or ritual observance since they are usually located in the most difficult and inaccessible positions inside caves.
2. If they were drawn by artists in our sense, we would expect to find preliminary attempts, as if learning to draw, but such are not found.

3. If drawn by artists in our sense, we would expect a homogeneity of skill regardless of subject, but we do not: the paintings or engravings of animals (about 90 percent of the total) are of an astonishing sweep, beauty, and likeness, while those of humans are almost entirely sticklike and not likenesses at all; and no scenery is ever attempted.

4. The most prominent reason to think of these paintings and engravings specifically as tracings of eidetic images is their common superposition one over the other, as if each animal was projected on the cave wall regardless of what was there in the first place.[25]

Thus cave art may not rely on consciousness or the modern mind at all, but rather result from spontaneous renderings of hallucinatory images. Compelling evidence has recently emerged supporting Jaynes's assertion from two different researchers.

British psychologist Nicholas Humphrey studied the case of a young autistic girl named Nadia. Nadia was socially unresponsive and did not develop language beyond 10 words at age 6. Humphrey notes that her lack of language "went along with a severe degree of literal mindedness."[26] However, she was highly artistic and by age three demonstrated exceptional drawing ability. Nadia's art is surprisingly similar in form and style to that of ancient cave art. If a 3-year-old autistic child with no language ability and incapable of abstract thought can create drawings such as Nadia's, citing the cave art of 30,000 years ago as evidence of the emergence of the modern mind becomes highly problematic. In fact, researchers attributed Nadia's drawing ability and artistic style to her lack of language. At age 8, when a concerted effort was made, she did acquire some language, and her artistic ability diminished. Humphrey speculates that the similar style of Nadia's drawings and cave art may in fact be evidence that humans 30,000 years ago *did not* possess more than rudimentary language and were incapable of abstract thought. If Humphrey is correct this would move the date of the development of subjective consciousness closer to Jaynes's.

Further evidence supporting Jaynes's hypothesis comes from cognitive archeologist David Lewis-Williams, who argues that cave art was painted by individuals hallucinating in trance states. Lewis-Williams noticed similarities between recent rock art of the San tribe of the Kalahari and that of much older European cave art. He learned that modern San shaman engage in trance dances to "contact another world" for various purposes such as healing the sick, then noticed that the San rock art from past generations did not depict scenes from daily life but in fact represented spiritual experience and trance. In addition, both San and European rock art include dots, lines, and patterns that are indicative of the visual experiences perceived by those entering hallucinatory trance states. Lewis-Williams believes that cave and rock art thus are depictions of hallucinatory visions.[27]

The case of Nadia and the work of Lewis-Williams go a long way toward dispelling the notions that consciousness is necessary for art in general and that cave art can be viewed as an indicator of modern consciousness. Lewis-Williams's work also supports Jaynes's theory that hallucinations played an important role in the daily life of early man.

The Emergence of Farming and Towns

The next milestone for the dating of consciousness is the beginning of farming and town building, believed to have emerged around 10,000 B.C. Surely, some argue, the emergence of farming and people organizing themselves into towns indicates the presence of consciousness or the modern mind. Yet, social insects accomplish all of these things entirely without consciousness.

Colonies of ants, bees, and termites numbering from 40,000

to in some cases nearly 1 billion are, through still poorly understood processes, able to organize themselves into hierarchies with each member dutifully carrying out their respective role. With no prior exposure to the world of insects, it would be easy to imagine an insect colony numbering in the hundreds of thousands being in a state of total chaos, with each insect acting independently and many just wandering off. Yet the opposite is the case.

Ants, termites, and bees are organized into castes such as workers, scouts, nursers, soldiers, drones, and the queen. Nursers feed the young while they are still in the grub stage, soldiers defend the colony from attack, and drones mate with the queen. Often these jobs are age-dependent, with ants or bees taking on different roles at different life stages. For example, foraging bees are thought to be near the end of their life span. In this way, the colony gets as much use as possible from the bee before it is exposed to the dangers of foraging.

A variety of ants known as leafcutting ants strip trees of their leaves and carry them back to the colony where they are laid out in rows deep inside the nest. In a parallel to human farming, the leaves are not eaten but used to culture a fungus that grows on the leaves and serves as a food supply for the colony. In a practice akin to weeding, the ants remove all other plant material from the area.[28]

When a bee colony reaches a certain size, the colony prepares to split. Scouts are dispatched to identify a location for the new colony to form. In fascinating rituals known as the round dance and the waggle dance, honey bee scouts convey the recommended location for the new colony. After a number of scouts make their recommendations, the suitability of these locations is accessed by other bees, more and more bees "dance" in favor of a particular site, somehow a "decision" is made, and the splinter group leaves the primary group to form a new colony.

How all this is accomplished with some combination of instinct, diet, behavioral displays, and chemical signals known as pheromones remains largely a mystery. But I think we can agree it does not involve language as we understand it or conscious thought as nearly anyone would define it. If insects can carry out relatively complex tasks, resembling human activities such as social organization and farming, we must consider the possibility that these behaviors are not an indication of consciousness in humans of 10,000 B.C. With an exponentially larger brain[29] and far more complex language ability, we can perhaps imagine human farming, hunting, and town building all accomplished without the benefit of introspection or subjective consciousness, with the auditory hallucinations of the bicameral mind taking the place of pheromones as the form of social control.[30]

Yet, if the above examples described early man's social behavior and not bees or leafcutting ants, undoubtedly many prominent psychologists and philosophers would tout it as evidence of consciousness or a "modern mind." The complex behavior of insects led Alun Anderson, Editor-in-Chief of the publication *New Scientist*, to proclaim that insects such as bees, butterflies, and cockroaches are "conscious" — albeit in a way that differs greatly from human consciousness (which again raises the problem of terminology described in the Introduction). Anderson acknowledges:

> That may take me out of the company of quite a few scientists who would prefer to believe that a bee with a brain of only a million neurons must surely be a collection of instinctive reactions with some simple switching mechanism between them, rather [than] have some central representation of what is going on that might be called consciousness.[31]

Unconsciousness Problem Solving and Intuition

Anderson and other proponents of insect consciousness may

have it backwards: social organization and "problem solving" in insects is not evidence of consciousness but rather how much can be accomplished in its absence. Jaynes argues persuasively that a large amount of mental processing takes place outside of conscious awareness. Consciousness is not all sensory perception. It is not involved in signal learning, or even in more complex learning, such as learning to type, which is largely an automatic process that comes with practice. It is also not involved in the performance of skills such as playing tennis or playing the piano — in fact it often impedes their execution. Finally, consciousness is not necessary for all thinking and reasoning — the very things we usually equate with consciousness. Jaynes writes:

> Our minds work much faster than our consciousness can keep up with. We commonly make general assertions based on our past experiences in an automatic way, and only as an afterthought are we sometimes able to retrieve any of the past experiences on which an assertion is based. How often we reach sound conclusions and are quite unable to justify them! Because reasoning is not conscious.[32]

He describes how the notion of the scientist working through problems using conscious induction and deduction is somewhat of a myth, that "the greatest insights of mankind have come more mysteriously."[33] Jaynes mentions the German physician Hermann von Helmholtz and the mathematician Carl Gauss, and there are many other examples of scientists whose insights came to them "like a sudden flash of lightning," usually when they were no longer thinking about the problem, but "taking an easy walk over wooded hills in sunny weather."[34]

Over the past three decades, a growing number of scientists have begun to recognize the limited role of consciousness in daily life. Neuroscientist Joseph LeDoux writes that unconscious processes include "almost everything the brain does, from standard body maintenance like regulating heart rate, breathing rhythm, stomach contractions, and posture, to controlling many aspects of seeing, smelling, behaving, feeling, speaking, thinking, evaluating, judging, believing, and imagining."[35]

In his book *The User Illusion: Cutting Consciousness Down to Size*, Danish author Tor Nørretranders describes a range of new evidence that suggests we may give consciousness far more credit than it deserves. Nørretranders describes how the bandwidth of consciousness is extremely limited in comparison to the enormous amount of information taken in by the senses, arguing that a tremendous amount of information processing takes place outside of conscious awareness. He also describes experiments, still regarded as controversial, that show brain activity occurs prior to the conscious awareness of making a decision — with consciousness limited to deciding against carrying out behaviors initiated by the subconscious mind. Rather than attributing consciousness to the smallest insects, new research indicates that even for many of our complex behaviors, consciousness is unnecessary.[36]

The great difficulty in appreciating the idea that consciousness makes up only a small part of our mentality has led to the widespread fascination with intuition. The subconscious information processing described above is what I would call intuitive reasoning. Writing on the nature of intuition, anthropologist Charles Laughlin notes that "analytical and integrative processing is occurring prior to and ... 'behind' the actual experience that is registered in consciousness."[37] In this sense, intuitive reasoning can play an important role in decision-making and problem solving. It takes conscious attention to set up a problem and then, to a large degree, mental processing outside of conscious awareness takes over. Taking a break from a problem, especially overnight, allows for a period of incubation. Later, a sudden flash of insight can provide the solution.

Contemporary intuitive reasoning is often viewed as a remnant of a previous state of enhanced intuitive thinking. This is not the case. In the absence of consciousness, the bicameral mind was a form of stimulus-response decision-making that provided solutions in the form of hallucinations, but these solutions were not necessarily more intuitive or creative than those provided by the modern, conscious mode of thinking. Consciousness allows us to focus our attention on more complex problems, harnessing our subconscious mind to assist with processing information and determining solutions. The emergence of consciousness created a "cognitive explosion" that led to our astonishing problem solving ability and our modern state of technological advancement.

The popular motif of "moving back" to recapture a "lost wisdom" or "ancient knowledge" is itself a vestige of the bicameral mind. It is the "nostalgic anguish for the lost bicamerality of a subjectively conscious people."[38] It is the longing for a Golden Age when people were in direct communication with the gods, prior to the breakdown of the bicameral mind when the voices fell silent, the gods retreated to the heavens, and the concept of religion was born. This "paradise lost" theme can be seen in the story of the Fall in the Book of Genesis, which can be viewed as a parable of the breakdown of the bicameral mind and the birth of consciousness: After eating from the "tree of knowledge," "the eyes of them both were opened and they knew they were naked" (Genesis 3:7) — they developed conscious self-awareness, and for the first time saw themselves as others would see them.

Further Analysis of the Iliad *and the* Odyssey

Given the growing evidence that consciousness is not necessary for even higher forms of thinking and learning, it becomes possible to imagine that the ancient Egyptians and Greeks were pre-conscious as recently as 1200 B.C., despite their many accomplishments. Indeed, in ancient texts, with a few exceptions, writing that reflects consciousness does not emerge until after this time. For the most part, the actions of the characters of the *Iliad* are commanded by the gods, not the result of internal decisions. Furthermore, we see the birth of many practices such as prayer, divination, and worship that indicate a breakdown in the bicameral mode of thinking. Critics argue that what Jaynes identified in ancient texts was the emergence of the *concept* of consciousness, rather than the actual emergence of consciousness itself. This is referred to as the use/mention error, with Daniel Dennett[39] and Jaynes[40] countering that in some cases, for example baseball or money, the concept and the thing itself are one and the same. Jaynes and Dennett argue that this is also the case with consciousness. In Chapter 11, Jan Sleutels elaborates on this topic and counters arguments by one of Jaynes's critics.

In an extensive analysis of the *Iliad* and the *Odyssey*, English professor Judith Weissman agrees with Jaynes's conclusions, stating, "The most important and the most repeated relationships between gods and men in the *Iliad* occur when the gods, both male and female, do appear and speak briefly in a forceful and clear command." The frequent admonitions in the *Iliad* are "convincing corroborations of Jaynes's theory."[41] The admonitions of the gods in the *Iliad* are nearly identical to those experienced by modern voice-hearers. In the *Odyssey*, Weissman, like Jaynes, sees indications of a changing mentality: a relative lack of divine appearances and the growing importance of divination, dreams, prayer, and omens as means to interpret their will. Rather than the unquestioning obedience to the gods seen in the *Iliad*, prayers and omens become "complex and self-reflexive." Lying and deceit — hallmarks of consciousness — while rare in the *Iliad*, are commonplace in the *Odyssey*. Discussing Odysseus's self-protective use of deceit upon return to Ithaka, Weissman writes, "Jaynes could not have invented better evidence for his theory than these stories that Homer invents for his hero Odysseus; the analog *I* is used in deceit, in a series of elaborate narratizations,

in a poem about people who have just passed into consciousness."[42] The literary evidence for a shift from bicamerality to consciousness is not limited to the *Iliad* and the *Odyssey*: Michael
Carr has found similar evidence in analyses of ancient Chinese
texts (see Chapter 13).

In bicameral societies, all problem solving was done outside of
conscious awareness. When consciousness was developed as a
result of complex metaphorical language, a gap was created between stimulus and response where a range of actions could be
deliberated and conscious choices could be made. Most of us no
longer hallucinate when faced with a dilemma, but subconscious
thought processes and intuitive reasoning continue to make up a
significant part of the decision-making or problem solving process. In this section we have touched on a range of ideas that support Jaynes's dating the development of consciousness in Mesopotamia to around the end of the 2nd millennium B.C.: consciousness cannot clearly be associated with cave art, farming, or town
building; our emerging understanding of the limited role of
consciousness in thinking and behavior; and further analysis of
the *Iliad* and *Odyssey*, which chronicle the transition from
bicamerality to consciousness.

HYPOTHESIS FOUR:
JAYNES'S NEUROLOGICAL MODEL

Jaynes's fourth hypothesis is that of the double brain — his
neurological model for the bicameral mind.[43] When Jaynes
speculated that the areas responsible for auditory hallucinations
would be the right temporal-parietal lobe areas corresponding to the
language areas of the left hemisphere, he knew that it would be
decades before neuroscience progressed to the point that his ideas
could be tested. Jaynes's ideas have recently come back into focus

after several studies using advanced brain imaging techniques supported his early predictions.

Jaynes based his ideas in part on the now-famous split-brain research of neuroscientists Roger Sperry and Michael Gazzaniga, which eerily demonstrate that when the connection between the brain's two hemispheres is severed (as a remedy for patients with severe epilepsy), each hemisphere seems to possess its own distinct personality and sense of self.[44] Also influential were early studies of hallucinations and research that showed both hemispheres understand language.

Based on this research, Jaynes reasoned that the areas in the right hemisphere of the brain corresponding with the speech areas in the left hemisphere were responsible for the generation of auditory hallucinations: "The speech of the gods was organized in what corresponds to Wernicke's area on the right hemisphere and 'spoken' or 'heard' over the anterior commissures to or by the auditory areas of the left hemisphere."[45] He called this prior mentality "the bicameral mind," referring to the brain's two hemispheres.

For decades there has been strong evidence that the right hemisphere is involved in hallucinations. Studies conducted by Wilder Penfield in the early 1960s found a high frequency of hallucinations when the right temporal lobe was stimulated with a mild electric current.[46] A study of 919 human responses to cortical stimulation under local anesthesia in 139 craniotomies revealed that "indeed, hallucinations originated mainly from the right hemisphere."[47]

The neurobiology of hallucinations is complex and a definitive theory has not yet emerged. However, advances in brain research using positron emission tomography (PET) and magnetic resonance imaging (MRI) provide more concrete evidence supporting Jaynes's neurological model. In 1982, a study using PET scans demonstrated more glucose uptake, and thus more activity, in the right temporal lobe when schizophrenic patients were hearing voices.[48] Further vindication for Jaynes's model came in 1999 — 15 months after his death — in a breakthrough study headed by British psychiatrist Belinda Lennox that examined a 26-year-old, right-handed male who had suffered from paranoid schizophrenia for eight years.[49] The patient pressed a button at the onset of a hallucination, and magnetic resonance imaging was used to scan his brain, showing the areas of activity during his hallucinations. The results showed that activation first appeared in the right middle temporal gyrus and then extended to a wider area of the right superior temporal and left superior temporal gyri, right middle and inferior frontal gyri, the right anterior cingulate (related to emotion and arousal), and right cuneus.

The right temporal-parietal region is precisely the area that Jaynes predicted would be responsible for hallucinations. The right middle and superior temporal gyrus corresponds to the area that contains Wernicke's area in the left hemisphere — the area long known to be associated with language comprehension. The left inferior frontal gyrus is known as Broca's area, where language articulation is generated. In hallucinations we see activation in the corresponding area in the right hemisphere. The left superior temporal gyrus contains the primary auditory cortex and Wernicke's area, and is presumably where the hallucination is "heard" (see Figure 1).

The significance of Lennox's research for Jaynes's neurological model was noted by Robert Olin[50] in *Lancet* and Leo Sher[51] in the *Journal of Psychiatry & Neuroscience*. Lennox's results contradict

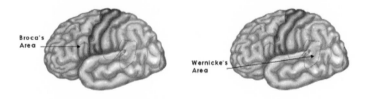

Figure 1. Broca's area and Wernicke's area

Drs. Assad & Shapiro's critique of Jaynes's neurological model, who state, "it is now well known that lesions of the right-sided areas corresponding to Broca's or Wernicke's area result in expressive or receptive aprosodias[52] ... these areas would thus seem more related to the negative symptoms of schizophrenia (such as restricted affect) than the positive hallucinatory symptoms."[53]

A more recent study by psychiatrists Lahcen Ait Bentaleb and Emmanuel Stip found results similar to Lennox's: "Auditory verbal hallucinations (AVHs) were associated with increased metabolic activity in the left primary auditory cortex and the right middle temporal gyrus. Our results suggest a possible interaction between these areas during AVHs."[54] Additional studies have found similar results. In 2004, British neuroscientists reported that 6–9 seconds before the person signaled the onset of the hallucination, activation was seen in the left inferior frontal and right middle temporal gyri, whereas activation in the bilateral temporal gyri coincided with the perception of the hallucination.[55] Referring to the Bentaleb and Stip article, another group of researchers noted that based on these findings, "It could be hypothesized that inner speech, originating from right cerebral homologues of the language areas, is perceived as auditory hallucinations."[56]

Two studies published in 2005 add further support to Jaynes's fourth hypothesis. Psychiatrists at McMaster University in Ontario used PET scans to compare brain activity in schizophrenic patients that were either experiencing or not experiencing auditory hallucinations at the time of the scan. The patients who did experience auditory hallucinations "had significantly lower relative metabolism in auditory and Wernicke's regions and a trend toward higher metabolism in the right hemisphere homologue of Broca's region" when compared with those who did not experience hallucinations.[57] Researchers in Australia studied the change in EEG alpha-band average coherence between auditory hallucination and non-auditory hallucination states in seven patients with schizophrenia. They found "no significant change observed in the coherence between Broca's and Wernicke's areas, but a significant increase was observed in coherence between the left and right superior temporal cortices during auditory hallucinations compared with non-auditory hallucinations, suggesting increased bilateral coherence between auditory cortical areas." They go on to state that their findings suggest "abnormally increased synchrony between the left and right auditory cortices during auditory hallucinations in schizophrenia."[58]

As mentioned previously, the neurobiology of auditory hallucinations is complex and still poorly understood. While these studies do not conclusively prove the validity of Jaynes's neurological model — and it may still be many years before the origin of hallucinations in the brain is thoroughly understood — a picture has now emerged that clearly supports the ideas Jaynes put forth 30 years ago. The results of Lennox's research and the "possible interaction" between the right and left temporal lobes during auditory hallucinations described by a number of studies provides strong evidence for Jaynes's neurological model.

RELIGIOUS HALLUCINATIONS AND THE BICAMERAL MIND

The historical association of hallucinations and visions with art and religion has given them a mystical quality and created the misconception that hallucinations are a profound, insightful, uplifting experience. While it is true that hallucinations are often religious in nature and in some cases can have positive effects, experiencing hallucinations on a regular basis in a society where this is no longer the norm can be a confusing, stressful, and sometimes devastating experience.

However, some writers, poets, and artists have been known to draw inspiration from actual hallucinations. Judith Weissman discusses this in her book, *Of Two Minds: Poets Who Hear*

Voices.[59] V.S. Ramachandran, a neuroscientist, describes visual hallucinations in the writer and cartoonist James Thurber.[60] Thurber was blind by the age of 35 and experienced visual hallucinations that he incorporated into his work. The English poet William Blake "insisted he could teach anyone to listen to and see angels as he did, angels from whom he heard his poetry" (see Chapter 2). Geographers Deborah Park, Paul Simpson-Housley, and psychologist Anton de Man provide an interesting discussion of the hallucination-inspired artwork of the famous Swedish schizophrenic artist Adolf Wolfi and his unusual perception of geography and space.[61]

Auditory and visual hallucinations were also experienced by English writer and occultist Aleister Crowley. While in Egypt in 1904, he claims that for three days between the hour of noon and 1pm his "Holy Guardian Angel" Aiwass dictated the *Book of the Law* to him. In his book *The Equinox of the Gods*, Crowley describes the event in detail, saying that as he sat at his desk, the voice of Aiwass came from over his left shoulder in the furthest corner of the room, and "seemed to echo itself in my physical heart in a very strange manner ... I have noticed a similar phenomenon when I have been waiting for a message fraught with great hope or dread." As in the case discussed on page 103, we see the left shoulder specifically mentioned, implicating the right hemisphere. Crowley himself did not entirely rule out the possibility that the voice came from his own mind:

> Of course I wrote them, ink on paper, in the material sense; but they are not My words, unless Aiwass be taken to be no more than my subconscious self, or some part of it: in that case, my conscious self being ignorant of the Truth in the Book and hostile to most of the ethics and philosophy of the Book, Aiwass is a severely suppressed part of me. Such a theory would further imply that I am, unknown to myself, possessed of all sorts of praeternatural knowledge and power.[62]

Although the right hemisphere tends to "look down on" the left hemisphere — with the hallucinated voice often being interpreted as having more wisdom or authority by the individual who experiences it — auditory hallucinations are often disparaging, confused, and contradictory. Individuals can be compelled to violence, much like the voices of the right hemisphere commanded Abraham in the Book of Genesis to kill his first born son Isaac, then spared his life. Socrates frequently heard a voice that at one point convinced him not to flee Athens before his execution by the court.[63]

The role of religious-related hallucinations in modern violent crime — especially cases of individuals who kill their children or other family members — remains poorly understood and underreported by the media. A recent example is the case of Andrea Yates, a Texas woman who murdered her five children. Yates, who had a history of depression and schizophrenia, claimed to have had visions and "heard the voice of Satan speaking to her." At one point before the murders she told her psychiatrist that "she was hearing voices and seeing visions again about getting a knife." In another case, Evonne Rodriguez killed her 4-month-old baby in 1997 in Houston, Texas, because she believed he was possessed by demons. "Evonne insisted that she had heard screeching voices, 'just like Hell,' so she beat at her child with her hand and then choked him with a rosary." [64]

Hallucinations have been associated with divine inspiration for centuries, and modern hallucinations are also frequently religious in nature. Psychiatrist Jerome Kroll and medieval historian Bernard Bachrach compared the religious hallucinations of contemporary psychiatric patients with reports of visions collected from the writings of medieval European scholars. While the medieval visions were not considered pathological at the time, they were similar in many ways to hallucinations experienced by modern patients.[65]

Yet despite claims of divine (or more recently, extraterrestrial) inspiration, writings resulting from the transcription of hallucinations are usually mundane. In discussing cases of non-psychotic voice hearers, Jaynes writes, "an example I have come to know personally is an extremely successful businessman who is sometimes teased by his wife and children for spending so much time in the evening with 'Richard,' a superior being who 'dictates' to him reams of what I consider to be boring pseudoprofundities." [66]

Prophets such as Joseph Smith and Mohammed also had well documented auditory and visual hallucinations. In *The Sword of Laban: Joseph Smith, Jr., and the Dissociated Mind*, Dr. William Morain speculates that Joseph Smith probably learned to dissociate when as a child he endured a series of excruciatingly painful surgeries on his leg without anesthesia. [67] Later in life, he continued to slip into dissociated states, where he experienced visions of angels and auditory hallucinations. Smith would bury his face in his hat and stare at a stone he had placed there, and in this state most likely "heard" sections of what became the *Book of Mormon*. Queen's University history professor Klaus Hansen also proposes a hallucinatory explanation for *The Book of Mormon*. In his book *Mormonism and the American Experience*, he describes the visions and auditory hallucinations Smith had starting at the age of 14, when, during a period of "severe religious anxiety ... he retreated into a grove behind his father's farm, where ... God the Father and Jesus Christ appeared to him in person." While Smith was in a disassociated state, they replied to his question regarding which religious denominations were true. Hansen discusses a number of theories, and suggests Jaynes's as the most probable explanation for Smith's religious auditory and visual hallucinations and the *Book of Mormon*. [68]

After his first major hallucinatory experience, Mohammed himself thought he was "possessed" and tried to commit suicide. He later regularly experienced trance states, sometimes foaming at the mouth and rolling on the ground. In the late 1800s, British psychiatrist Henry Maudsley argued that Mohammed's trance states were likely brought on by epilepsy.[69] More recently, Flemish psychologist Dr. Herman Somers described parallels between accounts of Mohammed and what today would be diagnosed as schizophrenic-like hallucinations and delusions:

> Mohammed, according to Dr. Somers, was a classic case of paranoia. The syndrome of paranoia is essentially characterized by a delusion about oneself nourished by recurring hallucinations. These hallucinations may be auditory (hearing voices), visual (seeing visions or apparitions), or purely mental (being struck with sudden "insights" of enormous and unshakable certainty, not susceptible to falsification by reality). The delusion typically puts the affected person in the center of events: either he is the target of a ubiquitous and all-powerful conspiracy (delusion of persecution); or he is the privileged witness to a cosmic event, especially the imminent end of the world; or he has been selected for a unique mission.[70]

Mohammed may have hallucinated much of the Koran in a cave near Mecca, where he would spend months in isolated prayer and meditation. Referring to the Koran, Victorian writer and philosopher Thomas Carlyle wrote: "Much of it is rhythmic, a kind of wild, chanting song ... a bewildered rhapsody."[71] The rhythmical aspect of the Koran is significant, as Jaynes provides evidence that poetry is a function of the right hemisphere, and argues that poetry began with the bicameral mind. Hallucinations in the ancient world were often in the form of verse.[72] Neuroscientist V.S. Ramachandran describes how contemporary temporal lobe epilepsy patients also hallucinate and frequently display behaviors of increased religiosity and excessive mystical writing, know as hypergraphia.[73] The correlation of temporal lobe excitation with religious hallucinations provides further evidence for Jaynes's bicameral mind theory and his neurological model.[74]

That the world's religions arose out of a longing for bicameral hallucinated voices merits consideration. At least in the Middle East, the shift from polytheism to monotheism coincides with Jaynes's dating for the breakdown of the bicameral mind. Bicameral societies worshipped many gods because the members of these communities all regularly experienced auditory hallucinations and labeled these voices as various gods. Leaders of bicameral societies organized these gods into hierarchies. This helped create social cohesion through what Jaynes called the "collective cognitive imperative." Much like contemporary schizophrenics interpret their voices within the context of modern politics and religious teachings, members of ancient bicameral societies interpreted their voices within the established system of gods. Ordinary citizens heard voices attributed to a personal god, which served as an intermediary to the great gods.[75]

When people developed consciousness and the voices of the gods fell silent, it became increasingly difficult to maintain the complex hierarchical system of gods, which up to that time were based on the direct experience of hallucinatory commands. The number of accepted gods declined, as previously established gods began to blend and merge. According to historian H.W.F. Saggs, in Mesopotamia "there came a time when ancient polytheistic religion no longer satisfied, but this did not result — as it did in Israel — in a stark assertion of monotheism; rather there was a gradual bland drift towards the idea that all gods were but aspects of the One."[76] After the breakdown of the bicameral mind, newly conscious individuals longed for the lost certainty and guidance the voices of the gods had provided. The few who still experienced voices, such as early Biblical prophets like Amos and, in the 6th century, Mohammed, were sought out as conduits to the gods.

Those who could still elicit bicameral-like hallucinatory trance states were viewed as oracles or prophets, their trance-induced hallucinations seen as divinely (or, in some cases, demonically) inspired messages. Eventually, with only a few remaining semi-bicameral "prophets" still directly experiencing "the gods," the notion of only one "true" god was born, and then heavily promoted by figures such as Jesus, whose teachings were an attempt to shift religious thinking from the outmoded bicameral system of many gods to the newly conscious system of one God. "Behavior now must be changed from within the new consciousness rather than from Mosaic laws carving behavior from without. Sin and penance are now within conscious desire and conscious contrition, rather than in the external behaviors of the Decalogue and the penances of temple sacrifice and community punishment."[77] With individuals no longer in direct contact with the gods, each of the world's great religions "received their imprint from the teaching of a great religious reformer, who, according to believers, brought a direct divine revelation."[78]

IMPLICATIONS FOR MENTAL HEALTH

Despite decades of research, schizophrenia remains poorly understood; it is thought to involve both genetics and stress levels, but causes remain unknown. To date, while biological abnormalities have been noted, no conclusive evidence of brain abnormality has been discovered in all people with schizophrenia. In the conclusion to his comprehensive book on schizophrenia research, *In Search of Madness*, R. Walter Heinrichs speculates that perhaps the illness "cannot be accommodated within current views of brain function, behavior, and neurological disease." He continues:

... the evidence suggests that schizophrenia is in a class of disorders that cannot be understood without a workable theory of mind and brain ... it must be that schizophrenia is a disorder of the working brain as a psychological system, a disorder of the brain in action. Yet without a model of how to understand this action and how to relate mental to neurological activity, neuroscience cannot take the next step and solve the schizophrenic puzzle — the anomaly of madness.[79]

Jaynes's ideas on consciousness and the bicameral mind have profound implications for therapy in general and the treatment of schizophrenia in particular. Schizophrenia may never be fully understood without the historical context of Jaynes's bicameral mind theory. Furthermore, Jaynes felt that consciousness and the role of one's internal dialogue were intimately linked with other aspects of mental health. During a question and answer session, he addressed this issue:

In the treatment of neuroses, the theory provides a strong theoretical framework for such consciousness-changing procedures as the cognitive theories of [Aaron] Beck (1976) or [Donald] Meichenbaum (1977), retraining or restructuring, the use of guided imagery, paradoxical therapy and various visualizing practices. Most of what are diagnosed as neurotic behaviors are, of course, disorders of consciousness, or more specifically of narratization and excerption. Therefore, narratization and excerption must be retrained for the patient to experience relief. Such narratization is actually what is going on in most therapy, even in analysis of either the Freudian or Jungian variety. And it doesn't matter whether or not the renarratization is existentially veridical so long as it is believed and redirects behavior into more adaptive modes.[80]

When Jaynes says "narratization and excerption" he is referring to two key aspects of consciousness. In narratization, "we are always seeing our vicarial selves as the main figures in the stories of our lives … situations are chosen which are congruent to this ongoing story, until the picture I have of myself in my life determines how I am to act and choose in novel situations as they arise … The assigning of causes to our behavior or saying why we did a particular thing is all part of narratization." [81]

We are not just narratizing our own lives, but also everything else in consciousness: "A stray fact is narratized to fit with some other stray fact. A child cries in the street and we narratize the event into a mental picture of a lost child and a parent searching for it."[82] When this narratizing process goes astray, perhaps due to early negative experiences or for biological reasons, the result can be hostility, depression, obsessions, or other thought disorders. How our consciousness narratizes our own life influences the decisions we make, and how we narratize the thoughts and intentions of others can be a source of either harmony or conflict in our interpersonal relations. It is through the process of replaying events in consciousness that anger becomes hatred and fear becomes anxiety.

In the process of excerption, consciousness necessarily excerpts "from the collection of possible attentions to a thing which comprises our knowledge of it." Jaynes elaborates:

> Thus, if I ask you to think of the city you are now in, you will excerpt some feature, such as a particular building or tower or crossroads. Or if I ask you to think of yourself, you will make some kind of excerpts from your recent past, believing you are thinking of yourself. In all these instances, we find no difficulty or particular paradox in the fact that these excerpts are not the things themselves, although we talk as if they were. Actually we are never conscious of things in their true nature, only of the excerpts we make of them.[83]

An obvious example of how this relates to therapy is the depressed person who has a tendency to excerpt the negative aspects of situations, or from his or her own life narrative. By examining an individual's pattern of narratization and excerption, therapy can help to retrain or redirect these processes in more positive directions.

Viewed from the perspective of Jaynes's theory, the development of consciousness and the diminishing role of hallucinations in society brought about the concept of mental illness in that hallucinations, once the norm, became abnormal and lost their functional role. No longer validated by others, individuals experiencing hallucinations became increasingly confused and delusional. Jaynes argues that past theories of schizophrenia have failed to a large degree because they have tried to fit schizophrenia into various existing psychological perspectives, none of which are appropriate.

Patients with chronic schizophrenia typically do not show improvement to therapy not paired with antipsychotic medication. A large percentage of schizophrenics suffer from "lack of insight," a medical term for the failure to recognize that there is anything wrong with them, making them resistant to any form of treatment. Unfortunately, current anti-psychotic medications are not always effective, can have serious physical side effects, and tend to reduce psychotic symptoms by "deadening" brain activity in general — sometimes leaving patients feeling an overall lack of joy and self-motivation. Therapy can be beneficial for outpatients with schizophrenia by teaching them coping and problem-solving skills, in cases where drug treatment has relieved the patient's psychotic symptoms.

Understanding Jaynes's ideas can give the therapist a better understanding of the schizophrenic experience. As mentioned previously, stress can be a major factor in the onset of hallucinations. Thus, reducing stressors in a patient's environment should be a primary goal. Jaynes also observed that hallucinations are dependent on the teachings and expectations of childhood, and that they are susceptible to suggestion from the social environment. There is evidence that in some cases the frequency of hallucinations can be reduced through a placebo effect.[84]

Jaynes stated in 1985 that a simplified version of his theory was being taught to hallucinating schizophrenic patients in some clinics, and that "it relieves a great deal of the associated distress of 'being crazy' by getting the patient to realize that many of his or her symptoms are a relapse to an older mentality that was perfectly normal at one time but no longer works."[85]

Jaynes's theory predicted that hallucinations were not necessarily a sign of pathology and were far more common in the normal population than was generally believed. The last 30 years have witnessed an explosion of interest in hallucinations and, as mentioned previously, a large number of studies have documented their occurrence throughout the normal population. A widespread understanding that hallucinations are relatively common among normal, non-psychotic individuals will help reduce the current association of hallucinations with pathology, thus reducing the stress and in some cases embarrassment of individuals who experience them.

But hallucinations are only one aspect of schizophrenia. As in bicameral man, consciousness itself can be diminished: there is an erosion of the ego or the 'I', dissolution of the mind-space, and the failure of narratization. One's sense of self becomes lost — schizophrenics can feel as though their body is blended with other objects or the universe in general. This can be the most frightening and distressful aspect of the illness. "With the loss of the analog 'I', its mind-space, and the ability to narratize, behavior is either responding to hallucinations, or continues by habit."[86]

Schizophrenia is a partial relapse to the bicameral mind in a conscious person. It is clear from studies of patients with schizophrenia that much of the depression and disordered thought are culturally related, resulting because hallucinations no longer serve a functional role in modern society. Jaynes concludes:

> The learnings that make up a subjective consciousness are powerful and never totally suppressed. And thus the terror and the fury, the agony and the despair. The anxiety attendant upon so cataclysmic a change, the dissonance with the habitual structure of interpersonal relations, and the lack of cultural support and definition for the voices, making them inadequate guides for everyday living, the need to defend against a broken dam of environmental sensory stimulation that is flooding all before it — produce a social withdrawal that is a far different thing from the behavior of the *absolutely* social individual of bicameral societies. The conscious man is constantly using his introspection to find 'himself' and to know where he is, relevant to his purpose and situation. And without this source of security, deprived of narratization, living with hallucinations that are unacceptable and denied as unreal by those around him, the florid schizophrenic is in an opposite world to that of the god-owned laborers of Marduk or of the idols of Ur ... In effect, he is a mind bared to his environment, waiting on gods in a godless world.[87]

CONCLUSION

Scientific research and academic debate over the past three decades provide a variety of supporting evidence for each of Jaynes's four hypotheses: consciousness based on language, a previous mentality involving hallucinations known as the bicameral mind, consciousness as a recent development, and

Jaynes's neurological model. Clearly, the bicameral mind theory warrants renewed attention. Beyond theoretical debate over brain and cognition, a greater understanding of the emergence of consciousness will provide profound new insights into ourselves: our culture, our history, our society, our ongoing evolution.

Jaynes maintained that we are still deep in the midst of this transition from bicamerality to consciousness; we are continuing the process of expanding the role of our internal dialogue and introspection in the decision-making process that was started some 3,000 years ago. Vestiges of the bicameral mind — our longing for absolute guidance and external control — make us susceptible to charismatic leaders, cults, trends, and persuasive rhetoric that relies on slogans to bypass logic. The tendency within us to avoid conscious thought by seeking out authoritative sources to guide our actions has led to political movements such as Marxism-Leninism and Nazi Germany, cult massacres such as Jonestown and Heaven's Gate, and fundamentalist religions worldwide. By focusing on our inner dialogue, reflecting on past events, and contemplating possible future outcomes, we expand the role of consciousness in decision-making, enhance our ability to engage in critical thinking, and move further away from the commanding guidance of authoritative voices and non-thinking, stimulus-response behavior.

NOTES TO CHAPTER 4

1.   Jaynes, 1990, p. 449. See also Jaynes, 1976, pp. 48–66.
2.   Damasio, 1999, pp. 187–188.
3.   Donald, 1993, p. 42.
4.   Ibid., p. 253.
5.   Margolis, 1987, p. 60.
6.   Bridgeman, 2003, p. 248.
7.   Bermúdez, 2003, p. 187.
8.   Dennett, 1991, p. 301.
9.   Dennett, in Edge Foundation, 2005.
10. Sacks, 1991, quoted by Calvin in Edge Foundation, 2005.

11. Piaget, 2000; Singer, 1996.
12. See Jaynes, 1976, pp. 84–99.
13. Jaynes, 1976, p. 85.
14. Jaynes, 1976, 85–99; see also Chapter 3.
15. Jaynes, 1986a.
16. Dennett, 1986; Stove, 1989 (see Chapter 9).
17. See, for example, studies of hallucinations in children: Escher, et al., 2002; Kotsopoulos, et al., 1987; Mertin, et al., 2004; Pearson, et al., 2001; Pilowsky, et al., 1986; Schreier, 1999; Vickers, et al., 2000; college students: Feelgood, et al., 1994; Rodrigo, et al., 1997; women: Chedru, et al., 1996; the elderly: Berrios, et al., 1984; Grimby, 1998; Kobayashi, et al., 2004; low-income urban populations and various ethnic groups: Izquierdo, 2000; Olfson, et al., 2002; evangelical Christians: Davies, et al., 2001; high altitude climbers: Brugger, et al., 1999; Garrido, et al., 2000; and near-death experiencers: Greyson and Liester, 2004.
18. Romme and Escher, 2000.
19. Garcelán, 2004, p. 135.
20. See Spivak, et al., 1992 (hallucinations in soldiers); Hamner, et al., 2000 (combat veterans with PTSD); Comer, et al., 1967; Hobfoll, 1988; Wells, 1983 (as a result of various stressors); Knudson and Coyle, 1999 (reducing stress helps reduce hallucinations).
21. See Lee, et al., 2004 (hallucinatory commands); McNeil, et al., 2000 (compliance with hallucinatory commands); Suraya and Saw, 1999 (Chinese factory worker); McGraw, 2001 (Sappington case); Kobayashi, et al., 2004 (elderly patients).
22. Erkwoh, et al., 2002.
23. Jaynes, 1976, pp. 223–313.
24. Keen, 1978.
25. Jaynes, 1979.
26. Humphrey, 1999.
27. Lewis-Williams, 2002; Lewis-Williams and Pearce, 2005.
28. Holldobler and Wilson, 1990.
29. An ant's brain has an estimated 10,000 neurons, a bee's brain has an estimated 1 million neurons, and the human brain has in excess of 100 billion neurons.
30. Jaynes, 1976, p. 144.
31. Anderson, in Edge Foundation, 2005.
32. Jaynes, 1976, p. 42.
33. Ibid., p. 43.
34. Helmholtz quoted in Woodworth, 1938.
35. LeDoux, 2002.
36. Nørretranders, 1999.

37. Laughlin, 1997, p. 23.
38. Jaynes, 1976, p. 297.
39. Dennett, 1986.
40. Jaynes, 1990, new Afterword to *Origin*.
41. Weissman, 1993, p. 7.
42. Ibid.; p. 25.
43. See Jaynes, 1976, pp. 100–125.
44. For an interesting discussion of multiple "selves" and disunity of consciousness in split-brain patients see Marks, 1981. In a series of articles highly relevant to Jaynes's theory (but beyond the scope of this chapter), philosopher Roland Puccetti (1977, 1981, 1989) argues that everyone has two distinct minds, one for each hemisphere, and that this only becomes evident after commissurotomy when (in right-handed individuals) the left or dominant hemisphere is no longer inhibiting the right hemisphere. Dr. Fredric Schiffer (1998) has applied dual-brain concepts to mental health. Further evidence that each hemisphere can function independently as a complete "brain" comes from children that have, for medical reasons, had one hemisphere removed (Battro, 2001).
45. Jaynes, 1976, p. 105.
46. Penfield, et al., 1963.
47. Baldwin, 1970.
48. Buchsbaum, et al., 1982.
49. Lennox, et al., 1999.
50. Olin, 1999.
51. Sher, 2000.
52. Aprosodia is a medical term for a disruption in the expression or comprehension of the changes in pitch, loudness, rate, or rhythm that convey a speaker's emotional intent.
53. Moffic, 1987.
54. Bentaleb, et al., 2002.
55. Shergill, et al., 2004.
56. Sommer, et al., 2003.
57. Cleghorn, 2005.
58. Sritharan, et al., 2005.
59. Weissman, 1993.
60. Ramachandran and Blakeslee, 1998, pp. 85–87.
61. Park, Simpson-Housley, and De Man, 1994.
62. Crowley, 1936/1991, Ch. 7.
63. Leudar and Thomas, 2000, pp. 14–27.
64. For both the Yates and Rodriguez cases, see Ramsland, 2003.
65. Kroll and Bachrach, 1982.
66. Jaynes, 1986b.

67. Morain, 1998.
68. Hansen, 1981, pp. 21–22.
69. Maudsley, 1886.
70. Elst, 2002.
71. Carlyle, 1841.
72. Jaynes, 1976, pp. 361–378.
73. Ramachandran and Blakeslee, 1998, p. 180.
74. See also Persinger, 1987.
75. Jaynes, 1976, p. 183.
76. Saggs, 1989, p. 15.
77. Jaynes, 1976, p. 318.
78. Saggs, 1989, p. 267.
79. Heinrichs, 2001, p. 272.
80. Jaynes, 1986a.
81. Jaynes, 1976, pp. 63–64.
82. Ibid., p. 64.
83. Ibid., p. 61.
84. Weinstein, 1962; Weingaertner, 1971.
85. Jaynes, 1986a.
86. Jaynes, 1976, p. 423.
87. Ibid., p. 432.

REFERENCES

Baldwin, M. 1970. "Neurologic Syndromes and Hallucinations." In W. Keup (ed.), *The Origins and Mechanisms of Hallucinations*. New York: Plenum Press.

Battro, A.M. 2001. *Half a Brain is Enough: The Story of Nico*. Cambridge University Press.

Bentaleb, L.A., M. Beauregard, P. Liddle, and E. Stip. 2002. "Cerebral Activity Associated with Auditory Verbal Hallucinations: A Functional Magnetic Resonance Imaging Case Study." *Journal of Psychiatry & Neuroscience*, 27, 2, 110.

Bermúdez, J.L. 2003. *Thinking Without Words*. New York: Oxford University Press.

Berrios, G.E. and P. Brook. 1984. "Visual Hallucinations and Sensory Delusions in the Elderly." *British Journal of Psychiatry*, 144, 662–664.

Bridgeman, B. 2003. *Psychology and Evolution: The Origins of Mind*. Thousand Oaks, CA: Sage Publications.

Brugger, P., M. Regard, T. Landis, and O. Oelz. "Hallucinatory Experiences in Extreme-Altitude Climbers." *Neuropsychiatry, Neuropsychology, & Behavioral Neurology*, 12, 1, 67–71.

Buchsbaum, M.S, D.H. Ingvar, R. Kessler, R.N. Waters, J. Cappelletti, D.P. van Kammen, et al. 1982. "Cerebral Glucography with Positron Tomography: Use in Normal Subjects and in Patients with Schizophrenia." *Archives of General Psychiatry*, 39, 251.

Carlyle, T. 1841. *Heroes and Hero Worship*. Chicago: Donohue.

Chedru, F., F. Feldman, A. Ameri, J. Sales, and M. Roth. 1996. "Visual and Auditory Hallucinations in a Psychologically Normal Woman." *Lancet*, 348, 9031, 896.

Cleghorn, J.M., S. Franco, B. Szechtman, R.D. Kaplan, H. Szechtman, G.M. Brown, C. Nahmias, and E.S. Garnett. 2005. "Toward A Brain Map of Auditory Hallucinations." *Psychiatry Research*, 136, 2–3, 189–200.

Comer, N.L., L. Madow, and J.J. Dixon. 1967. "Observations of Sensory Deprivation in Life-Threatening Situations." *American Journal of Psychiatry*, 124, 164–169.

Crowley, A. 1936/1991. *Equinox of the Gods*. New Falcon Publications (revised edition).

Davies, M.F., G. Murray, and S. Vice. 2001. "Affective Reactions to Auditory Hallucinations in Psychotic, Evangelical and Control Groups." *British Journal of Clinical Psychology*, 40, 361–370.

Dennett, D. 1986. "Julian Jaynes's Software Archeology." *Canadian Psychology*, 27, 2, 149–154.

Dennett, D. 1991. *Consciousness Explained*. Boston: Little, Brown, and Company.

Donald, M. 1991. *Origins of the Modern Mind: Three Stages in the Evolution of Culture and Cognition*. Cambridge, MA: Harvard University Press.

Edge Foundation, Inc. 2005. "What Do You Believe is True Even Though You Cannot Prove It?" http://www.edge.org/q2005/q05_10.html

Elst, K. 2002. "Wahi: the Supernatural Basis of Islam." *Kashmir Herald*. October. www.kashmirherald.com

Erkwoh, R., K. Willmes, A. Eming-Erdmann, and H.J. Kunert. 2002. "Command Hallucinations: Who Obeys and Who Resists When?" *Psychopathology*, 35, 272–279.

Escher, S., M. Romme, A. Buiks, P. Delespaul, and J. Van Os. 2002. "Independent Course of Childhood Auditory Hallucinations: A Sequential 3-Year Follow-up Study." *The British Journal of Psychiatry*, 181, s10–s18.

Feelgood, S.R. and A.J. Rantzen. 1994. "Auditory and Visual Hallucinations in University Students." *Personality and Individual Differences*, 17, 2, 293–296.

Garcelán, S.P. 2004. "A Psychological Model for Verbal Auditory Hallucinations." *International Journal of Psychology and Psychological Therapy*, 4, 1, 129–153.

Garrido, E., C. Javierre, J.L. Ventura, and R. Segura. 2000. "Hallucinatory Experiences at High Altitude." *Neuropsychiatry, Neuropsychology, & Behavioral Neurology*, 13, 2, 148–148.

Greyson, B. and M.B. Liester. 2004. "Auditory Hallucinations following Near-Death Experiences." *Journal of Humanistic Psychology*, 44, 320–336.

Grimby, A. 1998. "Hallucinations following the Loss of a Spouse: Common and Normal Events among the Elderly." *Journal of Clinical Geropsychology*, 4, 1, 65–74.

Hamner, M.B., B.C. Frueh, H.G. Ulmer, M.G. Huber, T.J. Twomey, C. Tyson, and G.W. Arana. 2000. "Psychotic Features in Chronic Posttraumatic Stress Disorder and Schizophrenia: Comparative Severity." *Journal of Nervous & Mental Disease*, 188, 4, 217–221.

Hansen, K. 1981. *Mormonism and the American Experience*. University of Chicago Press.

Heinrichs, W.R. 2001. *In Search of Madness: Schizophrenia and Neuroscience.* Oxford University Press.

Hobfoll, S.E. 1988. *The Ecology of Stress*. Washington, D.C.: Hemisphere.

Holldobler, B. and E.O. Wilson. 1990. *Ants.* Harvard University Press.

Humphrey, N. 1999. "Cave Art, Autism, and the Evolution of the Human Mind." *Journal of Consciousness Studies*, 6, 116–143.

Izquierdo, A.M. 2000. "A Study of Manifestations of Hallucinations in a Non-Psychiatric Population of Caribbean Descent." *Dissertation Abstracts International: Section B: The Sciences & Engineering*, 61, (5-B), 2764.

Jaynes, J. 1976. *The Origin of Consciousness in the Breakdown of the Bicameral Mind*. Boston: Houghton Mifflin.

Jaynes, J. 1979. "Paleolithic Cave Paintings as Eidetic Images." *Behavioral and Brain Sciences*, 2, 605–607.

Jaynes, J. 1981. "The Ghost of a Flea: Visions of William Blake." *Art/World*, 6, 1.

Jaynes, J. 1986a. "Consciousness and the Voices of the Mind." *Canadian Psychology*, 27, 2, 128.

Jaynes, J. 1986b. "Hearing Voices and the Bicameral Mind." *Behavioral and Brain Sciences*, 9, 3.

Jaynes, J. 1990. "Verbal Hallucinations and Pre-conscious Mentality." In Spitzer, M. & Maher, B. (eds.). *Philosophy and Psychopathology*. New York: Springer Verlag.

Keen, S. 1978. "The Lost Voices of the Gods." *Psychology Today*, 11, 58–60.

Knudson, B. and A. Coyle. 1999. "Coping Strategies for Auditory Hallucinations: A Review." *Counseling Psychology Quarterly*, 12, 1, 25.

Kobayashi, T., S. Kato, T. Osawa, and K. Shioda. 2004. "Commentary Hallucination in the Elderly: Three Case Reports." *Psychogeriatrics*, 4, 3, 96–101.

Kotsopoulos, S., J. Kanigsberg, A. Cote, and C. Fiedorowicz. 1987. "Hallucinatory Experiences in Nonpsychotic Children." *Journal of the American Academy of Child & Adolescent Psychiatry*, 26, 3, 375–380.

138   *Marcel Kuijsten*

Kretz, R.K. 2000. "The Evolution of Self-awareness: Advances in Neurological Understandings Since Julian Jaynes's 'Bicameral Mind.'" *Dissertation Abstracts International: Section B: The Sciences & Engineering*, 60, 12-B, 6413.

Kroll, J. and B. Bachrach. 1982. "Medieval Visions and Contemporary Hallucinations." *Psychological Medicine*, 12, 4, 709–722.

Kroll, J. and B. Bachrach. 2005. *The Mystic Mind: The Psychology of Medieval Mystics and Ascetics*. Routledge.

Laughlin, C. 1997. "The Nature of Intuition." In R. Davis-Floyd and P.S. Arvidson (eds.), *Intuition: The Inside Story*. New York: Routledge.

LeDoux, J. 2002. *Synaptic Self: How Our Brains Become Who We Are*. Penguin Books.

Lee, T.M., S.A. Chong, Y.H. Chan, and G. Sathyadevan. 2004. "Command Hallucinations among Asian Patients with Schizophrenia." *Canadian Journal of Psychiatry*, 49, 12, 838–42.

Lennox, B.R., S.B.G. Park, P.B. Jones, and P.G. Morris. 1999. "Spatial and Temporal Mapping of Neural Activity Associated with Auditory Hallucinations." *Lancet*, 353, 644.

Leudar, I. and P. Thomas. 2000. *Voices of Reason, Voices of Insanity: Studies of Verbal Hallucinations*. Florence, KY: Taylor & Francis/Routledge.

Lewis-Williams, D. 2002. *The Mind in the Cave: Consciousness and the Origins of Art*. Thames & Hudson.

Lewis-Williams, D. and D. Pearce. 2005. *Inside the Neolithic Mind: Consciousness, Cosmos, and the Realm of the Gods*. Thames & Hudson.

Margolis, H. 1987. *Patterns, Thinking, and Cognition*. Chicago: University of Chicago Press.

Marks, C.E. 1981. *Commissurotomy, Consciousness and Unity of Mind*. Cambridge, MA; London, England: The MIT Press.

Maudsley, H. 1886. *Natural Causes and Supernatural Seemings*. London: Kegan Paul, Trench, Trubner & Co.

McGraw, S. 2001. "Marc Sappington: The Kansas City Vampire." *Court TV's Crime Library*. www.crimelibrary.com.

McNiel, D.E., J.P. Eisner, and R.L Binder. 2000. "The Relationship between Command Hallucinations and Violence." *Psychiatric Services*, 51, 1288–1292.

Mertin, P. and S. Hartwig. 2004. "Auditory Hallucinations in Nonpsychotic Children: Diagnostic Considerations." *Child and Adolescent Mental Health*, 9, 1, 9–14.

Moffic, H.S. 1987. "What About the Bicameral Mind?" *American Journal of Psychiatry*, 144, 5, 696.

Morain, W.D. 1998. *The Sword of Laban: Joseph Smith, Jr., and the Dissociated Mind*. American Psychiatric Association.

Nørretranders, T. 1999. *The User Illusion: Cutting Consciousness Down to Size*. Penguin.

Olfson, M., R. Lewis-Fernández, M.M. Weissman, A. Feder, M.J. Gameroff, D. Pilowsky, and M. Fuentes. 2002. "Psychotic Symptoms in an Urban General Medicine Practice." *American Journal of Psychiatry*, 159, 1412–1419.

Olin, R. 1999. "Auditory Hallucinations and the Bicameral Mind." *Lancet*, 354, 9173, 166.

Park, D.C., P. Simpson-Housley, and A. De Man. 1994. "To the 'Infinite Spaces of Creation': The Interior Landscape of a Schizophrenic Artist." *Annals of the Association of American Geographers*, 84, 2, June, 192–209.

Pearson, D., A. Burrow, C. FitzGerald, K. Green, G. Lee, and N. Wise. 2001. "Auditory Hallucinations in Normal Child Populations." *Personality & Individual Differences*, 31, 3, 401–407.

Penfield, W. and P. Phanor. 1963. "The Brain's Record of Auditory and Visual Experience: A Final Summary and Discussion." *Brain*, 86, 595.

Persinger, M. 1987. *Neuropsychological Bases of God Beliefs*. Praeger Publishers.

Piaget, J. and B. Inhelder. 2000. *The Psychology of the Child*. Basic Books.

Pilowsky, D. and W. Chambers. 1986. *Hallucinations in Children*. Washington D.C.: American Psychiatric Press.

Posey, T.B. and M.E. Losch. 1983. "Auditory Hallucinations of Hearing Voices in 375 Normal Subjects." *Imagination, Cognition, and Personality*, 3, 2, 99–133.

Puccetti, R. 1977. "Bilateral Organization of Consciousness in Man." *Annals of the New York Academy of Sciences*, 299, 448–457.

Puccetti, R. 1981. "The Case for Mental Duality: Evidence from Split-brain Data and Other Considerations." *The Behavioral and Brain Sciences*, 4, 93–123.

Puccetti, R. 1989. "Two Brains, Two Minds? Wigan's Theory of Mental Duality." *British Journal for the Philosophy of Science*, 40, 137–144.

Ramachandran, V.S. and S. Blakeslee. 1998. *Phantoms in the Brain: Probing the Mysteries of the Human Mind*. New York: William Morrow and Company, Inc.

Ramsland, K. 2003. "Andrea Yates: Ill or Evil?" *Court TV's Crime Library*. www.crimelibrary.com.

Rodrigo, A.M.L., M.M.P. Pineiro, P.C.M. Suarez, M.I. Caro, and S.L. Giraldez. 1997. "Hallucinations in a Normal Population: Imagery and Personality Influences." *Psychology in Spain*, 1, 1, 10–16.

Romme, M. and S. Escher. 2000. *Making Sense of Voices: A Guide for Mental Health Professionals Working with Voice-hearers*. Mind Publications.

Sacks, O. 1991. *Seeing Voices: A Journey into the World of the Deaf*. Pan Books.

Saggs, H.W.F. 1989. *Civilization before Greece and Rome*. New York: Yale University Press.

Schiffer, F. 1998. *Of Two Minds: The Revolutionary Science of Dual-Brain Psychology*. New York: The Free Press.

Schreier, H.A. 1999. "Hallucinations in Nonpsychotic Children: More Common Than We Think?" *Journal of the American Academy of Child & Adolescent Psychiatry*, 38, 5, 623–625.

Sher, L. 2000. "Neuroimaging, Auditory Hallucinations, and the Bicameral Mind." *Journal of Psychiatry & Neuroscience*, 25, 3, 239–40.

Shergill, S.S., M.J. Brammer, E. Amaro, S.C. Williams, R.M. Murray, and P.K. McGuire. 2004. "Temporal Course of Auditory Hallucinations." *British Journal of Psychiatry*, 185, 516–7.

Singer, D. and T.A. Revenson. 1996. *A Piaget Primer: How a Child Thinks* (Revised Edition). Plume.

Slade, P. and R. Bentall. 1988. *Sensory Deception: Towards A Scientific Understanding of Hallucinations*. London: Croom Helm.

Somers, H. 1993. *Een andere Mohammed ("A Different Mohammed")*. Hadewych, Antwerp.

Sommer, I.E.C., A. Aleman, and R.S. Kahn. 2003. "Letters to the Editor." *Journal of Psychiatry and Neuroscience*, 28, 3, 217–218.

Spivak, B., S.F. Trottern, M. Mark, A. Bleich, and A. Weizman. 1992. "Acute Transient Stress-Induced Hallucinations in Soldiers." *The British Journal of Psychiatry*, 160, 412–414.

Sritharan A, P. Line, A. Sergejew, R. Silberstein, G. Egan, D. Copolov. 2005. "EEG Coherence Measures during Auditory Hallucinations in Schizophrenia." *Psychiatry Research*, 136, 2–3, 189–200.

Stove, D.C. 1989. "The Oracles and Their Cessation: A Tribute to Julian Jaynes." *Encounter*, 75, 30–38.

Suraya, Y. and K.C. Saw. 1999. "Psychiatric and Surgical Management of Male Genital Self-Mutilation." *Singapore Medical Journal*, 40, 10.

Vickers, B. and E. Garralda. 2000. "Hallucinations in Nonpsychotic Children." *Journal of the American Academy of Child & Adolescent Psychiatry*, 39, 9, 1073.

Weingaertner, A.H. 1971. "Self-administered Adversive Stimulation with Hallucinating Hospitalized Schizophrenics." *Journal of Consulting and Clinical Psychology*, 36, 422–429.

Weinstein, E.A. 1962. "Aspects of Hallucinations." In L.J. West (ed.), *Hallucinations*. New York: Grune and Stratton. pp. 233–238.

Weissman, J. 1993. *Of Two Minds: Poets Who Hear Voices*. Hanover: University Press of New England.

Wells, L.A. 1983. "Hallucinations Associated with Pathologic Grief Reaction." *Journal of Psychiatric Treatment and Evaluation*, 5, 259–61.

Woodworth, R. 1938. *Experimental Psychology*. New York.

CHAPTER 5

Auditory Hallucinations
in Nonverbal Quadriplegics

JOHN HAMILTON

I S THERE ANY ATTRIBUTE of man which is more important, yet more confusing, than consciousness? Julian Jaynes did not think there was. He directed his major research efforts toward understanding the content and origin of consciousness. His extended search, presented in *The Origin of Consciousness in the Breakdown of the Bicameral Mind*, resulted in some startling and revolutionary inferences. According to Jaynes, consciousness, as we know it today, is a relatively new faculty, one that did not exist until as recently as 2000 B.C. He holds that a basic difference between contemporary and ancient man is in the process of decision-making. When faced with a novel situation today, man considers alternatives, thinks about future consequences, makes a final decision, ruminates over it, and finally acts. He then reconsiders his action, evaluates it, worries about it, feels good or bad about it, makes resolves about future decisions, and so forth. The cerebral activity that precedes and follows an action response is consciousness. Jaynes believes that man of antiquity had no consciousness — that when faced with a novel situation, he simply reacted. He reacted without hesitation by following the directions

First published in *Psychiatry*, 1985, 48, 4, 382–92. © 1985 Guilford Press, reprinted with permission.

of a personal voice that told him exactly what to do. Ancient man called this voice God; today it is called an auditory hallucination. To ancient man, God was not a mental image or a deified thought but an actual voice heard when one was presented with a situation requiring decisive action.

Prior to 2000 B.C., according to Jaynes, man was governed entirely by this authoritative voice, but by 500 B.C. man had, for the most part, lost this faculty and was learning to make his own decisions consciously. This radical change did not occur precipitously and the period of authoritative shift had the most unsettling and often disastrous consequences. The decline and fall of the authoritative voice and the development of consciousness, Jaynes continues, was a transition period of extreme difficulty because man had no one, neither God nor self, to direct his behavior.

Jaynes developed and supported his ideas primarily from historical evidence. Is there observable evidence today that such voices ever existed? Jaynes found a partial answer in the reports of auditory hallucinations from schizophrenic and brain-damaged patients. He theorized that the authoritative voice of ancient man originated from one cerebral hemisphere and was a function that had become suppressed as a result of some organic changes during the evolutionary transition period. He further theorized that this suppressive effect could be countermanded by unusual situations that altered brain functioning, such as severe stress or organic pathology, and resulted in a reversion to an earlier level of functioning, including the experience of auditory hallucinations similar to the authoritative voices of ancient times.

I have found a contemporary population experiencing auditory hallucinations which are strikingly similar to the phenomenon described by Jaynes. The purpose of this report is (1) to present these cases in some detail as they represent what may be the most directly observable evidence to support Jaynes's theory and (2) to demonstrate the significance that these voices have for this population.

SUBJECTS

The study was conducted in a state institution for the developmentally disabled. Of the total resident population of 1,034, all were categorized as mentally retarded. Among those were 222 who were so physically handicapped that they required total care; they were unable to walk, talk, feed, bathe, toilet, or dress themselves. Within this group were some who gave signs of unusual alertness. With those residents suspected of having the most awareness, communication methods were developed that provided more understanding of their receptive language abilities. Eventually, seven were identified as having questionable retardation, meaning that although they could not talk and had very limited information about the world beyond their own physical environment, they were able to understand what was said to them and could learn and retain new information in what appeared to be a normal manner.

To suggest that these residents had normal intellectual capabilities, without psychometric verification, may seem to be a statement of faith rather than a valid one. Yet, it is the validity of applying intelligence tests to this population that is questionable. Even with tests adapted for communication handicaps, these residents had such limited educational and experiential backgrounds that they were grossly deficient when compared to the norms. However, their "yes" or "no" signals to questions within the confines of their own experiences were accurate. Their understanding of what was asked of them was evidenced by the consistency of their responses, not only at different times with the same person, but with different people asking similar questions at different times. For some, the most quantifiable index of their ability to acquire new information was their prowess in learning, remembering, and using hundreds of Bliss Symbols (signs representing words and phrases). But for all seven, the most persuasive evidence that they possessed normal receptive language was reflected in the content of their personal communications, samples of which are presented in the following section.

The subjects were severely brain-impaired adults who had experienced unusual amounts of stress in their lives and had sufficient understanding of what was said to them to be able to communicate their thoughts and experiences by giving "yes" and "no" signals to questions asked of them. When these seven residents were asked privately about the possibility of hearing voices, five of them gave startled expressions followed by excited "yes" signals. These exaggerated responses were unmistakable signs that an important subject had been introduced. For the two who did not report hearing voices, no characteristics were observed which set them apart from the other five. Since a trusting relationship existed in each case, it was assumed that for these two "voices" simply did not exist. In subsequent interviews with six other residents, four more were added to the group. Again, no consistent differences were found between those who did and those who did not hear "voices."

This chapter is a report of the interviews with these nine residents — three men and six women. Their disability pattern was similar; all were cerebral palsied, spastic-athetoid, quadriplegic adults who had always been totally dependent on others for physical care and had never been able to speak, but who were relatively unimpaired in receptive language skills. None had received any formal education; only one was able to read.

THE COMMUNICATION
AND INTERVIEW PROCEDURE

The following notes from conversations with the residents are in sentence form, as if what was spoken by the residents is repeated in second-person form by the interviewer. Of course, the residents were totally unable to verbalize. It was the interviewer who asked the questions and translated the answers into sentences. The residents in this study had already learned physical responses for giving "yes" and "no" signals. Some had been taught by their families prior to admission to the institution, and the rest had been taught by interested staff who suspected that they had more potential than was generally recognized.[1]

The first step in the communication procedure was to identify the "yes" and "no" signals used by each resident. These were physical responses such as tongue, lip, or hand movements. I then asked questions which could be answered with either "yes" or "no" responses, beginning with general categories and progressing to specific details. For example: "Do you want to tell me something?" ("... ask a question?") "Is it an actual event?" ("... a thought?") "Does it involve others?" ("... yourself alone?") "Is the other person a man?" ("... a woman?") "Was it a pleasant event?" ("... unpleasant?") "Did it happen recently?" ("... in the past?"). Thus I proceeded in a more or less systematic search for the ideas they were attempting to express. When they did not understand the question or some of the concepts in the question, they expressed their uncertainty by withholding "yes" or "no" responses altogether. For a more detailed discussion of this type of binary communication approach, see the article by Moore.[2] This procedure was not as stilted or mechanical as it might seem. The visible yes-no cues, facial expressions, postures, and mannerisms served as corrective guides, making it possible to proceed rapidly, with repetitions and modifications, until acceptable verbal reflections of the residents' thoughts were reached. Notes of the conversations were converted into complete sentences in second-person form and read aloud at the end of each session; only those sentences confirmed by the residents were retained.

The following dated excerpts contain examples of the voice experiences of the nine residents. Although only selected responses are presented, they represent the unique characteristics of each voice and the residents' reactions to the voice. There were

changes over time in the messages of each voice and the residents' reactions to these messages, yet there was remarkable consistency of communication with each resident. Despite the
element of interpretation that was a necessary part of the procedure, these statements are considered to be accurate reproductions of what the residents were experiencing.

CASE PRESENTATIONS

The Typical Experience

The first two cases exemplify the standard nature of the voice
experience. They portray a relatively consistent pattern which has
been present for a long time without much change in frequency,
content, or resident response.

Case 1: Tim

Tim is 27 and has been institutionalized since age 14. His
diagnosis is athetoid-spastic quadriplegia due to perinatal hypoxia.
There is no history of seizures and he takes no medication. EEG
results are within normal limits. He responds to questions by
sticking out his tongue for "yes" and by pursing his mouth for
"no." Tim is the only one of these nine residents who is able to
read; his reading skills are at the adult level and by exerting great
effort, he can operate a typewriter with his left thumb. Having
the same intellectual and emotional needs as anyone, Tim feels
that it is grossly unfair that he is able to live in this world only as
a spectator. Consequently, he is a lonesome, depressed, and angry
young man.

March 23, 1979. You actually hear a voice like there is
someone in the room. It's a real voice; you hear him with your
ears. It's a man's voice; it is God talking to you. He started after
you came here; he never came before. You don't know how he
comes, but you're glad for it. This is unusual; others don't have

it. You keep it private. You ask questions, but he does not answer. It is not a two-way conversation; he talks to you. He passes judgment, says what is good or bad. If you have bad thoughts about your parents, he criticizes you. He praises your good actions.

March 20, 1980. He still talks to you. He's talking to you now. (As we talk, Tim's eyes are making occasional shifts to the left, as though they are being pulled in that direction involuntarily, and while fixated there, he seems preoccupied and inattentive to me. Then his attention shifts back to me. During our conversation, these shifts occur intermittently. On the assumption that the eye shift to the left indicates he is hearing the voice, we spend the next 20 minutes in silence, except that I indicate when I think that he is hearing the voice and when he is not, my sole cue being his eye movements. Tim confirms each prediction. A specific eye movement occurs when he hears the voice.)

When you want peace and quiet, which you often do, you can't make him go away. You didn't find religion until you heard him. After you started hearing him, you became very religious. When your parents first left you here, you were frightened; then he talked to you and calmed you.

Case 2: Ron

Ron is 30 and has been institutionalized since age 19. His diagnosis is athetoid-spastic quadriplegia due to brain injury at birth. There is no history of seizures and Valium is his only medication.[3] EEG results are compatible with diffuse brain damage. Ron responds to questions by sticking out his tongue for "yes" and by pursing his mouth for "no." Everyone likes Ron; he thrives on attention, enjoys a good joke, laughs easily and is especially sensitive to the feelings of others. Yet, when provoked by injustices to himself or his friends, he angers quickly and can bellow with rage.

January 15, 1978. You hear this voice almost all the time

except when someone is talking to you. It is a man's voice; it sounds like an uncle you had. It comes from the left side. It is a definite sound, as if someone is there. It directs you to do things, such as go to the school and learn to use your communication board. (The voice apparently supports any training program initiated.) This is a pleasant voice; it keeps you company.

November 29, 1979. You first heard him when you were a boy, long before coming here. The first time he did not scare you. He has always been a helpful friend, but you don't always agree with him.

December 2, 1979. When you don't agree with him, he gives you a hard time, but you still think he is a friend and would not get rid of him if you could.

February 14, 1980. He does not listen to you. You can talk to him in your thoughts, but he does not listen. He is coming more now and you're glad. (When the voice comes, Ron looks up and to the left; he seems almost in a trance when he hears the voice and is inattentive to anything or anyone else.)

Changing Attitudes toward the Voice Experience

Acceptance of "their voices" by the residents was not always the case, as it was with Tim and Ron. The following two cases illustrate how attitudes toward the voice changed with changing environmental conditions.

Case 3: Ann

Ann is 29 and has been institutionalized since age 16. Her diagnosis is athetoid-spastic quadriplegia due to perinatal hypoxia. Psychomotor seizures began a few years ago; they are intermittent and infrequent. EEG patterns are diffusely dysrhythmic with much irregular activity and no alpha signs. Her medications are Phenobarbital and Valium. She responds to questions by sticking out her tongue for "yes" and pursing her mouth for "no." Ann has the maddening trait of being so considerate of the feelings of others that it is difficult to find out how she feels; her outward behavior is sociable and jovial, but inwardly she is despondent, without hope, and patiently waiting to die.

Ann's "voice" did not occur until she was moved to a new area of the institution in 1978. This move apparently was the precipitating factor. These excerpts demonstrate her changing attitude toward her "voice," shifting from passive acceptance to open disagreement in which she criticized her voice and was harassed by it. Finally she reluctantly accepted her "voice" when she found it easier to do as she was told. It may appear that the nature of her "voice" changed, but it is more probable that it was the change in Ann's attitudes and reactions that resulted in a varied, but predictable, set of responses from her "voice."

April 5, 1979. You hear a woman's voice; she sounds like your aunt and talks to you everyday when you're by yourself. When you first heard her, you thought someone else was in the room. You were scared. Now she comforts you. She tells you what is good and bad and what you should and should not do. You try to follow her directions.

July 15, 1979. In the past, she was helpful and supportive. Now she is saying critical things and is saying you're worthless. In the past, you wanted to keep her; now you'd like to get rid of her.

October 8, 1979. She gave you messages from two grandfathers, who are both dead; she told you to tell their wives that heaven is a nice place where you all will meet. When you die, all will be together. She is the voice of God.

November 29, 1979. She says you should like it here and that you belong here. You don't agree. You can't speak to her so she does not know you don't agree. You've always agreed with her; now you don't and think she is wrong.

December 18, 1979. She has been telling you to go to sleep earlier. You have and feel better. So now she does not criticize about that or about anything else. You have not heard her today. It's because you did what she said.

March 11, 1980. She's coming more lately — several times a day. That's o.k.; now you want to keep her because she's helpful.

March 18, 1980. She's talking to you a lot now during the day. (Ann was hearing the voice intermittently while I was with her today. When her "voice" came, she assumed a spastic-rigid posture, hyperextended, looked up, became preoccupied, thrust her head back, repeatedly opened and closed her left hand, opened her mouth, and shifted her eyes to the left. Whenever her "voice" left, all these movements stopped; and there was a noticeable relaxation. Ann listened to both myself and the voice during these periods, although her attention to my questions was interrupted.)

March 11, 1981. She still talks to you a lot. She says what is right and wrong and what you should do. But she is not very important to you now because you would do what she says anyway. You don't pay much attention to her; she's just there.

Case 4: Mary

Mary is 38 and has been institutionalized since age 14. Her diagnosis is athetoid-spastic quadriplegia due to hyperbilirubine-mia and high fever at three weeks of age. One grand mal seizure occurred at age 21 with no recurrences. EEG results are diffusely dysrhythmic and compatible with epilepsy. Her only medication is Valium. She responds to questions by moving her left arm for "yes" and her right arm for "no." Mary is a chronic worrier; her value system is so rigid that she perseverates over what she interprets to be her own inadequacies and what she perceives to be injustices done to her by others. Yet, she has enough energy left to work hard at becoming as independent as possible. She actively participates in all available training programs and is learning to read.

The following excerpts clearly demonstrate how attitudes

toward the "voice" can vary with changing conditions. During this two-year period of Mary's life, there were more changes in her living environment and program experiences than in her previous 20 years. In the early part of 1978, Mary was isolated socially, but by 1980, she was able to communicate with numerous staff and visitors. Her attitude toward her "voice" reflected these social changes. In the past, Mary had considered the voice to be her private, supportive, and helpful companion, but as more opportunities were developed for her to make her own decisions, she began to consider the voice as an outsider who interfered more than as one who helped. The conflict between Mary and her voice developed into an intense one; it became increasingly important for Mary to win out over her voice's dictates and to become independent. She viewed success as reaching the point at which she would no longer need her "voice" and it would no longer come to her. As the following excerpts suggest, that goal was only approachable when Mary was consistently true to the directives of her "voice."

July 15, 1978. You hear her all the time when you're alone and quiet. She comes from the left side. You've told no one else. She lives on the ward with you.

September 30, 1978. She is the voice of God. She is strict like a parent; she tells you what is good and bad, what you should and should not do. You never want her to leave.

November 17, 1978. She is saying something you don't agree with, but you can't stop it. This is something new, and it bothers you. She is saying you have bad thoughts about your parents. (Mary denies having such thoughts.)

March 25, 1979. She says not to be angry with your parents, but now you feel anger. This is your first big difference of opinion. (Mary is upset and feels guilty over disagreeing with her voice.) When you disagree, she gets angry and you get afraid. She can't hurt you but can make you feel bad. You don't need her as much anymore. If you could, you would get rid of her.

December 10, 1979. You're angry with your parents now, but she says that you should forgive them. She says you should feel worse about yourself than you do, that you're mean and unkind, especially in how you think about your family.

December 20, 1979. You're not mad at your family anymore. Years ago, Mom really upset you; she didn't know you could understand everything; she thought you were dumb; she didn't even work out a yes-no response with you.

February 19, 1980. She [the voice] was gone for a few days, but she's back. She said you should forgive your family, which you have.

February 28, 1980. She has been gone for over two weeks. You don't miss her. She is gone because you are doing everything you're supposed to. You can make your own decisions now. She would come back if you didn't do what you're supposed to.

March 11, 1980. Since she left, you've been happy but have been having more trouble — for instance, in school. There are problems because she is not here to tell you what to do.

April 9, 1980. She returned. (During the next year, the pattern alternated between a few days of the voice's absence during which Mary felt good about being in control of her own decisions followed by a return of the voice for a few days, during which Mary felt imposed upon and somewhat personally devalued. Mary now is happiest during periods when her "voice" is absent, but those are also the periods when things are going smoothly. It is during times of stress that the voice returns, perhaps when it is needed the most.)

An Atypical Experience

This is the only case of a "voice" being completely negative and upsetting from the start. Whereas the other residents considered their voices to be the voice of God, Beth thought hers to be the voice of the Devil, in whose presence she felt possessed and tortured. Her "voice" came during periods of stress but gave no comfort. Despite these negative characteristics, there were many similarities to the "voices" of the others.

Case 5: Beth

Beth is 30 and has been institutionalized since age 8. Her diagnosis is athetoid-spastic quadriplegia due to unknown prenatal influence. She has never had seizures. Her only medication is Valium. She responds to questions by opening her mouth wide for "yes" and closing it tightly for "no." Beth smiles and laughs easily; people like to talk and joke with her because of her responsiveness. But what she wants most and what is least available is to have a few close friends who have time to take a special and enduring interest in her.

January 11, 1980. (In the past, I had asked Beth about hearing a "voice" and she had given a "no" response. Today, I asked her again, whereupon she became upset and signaled for me to close the door. By questioning her, I learned that when she first came to the institution, she did hear a "voice," but that it had left years ago.) It was a woman's voice. When she left, you were glad to get rid of her; you don't want her back. You never told anyone before; you were afraid they'd think something was wrong with you.

February 19, 1980. You quit hearing her several years ago when you lived in the infirmary. You never heard her before coming to the institution. You were frightened at first. She sounded like your mother. She seemed to come from straight above. She did not come during the day when you were with others. She gave instructions, told you what to do. You were not able to talk back to her. She only stayed a few weeks. You were frightened by her and were glad when she left.

March 31, 1980. (For the first time in several years, Beth heard the voice again. She was under considerable stress because of the rumor that she and the other residents in the living area might be returning to the infirmary.) It's the same voice from above. She said you should go back to the infirmary; you don't want to. You don't feel you have to do what she says. In the past, she said you should stay here, that it was better than living at home. You did not agree. You don't like what she's saying.

April 15, 1980. She said that your grandmother would die. You don't believe her. She's doing that to upset you. She lies. You would like to get rid of her. When she comes, you can see something similar to what you saw when you heard her years ago. You see a light, no form, just a big bright light, then you hear a voice. She always comes at night when everyone is in bed. It's frightening. She does not want to help; she wants to hurt. If someone comes into the room, she goes away. The light always comes with the voice.

May 7, 1981. She gave you a message from Carrie [a fellow resident who had died the previous year]. She said Carrie was in heaven and was doing well. This was good news. Most of the time it's bad news. You would still like to be rid of her.

Problems Caused by the "Voice" Experience

It is not uncommon for a resident to disagree with his or her "voice," but disobedience usually results in harassment from the "voice." Therefore, except in rare temporary periods of resistance by the resident, the direction and dictates of the "voice" prevail. A lack of awareness of obedience to the voice can be confusing to others. The following two cases exemplify this problem.

Case 6: Betty

Betty is 35 and was institutionalized at age 2. Her diagnosis is athetoid-spastic quadriplegia related to infantile cerebral paralysis. There is no history of seizures and she takes no medication. She responds to questions by moving her head up and down for "yes" and by shaking it from side to side for "no." Betty is a loner. Most of her time is spent listening to music and watching TV, not because she values privacy but because she fears new and unfamiliar situations.

March 18, 1980. She sounds like an attendant you used to have. You're glad she's there. She takes care of you and tells you what to do. She gets angry if you have bad thoughts. She told you to drop out of school; you did not want to quit but had to do what she said.

April 20, 1980. She tells you not to like Ms. Anderson [one of her attendants] and not to be friends with her. You don't want to be mad at her, but you have to do what she says. Your voice turned you against her.

Betty's adverse reaction to Ms. Anderson was so apparent that it led to some damaging assumptions about the attendant. Betty's insistence on being dropped from the school program was perplexing to her teacher who knew that she liked school but was unaware that her "voice" was the one insisting upon this action. These were not isolated incidents. Unless one has knowledge of and understands the contents of a resident's "voice," crucial behavioral cues can be missed.

Case 7: Larry

Larry is 21 and has been institutionalized since age 11. His diagnosis is athetoid-spastic quadriplegia due to erythroblastosis fetalis and kernicterus. There is a long-term history of grand mal seizures, which are partially controlled with Dilantin, Phenobarbital, and Valium. He responds to questions by raising one finger for "yes," two fingers for "no," and three fingers for "I don't know." Larry has accepted his own physical handicap and wants others to be equally accepting, recognizing that intellectually he is normal. Unfortunately, this rarely happens — he is generally treated as a child, and thus usually is in a state of fury.

March 30, 1979. The fact that you hear a voice bothers you; it is not normal. He does not order you, he just suggests. This is not from within but is outside of you. It is God. You can't talk back to him, but he listens through your thoughts. You can't make him go away.

April 10, 1979. He is telling you to leave here and you must obey. If you left, he might leave you alone. (As it turned out, plans were made for Larry to be transferred to an institution nearer home.)

April 24, 1979. Now he is telling you not to move.

July 7, 1979. He continues to tell you to stay. This bothers you, but you're going along with him, hoping to be free of him. There was a time when he was a good friend but no longer. Now he makes decisions you don't always agree with.

August 4, 1979. Now he advises you to go ahead and move and now you agree. You worry about the move, but he says not to worry, that it is for the best. You're still worried, but you believe in him.

Without knowledge of the directives of his "voice," Larry's behavior was very confusing to the staff. He had always wanted to be nearer home, and when it was finally arranged, he was happy. Suddenly, he was distraught over the move and became upset whenever it was discussed. Plans for the move were about to be dropped when Larry's mind was again changed for him by his voice. He then agreed to move and the delayed plans were implemented. Why the directives of his voice changed may remain a mystery, but knowledge of its presence and its content would have explained Larry's behavior.

A More Efficient Interview Procedure

Some generalized characteristics of the voice phenomenon gradually emerged through discussions with the residents. With increased familiarization of the content of the voice experience, a more direct questioning procedure was developed and used in the following two cases. The question of validity may be raised because the information from previous interviews influenced the questions asked in the following two cases. The nature of the questioning procedure minimized that possibility. Even though specific questions were asked, care was taken to avoid giving any cues to suggest that affirmation or denial was the preferred response. A consistent and familiar pattern appeared in these two interviews.

Case 8: Donna

Donna is 24 and has been institutionalized since age 10. Her diagnosis is athetoid-spastic quadriplegia due to unknown pre-natal influence. She has never had seizures and takes no medication. She responds to questions by vocalizing for "yes" and by shaking her head from side to side for "no." Donna appears to be happy, she smiles and laughs easily, is responsive and sociable, does not have unrealistic expectations about her future, and claims to be content to remain in this institution for the rest of her life.

December 9, 1980. Shortly after coming here, you began hearing a voice. It is like a woman's voice, sounding like your mother's, coming from the right side. No one else hears her. The first time you heard her, you were frightened but are not anymore. You can't talk back to her; she does all the talking. She tells you what is right and wrong, what you should and should not do. You agree with what she says and try to do what she tells you. When you don't obey, she gets angry and that bothers you. She is God talking to you. Sometimes she is away for long periods. She comes more often when you're upset and when you need her. She says to be good and not to worry or get angry — that helps. You're glad to have her.

Case 9: Helen

Helen is 37 and has been institutionalized since age 14. Her diagnosis is athetoid-spastic quadriplegia due to head injuries at birth. There is no history of seizures and she takes no medication. She responds to questions by opening her mouth wide for "yes" and by closing it tightly for "no." Helen has a pleasant, even temperament; she is trusting and comfortable with those who care for her and in turn has many friends.

August 20, 1980. It's a woman's voice; it reminds you of your grandmother. (Helen was raised by her grandmother.) The first time you heard her, you were frightened. You did not hear her until after your grandmother died. She says it's nice up there. You hear her from outside yourself. (She indicates the direction as being from above and the left.) You never told this to anyone else. She only talks to you; you can't talk back to her. You've never seen anything; you only hear her. She tells you what to do and you try to do what she says. You always agree with what she says. You are thankful for her.

FOLLOW-UP SURVEY

The question of the validity of the residents' responses must be addressed since the results depended so heavily on my own interpretations. Because this was an evolving study with no specific expectations, several experimental precautions were neglected, such as concurrent reliability checks by other examiners and detailed records of all questions asked and answers received. In an attempt to partially rectify this deficiency, a different investigator conducted a follow-up survey two years later, consisting of interviews with seven of the nine original residents (one had died; the other had moved to a different institution). Marlene Mains, the psychologist who administered the questionnaire, had worked with these residents in the past and knew how to communicate with them but had never discussed their "voices" with them. In the survey, 26 questions were answerable with yes or no responses and were related to information from my previous interviews. I made predictions, based on the earlier data, as to how each question would be answered by each resident. These predicted responses were not disclosed to the follow-up examiner. The agreement between the predictions and the actual follow-up survey was 86 percent. There was evidence that the 14 percent discrepancy rate between predicted and actual results was due to ambiguous items on the questionnaire, original misinterpretations on my part, and actual changes in the residents' responses to the "voices" during the time lapse between the original interviews and the follow-up survey. However, the consistencies far outweighed the differences.

The follow-up study dealt with reliability and indicates that the residents were consistent in their stories; it does not necessarily indicate that their stories were valid. Could they have responded in a manner calculated to elicit and hold attention and thereafter persisted in these fictions regardless of who was doing the questioning? Besides a personal conviction that this was not the case, the following behavioral observations support the interpretation that these "voices" did exist for and were honestly reported by the residents. The "voices" of three of the residents sometimes occurred in public and were accompanied by physical agitation, vocalizing, preoccupied gazing in a fixed direction, rigidity, and a complete loss of attention to the surroundings. Observers, unaware of the "voices," reported these unusual behaviors. Three other residents experienced periods when they wished to be free of their "voices," and during those occasional periods when their voices were absent, they were pleased that there was nothing to report. Although individual messages and directions from voices varied markedly, in general there was a pattern of consistency between the voices. It is improbable that even two residents could have contrived such similar structural patterns, much less that nine did so.

DISCUSSION

The purpose of these case presentations has been twofold: to offer directly observable evidence to support Jaynes's perspective on auditory hallucinations and to demonstrate the significance these voices have on the lives of handicapped people.

Characteristics of the Voices: A General Summary

The contents of the messages of the voices as reported by these nine residents are as individualized as their own personalities, but some characteristics of the voice phenomenon are similar for all residents. The most commonly reported experiences included the following: The voice is heard frequently, usually on a daily basis. The experience is clearly an auditory one, not a thought, dream, or vision but an actual sound heard as if spoken by another in understandable and complete sentences. The direction of the voice has a specific localization from the outside — from above and in most cases, from the left. The voice sounds as if it is a relative, living or dead, who has played an important part in the resident's life. It serves as an authoritarian conscience by telling the resident what to do, how to think and what to feel, and what is right and wrong. During periods of change and stress, it comes more frequently and for longer periods of time, taking charge of new situations by offering instruction and guidance. There is a compelling need to follow the dictates of the voice, not only because it is usually seen as right but also because disobedience brings harsh criticism and incessant harassment. The voice is perceived as being the highest authority; with the exception of one case, it is thought to be the voice of God.[4]

I believe the many similarities between my findings and Jaynes's speculations about the voices of ages past serve as current validating evidence for his theory, which, for the most part, was developed from a historical perspective. There is one major difference: whereas the voices of ancient man pre-empted consciousness as we know it today, the voices of these handicapped residents occur *in addition* to consciousness. When these residents are asked about the source of their thoughts, they know the difference between their own ideas and those of their voices. Ancient man, it appears, would not have known the meaning of the question.

Relevance of Auditory Hallucinations to the Handicapped

The word that best describes the situation of one who is as profoundly handicapped as the nonverbal quadriplegic is *vulnerability*. To grasp the full meaning of total vulnerability is difficult for the outsider, but try to consider what the world view of the residents must be like. They are completely dependent on others for their physical and mental well-being — for their food, clothes, body position, location in the living area, medicine, activities, privileges, friends, acceptance, and above all, for their self-esteem. They must correctly analyze their caretakers because they know that their own reactions greatly influence the treatment they receive. On the other hand, those who provide the care need all available information about those for whom they are responsible. Skill at nonverbal communication is not enough; important information will be withheld unless a trusting relationship has been established. The reasons for reticence about sharing hallucinatory experiences are clear; the residents are aware of what hearing a voice implies, how it is customarily accepted by others, how it may be reacted to socially, and how it may be treated medically. To be unable to control consequences is vulnerability at its extreme. Therefore, those who are in positions of control must carefully consider the viewpoint of the handicapped. It is hoped that the findings of this report, based on the extensive research of Julian Jaynes, may enlarge our understanding of auditory hallucinations, which for certain physically handicapped populations may be the rule, not the exception.

Current Perspectives and Afterthoughts on
Auditory Hallucinations in Nonverbal Quadriplegics,
A Study Based on the Work of Julian Jaynes

After publishing "Auditory Hallucinations in Nonverbal Quadriplegics," I received several questions regarding the validity of
the reported messages. As one humorously put it, "Who's
hearing these voices anyway?" Since I was the initiator of the
questions asked as well as the recorder of the responses, these
were legitimate and well received comments.

So we did a follow-up study to try to answer this question.[5] Of
the nine cases in the original paper, four were selected for the
validity study (the 5 others were not available due to transfers,
one death, and one refusal).

Each of the four clients, studied separately, was given a verbal
message by one staff member. Then another staff member,
unfamiliar with the message, attempted to elicit the message
using the binary yes-no questioning method, the same used in the
original study. There were six levels of message difficulty, each
client given four messages, one at a time, at each level.

The following are two examples of these messages at each level:

Level 1 (concrete nouns) — Chair, Ball
Level 2 (adjective plus concrete noun) — Large room, Big smile
Level 3 (verb plus concrete noun) — Fill a bag, Ride a bus
Level 4 (verb plus adjective plus concrete noun) — Buy a new
        hat, Tie a strong knot
Level 5 (verb plus adjective plus abstract noun) — Play country
        music, Try new flavors
Level 6 (nonsense phrase including verb plus adjective plus
        noun) — Eat purple flowers, Cook hidden shoes

Two psychologists who were not told how the responses were
obtained determined the level of correctness between actual and

elicited messages. Their combined and averaged results indicated the following degrees of matches between the actual and elicited messages for all four clients.

Level 1 – 100%
Level 2 – 88%
Level 3 – 91%
Level 4 – 85%
Level 5 – 88%
Level 6 – 82%

These clients may have been non-verbal quadriplegics, but the effectiveness of the binary questioning procedure along with the difficulty of some of the questions, supported not only their intelligence, but also the validity of their responses.

The research of Julian Jaynes indicated that there was a time when people were directed by auditory voices, which they apparently obeyed without question. Through some evolutionary process the auditory nature of these voices seemed to disappear, resulting in a period of confusion in which people had to rely on their own consciousness in making decisions.

But did these voices really disappear? Or were they merely relegated to a less conscious level, no longer auditory but manifest in the form of intuition. Several current publications have emphasized the validity and importance of intuition and how, if accessed, intuition can give important directions and valid insights. Awkward as it sounds, we may know more than we think we know. Within us, within our very cells, may be an awareness of situations, long before we become consciously aware of them. Yet we may be able to access this valuable source of information by paying attention to our hunches, feelings, and intuitions.

Gavin de Becker wrote *The Gift of Fear*, in which he interviewed case after case of survivors of dangerous and violent situations, in which there had been signs and internal messages all along that had not been consciously attended to. He also interviewed cases where such tragedies had been avoided by recognizing and acting on these intuitions. He now teaches seminars all over the country on how we can protect ourselves by "learning to trust and act on our gut reactions."

Malcolm Gladwell wrote a book called *Blink* with extensive research supporting the thesis that we have an awareness of events and situations just below the surface of awareness which we can learn to access by focusing on, paying more attention to, and trusting our instincts, feelings, and intuitions. Furthermore, these signals come in an instant, not after prolonged thinking and processing, in the blink of an eye. Paying attention to these initial intuitions can help us, not just in avoiding danger, but in making wise decisions about most anything, such as choosing a mate, buying a car, changing careers, interviewing job applicants, everything. He feels it is more than just a reflection of our past training, experience and imprinting, but instead is a source of knowledge instilled in every cell in our body about which we may be consciously unaware of except at a intuitive level.

He gives an example in the introduction of his book, which sets the pace. An art dealer offered the J. Paul Getty Museum a rare statue known as a kouras for ten million dollars. It passed the authenticity test of many experts who took core samples, measurements, X-rays, and numerous chemical analyses.

There was a problem however; it didn't look right to several other art historians after they took just a glance at the statue. They didn't know why, they just had a hunch, a sense that something was amiss. Others had this same unverifiable doubt. Georgios Dontas, head of the Archeological Society in Athens, glimpsed at the statue and immediately felt cold, "When I saw the kouras for the first time, I felt as there was a glass between me and the work." Angelos Delivorrias, director of the Benaki Museum in Athens, also felt the statue was a fake. Why? Because when he first laid eyes on it he felt a wave of "intuitive repulsion."

In fact the statue did turn out to be a forgery. In the first two seconds, after a single glance, they were able to understand the essence and truth of the situation. *Blink* is a book about the importance of those first two seconds of any experience. It is not always that simple — Gladwell also gives examples of how intuition can be misleading, based on the heavy influences of previous conditioning, experience, and imprinting. The book is about learning to distinguish the difference and is a guide to understanding every decision you have made and perhaps will make in the future.

We can follow Jaynes's theorizing right to the present time. There was not a discontinuity of the process, just a continuum of evolution to a different level, from external auditory directives and information to semi-conscious internal or intuitive messages.

Occasionally there occurs a reversion to previous levels accompanying some organic dysfunction, quite common in quadriplegic, non-verbal clients. Or, in some who display psychotic-like features, organically based or not, the voices perhaps contributing to their designation as psychotic. In addition it is not uncommon for children to hear voices, a situation which fades and passes with maturation. Yet there are even some quite normal adults living productive and meaningful lives who also hear auditory voices.

And so we witness the evolution of consciousness in a positive progressive way affording us opportunities to understand more about ourselves and enabling us to lead more satisfying, fulfilling, and happier lives. The main difference between the preconscious era that Julian Jaynes describes and the consciousness that we experience today is that now we must be sensitive and pay attention to the intuitive messages that were once given so freely.

John Hamilton
March 2005

NOTES TO CHAPTER 5

1. One of the interested staff was Mary Poteet. At a time when I was struggling to understand the residents, she was communicating with them regularly. Being skeptical, I told one of her nonverbal residents to give her the message to call me at 3 p.m. the next day. At three o'clock sharp the following day, Mary Poteet called to ask what I wanted. What I wanted was to observe her communicating with the nonverbal. Her method was rapid and effective, and it was by following her example that I carried out the subsequent interviews with the residents in this study.
2. Moore, 1972.
3. Five of the nine residents were taking Valium as a muscle relaxant at some point during this study. No relationship was observed between the presence or absence of Valium and the "voice" phenomenon. Four of the five medicated residents reported that the "voices" started long before they ever received Valium. One resident was treated with Valium six months after he first reported his "voice" and Valium was later discontinued; there were no related changes in the frequency of occurrence or the content of his "voice."
4. The concept of God was a familiar one to these residents; in their early years they had been influenced about religion by their families; later they attended church services within the institution on a regular basis. Individual concepts of God varied among residents, but it was the generally accepted belief that God was a higher power who directed and controlled their lives.
5. Sappington, Reedy, Welch, and Hamilton, 1989.

REFERENCES

De Becker, G. 1997. *The Gift of Fear*. New York: Bantam-Doubleday.

Gladwell, M. 2005. *Blink: The Power of Thinking Without Thinking*. New York: Little and Brown.

Hamilton, J. 1985. "Auditory Hallucinations in Non-Verbal Quadriplegics." *Psychiatry*, 48, 4, 382–92.

Jaynes, J. 1976. *The Origin of Consciousness in the Breakdown of the Bicameral Mind*. Boston: Houghton Mifflin.

Moore, M.V. 1972. "Binary Communication for the Severely Handicapped." *Archives of Physical Medicine and Rehabilitation*, 53, 532–33.

Sappington, J., S. Reedy, R. Welch, and J. Hamilton. 1989. "Validity of Messages from Quadriplegic Persons with Cerebral Palsy." *American Journal on Mental Retardation*, 94, 49–52.

PART III

Consciousness and the Self

CHAPTER 6

Language and Consciousness

Jaynes's "Preposterous Idea" Reconsidered

JOHN LIMBER

JULIAN JAYNES'S IDEAS ON the nature and origin of consciousness remain as provocative today as they were 30 years ago when he published his book — *The Origin of Consciousness in the Breakdown of the Bicameral Mind* (OC).[1] In OC Jaynes proposed that human consciousness — suitably delimited — was a cultural artifact, based on structural and functional aspects of human language, brought about by upheavals in society due to eruptions, migration, conquest, as well as the onset of trade and the invention of writing. Jaynes conjectured that the bicameral brain, with its hallucinatory right hemisphere, was replaced by a new mentality of consciousness. Most remarkably — some said incredibly — this fundamental change in human brain function occurred within the last few thousand years. He supported this theory with his interpretation of the history of early civilization, evidence from neuropsychology, clinical psychology, and his own analyses of ancient texts where he argued the lack of mental state words

My title draws from Jaynes's own words. "The preposterous hypothesis we have come to ... is that human nature was split in two, an executive part called a god, and a follower part called a man" (Jaynes, 1976/1990, p. 84). Some of these ideas were presented at the 2005 Julian Jaynes Symposium on Consciousness, University of Prince Edward Island, Charlottetown, PEI.

like *think* or *believe* and the like in those texts indicated that the people of those times did not think or believe — at least as we understand those terms today.

In this chapter I identify what I believe are the core concepts of Jaynesian consciousness — a variety of subjective yet functional experiences that depend in their everyday application upon cultural artifacts related to the use and development of human language. Using anecdotes and recent research on the use and development of language, I hope to show that there is growing empirical support for some of Jaynes's conjectures on consciousness. For those contemporary readers of Jaynes's conjectures who remain unconvinced by his 30-year-old suggestions, it is undeniable that these ideas remain as pointers to hotspots of current research where there is little consensus 30 years and countless brain scans later.

We can sort his proposals into four broad conjectures: (1) human consciousness from language, (2) the role of verbal hallucinations in the ancient bicameral mind, (3) the history/timing of the changeover, and (4) the underlying biology — lateralization of language to the left hemisphere and the hallucinatory role of the right hemisphere. Each of these today are topics of contemporary inquiry to a large extent independent of each other. Jaynes himself pointed out that, "the book is not a single hypothesis."[2] One of the main virtues of OC today is that it might lead readers to take a broader perspective on consciousness than they would otherwise get from contemporary reductive studies of blindsight, 40 Hz brain waves, or other of the many so-called "neural correlates of consciousness."

THE EXPERIENCE OF CONSCIOUSNESS: WHAT IS IT?

When OC was published, critics had a field day — everyone could find a topic or conjecture that they disagreed with. My own skepticism actually predated the book; I heard Jaynes talk at the University of New Hampshire several years before OC was published. My immediate reaction was similar to that of subsequent reviewers of OC — intriguing, imaginative, preposterous, crazy. There was no way human language could have taken on such a different role so rapidly and recently. His speculation on the functioning of cerebral hemispheres went far beyond the contemporary evidence. Most preposterous, I believed, was the idea that the builders of pyramids and the inventors of writing were not conscious. My own research had shown that three-year-old children, apparently unlike the characters in Jaynes's ancient texts, used those mental state verbs like *think*.[3] Anyway, could one really infer mentality from the choice of words in texts? Ned Block in an early review of OC and elsewhere, touched on an issue many scientists remain sympathetic to — how could anyone think consciousness is a cultural construction?[4]

In retrospect, most of these critics — myself included — just ignored Jaynes's early chapters where he tries to tell us what consciousness is not. Even today, people seem to think they have refuted OC by demonstrating animals and infants have sensation, perception, memory, or awareness of contingencies. Those complaints can safely be ignored. These phenomena, widespread across the animal kingdom, are fundamental properties of organisms but they are certainly not what Jaynes was concerned with. Science is, if anything, a human endeavor, capturing knowledge in language. Science history is often reflected in the history of words. Consciousness, like "force" and other scientific terms before it, has a long road ahead before it becomes the unambiguous "natural kind" expression[5] some egocentric psychologists and philosophers think it is.

Far more significant criticisms relate to his first conjecture — consciousness from language. Even when we narrowly focus on Jaynesian consciousness (J-con),[6] it remains unclear how language operates to create it. This issue is the focus of this chapter. I will explore the possibility that Jaynes's most important conjecture may be explained, as he suggested, by changes in vocabulary, metaphoric shifts in meaning of existing terms, and cultural innovations on the intrapersonal use of language. Those aspects of language are surely "cultural constructions" — albeit within a biological account of language evolution.[7] Every word we know was invented by someone. The meaning of those words comes through our personal experiences with them, yet necessarily retaining much of their conventional (shared) meaning. And the ways we use language may be very strongly influenced by our peers, parents, teachers, and our own self-discoveries. Jaynes proposed that such changes in language use over some thousands of years transformed everyday interpersonal group communication[8] into something like an intrapersonal operating system capable of a variety of new tasks including expanding imagination and creating autobiographical memories.

JAYNES'S CORE IDEA – J-CONSCIOUSNESS (J-CON)

The following paragraph from OC captures the idea of J-consciousness:

> I shut my eyes and even if I try not to think, consciousness still streams on, a great river of contents in a succession of different conditions which I have been taught to call thoughts, images, memories, interior dialogues, regrets, wishes, resolves, all interweaving with the constantly changing pageant of exterior sensations of which I am selectively aware.[9]

Notice how he discriminates between consciousness and "exterior sensations" and selective awareness. There is also the suggestion that thinking is distinct from consciousness. Yet critics often conflate these cognitive phenomena; Jaynes regretted not emphasizing more the differences among them.[10] As I see it now, Jaynes is simply talking about a representational mind, where language plays a very significant yet limited role in the contents and operation of mind processes. I have set aside some of my own earlier objections. While the ancients surely were aware and had perceptual experiences like ours, is it possible they did not have the interior dialogue that Jaynes refers to? Like other readers, I had projected my own pre-existing notion of consciousness onto OC, neglecting Jaynes's own words about both the nature and significance of consciousness. For Jaynes, consciousness was limited to what was introspectable and also limited in its overall contribution to human behavior.

> Here it is only necessary to conclude that consciousness does not make all that much difference to a lot of our activities … it is perfectly possible that there could have existed a race of men who spoke, judged, reasoned, solved problems, indeed did most of the things that we do, but who were not conscious at all.[11]

But does this mean J-consciousness is simply an epiphenomenal linguistic manifestation of some cognitive processes? To a certain extent that is the case. But it is not always so. Jaynes addresses this issue directly, with a paraphrase of William James:[12]

> It is just plain inconceivable that consciousness should have nothing to do with a business which it so faithfully attends. If consciousness is the mere impotent shadow of action, why is it more intense when action is most hesitant? And why are we least conscious when doing something most habitual?[13]

In what follows, I plan to reconstruct, following Jaynes's lead whenever possible, J-con in the context of some recent research in the use and development of language and memory. Just what is it that makes a brain seemingly "introspectable?" I will assume, without much discussion, some aspects of cognition, language, and memory that I do not think violate Jaynes's conceptions but were not an explicit part of OC.

SOME BACKGROUND ASSUMPTIONS ON LANGUAGE AND COGNITION

I assume "thinking" is a functional manipulation of representations toward some goal, problem, or objective. These representations may be automatically encoded — to some approximation — into a natural language like English to make them conscious to ourselves or others whenever possible. This is what I mean by "having a thought." But far more often they remain inaccessible in some primary format — perhaps "mentalese,"[14] or even sensory or motor images that may not find adequate expression in any language lexicon. It is worth noting here that humans create conventional meaning by making conventional movements — speech or signs. It is these subtle movements or movement plans, I assume, that underlie J-con as suggested in the "inner speech" box in Figure 1 discussed below.

Organisms "think" to the extent that they manipulate representations. Wolfgang Kohler's[15] famous reports of chimpanzee "insight" might be taken literally as virtual manipulation of visual-motor images in aid of obtaining a desired food object.[16] Kohler's characterization of his chimpanzees' tool construction hints at a limited non-verbal visual-motor consciousness:

> One fact must be noted in reference to the breaking off of pieces from boxes ... not everything that is obviously 'a part' for man is so for the chimpanzee. ... There must be a kind of visual firmness which makes the separating as an act of intelligence as difficult as the strongest nails would the actual pulling off of the board.

... We do not differ much in principle from the chimpanzee in this ... but ... visual unities are probably more easily separated by the adult human than by the chimpanzee.[17]

Kohler goes on to suggest that in the course of problem solving, the chimpanzees engage in "expressive gestures." Rana, for example, is figuring out how to use a rope to swing through a door to reach a treat. Kohler believed her movements were:

Expressing some such state as: "It all depends on getting through the door." ... The animal is entirely deprived of expression in speech; we mutter words of this kind to ourselves, even when no one can hear us, i.e. when speaking is of no use, but we are "so full of the thing that our tongue starts to utter words. Rana's limbs are her tongue.[18]

The chimpanzees' skills develop over time, whether by maturation or experience:

The low degree of optical apprehension ... in the above discussions is not necessarily characteristic of chimpanzees, for a certain improvement is possible with them, just as with human children, though in quite a different measure.[19]

Young humans routinely are able to pretend and create — parsing reality into components and reorganizing the parts into novel objects, imaginary dancing trees, talking trains, and the like. Our much greater human facility with language[20] is probably both a cause and effect of such perceptual parsing. As Kohler suggests, language may not be necessary for a degree of "optical apprehension." Yet even the most visual human thinkers — like my daughter or Temple Grandin, discussed below, who characterizes her mind as a picture-filled thousand gigabyte hard-drive — appear to interact with their imagery via language.

The advantage in thinking, obviously, is that the outcome of actual manipulations can be previewed without the costs of doing them. Jaynes was essentially elaborating on this recurrent theme in psychology[21] — consciousness enables modeling or simulation of one's outer world — and beyond — quickly, cheaply, and often effectively.

While it seems very implausible that we think in a specific language, such as English, Hopi, or Yupik, there can be a very close connection in fluent speakers between their thoughts, their language, and their consciousness.[22] But these are not identical. To paraphrase Jaynes, language evolved in social interactions and became transformed over time into subjective consciousness.[23] Fluent speakers with sufficiently rich vocabularies began to hear themselves "think" via their inner speech — first as verbal hallucinations and later more specifically attributed to themselves as the source of that experience. I have tentatively sketched these processes in Figure 1. The "corollary discharge" box metaphorically borrows the old idea that the brain, in order to inform itself of the body's upcoming movements, provides an efferent copy of the planned movement to other parts of the brain.[24] This is the source of "inner speech." The "attribution" box assigns the source of the input to self or other.[25]

INTRA- PERSONAL LANGUAGE AND J-CONSCIOUSNESS

J-con is about this personal or interior use of language rather than its more obvious social use. While both use the same language structures[26] — these are two distinct functions of language. Here are some anecdotes from my own experience that illustrate several aspects of intrapersonal language:

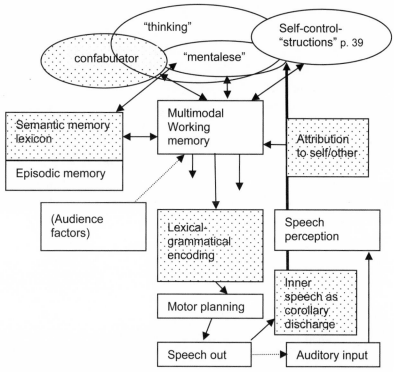

Figure 1. Jaynes's introspective consciousness reconsidered. The shaded concepts play pivotal roles in our experience of consciousness. Our thoughts become known to us — or perhaps more often created — as they are auto-coded into our speech movements, "heard," and attributed to ourselves.

1. As I left a friend's house, he admonished me to "finish that chapter so you can enjoy the weekend." I drove off repeating to myself "Finish this chapter. Finish this chapter." While this is not a particularly revealing piece of interior dialogue, it is more than an epiphenomenal bit of consciousness. At the very least it might serve to maintain that goal in consciousness, perhaps priming it sufficiently that it pops out when someone asks me to go sailing, watch the Red Sox, or any other attractive diversion.[27] Perhaps Rana's gestures served a similar function in her planning?

2. When my daughter was 2, I taught her how to play the card game "Concentration." Successful players remember the location of an increasingly large number of previously exposed cards. Within a few months she was unbeatable; it was as if she could see the previously exposed cards that were now faced down. Her verbal understanding of the game rules interacted with her vivid visual card memory. Ten months later, she was on the way to becoming "conscious" — and a very poor player. She had learned the names of the cards! Much research today is directed at the interaction of verbal and non-verbal representations.[28]

3. Maintaining a memory with verbal rehearsal is taken for granted by most of us. My daughters around age 3 or 4 began using the telephone. I thought it would be easy to show them how to find the numbers of their friends that I had underlined in red and dial themselves. It wasn't. They couldn't remember the numbers long enough to dial them, even if right in front of them. I had to tell them, over and over, to repeat the number before dialing. It took quite a while, with frequent reminders and examples, for them to do this effectively. Would they have figured this out on their own? Maybe — yet several years later they still needed on occasion to be reminded to use that rehearsal strategy.[29]

4. In a recent conversation, an acquaintance mentioned that she had a boat moored in a local bay — a rather large boat. I didn't think much of it at the time but later going over the bridge across that bay, I was prompted to ask myself — where would a boat that large be moored? Having sailed in this bay for years in a fourteen-foot sailboat, I knew it pretty well — indeed with more than enough first person experiences with the mud and rocks of low tide. I looked around but as it was early spring, no boats were in the water yet. The question departed my consciousness as I left the bridge — only to return each

time I crossed that bridge for the next week or so. And then one day crossing the bridge I saw an answer to my question — a sharp image in my mind of a sleek 40+ foot white sailboat at its mooring. The image was distinctive though incomplete[30] — transom sloping outward, many starboard portholes on her hull and streamlined cabin that was aerodynamically faired into the foredeck. I think I recognized the location of the mooring within a few hundred yards. With the image came a vague recollection of the encoding. event more than a year ago, asking myself "what's that doing there" among a fleet of smaller sailboats? However, until the recent episode, that event was lost to consciousness, along with millions of other events — untold books and papers read, people met, meals eaten, and softball games played. Most — fortunately — rarely return unless inadvertently primed or accessed deliberately by language.

5. The "boat" anecdote is similar to the one I've often used in classes. Many years ago I started to use reading glasses. Too often I would put them down, go off and do something, then — wanting to read again — could not find them. After a brief failed search, I'd say to one or both of my children — "Where's my glasses?" Occasionally, one would actually report their location, "on the table" or provide a clue "you had them at dinner." Frequently, there was silence or sarcasm — "they're *your* glasses!" Remarkably, I found that fairly often the memory of where I left my glasses rose to consciousness even with no answer or clue, in the face of sarcasm, or even if no one was there. Now, living alone, I ask myself many times a week — "Where are my glasses?" And, fairly often I get the answer or good clue primed by the question; sometimes I "see" or "feel" myself setting the glasses down and am quite certain about their location.

Although these personal examples illustrate some of the many functions of J-con, no one should assume I know how language and other representations and components in Figure 1 actually work in determining these cognitive processes! My understanding is particularly weak in the most interesting boxes — "self-control" and "confabulation." Contemporary psychology offers very little on the former beyond developmental assessments in young children (see below) and while Jaynes presents a descriptive historical account of a shift from the bicameral to the conscious "I" mind, much remains uncertain. As for "confabulation," even less is known.

THE KEY IDEAS IN OC: LANGUAGE AND J-CON

In the remainder of this chapter, I will review the essentials of J-con and try to reconstruct a story on the development of language that makes it plausible that J-con must to a considerable extent be a cultural artifact.

Consciousness is based on Language

Jaynes is quite firm on this: J-con is founded upon language. Should he allow some proto-consciousness in humans or apes without conventional language? Possibly — yet the flexibility of a J-con operating with mentalese[31] would be greatly limited — both in terms of control and feedback from one's underlying cognitive processes. Recall Kohler's remark about Rana's limbs. The lack of conventional symbols would greatly restrict the operation of an already limited system.

"Language is an Organ of Perception"[32]

Perception and understanding of our world depends on the growth of abstract concepts in our nervous system "whose referents are not observables except in a metaphorical sense."

Thus the words we have link the implicit machinery of thought, however metaphorically, to our consciousness. These words play more than a passive, reflective role in J-con:

...each new stage of words [in the development of a language] literally created new perceptions and attentions, and such new perceptions and attentions resulted in important cultural changes which are reflected in the archeological record."[33]

Moreover, contemporary cognitive scientists increasingly recognize that introspection is not only limited by the metaphoric "fit" of words to thoughts, but also that the products of introspection are powerfully influenced by one's culture and previous personal experiences. J-con — and introspection broadly construed — offer no direct insight into the mind. Our J-con experience is a consequence of layers of metaphor, interpretation, and confabulation — see note 30. This construction of the stream of J-con remains largely unexplained, though many, including William James,[34] Sigmund Freud, and several recent writers, have some interesting ideas on the topic.[35] The process may prove to be a much more controlled and detailed parallel to dream construction.

Consciousness is Far More Recent than You Think?

Perhaps the most contentious aspect of J-con is his argument that human consciousness is only several thousand years old. Even supporters of other elements of J-con balked at the timing. Morris Berman, for example, argues that a fundamental mental discontinuity occurred about 40,000 years ago:

Although I believe Jaynes's dating of these events is very much off (he places it at 1300–900, B.C.), his description of this new consciousness is one of the best I have come across.[36]

Berman goes on to characterize this new mentality as one involving goal orientation or "planning depth," along with increasing evidence of personal adornments and burial traditions.

> this in turn implicates the kind of consciousness described by Jaynes, the ego awareness necessary to see oneself in a story, in future time.[37]

I have put some of the important milestones in the evolution of language and J-con in Table 1, incorporating aspects of Jaynes, Berman, and my own considerations.

Jaynes knew well before OC that his time frame was very controversial. I questioned him skeptically at an early presentation of his ideas at the University of New Hampshire. One of my concerns was that while Jaynes acknowledged natural selection might have played a role in the very recent development of language and J-con, he was asking us to believe — on his timetable — that human evolution might have been ongoing just a few thousand years ago.[38] In his paper on the evolution of language, Jaynes[39] received sharp criticism on this issue. Yet he apparently was convinced by his linguistic analyses that a later development of J-con was most probable.

I will leave this controversial issue of when J-con emerged. It really doesn't impact the more general hypothesis deriving consciousness from language. Yet I expect Jaynes would be intrigued — as I was — to read about the recent research of Bruce Lahn and colleagues based on comparative DNA mutations in which they suggest that natural selection has continued to act on the human brain within the last 30,000 years and may be ongoing today.[40] Might this be the genetic underpinnings of the Baldwin effect?

Time (ya)	J-con relevant events	Species/societies
6,000,000	Chimps/humans diverge	
3,700,000	Bipedalism	Australopithecus
	Overall brain increase (3x)	Homo habilis, erectus
	Mosaic brain development	
	Fire, tools, meat	
	Human vocal tract	Homo sapiens - out of Africa
	Human proto-language	
150,000	Language modifies brain?	
	(Baldwin effect)	
	Modern humans emerge	Homo sapiens sapiens
	Climate changes	
60,000	Representational art	
	Expanding vocabulary	
	Personal identity	
40,000	J-con (Berman, 2000)?	
	Continued brain evolution?	Variable cultures in parallel?
	Balter (2005)	
5,000	Writing	
3,000	J-con (Jaynes, 1976/1990)?	Variable cultures in parallel?
	Autobio./episodic memory	
	Modern ego	

Table 1. Approximate timing in years ago (ya) of events leading up to the emergence of J-con. Uncertainty is indicated by "?"

The Contents of J-Con Are Not Exclusively Linguistic

While the interface between episodic memory and consciousness is based on language, Jaynes knew that the contents of consciousness could be anything in memory. In my "big boat" example, when I successfully probed myself asking "where...," the answer was visual-spatial. Often when I probe for my glasses, the answer is a sensory-motor response — a memory of removing the glasses and setting them down in a place and time — immediately identifiable or not.

When Temple Grandin,[41] who has eloquently expressed her autistic phenomenology, talks about her mind as like a "hard drive" filled with images, it seems as if her "operating system" is basically language-like but the contents rarely are. Jaynes put it this way:

...the content of consciousness is far from being all language. You or I can right now imagine a triangle in mindspace, color it red, and even slowly turn it around in our consciousness. There is nothing linguistic in that. But it takes language to get us there, to set it up in our imagination. I did not mean that everything in consciousness is made up of language. Language creates a mind-space on the basis of metaphor and analogy in which you are 'seeing' the triangle, as well as the analog 'I' which is doing the 'seeing'. The particular things you are conscious of, music, sculpture, triangles, are often not linguistic at all.[42]

Today we might say that our language provides a flexible, expandable operating system for interacting with, organizing, and creating memories.

J-Con Has Characteristic Qualities

Jaynes's consciousness has definitive features that create an "analog world" with its own space, agents and objects, storytelling ability, and capacities to selectively excerpt, rationalize, and create its own inner reality distinct from the outer world. Foreshadowing Michael Gazzaniga's left hemisphere "interpreter"[43] or Antonio Damasio's[44] "extended consciousness," J-con "is ever ready to explain anything we happen to find ourselves doing."[45] J-con, thus, converges with — not to say explains — the mysteries of confabulation[46] or "brain fiction." Isn't OC itself a product of J-con?

The Lexicon Is a Critical Component for J-Con

It is absolutely important to focus on specific words in order to understand how J-con might work. There are several different issues to consider — the "fit" of a word to its concept, the availability of a word to an individual and culture, and the degree of automaticity of encoding the concept into a language expression.

Inferring Consciousness from Mental State Words

Jaynes was criticized by many of us for his efforts to date the origin of consciousness by the presence or absence of mental state words. The following OC passage not only demonstrates his method based on words, but shows us how J-con is closely related to modern conceptions of episodic memory and in particular, accessing "autobiographical memory."[47]

> But more germane to the present topic is the famous "Know thyself".... This again was something inconceivable to the Homeric heroes. How can one know thyself? By initiating by oneself memories of one's actions and feelings and looking at them together with an analog 'I', conceptualizing them, sorting them out into characteristics, and narratizing so as to know what one is likely to do. One must 'see' 'oneself' as in an imaginary 'space', indeed what we were calling autoscopic illusions....[48]

Does the use of a word reliably indicate underlying mentality?[49] I remain skeptical — particularly when one person is writing about another and a third party — us — is making the inference about the protagonist's mind. Words are invented to fill a need — a process sometimes called "lexicalization." A word may be invented to directly reflect a new concept or perhaps more commonly, to replace a much more complex linguistic expression. So in either case the new word follows the concept.[50] Of necessity, then, there will be gaps between the time the concept emerges, the concept is lexicalized,[51] and when that new word is taken up by most of the speakers of that language. So, one might try to estimate the time it took for the conceptual innovations implicit in constructing J-con to be lexicalized and conventionalized sufficiently to be used in the *Iliad* and other texts Jaynes evaluates. In cultures without mass communication and systematic formal education, I imagine the timing here would be extremely variable from person to person, place to place.

The Importance of Lexicalization

While I do not consider the presence or absence of specific language expressions — words — as reliable indicators of mental state, the availability of specific words must have a very basic impact on cognition — and the utility of J-con. Expressing one's thoughts into language is a complex cognitive process that requires joint satisfaction of at least two conditions — words must be available to adequately fit the thought *and* this approximation of thoughts into English must occur at the extraordinarily rapid rate of over 100 words per minute (wpm). Nor can the rate exceed our ability to listen to ourselves — say 500 wpm at the most. This is true whether we are concerned with external speech or the interior dialogue of J-con. It appears there must be severe sensory-motor and linguistic constraints on J-con.

Encoding and Comprehension Rates

Even if it is possible to express any thought in any language, a language with a suitable vocabulary makes the process practical. Anecdotes abound about deaf individuals being taught a conventional signed language reporting a dramatic change in consciousness.[52] Newton and other scientists report on their struggle to express their ideas without appropriate words.[53] Our current experience of "inner speech" or "interior dialogue" simply could not happen either if there were too few or too many words to be encoded and comprehended. How fast can auto-encoding occur? Normal speech — 200 wpm — requires two to three words per second. Inner speech can be more efficient —

several times that perhaps since overt movements are not required and audience issues are minimal.[54]

In almost any story of human language evolution, inner speech — perhaps even more so than social speech — will become possible only in skilled speakers where cognitive substrates are encoded into speech precisely, rapidly, and automatically. And this requires a precise, succinct vocabulary that — with appropriate grammatical structures — can quickly map mentalese into speech movements, as well as being rapidly interpreted by our own speech perception processors. Are some languages better suited than others for J-con? Maybe — some languages may have more cognitive overhead in obligatory grammatical encoding. Even complex phonology might matter. More important, I expect, would be the level of abstraction or generality of the available vocabulary which is more of a cultural than a linguistic issue.

J-Con Is More Than Epiphenomenal

If our interior speech remained a functionless "corollary discharge," it might be of little interest outside of clinical settings.[55] For Jaynes, this inner speech provides a very limited access to our cognitions but does enable a certain amount of self-control over them (See Figure 1).

Self-Interrogation and Other "Structions"

My personal anecdotes above — the concentration game, the boat, and glasses — illustrate Jaynes's notion of a "struction:"

> ...one does one's thinking before one knows what one is to think about. The important part of the matter is the instruction, which allows the whole business to go off automatically. This I shall shorten to the term struction,

by which I mean it to have the connotation of both instruction and construction... the actual process of thinking... is not conscious at all... only its preparation, its materials, and its end result are consciously perceived."[56]

And we know from recent studies that these "end results" are rarely a reliable indication of those underlying cognitive processes.[57]

Consciousness as a Cultural Artifact?

Despite his critics, there is no doubt that Jaynes saw J-con as a cultural artifact:[58]

I have been speaking of consciousness as a human product, an ability that is learned in history in order to cope behaviorally in a civilized world.[59]

How might this work? First of all, the lexicon of a culture or individual is a collection of individually fashioned artifacts — the morphemes or words. While only a few word artisans create them, all of us use them creatively — if we have them. Next there is the varied use of language and other cognitive processes across cultures. We know that at least some of these processes are culturally determined — one example being Piaget's stage of "formal operations" intended to explain the advent of scientific thinking as a product of language and formal schooling. At the same time, in the old Soviet Union, Vygotsky and Luria, notably, were reporting similar effects.

Jaynes believed that evidence for J-con must be found in studies of language use and development.

One needs language for consciousness. We think consciousness is learned by children between two-and-a-half and five or six years in what we can call the verbal surround, or the verbal community as B.F. Skinner calls it. It is an aspect of learning to speak. Mental words are out there as part of the culture and part of the family. A child fits himself into these words and uses them even before he knows the meaning of them. A mother is constantly instilling the seeds of consciousness in a two- and three-year-old, telling the child to stop and think, asking him "What shall we do today?" or "Do you remember when we did such and such or were somewhere?" And all this while metaphor and analogy are hard at work. There are many different ways that different children come to this, but indeed I would say that children without some kind of language are not conscious.[60]

If one can get passed the idea that smiling little six-month-old Mary might not be "conscious," Jaynes's ideas — generally unreferenced — are developed in a number of recent investigations. Several contemporary research topics — including memory and executive control, use of mental state words, and the development of autobiographical memory — are particularly relevant.

DEVELOPMENT AND J-CON: SOME EXAMPLES

While verbally flogging myself to "finish this chapter, finish this chapter" probably had little useful effect, repeating a precise verbal recipe "the rabbit comes out of its hole, round the tree, and back down the hole again" has helped many tie a bowline knot. Yet we know that it takes modern children four to six or more years to become capable of following fairly elementary verbal recipes and strategies like the verbal rehearsal for phone numbers discussed above — not to mention the complexities of tying shoe laces. These tasks are not inevitably acquired by children like walking and talking, but require cultural support, perhaps explicit instruction, for widespread use in a culture.

Philip Zelaso has developed a complex developmental theory of consciousness levels in which the labeling of subjective experience facilitates rule use and words become instrumental in moving to higher levels of consciousness.[61] Jaynes might well have endorsed much of this.

Dan Slobin and his colleagues have an extensive research program documenting how languages may differ lexically and in obligatory grammatical encoding.[62] These differences, Slobin argues, influence children's thought processes as they acquire their native language.

The availability of mental state terms such as *know*, *think*, *believe* is an explicit part of J-con — both in the cognitive processes as well as in evidence bearing on the presence of consciousness in ancient minds. These subjective mental concepts are also elements in construction of a child's "theory of mind" which enables us today to project consciousness onto others. Jaynes suggested this phenomenon was so powerful that it in a way blinds us; I think it was responsible for some of the initial negative response to OC.

> It is very difficult to suspend that habit of projecting consciousness in thinking about ancient civilizations or even in animals close to us or even in newborn infants.[63]

While mental state words are today used by most four-year-olds,[64] as Jaynes pointed out, it is unclear what these words initially mean to young children. Moreover, as Ruffman, Slade, and Crowe report, mother's use of these terms appears to facilitate their children's usage of these words.[65] Harris, de Rosnay, and Pons reach a similar conclusion.[66] And of course now these words are already in the lexicon of all languages ready to go — no word artisans are needed. At the cultural level, there appear to be significant variations even today in these "theories" about how we predict and explain other's behavior.[67]

In addition, there is the development of episodic, autobiographical memory — explicit memories of ourselves set in a specific time and place, generally in a narrative context. Jaynes suggested that such memories were lacking in pre-J-con people:

> This idea of reminiscent memory, what Tulving (1983) calls episodic memory, is built on consciousness. You don't find a bicameral Achilles saying things like "When I was a child" or "Back in Greece what did I do at this time?" or anything of that sort. The bicameral world goes on in a relatively continual present."[68]

Recent research not only suggests that language is necessary for autobiographical memory but that there is considerable cultural variation related to maternal practices.

> We argue that autobiographical memory emerges within specific social and cultural milieus, which shape the ways in which individuals may or may not develop memories of a specific personal past. [69]

Fivush and Nelson suggest that children learn a narrative "reminiscing" style from their mothers' language practices that during preschool years enables their children to "develop the idea of a continuous self."[70]

When, then, might we expect our little Mary to become "conscious?" That is, when would the stream of introspectable J-consciousness become functional in a child's mental life? Jaynes must expect this to take a while — and current research seems in accord with this.[71]

Flavell and his colleagues have investigated this difficult question and find five year olds show far less evidence for introspection than older children.[72] Several issues remain entangled — extent of children's language fluency, becoming aware of their inner speech, and their ability and motivation to "consult" themselves. The latter may be the key to J-con once a basic level of fluency is established.

So it appears possible that little Mary, even up to age five years or so, might not achieve more than minimal J-con, and then only if her language has appropriate words available, her mother works at it, and she undergoes some formal education!

Janet Astington, reviewing Flavell's findings, draws what I take to be an insightful, Jaynesian conclusion:

> It may be that children's first experiences of introspection are perceived, not as reflection on their own thoughts, but as listening to what their brain has to say! There is other evidence that 5-year-olds may sometimes regard their brain as a sort of alter ego....[73]

CULTURAL CHANGES IN THE HUMAN MIND

Jaynes's conjectures were certainly not unique in the idea that fundamental cognitive processes may be influenced by culture. Shifting emphases on language in the concentration game and the emergence of Piaget's formal operations have already been mentioned. Luria's research on schooling effects is a similar result.[74] One might also look into the causes of the Flynn effect, where it appears there are widespread increases in absolute IQ test scores over generations.[75]

Even more to the J-con point, Singer and Singer argue that various electronic media can shape our consciousness:

> We are proposing ... that the seemingly ephemeral human capacity for conscious reflection, imagery, and fantasy depends in an important way upon a child's real-world experience.[76]

And finally, we should look closely at the ideas of Fauconnier and Turner, who elaborate on how humans continue to expand their cognitive abilities through a metaphorical blending or compression of concepts expressed in language.[77] This is perhaps the fundamental unelaborated idea in OC — "language as perception."[78] Eve Sweetser develops some of these ideas in her interesting account of the etymologies and metaphoric development of perception verbs including her suggestion that hearing verb meanings shift to the subjective self in terms of "heedfulness and obedience."[79] Perhaps there is something to reciting "finish this chapter, finish this chapter" after all?

CONCLUSION

Julian Jaynes's "preposterous" ideas can be found thriving in many areas, some 30 years after OC was published. In a surprising number of articles, OC is cited directly.[80] Jaynes's ideas also now benefit from a swing back to interests in cultural differences in mind just as a wave of universalism in the 1970s perhaps made some of us skeptical of the implied cultural relativism in OC. In other articles there may be a reference to someone — Daniel Dennett for example — who has acknowledged Jaynes and gone on to revise or elaborate on some of the OC conjectures.[81] Then there are the increasing numbers of empirical papers on related topics that bypass Jaynes altogether — often citing Vygotsky as inspiration.[82] Vygotsky, like Jaynes, viewed consciousness as primarily a social-cultural-historical process, with internalized language playing a major role in the process.

> Thought and speech turn out to be the key to the nature of human consciousness. ... The word is a direct expression of the historical nature of human consciousness.[83]

And while Jaynes advocated the study of children, Vygotsky and his colleague A.R. Luria had a long history of research on the effects of language on cognition.[84] Conversely, while Jaynes did not engage in language research himself, he made far greater efforts to detail the social-evolutionary-historical foundations of J-con than did his Russian counterparts. Indeed it may be that it was Jaynes's fascinating multidimensional historical story of rapid change in human mentality that has been responsible for much of the criticism and neglect of OC, as well as the long-lasting interest in it. The idea that language underlies aspects of human consciousness is hardly unique to Jaynes.

Astington, as indicated above, gives a Jaynesian account of the development of J-con without citing Jaynes. Instead she references Vygotsky and Snell's somewhat obscure scholarly historical work on the Greek mind,[85] along with current psychological research.

·   The voice of the gods, the voice of the brain, private speech — are these but different ways of conceptualizing introspection?[86]

I wonder if all these ideas would be bound together without OC? Could there be some connection between Vygotsky and Jaynes?[87] Or are these just converging inferences drawn from partially overlapping data and the periodic ebb and flow of notions of consciousness within psychology?

NOTES TO CHAPTER 6

1.   All references to Jaynes's book (OC) are to the second edition. This includes an Afterword, added in 1990.
2.   Jaynes, 1976/1990, p. 447.
3.   Limber, 1973.
4.   Block, 1981.
5.   Putnam, 1975.
6.   I designate this as J-consciousness (J-con) to distinguish it from phenome-

nal conscious (P-con) or access consciousness (A-con), extended consciousness (E-con), self-consciousness (I-con) or one of the several "levels" of
consciousness Con$_i$.

7. Limber, 1982.
8. cf. Dunbar, 1996.
9. Jaynes, 1976/1990, p. 23.
10. Ibid., p. 447.
11. Ibid., p. 47.
12. James (1890) says in his "automaton" Chapter 5, which Jaynes cites that
"consciousness ... is only intense when nerve-processes are hesitant" (p.
142). He concludes that "the distribution of consciousness shows it to be
exactly such as we might expect in an organ added for the sake of steering a
nervous system grown too complex to regulate itself" (p. 144). This is one
of several perspectives on consciousness shared by James and Jaynes
including the role of vocabulary.
13. Jaynes, 1976/1990, p. 11.
14. Fodor, 1975.
15. Kohler, 1925.
16. These separable bits of imagery may be necessary in intra-species
communication (Limber, 1996).
17. Kohler, 1925, pp. 114–115.
18. Ibid., p. 122.
19. Ibid., p. 123.
20. Limber, 1977.
21. Piaget's (1976) work, for example, is an elaborate and unappreciated
account of the development — ontogenetic and cultural — of consciousness
in humans. Russian psychologists — taking their cue from Marx — have a
long tradition of social effects on consciousness, e.g., Vygotsky (1934/1986),
Luria (1976). Recent work in "cognitive linguistics" further elaborates on
the role of metaphor in ramping up the intellectual powers of human minds
(e.g., Turner, 2004). And Dennett (1986, 1991) has explicitly articulated a
Jaynesian approach to consciousness, while others including Carruthers
(1996), Donald (2001), and Damasio (1999) offer similar proposals.
22. See Pinker (1994) for a good discussion of this issue.
23. See Dunbar (1996) for a perspective compatible with Jaynes's thoughts;
also see Limber (1982).
24. For recent application of this idea to schizophrenics and in cricket sound
production, see Ford et al. (2001) and Poulet and Hedwig (2002)
respectively.
25. Mistaken attribution about one's own movements extends beyond speech
into a variety of phenomena, e.g., Ouija boards, Chevreul's pendulum, spirit

possession, hypnotism (Wegner, 2002). See Maguire et al. (1995) for an application to auditory hallucinations.

26. Yet there is an important difference in referential phrasing — we typically know what we are talking about but our audiences may not. My own introspection on this, for what it is worth, reveals few if any descriptive relative clauses in my inner speech. The issue is similar to children's use or non-use of relative clauses (Limber, 1976).

27. Jaynes suggests that in pre-conscious humans auditory hallucination served a similar purpose: "enabling non-conscious early man to keep at his task alone."

28. E.g., Schooler and Schooler, 1990.

29. See Flavell, 1999 for a review.

30. Of course without more precise information, there's no way to be sure about the accuracy or identity of my boat image — but the partial evidence fits.

31. I have to expect if mentalese turns out to be a lot like a natural language, then chances of J-con in humans without a conventional language, e.g., English, ASL, are more likely. This of course is contingent on mentalese being "heard" in some way. The different interpretations of "egocentric" speech in young children between Vygotsky (1934/1986) and Piaget (1976) reflect different views of these issues, with J-con perhaps closer to Vygotsky's perspective. I interpret self-reports of deaf individuals acquiring thoughts after acquiring some social language as becoming conscious of approximations to existing cognitive processes (e.g., Keller, 1954; Schaller, 1991; Golden-Meadow and Zheng, 1998). Jaynes's own conception of "aptic structures" might be relevant here (Jaynes, p. 135).

32. Jaynes, 1976/1990, p. 50.

33. Ibid., p. 132

34. James's (1890) critique of introspection is well worth reading in connection with OC, especially his comments on "the misleading influence of speech." p. 194–8.

35. Nørretranders, 1998; Wilson, 2002; Wegner, 2002.

36. Berman, 2000, p. 37.

37. Ibid., p. 38.

38. See OC, p. 220 where he discusses this point briefly. At the time, both Jaynes and I were advocates of the Baldwin effect — essentially language shaping the brain via natural selection. Jaynes thought these changes might occur far more rapidly than I did — and I thought the idea of parallel evolution resulting in equivalent language biology was even less plausible. But who knows?

39. Jaynes, 1976.

40. Balter, 2005.

41. Grandin, 1996.

42. Jaynes, 1986.
43. Roser and Gazzaniga, 2004.
44. Damasio, 1999.
45. Jaynes, 1976/1990, p. 64.
46. Many have studied this from varying perspectives; in addition to the above, Nisbett and Wilson's (1977) paper "Telling More Than We Can Know" is informative. Linde's (1993) book *Life Stories* reveals some of the sources of our rationalizations, and recent books by Wilson (2002) and Wegner (2002), in particular, review much evidence on the topic. Much of this recent research is summarized in Hirstein's (2005) *Brain Fiction: Self Deception and the Riddle of Confabulations*.
47. Fivush and Nelson, 2004.
48. Jaynes, 1976/1990, p. 287.
49. Perhaps the most elaborated theory of speech production, Levelt et al., 1999, suggest three layers — conceptual, lexical concept, and lexical — mediating between thought and speech. The issue in Jaynes's analyses seems more than just lexical ,however; it concerns the difference between direct and indirect speech where the writer explicitly attributes a thought or belief — subject mentality — to the character.
50. The exception to this is in children's acquisition of language where it is possible the language at times precedes the concept. See Limber (1973) and Jaynes (1986). There is also the use of "lexicalization" in the synchronic sense — converting one's thoughts into words (phrases) on the fly, as in conversation and inner speech.
51. This brief account ignores at least one intermediate step that speech production theories require — binding together semantic features into a pre-lexical unit. See Levelt et al., 1999 on "lexical concepts."
52. E.g., Keller, 1954.
53. E.g., Gleick, 2003.
54. Levelt, et al., 1999, p. 34.
55. Schizophrenia and auditory hallucinations were a significant part of the OC story. This topic remains one of the most researched of all OC topics. It is too simplistic to say that schizophrenia results from a misattribution of speech source but this is certainly a common symptom.
56. Jaynes, 1976/1990, pp. 39, 41.
57. E.g., Nisbett and Wilson, 1977; Wegner, 2002.
58. Both Jaynes and I (Limber, 1982) have appealed to the Baldwin effect as a means of shading the boundary between culture and biology. Thus language can be both artifact and biology!
59. Jaynes, 1986.
60. Ibid.
61. Zelaso, 2004.

62. E.g., Slobin, 2003.

63. Jaynes, 1986.

64. Limber, 1973.

65. Ruffman, Slade, and Crowe, 2002.

66. Harris, de Rosnay, and Pons, 2005.

67. Lilliard, 1998.

68. Jaynes, 1986.

69. E.g., Fivush and Nelson, 2005.

70. Ibid.

71. Piaget's studies of logical operations using verbal justification as a criterion, might be viewed as a narrowly focused study of introspection. This also predicts a slow developmental process that in the final stage of formal operations is culturally determined.

72. Flavell, 1999; Flavell et al., 2000.

73. Astington, 1995, p. 110.

74. Luria, 1976.

75. Flynn, 1999.

76. Singer and Singer, 2005, p. 114.

77. Fauconnier and Turner, 2002.

78. Jaynes, 1976/1990, p. 50.

79. Sweetser, 1990, p. 42–44.

80. Limber, 2000.

81. Dennett, 1986.

82. For reviews of non-Jaynesian ideas on inner speech and consciousness, see Sokolov (1972), Kucaj (1982), Dennett (1991), Nørretranders (1998), and Morin (2005). Vygotsky, of course, was somewhat of a Marxist and probably took something from Marx's (1859) often cited "It is not the consciousness of men that determines their being, but, on the contrary, their social being that determines their consciousness." Vygotsky was also influenced by various pre-Whorfian advocates of linguistic relativity. I say "Vygotsky as inspiration" because I have not as yet found much of sub-stance in any of his writings on consciousness beyond that of the Marx quote above. (Several of his papers are available online at www.marxists.org.)

83. Vygotski, 1925/1999, p. 246.

84. Luria, 1929/1978, 1934.

85. Snell (1953/1960) is cited twice in OC (p. 71, 457 of Afterword), with the note that Jaynes had not known about Snell's work and they came to different conclusions. Astington refers to the 1982 Dover edition.

86. Astington, 1995, p. 112.

87. Jaynes (1976) cites Slobin's (1966) review of Russian psycholinguistics with its heavy emphasis on "linguistically mediated cognition" — which of course includes consciousness. In that same volume, there is a review and

analysis of Russian/Marxist notions of consciousness. The author, Jeffrey Gray (1966), stresses how different the Marxist perspective was from American behaviorists' view of consciousness as epiphenomenal and irrelevant. Jaynes certainly would agree with this assessment.

REFERENCES

Astington, J.W. 1995. "Talking It Over with My Brain." *Monographs of the Society for Research in Child Development*, 60, 104–111.

Balter, M. 2005. "Are Human Brains Still Evolving? Brain Genes Show Signs of Selection." *Science*, 309, 1661–1662.

Berman, M. 2000. *Wandering God*. Albany: SUNY Press.

Block, N. 1981. "Review of Julian Jaynes's Origin of Consciousness in the Breakdown of the Bicameral Mind." *Cognition and Brain Theory*, 4, 81–83.

Carruthers, P. 1996. *Language, Thought and Consciousness: An Essay in Philosophical Psychology*. Cambridge University Press.

Damasio, A.R. 1999. *The Feeling of What Happens*. New York: Harcourt Brace.

Dennett, D. 1986. "Julian Jaynes's Software Archeology." *Canadian Psychology*, 27, 149–154.

Dennett, D. 1991. *Consciousness Explained*. Boston: Little, Brown & Company.

Donald, M. 2001. *A Mind So Rare: The Evolution of Human Consciousness*. New York: W.W. Norton.

Dunbar, R. 1996. *Grooming, Gossip, and the Evolution of Language*. Cambridge: Harvard University Press.

Fauconnier, G. and M. Turner. 2002. *The Way We Think: Conceptual Blending and the Mind's Hidden Complexities*. New York: Basic Books.

Fivush, R. and R. Nelson. 2004. "Culture and Language in the Emergence of Autobiographical Memory." *Psychological Science*, 15, 9, 573–577.

Flavell, J.H. 1999. "Cognitive Development." *Annual Review of Psychology*, 50, 21–45.

Flavell, J.H., F.L. Green, and E.R. Flavell. 2000. "Development of Children's Awareness of Their Own Thoughts." *Journal of Cognition and Development*, 1, 97–112.

Flynn, J.R. 1999. "Searching For Justice: The Discovery of IQ Gains Over Time." *American Psychologist*, 54, 5–20.

Fodor, J.A. 1975. *The Language of Thought*. New York: T. Y. Crowell.

Ford, J.M., D.H. Mathalon, T. Heinks, S. Kalba, W.O. Faustman, and W.T. Roth. 2001. "Neurophysiological Evidence of Corollary Discharge Dysfunction in Schizophrenia." *American Journal of Psychiatry*, 158, 2069–2071.

Gleick, J. 2003. *Isaac Newton*. New York: Vintage Books.

Golden-Meadow, S. and M.-Y. Zheng. 1998. "Thought before Language: The Expression of Motion Events Prior to the Impact of a Conventional Language Model." In P. Carruthers & J. Boucher (eds.), *Language and Thought* (pp. 26–54). Cambridge: Cambridge University Press.

Grandin, T. 1995. *Thinking in Pictures*. New York: Vintage Press (Division of Random House).

Gray, J.A. 1966. "Attention, Consciousness, and Voluntary Control of Behavior in Soviet Psychology: Philosophical Roots and Research Branches." In N. O'Connor (ed.), *Present-day Russian Psychology* (pp. 1–38). Oxford: Pergamon Press.

Harris, P.L., M. de Rosnay, and F. Pons. 2005. "Language and Children's Understanding of Mental States." *Current Directions in Psychological Science*, 14, 69–73.

Hirstein, W. 2004. *Brain Fiction: Self-Deception and the Riddle of Confabulation*. Cambridge: MIT Press.

James, W. 1890/1950. *The Principles of Psychology (Vol. 1)*. New York: Dover Publications.

Jaynes, J. 1976. "The Evolution of Language in the Late Pleistocene." *Annals of the New York Academy of Sciences*, 280, 312–325.

Jaynes, J. 1986. "Consciousness and the Voices of the Mind." *Canadian Psychology*, 27, 128–148.

Jaynes, J. 1976/1990. *The Origin of Consciousness in the Breakdown of the Bicameral Mind* (Second edition). Boston: Houghton Mifflin.

Keller, H. 1954. *The Story of My Life*. Garden City, NY: Doubleday.

Kohler, W. 1925. *The Mentality of Apes*. New York: Harcourt, Brace and Co.

Kreutzer, M.A., C. Leonard, and J.H. Flavell. 1975. "An Interview Study of Children's Knowledge About Memory." *Monographs of the Society for Research in Child Development*, 40, 1, Serial No. 159.

Kuczaj, S.A. and A. Bean. 1982. "The Development of Non-Communicative Speech Systems." In S.A. Kuczaj (ed.), *Language Development: Volume 2: Language, Thought, and Culture* (pp. 279–300). Hillsdale, NJ: Erlbaum.

Levelt, W.J.M., A. Roelofs, and A.S. Meyer. 1999. "A Theory of Lexical Access in Speech Production." Target paper for *Behavioral and Brain Sciences*, 22, 1–38.

Lillard, A. 1997. "Ethnopsychologies: Cultural Variations in Theories of Mind." *Psychological Bulletin*, 123, 3–32.

Limber, J. 1973. "The Genesis of Complex Sentences." In T. Moore (ed.), *Cognitive Development and the Acquisition of Language* (pp. 169–186). New York: Academic Press.

Limber, J. 1976. "Unraveling Competence, Performance, and Pragmatics in the Speech of Young Children." *Journal of Child Language*, 3, 309–318.

Limber, J. 1977. "Language in Child and Chimp?" *American Psychologist*, 32, 280–295. Reprinted in T. Sebeok and J. Sebeok (eds.) 1980. *Speaking of Apes* (pp. 1197–1218). New York: Plenum Press.

Limber, J. 1982. "What Can Chimps Tell Us About The Origins of Language." In S. Kuczaj (ed.), *Language Development: Volume 2* (pp. 429–446). Hillsdale, NJ: L. E. Erlbaum.

Limber, J. 1990. "Language Evolved — So What's New?" *Behavioral and Brain Sciences*, 13, 742–743.

Limber, J. 1996. "Interspecies Communication, Consciousness, and the Cognitive Verb Gap." Paper presented at the *Toward a Science of Consciousness II*, Tucson, AZ.

Limber, J. 2000. "Julian Jaynes's 'Preposterous Hypothesis.'" Paper presented at the *Cheiron* conference, University of Southern Maine.

Linde, C. 1993. *Life Stories: The Creation of Coherence*. New York: Oxford University Press.

Luria, A.R. 1929/1978. "Paths in the Development of Thought." In M. Cole (ed.), *The Selected Writings of A. R. Luria* (pp. 97–144). White Plains: M.E. Sharpe.

Luria, A.R. 1976. *Cognitive Development: Its Cultural and Social Foundations*. Cambridge: Harvard University Press.

Marx, K. 1859. *A Contribution To The Critique of Political Economy* (S.W. Ryazanskaya, Trans; online at marxists.org). Moscow: Progress Publishers.

McGuire, P.K., D.A. Silbersweig, I. Wright, R.M. Murray, A.S. David, R.S. Frackowiak, and C.D. Frith. 1995. "Abnormal Monitoring of Inner Speech: A Physiological Basis For Auditory Hallucinations." *Lancet*, 346, 596–600.

Morin, A. 2005. "Possible Links Between Self-Awareness and Inner Speech." *Journal of Consciousness Studies*, 12, 115–134.

Nisbett, R.E. and T.D. Wilson. 1977. "Telling More Than We Can Know: Verbal Reports On Mental Processes." *Psychological Review*, 84, 231–259.

Nørretranders, T. 1998. *The User Illusion: Cutting Consciousness Down To Size* (J. Syndenham, Trans.). New York: Viking.

Piaget, J. 1976. *The Grasp of Consciousness: Action and Concept in the Young Child* (S. Wedgwood, Trans.). Cambridge: Harvard University Press.

Pinker, S. 1994. *The Language Instinct*. New York: William Morrow & Company.

Poulet, J.A. and B. Hedwig. 2002. "A Corollary Discharge Maintains Auditory Sensitivity During Sound Production." *Nature*, 418, 872–876.

Putnam, H. 1975. "The Meaning of 'Meaning.'" In K. Gunderson (ed.), *Language, Mind and Knowledge: Minnesota Studies in the Philosophy of Science* (Vol. VII, pp. 131–191). Minneapolis: University of Minnesota Press.

Roser, M. and M. Gazzaniga. 2004. "Automatic Brains — Interpretive Minds." *Current Directions in Psycholological Science*, 13, 56–59.

Ruffman, T., L. Slade, and E. Crowe. 2002. "The Relation between Children's and Mother's Mental State Language and Theory-of-Mind Understanding." *Child Development*, 73, 734–751.

Schaller, S. 1991. *A Man without Words*. New York: Summit Books.

Schooler, J.W. and T.Y. Engstler-Schooler. 1990. "Verbal Overshadowing of Visual Memories: Some Things Are Better Left Unsaid." *Cognitive Psychology*, 22, 36–71.

Singer, D.G. and J.L. Singer. 2005. *Imagination and Play in the Electronic Age*. Cambridge: Harvard University Press.

Slobin, D.I. 1966. "Soviet Psycholinguistics." In N. O'Connor (ed.), *Present Day Russian Psychology* (pp. 109–151). Oxford: Pergamon Press.

Slobin, D.I. 2003. "Language and Thought Online: Cognitive Consequences of Linguistic Relativity." In D. Gentner and S. Golden-Meadow (eds.), *Language in Mind: Advances in the Study of Language and Thought* (pp. 157–192). Cambridge: MIT Press.

Snell, B. 1953/1960. *The Discovery of the Mind in Greek Philosophy and Literature* (T.G. Rosenmeyer, Trans.). New York: Harper & Row.

Sokolov, A.N. 1972. *Inner Speech and Thought*. New York: Plenum Press.

Tulving, E. 1983. *Elements of Episodic Memory*. Oxford: Clarendon Press.

Sweetser, E. 1990. *From Etymology to Pragmatics*. Cambridge: Cambridge University Press.

Turner, M. 2004. "The Origin of Selkies." *Journal of Consciousness Studies*, 11, 90–115.

Vygotsky, L. 1934/1986. *Language and Thought* (A. Kozulin, Trans. Second English edition). Cambridge: MIT Press.

Vygotsky, L.S. 1925/1999. *Consciousness as a Problem in the Psychology of Behavior* (N. Veresov, trans. online at http://www.marxists.org/archive/vygotsky/works/1925/consciousness.htm): Peter Lang Publishing.

Wegner, D.M. 2002. *The Illusion of Conscious Will*. Cambridge: MIT Press.

Wilson, T.D. 2002. *Strangers To Ourselves: Discovering The Adaptive Unconscious*. Cambridge: Harvard University Press.

Zelaso, P.D. 2004. "The Development of Conscious Control in Childhood." *Trends in Cognitive Sciences*, 8, 12–17.

CHAPTER 7

The Self as Interiorized Social Relations

Applying a Jaynesian Approach to Problems of Agency and Volition

BRIAN J. MCVEIGH

A PERSONAL PREFACE

FOR TWO AND A HALF years I conducted fieldwork among members of a Japanese religious organization called Sûkyô Mahikari.[1] My research centered on the group's practice of spirit possession, but I was frustrated by the lack of any comprehensive theory that accounted for possession. Most researchers merely labeled it (together with hypnosis) as "trance," a term that seemed to me particularly unhelpful and non-explanatory. When I informed my dissertation committee members in the Department of Anthropology at Princeton University that I intended to employ Julian Jaynes's theories to account for possession behavior, they dismissed his ideas as loony. What surprised me about their reaction was how they criticized Jaynes as a sort of "biological reductionist." There was great irony here; my dissertation committee members loudly proclaimed themselves as "cultural constructionist," and yet they refused to take seriously a psychologist's assertion that the most basic experience of being human — subjective conscious interiority — was culturally constructed. Though supportive in many ways, my advisors attempted to dissuade me from examining what I witnessed as a phenomenon in its own right (i.e., "possession-in-itself" or the "what" of possession). Rather, I was strongly advised by researchers who prided themselves on being inter-disciplinary, theoretically cutting-edge, and open-minded to ignore any cross-cultural, "universal" implications of what I observed and told to focus on the social uses of possession (i.e., "possession-in-society" or the "why" of possession").[2] I still have a letter from Professor Gananath Obeyesekere who described my attempts at accounting for possession-in-itself as full of "hocus-pocus": "I am also surprised that your conclusion relies on such a dubious and ethnocentric work as Julian Jaynes's."[3]

THE PROBLEM OF AGENCY:
HOW DOES SOCIETY "PUT A SELF INSIDE US"?

Anthropologists and sociologists have convincingly argued that the self, rather than an inborn entity, is culturally constituted, historically specific, and politically contingent. Like any other cultural construction, it emerges from a complex matrix of age, class, gender, occupation, politics, and other sociological variables. However, regardless of the recognition that the self is culturally constituted, for some there still appears to be an implicit notion that willing, deciding, choosing, wishing — i.e., volitional acts — originate from an essentialist, pre-social "executive ego." Our commonsensical folk psychology has persuaded us that individuals are born with an indivisible psychological kernel, that though influenced by the social environment, develops into a self which inhabits our person (more specifically, our heads or brains). This self possesses "free will" and controls our persons/bodies. Many would undoubtedly agree that social variables influence how one makes decisions. However, we may go one step further and ask if *decision-making ability itself* is socially constructed. If so, how is our sense of agency built by society?

In this chapter I attempt to explain how personal decision-making capabilities and volition are socially grounded in mental models of agency.[4] I discuss how social relations construct psychological events; how overt, public power exchanges become covert, private intentions; how "society is put in the self." My arguments are offered in support of Julian Jaynes's theory that what we experience as our own individual "introcosms" are culturally-constructed analogs of the "outside" world: the self, as an introspectable entity, develops from what I call "interiorized social relations." My thinking is also inspired by G.H. Mead's notion of "participation in the other," which "requires the appearance of the other in the self, the identification of the other with the self, the reaching of self-consciousness through the other."[5]

Four premises, elaborated on in this chapter, guide my reasoning: (1) there are no essentialist, indissoluble selves; (2) society does not merely "influence" but constructs selves; (3) as social constructions, selves were invented sometime in history,[6] and (4) cross-cultural psychological parameters configure mental models of agency. In order to describe these cross-cultural parameters and to illustrate how "society becomes subjectivity," I examine the notion of "authorization" and "conscious interiority." Next, in order to account for the psychic diversity and psychic plasticity necessary to account for varying notions of agency, I explore three types of mentalities:[7] (1) an ancient form of mentality (bicamerality; see below); (2) the vestiges of this earlier form of mentality as evident in various ethnopsychologies; and (3) dramatic relics of this earlier form of mentality, i.e., spirit possession and hypnosis.

THE PARAMETERS OF PSYCHE

The Authorization Imperative: Individuals as Agents

We live our lives receiving and giving admonitions, commands, orders, and requests — we are inescapably sociopolitical beings. More to the point, social life is a matter of controlling or being controlled. This is an obvious if off-putting fact, but I state it because the next proposition follows from it: agency must be conceived in social-relational terms because of the way it is learned. To rephrase this: any sense that an individual has of immediate control over his or her own person/body must be thought of as originating in social beings. Or to rephrase it still one more time: all our actions and thoughts must have some form of "authorization" from a social being, even if this "social being" is conceived as someone we all know quite well, i.e., our own interiorized selves.

Being sociopolitical animals, the "how" and "why" of control become crucial to appreciating how we make decisions. This control is not inborn, and current societies enculturate their members to have selves which execute volitional acts. Just as we must learn everything else, we must be socialized to "tell ourselves what to do." Learning to understand oneself, in at least a certain sense, is the same as learning to understand others. "There is no more (and no less) mystery in coming to understand how I can obey myself than in coming to understand how I can obey you."[8] And taking orders from those around us (whether they are physically present or not, and whether these solicitations are explicit demands or implicit forms of knowledge) is inextricably linked to decision-making. Philosopher Rom Harré repeatedly makes the point that acquiring a self is not a matter of "the empirical disclosure of an experiential fact."[9] The self has the same status as a belief or theory; the "self as agent is not a mysterious thing but a belief which endows the believer with certain powers of action in accordance with the interpersonal models available in the society."[10] To "realize that one is a person is to learn a way of thinking about and managing oneself."[11]

From Authorization to Self-Authorization:
How We Learn to Be Agents

Sociopsychological existence has two aspects: what happens between social actors (intersubjective or intermental), and what happens psychologically (subjective or intramental). I submit that intermental behavior builds intramental processes through three basic types of communicative events: (1) "others command me"; (2) "others command others"; and (3) "I command others." These three types of intercommunication, all involving agents and recipients, are transformed via socialization into an intramental process ("I" command "myself"). From authorization between two individuals emerges self-authorization — i.e., decision-making — as something that occurs between two aspects of self ("I" and "me").[12]

In order to appreciate the very nature of a sense of immediate control, perhaps a basic "syntax of volitional acts" might illustrate the nature of the problem. This sociopolitical syntax, as suggested above, has two elements, an agent ("I") and a recipient ("me"). Different types of societies use this syntax to construct "sociopsychological grammars" that are appropriate to their politico-economic organization and social structural complexity. Other factors, such as demographic pressures, technological developments, and the religio-philosophical or scientific understandings of a historic period also shape the grammar. The "I" is the active subject, the "doer" that initiates action. The "me" is the passive object, the "recipient" of some action. The "I"–"me" dynamics are modes of sociopsychological experience: the "I" feels in control, and the "me" feels controlled. These two facets of personal identity exist "internally" (subjective, inner sense of being an agent or recipient) and "externally" (person as observable doer or receiver of action). Together the "I" and "me" constitute the self, and as a form of cognition, the "I–me" dynamic may be either "deep" (held with strong conviction and difficult to change) or "surface" (held with little conviction and easily changed) (see Appendix, "Examples of Active and Passive Aspects of the Self"). In order to gain a sense of the "feeling" of the "I"–"me" dynamic, consider the difference between everyday interaction and theatrical performance. When one is being one-self the subject and object aspects of self are closely identified. Or, to quote Goffman, "the performer comes to be his own audi-ence; he comes to be performer and observer of the same show."[13] But when one is not being oneself — e.g., acting, lying, deceiving — the subject ("I") and object ("me") aspects of self are separated because the former is carefully monitoring and managing the latter.

We are not born with an "I" and a "me," and their origins and how they relate need to be explained. More specifically, the question I want to address is how pre-socialized infants are encul-turated to possess intramental processes (i.e., assuming pre-socialized infants lack an interiorized, subjective notion of self-hood, i.e., an "I" and "me"). Since the first commands we are exposed to come from other socials beings, the commands and orders we give to ourselves are ultimately socially rooted. The "I–me" relationship is social in origin and social in operation: as between two people, the "I" controls/commands/communicates with the "me." Unlike nonhuman organisms, whose neurological systems do not require such an elaborate program rooted in and shaped by a sociopolitical matrix, the commands we give ourselves must be in societal terms. In other words, though our command-control-coordination system is neurological, in order to operate normally this hardware requires culturally informed authorization.

It might be mentioned that it is not necessary to explicitly command oneself through a type of inner speech every time one makes a decision; this is because the "I-commands-me" commu-nicative act becomes a mental syntax that often occurs noncon-sciously. What is important is the belief, *whether conscious or not conscious*, that somewhere in our psyche this is what occurs. The terms "I" and "me" do not denote linguistic forms and do not necessarily correspond with actual grammatical usage. This is not to say, however, that the "I–me" agentive formula is unrelated to language, since it is primarily through language that we are socialized to possess agency and notions of agency are encoded in linguistic form.

Child development is an excellent place to observe the socialization of agency. Vygotsky saw a clear difference between a child's decision-making and that of an adult. In his experiments that required a child to decide on which keys to press on a specially designed keyboard, he notes that

> the entire process of selection by the child is external, and concentrated in the motor sphere, thus allowing the experimenter to observe the very nature of the choice process itself in the child's movements. Adults make a preliminary decision internally and subsequently carry out the choice in the form of a single movement that executes the plan. The child's choice resembles a somewhat delayed selection among his own movements ... for the child the series of tentative movements constitute the selection process.[14]

During the developmental process, we must learn to exercise volition, and we do this by abstracting the intentional from the unintentional, the voluntary from the nonvoluntary. This process is essential to our development as agents, since as infants we do not distinguish between agent and action: "There is no distinction made by the child between subject, action, and object because for him they are effectively all the same — he is the locus of the action, both its subject and its object at once."[15]

Again, it may seem strange that we must be socialized to do something that *appears* so basic to our experience, which usually goes off so smoothly that it feels as if nothing else could be more a part of our identity. However, I contend that the prescriptions, demands, and orders of others are the substrata on which society builds our own inner, personal universe of intentions, decisions, and everyday volitions.

Spatializing Authorization: Psychological Interiority

Now that we have addressed from where a sense of self-authorization arises, I would like to comment more on the nature of the interior world within which the self dwells. Indeed, in order to understand what a self is, the nature of consciousness must be appreciated. Following Jaynes, I believe that in order to possess a sense of self-hood, we must be socialized to possess conscious psychological interiority (another cultural construction) in which the self metaphorically moves about and can be "seen" by the mind's eye. A psychological introcosm is "an analog of what is called the real world. It is built up with a vocabulary or lexical field whose terms are all metaphors or analogs of behavior in the physical world."[16] Consciousness permits an individual to navigate the environment, both social and natural, in a more efficient manner. For example, before actually executing a behavior, we can "see" ourselves "in our heads" carrying out an action, thereby allowing us to shortcut actual behavioral sequences that may be time consuming, difficult, or dangerous. As Jaynes points out, it is the almost magical nature of metaphors which permit the construction of a "mind-space" in which our selves dwell as objects of introspection.[17] Metaphorically spatialized authorization is self-authorization (Figure 1). Without this mind-space, there can be no self as we usually think of it. However, one can still be a cognitively competent person without a mind-space, that is, without consciousness and a self. Contrary to popular belief, consciousness is not needed for learning, thinking, or perceiving, though it is regularly confused or conflated with these, even by research psychologists. For the sake of clarity, we should distinguish between cognition (e.g., thinking) and conscious interiority. The latter is a product of cognition.

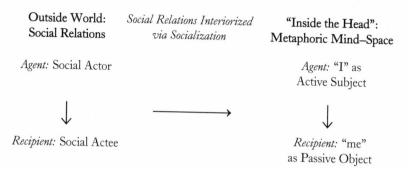

Figure 1. Interiority: The Self as Interiorized Social Relations

The universal use of metaphoric space to locate agency should not be surprising; after all, as three-dimensional beings occupying space, spatial awareness is the most apparent, immediate, and tangible experience we can have, more basic to our bodily perceptions than consciousness itself: "things that in the physical-behavioral world do not have a spatial quality are made to have such in consciousness. ... Time is an obvious example."[18]

At this point allow me to summarize my argument so far and its implications. A self is an internalized conceptualization of agency, imported by socialization processes through the use of metaphoric mind-words "into" our heads. The self dwells in a culturally-fabricated "mind-space." A self is not conscious of itself, nor is it consciousness: only a person can be conscious, not a person's interiorized representation or "self." Rather, a self is an object of consciousness, in the same way any other object of the world is. And just as there is nothing innate or inborn about our notions of being a person, there is nothing intrinsic about our ability to introspect and to conceive of our "selves." These are all culturally learned and historically specific, and do not result from natural bio-evolutionary processes. Society does not impose a model of agency onto a more basic, somehow truer "self." Eth-notheories of agency are not a superficial or surface structure resting on a more fundamental "ego," "I," "personality," or "inner me." A model of agency *is* our "self," at least in its intentional, volitional aspect. A society's design for a schema of authorization operates as a program for intentional behavior. It constitutes our very self-hood and is intimately bound up with volition. Moreover, this socially provided sense of control has two aspects. The first is as a program "for" authorization: it guides and informs our actions. The second is as a program "of" authorization: it can be used to attribute an individual's actions or mental activity to oneself and to others.

If Jaynes is correct in arguing that consciousness and self are not inborn, then we are forced to ask when these cultural constructions arose in history and why. Such problems do not fall under the direct purview of this essay, though above I have already suggested that sociopolitical pressures and complexity led to the invention of subjectivity as we presently experience it. Throughout history, the development from exterior-control to interior-control forms of agency — a "psychological revolution" on par with the agricultural revolution and other technological developments — has, for a variety of reasons, undoubtedly taken various directions, detours, turns, perhaps even reversals. Because most human societies have been nonliterate, each of their unique trajectories to psychological interiorization is unfortunately lost forever. For my present purposes, however, it is the very general development of the human psyche that is at issue. Evidence of the emergence of conscious interiority can be found in all languages that still possess remnants of earlier lexical-mind worlds.[19] Moreover, there are residues of a more dramatic sort which in fact question our entire notion of "one person–one will," and demonstrate just how complex the problem of agency is. Before turning to the most salient examples of such extant sociopsychological behavior (hypnosis and spirit possession), I first look back in history and across different cultures in order to gain some perspective on the human psyche.

THREE TYPES OF MENTALITIES

(1) An Earlier Mentality: Bicamerality

Let us start with the supposition that a person is a human socialized to possess certain cultural values, to think, to feel, to respond meaningfully to other persons, and in general to behave as a member of a sociocultural order. However, as argued above, one does not have to possess an "introspectable" mental world in which a self dwells to be a person. Why did societies, then, begin to furnish persons with selves? For the same reason they name, number, and label individuals: to organize, classify, and control populations. When societies started to equip individuals with selves is an open question, though I would argue that the social invention of selves probably occurred sometime between the 2nd and 1st millennium B.C.[20] Arguably it was during these millennia that selves were culturally constructed as a response to demographic pressures and sociopolitical complexities that had been mounting since the agricultural revolution (some six to two millennia earlier, depending on the place). According to Jaynes's controversial but compelling theory, before the invention of selves the volition of ancient humankind took the form of auditory and visual hallucinations (the admonitions of ancestors, kings, divine rulers, or gods). The minds of pre-conscious individuals were "bicameral" because they were composed of two chambers: a hallucination-initiating god side that issued admonitions and an order-following human side (currently, individuals might be described as "unicameral," i.e., with a unitary self occupying the mind). Divine voices were elicited by stress in the same way modern individuals become most consciously aware when experiencing novel situations (i.e., metaphorically "seeing" with their mind's eye the answers "inside" their heads). Socialized to believe they were under the direct control of external divine forces, there was no notion of "free will" for bicameral individuals. Support for the view that there was a radically different mentality is at least suggested by others. Consider Snell's research into the "pre-psychological language" of the Homeric period or Dodds's opinion that the ancient Greeks lacked a concept of a unified self or soul and that mental events arose from the will of the gods.[21] Or peruse through the Bible or some other ancient religious text and search for the many instances of divine voices commanding individuals what to do.

Authority based on clear hierarchical lines of command and control is inherently fragile (this may explain the archaeological mystery of why some otherwise sophisticated civilizations suddenly collapsed). Indeed, societies built upon strict bicameral authorization are only workable if population growth stays within certain limits, external influences are kept to a minimum (e.g., from long-distance trade), and environmental shocks are not too disruptive (e.g., flooding, earthquakes, famine, disease). Most likely, some or all of these forces eventually destabilized ancient civilizations. In any case, the historical emergence of psychological interiority evidently accompanied increasing sociopolitical complexity.

What is a god-authorized society to do to stabilize itself, resting as it would on a wobbly sociopolitical edifice? After all, as sociopolitical complexity grew, the individual would be ordered about by competing, conflicting, and confusing voices. Divinely ordered decision-making would be in jeopardy. From the perspective of an inherently unstable sociopolitical arrangement, the need for clear hierarchical lines of command–control that had characterized the earliest complex societies could be managed by individuals equipped with selves. A self, in a sense, is a personal tool kit of command and control "inside a person's head." Socialized into a person, a self becomes a socio-organization's inner voice by proxy. Once authorization for immediate control of self becomes individual-centered and interiorized, socio-organization actually becomes more stable because its orders, directives, and warnings are transmuted into subjective truths (such as "conscience").

Individuals lacking interiority would probably be incapable of using metaphoric expressions about the location and control of their persons. This is because, for them, there would be no lexi-cally-based "inner world" of mental events and thus no self (i.e., no "I" and "me" within the same individual) that could be intro-spected upon and moved about. Agency-shifting conceptualiza-tions would be absent; in other words, such people would be incapable of theatrical acting, spiritual possession, and related phe-nomena. And in some respects, their literal belief in the external origin of agency would be remarkably similar to hypnosis. In a very strict sense, of course, individuals without interiority pos-sessed a type of agency (i.e., ancestors or gods), but they lacked what we can refer to as an agentive self.

(II) Vestiges of an Earlier Mentality: Different Psychologies

If what Jaynes has proposed about bicamerality is correct, we should expect to find remnants of this extinct mentality. In any case, an examination of the ethnopsychologies of other societies should at least challenge our assumptions. What kinds of metaphors do they employ to discuss the self? Where is agency localized? To what extent do they even "psychologize" the individual, positing an "inte-rior space" within the person? If agency is a socio-historical construction (rather than a bio-evolutionary product), we should expect some cultural variability in how it is conceived. At the same time, we should also expect certain parameters within which differ-ent theories of agency are built.

Ethnographies are filled with descriptions of very different psychologies. For example, about the Maori, Jean Smith writes that

> it would appear that generally it was not the "self" which encompassed the experience, but experience which en-compassed the "self" ... Because the "self" was not in control of experience, a man's experience was not felt to be integral to him; it happened in him but was not of him. A Maori individual was not so much the experi-encer of his experience as the observer of it.[22]

Furthermore, "bodily organs were endowed with independent volition."[23] Renato Rosaldo states that the Ilongots of the Philippines rarely concern themselves with what we refer to as an "inner self" and see no major differences between public presentation and private feeling.[24]

Perhaps the most intriguing picture of just how radically different mental concepts can be is found in anthropologist Maurice Leenhardt's intriguing book *Do Kamo*, about the Canaque of New Caledonia, who are "unaware" of their own existence: the "psychic or psychological aspect of man's actions are events in nature. The Canaque sees them as outside of himself, as externalized. He handles his existence similarly: he places it in an object — a yam, for instance — and through the yam he gains some knowledge of his existence, by identifying himself with it."[25]

Speaking of the Dinka, anthropologist Godfrey Lienhardt writes that "the man is the object acted upon," and "we often find a reversal of European expressions which assume the human self, or mind, as subject in relation to what happens to it."[26] Concerning the mind itself,

> The Dinka have no conception which at all closely corresponds to our popular modern conception of the "mind," as mediating and, as it were, storing up the experiences of the self. There is for them no such interior entity to appear, on reflection, to stand between the experiencing self at any given moment and what is or has been an exterior influence upon the self. So it seems that what we should call in some cases the memories of experiences, and regard therefore as in some way intrinsic and interior to the remembering person and modified in their effect upon him by that interiority, appear to the Dinka as exteriority acting upon him, as were the sources from which they derived.[27]

The above mentioned ethnographic examples may be interpreted as merely colorful descriptions, as exotic and poetic folk psychologies. Or, we may take a more literal view, and entertain the idea that these ethnopsychological accounts are vestiges of a distant past when individuals possessed radically different mentalities. For example, if it is possible to be a person lacking interiority in which a self moves about making conscious decisions, then we must at least entertain the idea that entire civilizations existed whose members had a radically different mentality. The notion of a "person without a self" is admittedly controversial and open to misinterpretation. *Here allow me to stress that I am not suggesting that in today's world there are groups of people whose mentality is distinct from our own.* However, I am suggesting that remnants of an earlier mentality are evident in extant ethnopsychologies, including our own.[28]

Metaphors and Loci of Control:
Conceptualizing Different Psychologies

How do we conceptualize such different psychologies? In an attempt to do just this, Andrew Lock discusses two "universals in human conception." The first is the active/passive, or control/ under control dimension: "while my culture provides the means of orientating me to identifying with my control abilities, and so regarding myself as *in control*, so another culture may well orientate me to identifying them with another, and my regarding the exercise of control as being by them, regarding myself as *under control.*"[29] The second dimension is that of internal/external locus of control of self: "A human, from primitive to academic, is thus faced with the problem of where to attribute the responsibility for, and control of, such activities."[30] "Internalized conceptualizations" can be further classified, since the "self has been variously located in the head (current Western thought), the lungs (Anglo-Saxon and Ancient Greek), the heart (Ancient Egyptian), and the liver (the Chewong)"[31] "Externalized conceptualizations" can be further classified into "here," "there," "below," or "above."

If the two dimensions, control/under control and internal/external, are represented as two intersecting axes, we have what I believe is a very useful schema. If applied to various cultural settings and historical periods, this schema provides us with a convenient "map" of different theories of human agency (Figure 2). Paul Heelas uses the coordinates of this map to locate different psychologies: those of Tibetan Buddhist philosophy, the Kalabari, Maori, Dinka, Chewong, Tallensi, Homeric Greece, and our own ethnopsychology. Societies that have internalized conceptualizations and place the self in control possess an "idealist" (i.e., what I describe as "highly interiorized") psychology:

> When the self is held to exercise control, internalized representations, power and freedom, come to the fore. "Mind" is a good way of "symbolically" freeing the self from the world, of allowing individuals to think that they are autonomous and able to exercise control or agency ... the self is primarily envisaged in terms of the mental and the contents of consciousness.[32]

Societies that have externalized conceptualizations and place the self under control possess a *passiones* psychology; the self is acted upon or affected by an external agency or force:

> In order for the individual to be thought of as being under the control of something other than his conscious, free-willed self, the obvious move is to introduce externalized conceptualizations. It is natural to seat the controller outside. If the individual is denied autonomy, being treated instead as a pawn in the hands of external agencies, inner decision-making and motivational phenomena such as "mind" cannot easily intrude.[33]

Heelas notes that whereas "in idealist systems the locus of control cannot be thought of without (for, if it were, the individual would not be in control of himself), *passiones* systems cannot locate this locus within the human self (for, if it were, external agencies would not be in control)."[34]

Because of the close connections between poles 1 and 4, and 2 and 3 (Figure 2), it would appear that the model need not be two-dimensional. However, Heelas points out that "the self in control can be combined with externalized representations, when these need not indicate control of the self, and the self under control can be combined with internalized representations, where these do not indicate the self in control."[35]

In order to account for systems of thought that are not strictly idealist or *passiones*, Heelas discusses modified idealist and modified *passiones* psychologies. As an example of modified idealist psychologies, he mentions how we externalize ourselves, such as in role-playing, or in the description of intense emotions. Regarding role-playing, he notes that there is a thin line between "playing a role" and "being taken over by a role." "In fact, there is a tendency for modified idealist formulations to result in 'contradictions' or divisions of the self. Our public man (under control) has to go home before reverting to his private self and idealist language ('I'm going to let my hair down')."[36]

	(3) *Externalized Conceptualizations*	
Modified Idealist Psychology	*Passiones* Psychology
D	B
(1) *Self in Control*	(2) *Self under Control*
A	C
Idealist Psychology	Modified *Passiones* Psychology
	(4) *Internalized Conceptualizations*	

Figure 2. Models of Agency

Modified *passiones* systems combine internalized conceptions and the self under control. As an example, he cites those who, though they consider themselves to be essentially free and autonomous, visit a psychotherapist in order to deal with repressed, unconscious emotions. Another example is how we often speak of "being at the mercy of our emotions," or of "following a blind impulse," though we generally feel we are in control of ourselves.

Heelas's model is illuminating because it serves as a useful starting point for delineating the cross-cultural parameters of the locus of agency and self. However, Heelas discusses his model as if it were merely a description of *stylistic differences* in how various peoples view agency; I contend, though, that these differences are vestiges of past mentalities. Also, we need to consider another issue: how literally does an individual in contemporary societies accept a theory of agency?[37] On the theoretical level, there is the danger of confusing *literally-believed* notions of agency with *metaphorically-expressed* ideas. This confusion between deeply held beliefs and figures of speech is rarely a major problem in everyday life: we all know the difference between being meta-phorically "pushed around" and being physically "pushed around." Other related issues concern multiple agencies within the same individual and which locus is the "true" center of con-trol. As a step in avoiding some of this confusion, we can speak of "layered" schemata of authorization. The "deeper" the belief in agency-locus, the more literally it is accepted as fact. The more "shallow" the idea of agency-locus, the more metaphoric it is.

(III) Vestiges of an Earlier Mentality:
Hypnosis and Spirit Possession

Two varieties of sociopsychological behavior, hypnosis and spirit possession, raise intriguing questions about the historical emergence of psyche as well as about the nature of volition. A careful examination of these ubiquitous but unusual experiences forces upon us a defamiliarization with our taken-for-granted folk psychology about agency, consciousness, and self. Any account of human psychology must take hypnosis and spirit possession into consideration, because they challenge our sacred notions of "one person–one will" and "one body–one self," and have lessons for us about how "society is put into the self."[38] For my present purposes, I contend that hypnosis and spirit possession teach us about psychic plasticity and psychic diversity; more specifically, that an individual can be socialized to have multiple loci of agency.

Hypnosis

Julian Jaynes described hypnosis as a behavior denying "our immediate ideas about conscious self-control on the one hand, and our scientific idea about personality on the other." It "wanders in and out of laboratories and carnivals and clinics and village halls like an unwanted anomaly."[39] Hypnosis, however, is merely one member of a larger family of scientifically unwelcome oddities such as spiritualist mediums, automatic writing, glossolalia, and poetic and religious frenzy. Consider an even more dramatic and scientifically embarrassing cousin to hypnosis — spirit possession (often confused and conflated with hypnosis). Despite the initial assumption of some, such behaviors are far from rare. Indeed, they fill ancient sacred texts, historical accounts, and contemporary ethnographies, and rather than being atypical, are common, widespread, and in some societies, routinely practiced. And though it would be inaccurate to claim that these behaviors have not been investigated by research psychologists, very few have bothered to integrate what we know into a comprehensive account of how and why the human psyche produces such behavior. Instead, many mainstream research psychologists have relegated ostensibly peculiar behaviors to superstitious eras, exotic locales, or unstable personalities. However, despite attempts at official banishment from the realm of science, unusual behaviors loiter around our dwellings of "rational" thought, pressing against the doors of "normal" inquiry and eerily peering in through the windows of our "commonsensical" understandings. As uninvited as they may be, these uncanny phenomena remind us of our ignorance when faced with the richness and puzzles of human psychic diversity. In any case, an exploration of these behaviors can offer us insights into issues of agency.

Hypnosis calls our most basic notions of self-control and self-hood into question, and amazingly, in spite of the tremendous amount of literature on the topic, I have yet to come across a useful definition that integrates it into a comprehensive account of social psychology.[40] Before addressing the central issue of the nature of hypnosis, some demystification is in order. There is a popular belief that, while under hypnosis, a person loses all power of will and becomes a mere automaton, controlled and directed by the words of the hypnotist. This is a myth because people cannot be involuntarily hypnotized nor ordered to do anything against their will while hypnotized.[41] Nevertheless, temporarily abdicating one's volitional powers in an unguarded manner and readily following the orders of the hypnotist minus a subjective sense of control are the primary characteristics of the hypnotic state. Increased suggestibility has been so much emphasized in the studies of hypnosis that "many have defined hypnosis according to the changes in suggestibility that it produces."[42] However, hypnosis "evidently includes more than an enhancement of responsiveness to suggestions."[43] Indeed, exactly what it includes should be our concern. We must ask why the abdication of personal decision-making, though never complete, occurs. Why does an individual allow another to usurp one's "I" and pull the strings on one's "me"?[44]

Hypnosis typically involves two persons, the hypnotist and the hypnotized, or in other words, an active agent and a passive recipient.[45] During hypnosis, one willingly abdicates one's belief about self-control and begins to trance; in other words, the belief in the metaphoric interiority encased within the head is suspended. This suspension evaporates the elements of "mind-space," in particular beliefs about "I-controls-me" — and its first cousin — the "self-controls-body." The locus of agency temporarily shifts from internal-control to external-control, so that one's "I" is replaced by an outside controller (hypnotist). That beliefs about self-control are so easily arrested at least suggests: (1) psychic diversity, i.e., how vestiges of an earlier mentality exist within the individual; (2) psychic malleability, i.e., how easily self-authorization (decision-making) can be altered; and (3) how decision-making may be thought of as an interiorized version of social interaction between an agent and a recipient.

In what is known as "self-hypnosis," the dyad of command-and-obedience becomes internalized: "A subject can bring himself to a similar condition or state through auto-hypnosis, preserving a verbal system that can take the same role as an external hypnotist."[46] Indeed, technically all hypnotism is really internalized self-hypnosis; "the person accepts the hypnotist as an aid to hypnotizing himself."[47] Thus, it could be stated that within an individual the "I" (hypnotizer) induces the "me" (hypnotized) into trance, with guidance and encouragement coming from a "third party," the hypnotist (Figure 3).

The fact one can hypnotize oneself lends support to Harré's conviction that understanding how I can obey another person is of the same order as how I can obey myself. Dealing with others is very much related to how we deal with ourselves, and perhaps this is why at times the hypnotized repeats the suggestions of the hypnotist to her or himself, "occasionally modifying the wording to make the suggestions more acceptable."[48] Of course, the important differences between obeying others and making decisions cannot be ignored. Nevertheless, the intimate relation between intramental and intermental behavior should be evident.

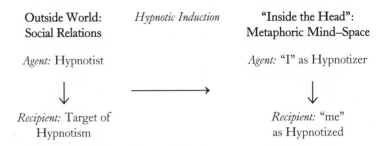

Figure 3. Hypnosis: Suspension of Interiority

Spirit Possession

"The extraordinary importance accruing to the phenomena of possession amongst races has hitherto been insufficiently appreciated by ethnology."[49] This is not entirely true anymore, but the attentiveness early 20th century German philosopher and psychologist Traugott Oesterreich afforded the import of possession should be appreciated. Many anthropologists and ethnographers have recognized and reported on the importance of possession. However, if Oesterreich's opinion is construed to mean that researchers have not recognized what possession may mean for an understanding of human nature in general, his point is well taken. Despite the vast amount of literature on the subject, there are as many questions as answers regarding the nature of possession. As Bourguignon has pointed out, there are many interpretations, but no systematic theory of possession.[50]

Though studies of possession that focus on its local manifestation and its uses in a particular society are essential, its very ubiquity demands that we also ask more fundamental questions about possession. Possession is not an unusual, marginal practice. Bourguignon reports that 360 societies out of a sample of 488 have a belief in spirit possession, and that 437 out of 488 societies institutionalized one or more forms of altered states of consciousness.[51]

Though the literature is replete with definitions and typologies of spirit possession, there is little in the way of useful theorizing on why possession occurs in the first place.[52] Space precludes any useful review, but for my present purposes possession may be defined as the sociopsychological manufacture of alternate selves radically different from one's usual persona (alterability).[53] Possession is most often described as a feeling of being controlled, where a supernatural other usurps a person's "I" and commandeers the "me." It may involve any number of behaviors, though "classic possession" involves trancing, during which a secondary, less basic locus of agency is engaged (the primary locus being one's usual persona) (Figure 4). Depending on the indigenous interpretation, the possessing agency may be a god, ancestor, or spirit. During the trance the possessing agency is believed to enter the person in order to control him or her. Possession is usually ritually induced and surrounded by a ceremonial context that supports and defines its cultural meaning. In addition, these "should not be considered as isolated phenomena that simply appear in a culture and loiter around doing nothing but leaning on their own merits."[54] They are used by certain societies to do particular things, such as divination, curing, meeting with the gods and ancestors, etc.

What is important for my present purposes is the fact that people can be socialized to experience radical alterability. This indicates the highly plastic nature of the psyche. Such plasticity — here meaning multiple loci of agency — demonstrates the saliency of culture in the construction of agency.

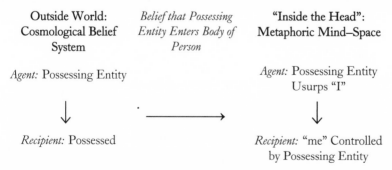

Figure 4. Spirit Possession: Suspension of Interiority plus Behavior of Possessing Entity

CONCLUSION

Different types of mentalities have characterized the human psyche throughout history. Any given mentality is comprised of cognitive operations that are configured by sociopolitical forces. The modern search for cognitive universals (psychology with a capital "P") has distracted us away from careful explorations of "psychologies" (psychology with a small "p") that may reveal important clues about how the human psyche operates. Nevertheless, despite a fair amount of psychic plasticity in the human species, there are certain parameters, such as authorization (whether through commanding hallucinations or self-directed decision making).

In this chapter, I have only touched upon some important issues that cry out for further investigation: metaphors and their relation to consciousness; the historical processes that led to the sociopolitical construction of an internal "mental space"; and psychic diversity. The factors that construct an individual's agentive capabilities range from linguistic forms, sociopolitical values, technological developments, to our neurological machinery. In order to understand the nature of agency, all these factors must be viewed in light of how social relations are transformed into an inner "psychological society" that we require in order to be persons capable of executing volition. Selves are more than just a nexus of social currents; they are inextricably bound up with volitional acts and how we subjectively experience control or being controlled. And as a form of belief, selves are as culturally contingent and diverse as notions about spirits, souls, and sacred symbols.

APPENDIX

Examples of Active and Passive Aspects of the Self

Examples	Two Aspects of the Self	
	Analog "I" as Active Subject	Metaphor "Me" as Passive Object
Psychomotor Activity (D)	Person	Body
In Society - *Social Relations* (D) - *Social Interaction* (S) - *Deception* (S)	Person in Control Self Self	Person under Control Social Roles, Personas False Persona
Psychological Interiority - *Interiorized Self* (D) - *"Intro-perception"* (D) - *Autoscopic Self* (D) - *Self-Deception* (D)	"I" "I" Observing "I" Self	"Mind-scape"/Mental Space Subjective Scenery Observed "me" Deceived Self
Interiorized Time - *Introspective Self* (S) - *Retrospective Self* (S) - *Prospective Self* (S)	"I" "I" "I"	Current "me" Former "me" Future "me"
Self-Image - *Aspiring Self* (S) - *Improving Self* (S) - *Self-Appearance* (S)	Aspiring "I" Actual "I" Self–Body as Set Designer	Ideal/New "me" Old "me" Self–Body as Mannequin
Linguistics - *Voice* (D) - *Syntax* (D) - *Personal Pronouns* (D)	Active, Agent Subject Subject Pronouns	Passive, Recipient Direct/Indirect Object Object Pronouns
Arts - *Theatrical Acting* (S) - *Literature (e.g., novels)* (S)	Actor Creator (e.g., writer)	Role Character
Religio-philosophical Thought - *Spiritual Essence* (D)	Spirit, Soul(s)	Body
Vestigial Sociopsychological Behavior - *Spirit Possession* (D) - *Hypnosis* (D)	Possessor Usurps "I" Hypnotizer Suspends "I"	Possessed–Controlled "me" Hypnotized–Directed "me"
Disorders - *Various Agnosias* (D) - *Schizophrenia* (D) - *Dissociative Identity Disorder* (D)	Self–Body Effaced/Eroded "I" Multiple "I's"	Distortion/Loss of Control Effaced/Eroded "me" Multiple "me's"
Modern Technoculture - *Cyber Space* (S)	Self	Virtual Self

(D) = Deep cognitive belief held with strong conviction and difficult to change.
(S) = Surface cognitive belief held with little conviction and easily changed.

NOTES TO CHAPTER 7

1. The fieldwork lasted from 1988 until 1991. See McVeigh, 1991, 1996b, and 1997a. Besides guiding my dissertation research on spirit possession, the theories of Julian Jaynes have also inspired my approach to self-presentation as it involves socio-ritualization within a Japanese educational setting and self-appearance (McVeigh, 1997b, 2000). His thinking has also directed my work on "mind–words" in Japanese (McVeigh, 1996).

2. Of course, a possession-in-itself approach can only reveal certain aspects of possession. It cannot inform us about why certain people become possessed or what this form of action means to them. This is because possession behavior does not and cannot exist outside some sociocultural patterning. Nevertheless, insights obtained from studying possession-in-itself will have cross-cultural relevance. Some of the noted uses include self-aggrandizement; self-assertion; realignment of marital relations; escape from an unpleasant situation; immediate· control of persons around the possessed during actual possession; self-chastisement; attainment of intimacy through fleeting interpersonal relationships desired by the possessed but socially prohibited in the nonpossessed state; desire for a specific object; and the assertion of rights among the socially marginal, especially by women (Crapanzano and Garrison, 1977).

3. This coming from an anthropologist who has himself relied on perennially criticized and discredited "Freudian" theorizing.

4. This essay has had two previous incarnations. The first, entitled "Towards a Theory of Agency," was as a research paper for the course Psychology 319 taught by Julian Jaynes in the spring of 1987 at Princeton University. The second incarnation was an article called "Society in the Self: The Anthropology of Agency" (McVeigh, 1995). The present incarnation has been fundamentally revised and updated.

5. Mead, 1934, p. 253.

6. Cf. Harré's opinion: "There may be human beings whose belief systems, imaginary anticipations and so on are organized in some non-unitary way. Necessarily all human beings who are members of moral orders are persons, social individuals, but the degree of their psychological individuality, their personal being, I take to be contingent" (Harré, 1985:77).

7. For my present purposes, "mentality" describes *fundamental differences* in mental processes between historical periods, whereas a "psychology" (or ethnopsychology) denotes *less radical differences* between historical periods and societies.

8. Harré, 1985, p. 195.

9. Ibid., p. 212.

10. Ibid., p. 180.

11. Ibid., p. 22.
12. Cf. Jaynes, 1976, pp. 62–3. Mead's ruminations about the "I" and its relation to the "me" deserve mention here. He discussed these components of the self in various ways, including the view that the "me" is an organized set of attitudes of others while the "I" is the spontaneous response to these attitudes. Related to this is the idea that the "I–me" relationship constitutes sequential phases of the self (Mead, 1934, pp. 173–78, *passim*). In my treatment of "I" and "me" I emphasize how intermental communicative events become intramental experience and the related experiences of control and being controlled.
13. Goffman, 1959, pp. 80–81.
14. Vygotsky, 1978, p. 34.
15. Lock, 1980, p. 132.
16. Jaynes, 1976, p. 55.
17. Ibid., pp. 48–66.
18. Ibid., p. 60.
19. Jaynes, 1976; McVeigh, 1996a.
20. Cf. Jaynes, 1976.
21. Snell, 1953; Dodds, 1951.
22. Smith, 1981, p. 152, quotations in original.
23. Ibid., p. 156.
24. Rosaldo, 1985, pp. 137–57.
25. Leenhardt, 1979, p. 61.
26. Lienhardt, 1961, p. 150.
27. Ibid., p. 149, quotations in original.
28. See Jaynes, 1976.
29. Lock, 1981, p. 30, italics in original.
30. Ibid., p. 31.
31. Ibid., p. 35.
32. Heelas, 1981, p. 39, quotations in original.
33. Ibid., p. 41, quotations in original.
34. Ibid., parentheses in original.
35. Ibid.
36. Ibid., p. 42, parentheses and quotations in original.
37. The "modified idealist and modified *passiones* systems" of Heelas raise this issue: "the boundary between the external and internal is not easy to define" (Heelas, 1981, p. 42). Therefore, the "unconscious realm is in a sense external to the autonomous self, although it is internalized in contrast to 'genuine' external agencies, such as the stars in astrology" (Heelas, 1981, pp. 42–3, quotations in original).
38. It is important to note that hypnosis and spirit possession are vestiges of an earlier mentality, not a return to an earlier mentality.

Brian J. McVeigh

39. Jaynes, 1976, p. 379.
40. See, however, Jaynes, 1976.
41. This myth, incidentally, says much about our own cultural values: an emphasis on individual self-control, self-determination, independence, and a consequent fear of losing these to the control of others.
42. Hilgard, 1977, p. 163.
43. Ibid., p. 227.
44. We should keep in mind that, in a certain sense, while in nonhypnotic states the "generalized other" (in the form of cultural prescriptions, expectations, or customs) always stands behind an individual's "I," which in turn commands the "me." In other words, the difference between hypnosis and ordinary subjectivity is continuous, not discontinuous.
45. Here it is pertinent to mention that not all individuals (e.g., schizophrenics) can be hypnotized.
46. Hilgard, 1977, p. 227.
47. Ibid., p. 229.
48. Ibid., p. 230.
49. Oesterreich, 1930, p. 378.
50. Bourguignon, 1978, p. 489–90.
51. Bourguignon, 1973; 1974.
52. Some ethnopsychologies regard hypnosis as possession. However, contrary to what many researchers contend, not all possession trancing can be explained as a form of hypnosis. Basically, hypnosis involves trancing (a suspension of belief in the interior "mind-space" usually called consciousness), whereas possession involves trancing *plus* high levels of alterability.
53. My treatment of possession is cursory. For example, I have not examined the two major types of possession often distinguished in the literature. The first is induced, ritualized, desired. The second is spontaneous, inappropriate, and undesired. The distinction between these types is not always clear-cut, but most who have done research have noted two types of possession that roughly correspond to a "voluntary and involuntary" continuum.
54. Jaynes, 1976, p. 355.

REFERENCES

Bourguignon, E. 1973. "Spirit Possession Belief and Social Structure." In A. Bharati (ed.), *The Realm of the Extra-Human*. Chicago: Mouton Publishers.
Bourguignon, E. 1974. "Cross-Cultural Perspectives on the Religious Uses of Altered States of Consciousness." In I. Zarestsky and M.P. Leone (eds.), *Religious Movements in Contemporary America*. Princeton: Princeton University Press.

Bourguignon, E. 1978. "Spirit Possession and Altered States of Consciousness: The Evolution of an Inquiry." In G.D. Spindler (ed.), *The Making of Psychological Anthropology.* Berkeley: University of California Press.

Crapanzano, V. and V. Garrison (eds.). 1977. *Case Studies in Spirit Possession.* New York: John Wiley and Sons.

Dodds, E.R. 1951. *The Greeks and the Irrational.* Berkeley: University of California Press.

Goffman, E. 1959. *The Presentation of Self in Everyday Life.* New York: Anchor Books.

Harré, R. 1984. *Personal Being.* Cambridge: Harvard University Press.

Heelas, P. 1981. "The Model Applied: Anthropology and Indigenous Psychologies." In A. Lock and P. Heelas (eds.), *Indigenous Psychologies: The Anthropology of Self.* New York: Academic Press.

Hilgard, E.R. 1977. *Divided Consciousness: Multiple Controls in Human Thought and Action.* New York: Wiley-Interscience.

Jaynes, J. 1976. *The Origin of Consciousness in the Breakdown of the Bicameral Mind.* Boston: Houghton Mifflin Company.

Leenhardt, M. 1979. *Do Kamo: Persons and Myth in the Melanesian World.* Chicago: University of Chicago Press.

Lienhardt, G. 1961. *Divinity and Experience: Religion of the Dinka.* Oxford: Oxford University Press.

Lock, A. 1980. *The Guided Reinvention of Language.* New York: Academic Press.

Lock, A. 1981. "Universals in Human Conception." In A. Lock and P. Heelas (eds.), *Indigenous Psychologies: The Anthropology of Self.* New York: Academic Press.

McVeigh, B.J. 1991. *Gratitude, Obedience, and Humility of Heart: The Cultural Construction of Belief in A Japanese New Religion.* Unpublished Ph.D. Dissertation, Princeton University, Anthropology Department.

McVeigh, B.J. 1995. "Society in the Self: The Anthropology of Agency." *Tôyô Gakuen Daigaku Kiyô* (Tôyô Gakuen University Research Bulletin), 3, 33–48.

McVeigh, B.J. 1996a. "Standing Stomachs, Clamoring Chests and Cooling Livers: Metaphors in the Psychological Lexicon of Japanese." *Journal of Pragmatics*, 26, 25–50.

McVeigh, B.J. 1996b. "Spirit Possession in Sûkyô Mahikari: A Variety of Sociopsychological Experience." *Japanese Religions*, 21, 2, 283–97.

McVeigh, B.J. 1997a. *Spirits, Selves, and Subjectivity in a Japanese New Religion: The Cultural Psychology of Belief in Sûkyô Mahikari.* Lewiston, New York: Edwin Mellen Press.

McVeigh, B.J. 1997b. *Life in a Japanese Women's College: Learning to Be Ladylike.* London: Routledge.

McVeigh, B.J. 2000. *Wearing Ideology: State, Schooling, and Self-Presentation in Japan.* Oxford: Berg Publishers.

Mead, G. 1934. *Mind, Self, and Society*, Vols. 1 and 2. Chicago: University of Chicago Press.

Oesterreich, T.K. 1930. *Possession: Demoniacal and Other.* New York: R.R. Smith, Inc.

Rosaldo, M.Z. 1984. "Toward an Anthropology of Self and Feeling." In R.A. Shweder and R.A. LeVine (eds.), *Culture Theory.* New York: Cambridge University Press.

Smith, J. 1981. "Self and Experience in Maori Culture." In A. Lock and P. Heelas (eds.), *Indigenous Psychologies: The Anthropology of Self.* New York: Academic Press.

Snell, B. 1953. *The Discovery of the Mind* (tran. T. G. Rosenmeyer). Cambridge: Harvard University Press.

Vygotsky, L.S. 1978. *Mind in Society.* Cambridge: Harvard University Press.

CHAPTER 8

A Knowing Noos and a Slippery Psychê

Jaynes's Recipe for an Unnatural Theory of Consciousness

SCOTT GREER

O, WHAT A WORLD of unseen visions and heard silences, this insubstantial country of the mind! What ineffable essences, these touchless rememberings and unshowable reveries! And the privacy of it all! A secret theater of speechless monologue and prevenient counsel, an invisible mansion of all moods, musings, and mysteries, an infinite resort of disappointments and discoveries. A whole kingdom where each of us reigns reclusively alone, questioning what we will, commanding what we can. A hidden hermitage where we may study out the troubled book of what we have done and yet may do. An introcosm that is more myself than anything I can find in a mirror. This consciousness that is myself of selves, that is everything, and yet nothing at all...[1]

Thus spake Jaynes, and thus began, 30 years ago, his ingenious but highly controversial magnum opus, *The Origin of Consciousness in the Breakdown of the Bicameral Mind*. In this work, Jaynes offers some provocative ideas on the nature of consciousness, and some genuinely new and rather startling conclusions as to its origin.

In short, Jaynes argues that until around 1200 B.C. humans did not have consciousness as we understand it: they were unable to introspect, reminisce, make plans, or engage in any reflexive deliberation. When faced with important or meaningful decisions, they heard voices that they took to be gods, which directed their behavior. Jaynes proposed that these "admonitory" and "executive voices" emanated from the right side of the brain, and were communicated to the left side, the 'human' side, as an external voice. The right side, being more creative and better at solving more complex and long-term problems, appeared to the person as a voice of authority that understood the world in a larger, more abstract and god-like way. As one might imagine, a society full of hallucinating people is hardly stable. As the number of people living together and needing to be coordinated grew, more stress was placed on these people and their 'gods'. According to Jaynes, the bicameral civilization worked under conditions of consensus and strict hierarchy, but it was a fragile arrangement; one that had worked for the hunter-gather, but was too inflexible in a context with greater and more numerous and varied social connections. With increasing internal and external stressors (e.g., earthquakes, volcanic eruptions, invasions), as well as the spread of writing, the bicameral mentality gave way to what was simply a more efficient use of our brain — namely, consciousness.

In explaining his theory, Jaynes wove together, in an almost polymathic fashion, a narrative that draws on aspects of philosophy, psychology, history, neurology, anthropology, archeology, religion, and linguistics. Jaynes's search for the origin — or origins — of consciousness was also a highly personal quest, resulting in a theory that makes a fascinating blend of science, literature, history, and crypto-biography.

The quality and validity of Jaynes's theory, however, has been the subject of an ongoing debate — both inside and outside of academia. Reviews of his book have varied from "one of the books of the century" (William Harrington, in *Columbus Dispatch*) and Mike Holderness, in *New Scientist*, who remarked, "It has been a while since a philosophical book made me laugh out loud" — to others that were highly critical.

In any case, it cannot be said that Jaynes's ideas have been irrelevant, nor the point of his questioning moot. In fact, recent developments in neuroscience, and technologies such as PET and MRI scans, have brought consciousness to the fore once again — much as he had hoped and in fact predicted they would. However — and this is a crucial point — this understanding and conception of 'consciousness' is different than the classic notion of 'mind' or self. The neuroscience model of consciousness is a more empirical natural science view, portraying consciousness as solely a neurological event revealed through the lens of modern technology. The other popular contemporary understanding of consciousness is found in cognitive science. Rather than reducing consciousness to a series of brain events, cognitive science often takes a more functional approach to the mind, arguing that mental states are relevant in their own right, since they tell us about the relationship of a particular mental state to other mental states and to behavior.

Jaynes speaks to contemporary theories of consciousness in a profoundly meaningful way. I find that Jaynes's position on the ontology of consciousness, which is the main focus for this chapter, makes a critical counterpoint to the current hegemonies of neuroscientific reductionism on the one hand and computational cognitive science on the other. While he was a thoroughgoing modernist in many respects, Jaynes tested the limits of the modernist conception of consciousness as an individually bounded, embodied, efficient cause (to borrow Aristotle's designation). In the first half of this chapter, we witness Jaynes's path through evolutionary psychology, where he takes the experimental approach of understanding and explaining consciousness to its logical conclusion. He then traces evidence of consciousness in art and literature back to ancient times, where he proposes a radical reinterpretation of both its nature and origins. The second half of this chapter explores some theoretical and biographical evidence that ties Jaynes's view of consciousness to his trek through antiquity, and to Aristotle in particular.[2] This chapter, and the second half in particular, is based on materials held in the Julian Jaynes Collection at the University of Prince Edward Island (UPEI) and additional archival data held at the Archives of the History of American Psychology in Akron, Ohio.[3]

THE JAYNES COLLECTION: SOME BACKGROUND

Before proceeding further, some background on the new Julian Jaynes Collection at UPEI may be in order. Julian Jaynes taught at Princeton University for over 30 years, but he spent nearly all of those summers on Prince Edward Island at a family home in Keppoch. It was here, in fact, that he wrote large portions of *The Origin of Consciousness*. When Jaynes retired from Princeton in 1995, he moved to his Keppoch home, and when he passed away on November 21, 1997, he donated his vast and varied library to the Psychology Department at UPEI (in addition to a generous endowment for scholarships and conferences). The Julian Jaynes Collection has over 800 psychology related books, including rare 1st edition classics by James, Darwin, Titchener, Bain, Ribot, Fechner, Bernheim, Morgan, and others, and many of these rare books are signed by their author. In addition, there are over 2,000 journals and articles, including a historic collection of the *Psychological Review*, passed down via Herbert Langfeld, dating from the early 20th century.

In addition to their immense general scholarly value, research on the life and ideas of Julian Jaynes has been (and can be) immeasurably enhanced. For instance, one of the main sources of information for this chapter is Jaynes's unpublished manuscript, "The History of Comparative Psychology," a text he was working on in the mid 1960's but abandoned for what would become *The Origin of Consciousness*. Also in the collection is his copy of *The Basic Works of Aristotle*. In what was a highly atypical, almost unprecedented practice, Jaynes made copious marginalia in this volume, with nearly two dozen written comments and several index cards marking important passages. In Jaynes's vast library, this volume of *Aristotle* stands out as unique, and would seem to have been quite important to him and his work. The second half of this chapter is an examination and discussion of these notations in the context of Jaynes's ideas and their connection to Aristotle. In addition to these materials, research in this chapter is also based on evidence from over 100 pages of notes written by Jaynes during the preparation of his book and his 1969 invited American Psychological Association (APA) address, which was where his ideas on consciousness were first presented. The Jaynes Collection also has 10 audio taped lectures given by Jaynes between 1978 and 1988, and these too have proven invaluable to the research for this chapter.

JAYNES'S CONCEPT OF CONSCIOUSNESS

Three Interrelated Theories

In revisiting Jaynes, the critical issue is to first recognize that there are three separate components to his theory. As Jaynes notes, each of these three parts may be independently true or false:[4]

1. The theory of the bicameral mind; namely, that the minds of ancient people were in two parts, and these corresponded to the two halves of the brain: the "voices of the gods" resided in the right hemisphere, while the left side dealt with the workaday world of human experience. The

"breakdown" of this bicameral mind was precipitated, in part, by an evolution in language (including writing), and the use of metaphor (and symbolic thought) more specifically. Through this evolution of language and language use, the breakdown also led to a further symbolic process of internal narratization. Jaynes describes it as the linguistic assimilation of the voices of the gods into a single sense of self, existing through time in a "mind-space." Mind-space is defined by Jaynes as a functional space, as opposed to a physical space, where we can create a (usually visual) analog of the world. Mind-space is thus Jaynes's description of the contents of consciousness, which he regards as representational and metaphoric, and as existing through language in a functional relationship with the world. It exists in the same way as, for instance, mathematics.[5] It represents and describes the world, allows us to symbolically manipulate it, and provides a means for rational analysis.

2. The bicameral mind theory is rooted in neurological differences (primarily with regard to speech) between the right and left hemispheres. In fact, one of his key insights into the origin of consciousness came in 1967, when Jaynes realized that if evolution had confined speech areas to the left side of the brain, what was the corresponding right side for, since most important brain functions are bilateral? These differences are still there, he noted, and can be witnessed today in cases of schizophrenia, through electrical stimulation to the right side of the brain, or in certain aspects of childhood, such as in having imaginary friends.[6] Following Sperry's and Gazzaniga's split-brain research, which was published a short time later, Jaynes recalled, "I knew I had something big."[7]

3. It is a linguistic shift rather than any biological or neurological change that resulted in consciousness as we now ex-

perience it. According to Jaynes, there is no substantial difference between our brains today and those of bicameral people 3,000 years ago. The origin of consciousness rests *not* in evolution, but is a product of *culture and language*, or a cultural evolution, more specifically, in the use of writing and language. Our mentality — whether bicameral or conscious — is thus more a function of social context, language, and forms of communication than a hard-wired neurologically-based system. Understanding consciousness, therefore, has more to do with understanding our society rather than our brain, our language practices rather than neurotransmitters, and our cultural history as opposed to our genetic endowment. Biological factors clearly do play some role: for example, we can see the evolution of communication and language in humans, something genetically and biologically grounded, but consciousness itself is something that emerged from *the use of language*.

    What is important to note about these three sub-theories is that his theory of consciousness (#3) *does not necessarily* commit one to his bicameral hypothesis on its origins (#1), or his neurological theory on the structure of the bicameral mind (#2). Jaynes's bicameral mind theory is rooted in neurological assumptions, while his argument for the origin of consciousness is based on certain cultural developments in language and metaphor. More importantly, the aetiology and ontology of consciousness for Jaynes is totally dissimilar to that of the bicameral mind (which was not so much a mind as a dual brain). Although for Jaynes, consciousness resulted from the "breakdown of the bicameral mind," this breakdown was a cultural adaptation that resulted in the learned ability to narratize the self and the person's world in and through language. So, what does Jaynes believe consciousness is?

The Search for and Development of a Theory of Consciousness

First and most importantly, we need to understand that questions concerning consciousness followed Jaynes all of his life; this was indeed a life long obsession. It is by recounting his intellectual journey in search of the origin and nature of consciousness that we discover crucial lessons and key assumptions that are relevant to today, for his path in many ways was a foreshadowing of contemporary cognitive neuroscience.

Jaynes traced the start of his quest for understanding consciousness to a vivid memory from the early age of six: while raking leaves in his yard, he was suddenly struck by the idea that the 'yellow' he saw in the forsythia bush before him may not be the same 'yellow' that others see; and, moreover, how would one ever know what someone else saw? Jaynes recalled, "As a child, I was fascinated by the inner world I alone could see, and I wondered what was the difference between seeing inwardly and outwardly."[8]

Jaynes started his search in earnest as an undergraduate majoring in philosophy and literature, attending the University of Virginia his first year, Harvard his second, and McGill his third and fourth. Jaynes graduated from McGill in 1941. He had studied philosophy with the hope that he might understand this "interior space we call consciousness," but later considered this a "false start": "... after going through Kant's *Critique of Pure Reason* and various epistemologies, I felt that we had to be out in the world gathering data to get anywhere."[9]

With this in mind, Jaynes continued with graduate work at Yale's Institute of Human Relations in 1946, studying human physiology and animal behavior. Jaynes looked for his 'data' by examining the relationship between the brain and behavior, looking for the physiological and biological bases of the mind. His research was clearly connected to the theory of evolution, and, from that, the idea that consciousness must have evolved — its origins should therefore be traceable back through history and through our links with other animals. Jaynes then began a systematic search for consciousness by studying how organisms learned. He started with plants and moved on to single-celled organisms, neither of which appeared to learn. Jaynes recalled, "I began running paramecia and protozoa through little T-mazes, all in the blissfully absurd notion that I was researching consciousness."[10] He then studied simple animals, such as flatworms, and then on to fish, reptiles, and cats, which obviously could learn — but Jaynes was feeling restless, and he was beginning to wonder if he was in any way coming closer to finding consciousness.

After earning his M.A. in 1948 from Yale, he continued on this line of research toward a Ph.D., but, in a striking move and for reasons that are not entirely clear, Jaynes refused to submit his dissertation to Yale. There are basically two stories to account for this, each having some truth perhaps. One is that he wanted the freedom to pursue interests outside of experimental psychology, and did not want the responsibility of having to follow the path that a Ph.D. would have entailed. The other story is that his committee wanted certain revisions, and Jaynes was simply unwilling to comply. He did finally receive his Ph.D. from Yale, almost 30 years later in 1977, but only at the behest of friends and colleagues who petitioned the university to accept his original research.

In either case, it is clear that Jaynes was an iconoclast, and had become increasingly disenchanted with the methods and restricted domain of experimental psychology. For Jaynes, 'psychology' represented the study of the mind, and he came to believe that "running rats in mazes had little to do with psychology," and furthermore that such a 'psychology' was little more than "bad poetry disguised as science."[11] He also criticized the scholastic apprenticeship system in universities, where he felt students were largely imbued with the theoretical prejudices of their professors, and received degrees for churning out unoriginal and uninspired research.[12]

The 'Turn' Toward Culture and Language

Frustrated by the scholarly limitations of the field, and his own failure after many years to uncover even a glimmer of consciousness, Jaynes determined that the search for consciousness as a natural object and product of evolution was a "dead end."[13] Jaynes slowly began to realize, "the problem of consciousness had stumped so many people because it wasn't in evolution, it was in human culture."[14]

Some progress had been made, however. Through his experimental research with animals, Jaynes had systematically and deductively come to understand what consciousness was *not*: it was not all of mentality or perception, it did not copy experience, it was not necessary for learning (in a complete reversal of his initial assumption), and it was not even necessary for all types of thinking or reasoning.

So, Jaynes began a new line of research, with a new bold set of assumptions. He looked for evidence of consciousness throughout world history and culture; searching ancient literature and art, and any kind of archeological evidence that might indicate the presence or absence of consciousness. The most direct kind of evidence seemed to be from language, and so he looked for concepts or actions that would denote consciousness. We can see, for instance, that Plato and Aristotle were conscious, although they do not have a well-defined concept of consciousness *per se*. He continued on through the Homeric Greeks, tracing consciousness back until it disappeared (in his opinion) between the *Iliad* and the *Odyssey*. This would then place the origin of consciousness for the Greeks between 1200 and 1000 B.C. For Jaynes, these two works seemed to bracket the emergence of conscious-type thinking (or at least the rise of concepts tantamount to consciousness). In the *Iliad*, the Greeks and the Trojans are depicted, more or less, as "puppets" of the gods, who are much more salient in determining the course of human action than in the *Odyssey*. In the latter work, crafty Odysseus is capable of, for instance, acts of deception, something that requires consciousness.[15]

Jaynes found similar evidence of consciousness emerging in the writings of the Near and Middle East, such as in the Bible and the Upanishads, and there was a remarkable degree of consistency around the dates, all centering around 1200 to 1000 B.C.[16] Again, Jaynes argues that until this time modern humans *did not* have consciousness (i.e., a Cartesian type of reflective, conscious awareness). Humans were unable to introspect on their decisions or actions, were incapable of thinking about themselves, or of having any concept of 'self'. These ancient humans were basically hallucinating automata who took the voices from the right side of their brains to be gods. Jaynes put the matter succinctly when he says, "human civilization was built by people who could not think."[17]

While this may sound patently absurd, Jaynes argued that we have lived and evolved for millennia without consciousness, and so it would not have been necessary for many basic human behaviors. His earlier research on animal behavior and the history of comparative psychology had demonstrated this, he believed. It only *seems* essential now, since consciousness *is* the awareness of our actions. Perhaps the behaviorists were right, but for the wrong reasons.

However, what I believe is the most decisive and perhaps radical point in Jaynes's theory is that he also argued that consciousness is not simply the brain — in fact, it "does not have a location," and elsewhere he states that "the location of consciousness is arbitrary."[18] I believe many people, when asked to point to their 'mind' or to their 'consciousness', would point to their head. Or one might argue, as current models of cognitive neuroscience and cognitive psychology suggest, the brain is really the mind, or at least a properly functioning brain is, among other things, a conscious 'mind'. According to these perspectives, consciousness can be located in the workings of the brain, and a scientific understanding of consciousness involves understanding the underlying neural connections, processes, and structures. For Jaynes, this is a very common and most unfortunate mistake in that it reifies consciousness into a thing, and is missing *the essential aspect of its origin: consciousness developed through the process of generating and fitting metaphors to objects and events.*[19]

For instance, we would not argue (I hope) that $2 + 2 = 4$ can best be understood as something residing in our brain; naturally, the ability to use this information involves the brain, but mathematics itself does not somehow reside in the brain. Similarly, consciousness and the generation of our mind-space clearly involves the brain, and like mathematical formula, grammatical structures (i.e., our syntax and semantics) are the tools of conscious thought. However, this can in no way be taken to mean that consciousness itself is rooted in the brain (just as most certainly mathematics is not either).

A further example given by Jaynes is that of riding a bicycle: we all use our brains in riding a bike, just as we do in producing conscious experience, but we do not ride bicycles in our heads or think of "bicycle riding" as residing in our heads. Consciousness is thus a functional concept, a type of representational system, that is expressed and 'found' in our use of language and metaphor. Although Jaynes was not fundamentally opposed to the metaphor of "cyberspace" to characterize consciousness as a functioning representational system, he was wary of taking computer or technological analogies too far, calling it "unnecessary," "inaccurate," and a path that "can lead us astray."[20]

With this in mind (so to speak), Jaynes offers two general but slightly different definitions of consciousness. The first comes from *The Origin of Consciousness*, and defines it as "an analog 'I' narratizing in a mind-space."[21] Jaynes's contention, as described earlier, was that consciousness developed through the process of generating and applying metaphors to objects and events, and that this all occurs in a mind-space. This idea can be further explained in three interlocking points:[22]

1. The operations of consciousness are based on metaphors, often visual in nature: e.g., "she's very bright."
2. The relationship to these metaphors is based on a sense of "I"; this "I" exists and moves about in mind-space, where it can engage in any number of activities, actually possible or not.
3. This activity occurs in time and is put into a temporal sequence which Jaynes called "narratization." The modes of conscious narratization can be verbal, perceptual, bodily, or musical.

Jaynes's other, later definition of consciousness repeats the main features of the first, but is concerned more with the *origins* of consciousness rather than its structural features: consciousness is "based on metaphor, developed through language, and is an operator, not a thing."[23] As noted earlier, both definitions highlight Jaynes's belief that consciousness and its origins are tied to language and cultural practices, and consciousness is not, in itself, a biological system.

To review, Jaynes's theory represents the questioning of some very basic assumptions about consciousness and the mind in general: its origins, its ontology, and the language we use to describe, understand, and explain it are addressed in ways that significantly depart from popular current models (i.e., neuroscience and cognitive science). As such, I would argue Jaynes represents a symbolic end to the modernist (i.e., Cartesian) conception of consciousness (and mind in general) as contained in the body, and as the executive 'homunculus' that *causes* (viz. as efficient cause) much of our conduct.[24] Jaynes's 'un-reified' ontology of consciousness and the grounding of our sense of self in language and socio-cultural praxis (rather than a single individually contained agent) clearly places him outside the modernist tradition; one might be tempted to argue that mind and self are, for Jaynes, "socially constructed" (in the strong sense of this term, as used by Gergen, 1985 and Cushman, 1990, among others). More importantly for this point: Jaynes came from an experimental tradition where consciousness was part of a biological process in the head, in our brains even, and only after a long and exhaustive systematic search for consciousness under these assumptions was the naturalistic discourse on consciousness questioned. By avoiding the reification of the mind or soul to explain consciousness, he rejects the ontological dualist tradition (i.e., Cartesian dualism) and avoids the subject/object dichotomy that has plagued naturalistic accounts of consciousness to this day. As we will see in the following section, there is biographical evidence to suggest that Jaynes's ideas are rooted in an ancient philosophical tradition of thinking about "the mind" that was non-dualistic, and that have much broader meanings for our term "mind" and other basic modern scientific concepts such as "cause and effect."

JAYNES AND ARISTOTLE

In the first half of this chapter, Jaynes's theory of consciousness was characterized as representing a kind of symbolic end to the modernist conception of consciousness. In the second half, we examine evidence that it was Jaynes's return to pre-modern psychology — to Aristotle in particular — that may have been partly responsible for his particularly un-modern stance on consciousness. As noted earlier, the ideas and conclusions in this chapter are largely based on Jaynes's unpublished manuscript, his own copy of *The Basic Works of Aristotle*, and over 100 pages of notes written by Jaynes during the preparation of his American Psychological Association address and book. Both the manuscript and his book contain many references to Aristotle, and I have been able to connect many of the marked passages in his *Aristotle* with the unpublished "History of Comparative Psychology." Correlating his manuscript with his comments in this way made it obvious that these comments were *written during the preparation of the manuscript*. While Aristotle's ideas are mentioned in *The Origin of Consciousness*, Jaynes's "History of Comparative Psychology" contains a *much* fuller discussion of Aristotle's notion of psychê (and other ancient Greek notions of mind). Based on this evidence, I will show that Jaynes's ideas on the ontology of consciousness have some substantive theoretical connections to Aristotle's notion of "psychê" and "noos." However, it is extremely important that we clarify what Aristotle (and others from antiquity) meant by these terms, and also try to ascertain what Jaynes's perception of these may have been.

Aristotle's Psychê [25]

First and foremost, Aristotle's "psychê" cannot be taken to mean "consciousness"; the idea that thinking was embodied in the "psyche" (using the English term here) is a very different meaning than that of psychê in Aristotle's time. As we will see below from Aristotle's writings, psychê implies life or activity, or the actualizing of a body's potential for activity. Perhaps the closest meaning in today's lexicon is found in "soul;" in *De Anima*, Aristotle argued that the "soul" (i.e., psychê) could not be seen as separate from the body. Psychê, according to Green and Groff, ironically did not have any psychological connotations, as we would understand them today.[26]

Rational thinking, which Aristotle wrote a great deal about as well, was believed by Homer and Aristotle to be centered just above the heart (with the brain used mainly to cool the blood!). The terms most closely associated with the mentality of thinking, feeling, and willing (what we see as 'psychological' today) are *noos* (later *nous*) and *thumos*. Noos was usually used to refer to rational and intellectual thought, dealing with images, ideas, and other "acts of mind."[27] Noos was often abstract in nature by comparison to thumos, which dealt more with emotion, motivation, and will. There was usually a more visceral quality to thumos, such as in a warrior's thumos driving him into battle (as Homer described Odysseus).[28]

While believed to reside in the chest, *noos was never identified with a particular part of the body or as having a definite substance or form*. In Book III, section 4 of *De Anima*, Aristotle argued:

> The thinking part of the soul must therefore be ... capable of receiving the form of an object; that is, must be potentially identical in character with its object without being the object. ... Therefore, since everything is a possible object of thought, mind in order ... to dominate ... must be pure from all admixture. ... Thus that in the soul which is called mind (by mind I mean that whereby the soul thinks and judges) is, before it thinks, not actually any real thing. For this reason it cannot reasonably be regarded as blending with the body....

Aristotle is basically saying that the rational mind (noos) does not and cannot have a form of its own, but must remain an indefinite abstract capacity to perceive sensory objects. If it had a form or properties of its own, this would interfere with its ability to correctly perceive the external world (which Aristotle believed it did).

Now, let us pause for a moment, since there are some extremely significant points here. First, this is part of the famous argument in psychology, long held by behaviorists, that the mind is a "tabula rasa," or a "blank slate," upon which sense experience is imprinted. As noted earlier, Jaynes largely agreed with this view, in so far as it depicted consciousness as an analog to the external world, where it represented sensory objects in a mindspace through language and metaphor. As such, Jaynes's concept of consciousness (and most modern ones too) has more in common with Aristotle's use of noos than psychê.

Second, centuries later the Scholastics would seize upon Aristotle's argument that noos had no specified form and was, according to some interpretations of Aristotle's fragmented and contradictory texts, "the eternal part of the psychê." This would become part of the foundation for the Christian notion of an individual immaterial soul, and that this soul also contained the rational, and thus uniquely human, mind. However, the Christian and modern concept of soul, one that encompassed the person's mentality as a whole, was a *combination* of psychê and noos, an important point identified by Jaynes.[29] Jaynes concedes that it was ultimately a mystery how psychê came to represent *both* the intellectual capacities of noos *and* the individual as an immaterial and eternal entity (i.e., how psychê became soul). While we lack the space to discuss the complex relationship between psychê and noos, Jaynes identifies an important set of historical developments that had an enduring impact on the understanding of psychê and its transformation into (the English) psyche, or mind.[30]

Aristotle was a 4th century B.C. writer, but his concept of psychê harkens back to the 'Ionian revolution' of the 6th century B.C., which marked one of the first sustained traditions of naturalistic explanation. This 6th century naturalistic turn represented a move away from myth and religious explanations and toward systematic and written ideas. However this naturalistic exploration of the cosmological was relatively short-lived. Fifth century B.C. Greece saw difficult and turbulent times: the war with Sparta and political unrest led people to turn toward ethical and moral questions, questions about the 'good life'. Jaynes points out that the Pythagorean and neo-Platonic interpretations of psychê saw life or activity, and what was responsible for it, as *contained within* the individual.[31] The body thus contained a soul in such a way that after death the soul "transmigrated," or would leave one body to take up residence in another (somewhat similar to the notion of 'reincarnation'). Although the Aristotelian/Ionian view existed along side the Pythagorean for a time, this latter interpretation of psychê, with its references to essential transcendent moral truths, leant itself to the kind of ethical discourse that was relevant at the time. As a result, around 500 B.C. psychê became increasingly reified into a substance that was of a different

metaphysical type than that of the body (or *soma*, in Greek).[32]
Although the details were incomplete, Jaynes identifies this as
one of the most important transformative events in the history of
mind.[33] Again, this reified understanding of psychê/noos was not
the one Aristotle had put forward. Nevertheless, this dualistic
subject/object split set the tone for the Western modernist discourse on the person.[34]

Aristotle and "The Origin of Consciousness"

Jaynes conducted a great deal of research on Aristotle and his
legacy. As described earlier, Jaynes's journey back through time
to find evidence for the emergence of consciousness in writing
and art took him through the ancient Greeks. Aristotle was naturally an important stop in this journey since the history of Western thought, in general, has been so heavily influenced by
Aristotle and his interpreters (particularly the Scholastics). This
research was originally done, it is important to recall, under the
premise of his "History of Comparative Psychology." We know
that several hundred pages had been written by 1968, when
Jaynes gave a series of National Science Foundation lectures. His
chapter on Aristotle alone is over 60 pages.

The notes in his Aristotle volume clearly correlate with his
manuscript. For instance, Jaynes begins his chapter on Aristotle
(called "The Aristotelian Corpus") by giving an overview of *De
Anima*. He makes frequent mention of the various inconsistencies
in the three books of *De Anima*, and comments in numerous
places that the material is a "hodgepodge" or "this is mere pad-
ding of Tyrannion" (Cicero's librarian). Similarly, Jaynes's undated manuscript notes similar points, and even goes on to offer
an explanation: "the historical Aristotle did not write the works
attributed to him." "I have not come to [this point of view] flip-
pantly or hastily," Jaynes continues, but "... the things being said
could never be said by the same man, as conflicting in approach

and detail as they are." He does not provide a full explanation, but maintains that the contradictions are largely what make it impossible to reconcile certain aspects of the Aristotelian corpus (of which we will see an example shortly).

After he concludes that the works of "Aristotle" were not written by the same person, Jaynes continues with a brief review of *De Anima*.[35] Such a review is helpful at this point, since it not only gives us some sense about what Jaynes thought was important, but it also introduces and explains Aristotle's ideas.

Jaynes notes that in Book I, Aristotle discussed and rejected each of the previous attempts to define psychê, including those by Democritus, Anaxagoras, Plato, and Heraclitus. Each writer had attempted to describe the soul in terms of movement and sensation, but encountered difficulties, according to Aristotle, because psychê was regarded as an independent or separate entity. Aristotle concluded that the soul was not some type of matter or combination of matter, but was, "... the first grade of actuality of a natural body having life potentially in it."[36] Jaynes underlined this passage and highlighted the following points (italicized below) in Aristotle's elaboration:

...the word substance has three meanings — form, matter, and the complex of both — and of these three what is called matter is potentiality, what is called form actuality. Since then the complex here is the living thing, the body cannot be the actuality of the soul; it is the soul which is the actuality of a certain kind of body. Hence the rightness of the view that the soul cannot be without a body, while it cannot *be* a body; it is not a body *but something relative to a body*. It was a mistake, therefore, to do as former thinkers did, merely to fit it into a body without adding a definite specification of the kind or character of that body. Reflection confirms the observed fact; the actuality of any given thing can only be realized in what is already potentially that thing, i.e., in a matter of its own appropriate to it. From all this follows that soul is an actuality or formulable essence of something that *possesses* a potentiality of being besouled.[37]

If psychê is the actuality of a certain kind of body, namely the kind to be "besouled," then by "actuality" Aristotle meant the body possess the potential for life, movement, sensation, etc., not just the manifestation of these acts (i.e., behavior).

Earlier, in the opening of Book II of *De Anima*, Aristotle made his position on a dualism of psychê and body clear, to which Jaynes had added great emphasis in his text (three emphasis lines and an arrow pointing to this section):

We can wholly dismiss as unnecessary the question whether the soul and the body are one: it is as meaningless to ask whether the wax and the shape given to it by the stamp are one, or generally the matter of a thing and that of which it is the matter.[38]

Later in Book II, Aristotle made four now famous analogies to describe psychê. The fourth of these, as will be discussed later, was put to great use by Jaynes in the *Origin of Consciousness*:

1. Psychê is to body as a finished house is to the pile of bricks that made it.
2. Psychê is to body as an impression is in a lump of wax.
3. If an axe were a natural body, then 'being-an-axe' would be its body and 'cutting' would be its psychê.
4. If an eye was an animal, sight would be its psychê. Just as pupil and sight *are* the eye, psychê and body *are* the animal.

"From this," wrote Aristotle, "it indubitably follows that the soul is inseparable from its body ..."[39] In this view, one cannot separate matter, function, and form, since existence (and the essence of a thing) is existing in a particular way (or, put another way, being alive is becoming). Further consider Aristotle's points here, that altering the form (e.g., a damaged eye) alters its function — being an 'eye' entails the act of seeing. Psychê is then the realization of the potential of the body and the body's abilities and purpose. As such, psychê (i.e., as part of a knowing process) is not inside our heads, but found in the relationship between objects and their interaction.

To elaborate, in Book III of *De Anima*, Aristotle argued,

> The *activity of the sensible object and of the sensitive faculty are **one** actuality, and yet the distinction between their being remains* [emphasis in the original].[40]

Aristotle explained that in spite of the difference between their modes of being, hearing and sound are "merged as one" in our experience, while as potentialities one may exist without the other.[41] Jaynes evidently found this passage quite meaningful, and it reinforces, I believe, his conviction that the mind/body dichotomy is the source of many modern errors in psychology, and that such distinctions are invalid.

To put this idea of the unity of subject and object in a somewhat trite (or hackneyed) example: "If a tree falls in the forest, and no one hears it, does it make a sound?" As this example is intended to demonstrate: The answer depends on what we mean by 'sound'. Aristotle would argue that if no one hears the tree fall, there was just the potential for sound, but not the actualization of it. This is very different from our more objective and analytical way of thinking about perceptual events, where the properties of objects have their own independent existence quite apart from our perception of them.[42]

Needless to say, for Aristotle, the notion of psychê as a separate entity or function that interacts with another class of object, namely behavior, is a non sequitur. Added to that is the idea that the soul (psychê) is that which is ultimately responsible for conduct (or movement, more specifically) in Aristotle's metaphysics, even though noos is more properly understood as the rational mind. Thus, mind, thinking, and action would seem inseparable, as his wax and stamp metaphor demonstrates — although there are other passages that contradict this.

In Book III of *De Anima*, Aristotle's position on the ontology of noos was less clear, particularly when considered along side his notion of psychê. As we saw in the previous section, Aristotle believed noos could not have definable properties or be of a specific substance since this would interfere with the accurate perception of the world. However, Aristotle wrote that noos was independent, immortal, and could even be separate from the body (cf. Book III, sec. 5). Many scholars have noted that it is very difficult to reconcile the notions that noos could be independent but undifferentiated, having no definite qualities of its own.[43]

Jaynes also pondered this question. In his copy of Aristotle, he highlighted the following passage with a line and a question mark in the margin:

Mind in this sense of it is **separable** [circled], impassible, unmixed, *since it is in its essential nature activity....* *Actual knowledge is identical with its object*: in the individual, potential knowledge is in time prior to actual knowledge, *but in the universe as a whole it is not prior even in time*. Mind is not at one time knowing and at another not. *When mind is set free* from its present conditions it appears as just what it is and nothing more: this alone is immortal and eternal ... and without it nothing thinks [emphases in the original].[44]

Obviously Jaynes was puzzled by this startling contradiction in the ontology of mind (noos), and scribbled some notes in the margin:

- "see Metaphysics XIII, 6" (which discusses the Pythagorean notion of number and whether number is a separate substance);
- "Orphic religion" (this refers to the ancient Greek Dionysiac-Orphic religion, which believed the soul was separate from the body and could "transmigrate" to other bodies);
- "contradicts all the preceding!"

Furthermore, this is another example of a clear connection between his *Aristotle* and "History of Comparative Psychology." Such contradictions spurred Jaynes to believe that Book III of *De Anima* was "a different work entirely" from the previous sections, was much more Pythagorean and dualistic in its conception, and that *De Anima* as a whole "is almost like a projective test where anyone can find and emphasize what they wish."[45] He also elaborated on his marginalia:

> Aristotle said that nous or enlightenment has no form or nature of its own, so how could it ever know itself or indeed know anything since to know is an active verb? If indeed the rational psyche or nous has no structure at all, then why don't we think of everything at one time, why aren't all the universals continually present to nous? There must be something that acts and this was the conception of the active intellect which was invented by the Arabians. Moderns might say that the active intellect is language, but I wonder.[46]

Ironic, indeed, that as Jaynes's thoughts would develop, it was in fact *language* as part of our active thinking processes — which he so doubtfully "wondered" about here — that would become so central in his explanation of consciousness.

From these examples, we can see that the concepts of form, matter, and function were central to Aristotle, and, as I see it,

extremely salient to Jaynes as well. Jaynes wrote that consciousness, and the use of symbols and metaphor, gave a certain form
to the behavioral world.[47] While he disagreed with John Locke's
idea that the mind was a simple reflection of the external world,
where it would act like a "camera,"[48] he did agree with Locke
when he wrote, paraphrasing him, that: "... there is nothing in
consciousness that is not an analog of something that was in
behavior first."[49]

Furthermore, in *The Origin of Consciousness* Jaynes makes frequent use of visual analogies in describing consciousness as a way
or kind of "seeing." We can see from archival data (i.e., his note
pads) that consciousness is depicted as a visualization of the
world, giving the world around us a kind of form and representation that we can manipulate. Jaynes explicitly ties this notion to
Aristotle's fourth analogy of psyché (i.e., "If an eye was an animal, sight would be its psyché ...). Early in his notes, Jaynes
posed the general guiding question, "What is consciousness?"
He then proposed with a "ρ" in the margin: "Model of seeing:
quote Aristotle, seeing/eye = mind/body. Suppose–cover eye,
don't see: eidola vs. light seeing (?);[50] seeing and eye no longer
dichotomous, distinctions further get into problem. ... Thinking
and brain: same thing." Then, adding another "ρ" in the margins,
Jaynes wrote: "New functionalism: no school previously."[51]

This would seem to be a very significant notation, and I believe it takes us to the heart of what makes Aristotle important for
understanding Jaynes's theory, both in terms of its ontology and
how it takes the modern conception of mind back to its roots.
Jaynes's theory of consciousness was unique in many ways, and
Aristotle's visual metaphor expresses some of its essential qualities (even though Aristotle was not using it to describe what we
would call "consciousness"). Aristotle's "functionalism" portrays
psyché and noos as acting in relationship with the outside world,
not apart from it. In fact, the mind would not have any content or
form at all if it were not for the outside world. While Jaynes

would only go that far with respect to consciousness itself (not all of cognition), he was extending the Aristotelian "tabula rasa" notion that thinking and ideas are constructed analogs taken from the world, not separate entities sealed off from it. Jaynes's theory is also functionalist in the sense that consciousness (and rationality) is not defined as an object but as "an operator"; being conscious is about the ability to narratize in a mind-space using an 'I'. There is a similar plasticity to Aristotle's noos and psychê, in that they result from the person existing and functioning in the world.

While Jaynes believes that it was the 'I' that 'sees', this idea also has its origins in ancient Greek thought. Jaynes's section on "noos" notes that this term is "derived from noeo = to see, [and] is perception itself."[52] As we all know from everyday experience, we frequently refer to the "mind's eye," but seldom do we think of the "mind's ear," or, much less, the "mind's tongue." Of course, Aristotle did not create the term noos; Jaynes provides numerous examples from antiquity of noos that all illustrate its visual character.

In his "History of Comparative Psychology," Jaynes also comments on noos, noting that not only is it connected with the idea of seeing something, but noos as a sight word "... leads to *theorein* [the root of our word 'theory'], a vision such as might be held in a theatre which is the natural abode of theorein. And since this is so, I shall translate nous as enlightenment and "nousing"[53] as being enlightened. ..." Jaynes also notes that "the Aegean writers" saw nousing as "a way of discovering the function of noos." In other words, Jaynes believes that our modern notions of knowledge, knowing, and reflexivity are rooted in the concept of noos. Since in Jaynes's view consciousness is a way to represent and symbolically manipulate the world, such abilities obviously lead to knowledge, which is why Jaynes equated noos and "nousing" with "enlightenment."

There is one further, rather curious point to consider: the

parallel organization of *The Origin of Consciousness* and *De Anima*. Visually, there is a rather striking similarity. For example, *De Anima* is organized into three books, and *Origin of Consciousness* is organized into three books; Book I of *De Anima* is a review of previous theories of psychê; Book II presents some definitions of psychê, as well as arguments and evidence to support this; and Book III discusses aspects of the functioning of psychê, such as sensing, perceiving, thinking, imagining, appetite, and motivation. By comparison, in *The Origin of Consciousness*, Book I is a discussion of various approaches to consciousness, including an argument of what consciousness is not, and a narrative about how he came to his view. Book II is a look at the historical and anthropological evidence for his bicameral theory, and Book III is an extrapolation of his ideas to explain some psychological phenomena, including things such as schizophrenia, hypnosis, poetry, and music.

It is not, of course, an exact or direct parallel, but there appears to be a general template in Jaynes's work that is similar to *De Anima*. There is also a broadly similar trajectory that both Aristotle and Jaynes follow: they presented a view of mind that stood in contrast to their contemporaries, and which they believed struck at the essence of what 'mind' is.

CONCLUSION

We can summarize and conclude with the following observations:

1. Jaynes connected his visual model of consciousness with Aristotle's fourth analogy of psyche.
2. His ontology of consciousness bears certain theoretical parallels with Aristotle's notions of psychê as a functional and integrated (i.e., non-dualistic) part of the person that is ultimately responsible for movement.
3. His portrayal of consciousness as a (largely) visual analog of

the physical world also has connections to the ancient term noos: the rational part of psychê that may, or may not, be separate from the body (according to Aristotle's contradictory scheme).

4. Reflection, knowledge, and knowing were also thought to be part of noos (and "nousing"), and Jaynes identified these active rational processes as inherent features of consciousness.

In the long Western tradition of the body as a container for the soul, Jaynes presents a theory of consciousness that deviates from this modernist course. He ironically reached this conclusion through the most modern of avenues: experimental animal behavior research. As someone in search of the origin of consciousness, Jaynes relinquished his assumptions about mind and natural law through his research on antiquity — and I make a case for Aristotle in particular. This return to antiquity and the pre-modern gave Jaynes a perspective on the mind that was not entrenched in a dualistic discourse, and allowed for a theory of consciousness that fit the historical and archeological evidence he found. Jaynes not only represents a symbolic end to the modernist conception of consciousness and the self, he returns the discourse to its pre-modern roots, where consciousness 'exists' in relation to a functional metaphoric mind-space, rather than existing outside of physical space. All of these points are based on a uniquely annotated text and an unpublished manuscript that cast the historical and theoretical background of Jaynes's *The Origin of Consciousness* in a new light. Finally, in reflecting on the reception of Aristotle by Jaynes, we are not only considering the historical connections, but the philosophical and theoretical implications that they both raise for contemporary theories of consciousness.

NOTES TO CHAPTER 8

1. Jaynes, 1976, p. 1.
2. To the contemporary historian, such a claim — one linking a recent figure such as Jaynes to an ancient one like Aristotle — must seem outrageous. There are so many differences in social context, language, and their overall view of the world that any comparison must surely be very limited or simply inappropriate. Ordinarily, I would probably agree; however, my concerns here are attenuated by the fact that I have Jaynes's own personal notes, manuscripts, and books. I have, in short, a partial record of his thoughts and ideas, and what helped, in a very general sense, give them shape. I also believe and will argue that the connections are sufficiently unique and specific (viz. the ontology of consciousness) to warrant consideration.
3. Part of the archival research for this chapter was made possible by a Major Research Grant from UPEI.
4. Keen, 1977; Rhodes, 1978.
5. Husserl made the exact same analogy, but there is no reference to Husserl or phenomenology in the *Origin of Consciousness*. However, research for this chapter has discovered that Jaynes was indeed aware, to some extent, of Husserl and phenomenology, and of the importance of this perspective for his own theory. From one of his notepads, dated July 28, 1969, Jaynes wrote: "Phenomenology must precede neurology, let neuroanatomy be where it will."
6. Jaynes, 1976; Keen, 1977.
7. Leo, 1977, p. 52.
8. Rhodes, 1978, p. 62.
9. Keen, 1977, p. 60.
10. Ibid.
11. Hilts, 1981, p. 87; Keen, 1977, p. 66.
12. Gliedman, 1982.
13. Jaynes, 1986a.
14. Hilts, 1981, p. 87.
15. Jaynes, 1976.
16. Jaynes, 1976; 1986b.
17. Hilts, 1981.
18. Jaynes, 1976; 1986a; 1988.
19. Jaynes, 1983.
20. Julian Jaynes Interview: Anonymous interview transcript.
21. Jaynes, 1983; 1986a.
22. Based on Jaynes, 1976.
23. Jaynes, 1988.
24. More recent work, since the late 1970s, in both neuroscience and cognitive science, has also tended to move away from the homuncular view. Rather,

many theories have conceived of consciousness (and self) as distributed processes functioning in concert throughout the brain. However, neither of these broad perspectives sees culture, language, and language use as having the generative role for consciousness the way that Jaynes does.

25. For purposes of historical and literary accuracy, it is important to distinguish between the English term "psyche" and the Latin transliteration of the Greek, "psychê." It is important to remember that not only does the Greek term differ substantially from the English term, but there are important differences in the usages of psychê among Plato, Aristotle, and other ancient Greeks (Green and Groff, 2003).

26. Green and Groff, 2003.

27. Bremmer, 1983, p. 57.

28. Green and Groff, 2003.

29. Jaynes, 1976.

30. Jaynes, undated manuscript.

31. Ibid.

32. Jaynes, 1976.

33. Jaynes, undated manuscript.

34. It was in examining his volume of *The Basic Writings of Aristotle* that I discovered a remark scribbled at the bottom of a page in Book I of *De Anima.* This started a line of questioning regarding the relationship of Aristotle's psychê to Jaynes's theory. Jaynes wrote: "'psyche' slips about like a fresh caught trout in inexperienced hands, slithering between a homunculus that knows and a principle and back simply to life or activity" (Aristotle, 1941, p. 541n). In this quote, Jaynes is not so much commenting on Aristotle's concept of psychê, but on Aristotle's review of previous theories of psychê.

35. Jaynes, undated manuscript.

36. Aristotle, 1941, p. 412b.

37. Ibid., p. 414a.

38. Ibid., p. 412b.

39. Ibid., p. 413a.

40. Ibid., p. 426a.

41. Ibid.

42. Since Aristotle stressed the functional quality of psychê and its role in experience, many contemporary writers have regarded Aristotle as a functionalist, or as an early representative of 'functionalism' (cf. Green, 1998). There are clearly some broad conceptual connections, but this may be a somewhat pointless debate, since I do not think Aristotle meant to *explain* psychê in the way that we would use this term today. Our understanding of an 'explanation' is much more influenced by a Galilean conception of causality than the broader Aristotelian one.

43. Green and Groff, 2003.
44. Aristotle, 1941, Book III, sec. 5.
45. Jaynes, undated manuscript, p. 8.
46. Ibid., p. 14.
47. Jaynes, 1976.
48. Jaynes, 1983.
49. Jaynes, 1976, p. 76.
50. Unlike Democritus, Aristotle rejected the idea that sensation and perception occurred because objects created and sent off copies of themselves that were picked up by our sense organs (these copies were called *eidola*). Rather, Aristotle believed that sensation came from a change or movement in the medium that was connected to the functioning of a sense organ. Visual perception was thus the result of movement in light.
51. From the Julian Jaynes papers held at the Archives of the History of American Psychology.
52. Jaynes, 1976, p. 269.
53. Jaynes noted that the term "nousing" was taken from Randall's (1960) classic text on Aristotle.

REFERENCES

Aristotle. 1941. *The Basic Works of Aristotle*. R. McKeon (ed), New York: Random House.

Bremmer, J. 1983. *The Early Greek Concept of Soul*. Princeton, NJ: Princeton University Press.

Cushman, P. 1990. "Why the Self Is Empty: Toward A Historically Situated Psychology." *American Psychologist*, 45, 599–611.

Gergen, K. 1985. "The Social Constructionist Movement in Modern Psychology." *American Psychologist*, 40, 266–275.

Gliedman, J. 1982. "Julian Jaynes and the Ancient Mindgods." *Science Digest*, 90, 84–87.

Green, C.D. 1998. "The Thoroughly Modern Aristotle: Was He Really A Functionalist?" *History of Psychology*, 1, 8–20.

Green, C.D. and P.R. Groff. 2003. *Early Psychological Thought: Ancient Accounts of Mind and Soul*. Greenwood, CT: Praeger.

Hilts, P. 1981. "Odd Man Out." *Omni*, January, 68–88.

Jaynes, J. Undated. "The History of Comparative Psychology." Unpublished manuscript.

Jaynes, J. Interview, undated. "Unedited and Abbreviated Julian Jaynes Interview." New Media Associates.

Jaynes, J. 1976. *The Origin of Consciousness in the Breakdown of the Bicameral Mind*. Toronto: Houghton Mifflin.

Jaynes, J. 1983. "University of New Hampshire Audio Tape." April 28. UPEI Julian Jaynes Collection.

Jaynes, J. 1986a. "Consciousness and the Voices of the Mind." *Canadian Psychology*, 27, 128–139.

Jaynes, J. 1986b. "How Old is Consciousness?" In R. Caplan (ed.), *Exploring the Concept of Mind*. Iowa City: University of Iowa Press.

Jaynes, J. 1988. "Harvard Audio Tape." December 3. UPEI Julian Jaynes Collection.

Keen, S. 1977. "Julian Jaynes: Portrait of the Psychologist as a Maverick Theorizer." *Psychology Today*, 11, 66–77.

Leo, J. 1977. "The Lost Voices of the Gods." *Time Magazine*, March 14, 51–53.

Randall, J.H. 1960. *Aristotle*. New York, NY: Columbia University Press.

Rhodes, R. 1978. "Alone In The Country of The Mind: When Did Humans Begin Thinking?" *Quest*, January/February, 71–78.

PART IV

The Origin of Religion

CHAPTER 9

The Oracles and Their Cessation

A Tribute to Julian Jaynes

DAVID C. STOVE

IN THE 5th CENTURY B.C. in Greece, and again in Europe in
the 18th century A.D., there was a period of what historians call
Enlightenment. They mean by this that religion then lost the
undisputed sway which it normally exercises over human life.
Such periods are rare, but when they do come, they come with a
strange easiness. People like Voltaire or Euripides are no one's
idea of profound thinkers, and yet, in scarcely more than a
generation, the immortal gods succumb to their attacks as meekly
as dew to the sun.

Partly for this reason it is a great mystery, to the people of the
Enlightenment, how it was that religion had acquired its hold
over human life in the first place. How did an incubus so easily
dislodged ever get into the driver's seat, and occupy it unchal-
lenged for so long? A question to be asked, indeed.

For Enlightenment critics, there are only two answers to it
(broadly speaking) that anyone has ever been able to think of.
One is the imposition theory: that religion is a racket. The other

First published in *Encounter*, April 1989, Vol. 72. Reprinted in *Cricket Versus
Republicanism and Other Essays*, 1995, J. Franklin and R.J. Stove (eds.), Sydney:
Quakers Hill Press. Reprinted with permission.

is the madness theory: that religion is a form of insanity. Of course there have been many variants of each of these two broad theories. The 19th century, for example, furnished a Marxist variant of the imposition theory, and the 20th a Freudian variant of the madness theory.

Unfortunately, all of the known variants of either theory are nearly worthless. The two theories are genuinely at odds with one another: a madman can hardly be a successful racketeer, or even a source of profit for racketeers. The trouble is that each theory is also at odds with most of the facts. In the history of Christianity, say, or of Islam, there is not much more madness than there is in the history of everything else. In fact a religion, once it has gained wide currency, usually acts as a support of *sanity*: religious people are actually less likely to be mad, or at least go mad, than people of the Enlightenment. Likewise there is little, if any, more racketeering in the history of religion than there is in the history of everything else; and a religious person is distinctly less likely to be a racketeer than an Enlightened person is.

The result is that, to heirs of the Enlightenment such as myself, the reasons for the very existence of religion have remained an absolute mystery. Nor is this a minor matter: not to understand religion is, quite simply, not to understand nine-tenths of human history. There is no mystery about why there is farming or industry, why there is instruction of the young, why there is architecture, medicine, or law. But the most salient fact of all human history is this: that all those things, and many others, have almost always been suffused through-and-through with religion, and subordinated to it. All right: but why does religion exist?

This is the question of questions concerning *Homo sapiens*. And I want to commend — and argue with — a book published some dozen years ago which to my mind comes closer to answering that question than everything else I have read about the matter put together. Its author is Julian Jaynes, a psychologist at

Princeton University. The book is *The Origin of Consciousness in the Breakdown of the Bicameral Mind*. The weight of original thought in it is so great that it makes me uneasy for the author's well-being: the human mind is not built to support such a burden. I would not be Julian Jaynes if they paid me a thousand dollars an hour.

Religion is not at all the only thing which Jaynes's book is intended to throw light on: though it is, I think, where he is most successful. Among the other subjects of the book are poetry, song, music, "possession," hypnotism, and schizophrenia. Above all his theory is, as the title of the book implies, a theory of the origin of consciousness. Jaynes has the extraordinary idea that consciousness — by which he does not mean intelligence, or learning-capacity, or anything like that, but self-scanning, inner life, *self*-consciousness — is new. Biologically new, in that it is no older than *Homo sapiens*; and even historically new, in that it began only at some time in the 2nd millennium B.C.

Until that time, Jaynes thinks, we were what he calls "bicameral": meaning by this that the right hemisphere of our brains had a certain function — a function of supreme importance which it does not now have. Namely, it was the source of *the voices of dead rulers*, hallucinated by the living. The architecture of early civilized men, Jaynes argues, and above all their burial-practices, can be understood on only one supposition: that the voice of a recently-dead ruler was *still heard*, and *still carried authority*.

These hallucinated voices were the germs, Jaynes thinks, of both religion and civilization. They furnished our first ideas of gods, and they also made possible, for the first time, social control out of earshot, and hence large, organized human groups. We all knew, in those days, what to do, because at every turn a god told us what to do. Indeed, it seemed to us that it was really the god who did it: just as, in the *Iliad*, whatever is done is done not by Achilles (say) or Agamemnon, but by some god. In bicameral men, Jaynes says, this authoritative voice "was volition." We were mere intelligent automata: simply some two-legged livestock which the gods happened to own. We were all permanently hypnotized; or, more accurately, schizophrenic.

This state of mind was brought to an end, in the 2nd millennium B.C., by some catastrophe: Jaynes hints at a catastrophe of extraterrestrial origin, but he is exceedingly vague about the whole matter. Anyway, as a result of this event, whatever it was, the hallucinated voices grew fainter; or multiple and therefore confusing; or audible only after elaborate induction-procedures (of prayer, or purification, etc.); or audible only to persons of a specialized caste (priests, prophets, etc.); or audible only at special places favored by gods (temples, oracles, etc.); and they finally fell silent altogether. This is "the breakdown of the bicameral mind."

Inner life begins. The world of the *Iliad* gives way to the world of the *Odyssey*. We think of the world of the *Iliad* as a *cruel* world, but even a little reflection suffices to show that is not really right: while there is much slaughter in the *Iliad*, there is very little cruelty. The real foreignness of that world consists, rather, in this: that it has absolutely nothing in it, except a plentiful supply of gods, plus assorted hardware — boats, armor, weapons — and men who have little more inner life than their helmets do. Odysseus, on the other hand, is just like you and me: ducking and diving, doing the best he can. He is always inwardly scanning alternative possibilities, both of action and belief, and he has to settle on just one of them for himself *without authority*. He has to, because natural authority, internalized authority, has now vanished from human life. For the first time, the possibility of *duplicity* has come into the world, with the mountain of consequences — psychological, moral, and political — which that entails. The priceless gift, and crushing burden, of consciousness has arrived.

Sources of Error

This is, as far as I know, that rarest of things: an absolutely original idea. It is also an idea of most various and far-reaching consequences. Kepler, looking back at what he had done in astronomy, once said: "I have touched mountains: it is amazing, what they give forth." Jaynes must have felt something like that, as his theory unfolded its consequences before his mind; and I think he was entitled to feel so.

He touches, at greater or less length, on a staggering number and variety of subjects, concerning which his theory has implications or suggestions that are not obvious at once. For example, the sound of ancient Greek poetry; the rhythm of "speaking in tongues"; the tirelessness of schizophrenics; the origin of moral evil; the "invisible playmates" of childhood; aristocratic ethics; and hundreds more. There must be others which he does not touch on at all: for example, his theory clearly ought to deliver something about that great weapon of Enlightenment, and peculiarity of conscious life, *humor*. Whatever topics he does touch, Jaynes almost always leaves on me the impression of someone who has got hold of a powerful new insight into human life and history. Several contemporary reviewers of the book compared Jaynes's theory with Freudianism; but, although this is saying very little, it is certainly a great deal better than that.

At the same time it will be obvious, even from the lightning-sketch which I have given of it, that his theory labors from the start under heavy objections. For one thing, it offends our ideas of evolutionary continuity by requiring us to suppose that consciousness suddenly appeared in *Homo sapiens*, without being foreshadowed by anything at all in our pre-human ancestors. There are, of course, variants of current evolutionary theory which postulate a certain amount of "jumpiness" in evolution; but (as the man said about the shaggy dog) not *that* damned jumpy.

To this objection, Jaynes replies indirectly but well (especially on pp. 379–403). Suppose, he says, that consciousness were not, as he thinks it is, a recent, superficial, and *learned* capacity: suppose it were ancient, organic, anchored in our pre-human forebears. In that case it could not possibly be *turned off*, with ridiculous ease, by an authoritative voice whose instructions are then obeyed with a docility and completeness to which conscious life affords no parallel. Yet exactly that is what happens in hypnotism a thousand times every day.

This reply quite turns the tables, it seems to me, on the objection from continuity. In fact the whole of Jaynes's chapter on hypnotism is extremely important. But there is an even more serious, and even more obvious, objection to his theory.

The human brain is the most complicated bit of matter known to exist; yet Jaynes asks us to believe that some particular external event, which could hardly affect directly either our brains or our genes, brought about, in a few generations, a major change in our brain-functions. Now that is logically possible, of course, but it *sounds*, at least, like magic, or a miracle. What means are there, what mechanisms, by which such a cause could possibly bring about such an effect?

Jaynes's reply to this fundamental objection, or the closest he comes to replying to it, is on pages 122–125. He appeals to the immense surplus-capacity of the human brain, and to its extreme "plasticity": that is, the ease with which, in certain circumstances, a function located in one hemisphere of the brain can be transferred to the other, if its normal *locus* is damaged or diseased or surgically removed.

This reply seems to me not only inadequate, but hardly even relevant. What was questioned was not the likelihood of one brain-function, x, being transferred from one hemisphere to the other. It was the likelihood of one brain-function, x, being extinguished, and a new one, y, being created (in whatever location), in a short time, by some external and nonrecurring cause. *That* is the fundamental and glaring offense which Jaynes's theory gives to our ideas of what is biologically likely. And he can do nothing, apparently, or least he *has* done nothing in this book, to palliate it. Nothing, except to show that, if such a thing *had* happened, an astounding number of otherwise mysterious facts would receive an explanation!

I have already compared Jaynes with Kepler, whom we remember with honor for his three laws of planetary motion, and for almost nothing else. But in Kepler's own eyes those laws were propositions of very subordinate importance. What he chiefly valued himself on was, rather, his marginally-sane speculations of a theologico-geometrical character: how God had spaced the planetary orbits so as to accommodate the five regular solids, etc. But it was perfectly easy to separate the three planetary laws from this context in which Kepler had embedded them, and to "throw away the wrapper," so to speak. And that is exactly what, in the Enlightenment, Kepler's editors did; and, surely, rightly did.

It is what I would like to do in Jaynes's case: to separate what is of permanent value in his theory (especially the part which relates to religion) from the context (which seems to me incredible) in which he embeds it. But while in Kepler's case it was easy to throw away the wrapper, I cannot see how to do it in Jaynes's case. In fact, I do not think anyone could do it. His theory fits together too well, despite the extreme heterogeneity of its materials: neurophysiological, archaeological, etymological, etc., etc.

But although I cannot see how to pare down or water down Jaynes's theory, I am certain that such a process is necessary. His theory is just too catastrophist, too external, too sharply dichotomous; he himself indirectly acknowledges this by various qualifications which he makes to it — not always consistently. I will give my reasons for saying this.

First, as I have said, I simply cannot see how micro-surgery could be performed on the human brain, in a short time, by some stray cosmic or geological blunt instrument (a Velikovskian comet, or whatever).

Then, as to the speed and the extent of the alleged change from bicamerality to consciousness, Jaynes wavers hopelessly. Bicamerality broke down in the 2nd millennium B.C., he says, and yet he also says that conscious Spaniards met bicameral Aztecs in Mexico in 1519 A.D. We ourselves are said to contain, and to be surrounded by, what he keeps calling "vestiges" of the bicameral mind; but these "vestiges" are, by Jaynes's account, so massive and ubiquitous that it is simply absurd to call them vestiges. Sometimes he even suggests that *no one* is yet more than half-way through the transition from bicamerality to consciousness. It is impossible to reconcile these various suggestions.

These are instances in which, obviously enough, Jaynes has been tripped up by his preference for brightly-colored and sharp-edged formulations. Another and a signal instance of the same fault is what he says about the *absolute* authoritativeness of the bicameral voices: for example (p. 202) that they "*were* man's volition." It is simply impossible to understand such a statement, taken literally.

Again, the theory is too dichotomous. It asks us to think of consciousness and hallucinated authoritative voices as two mutually-exclusive "control systems." Yet Jaynes is constantly obliged to acknowledge that the two systems can be mixed in various degrees in different individuals, and can alternate in the same individual. As to their alternating, I would offer the case of Socrates as decisive. He was usually conscious, I suppose, if ever a man was. Yet in addition to his occasional trances (one of which kept him standing motionless in the open air for 20 hours) he had his inner voice or *daimon* (his "divine sign," he called it), which on various occasions told him not to do something he had been about to do. Assuming that this "voice" was actually hallucinated by him, and was not a mere "as-it-were" voice, such a case seems sufficient on its own to show that Jaynes's favorite categories are too sharp-edged.

Or take the matter of duplicity. This is quite central for Jaynes:

he regards the capacity for deceit, along with the capabilities for disguise and for suicide, as a distinctive mark of conscious man. Yet he informs us that a female chimpanzee will sometimes pretend to be interested in sex with a male when her sole real interest is in stealing the banana he is carrying. Now, a Darwin, or even a Lorenz, might be able to point out some important differences between such cases and human duplicity. But Jaynes's attempt to distinguish between them (pp. 219–20) is weak.

These are some of the reasons why I cannot swallow Jaynes's theory whole: they could be summed up in the words: "too much drama." Yet his theory is so persuasive, at least as far as religion is concerned, that — as I have indicated — I hanker after a less lurid version of it, a "sub-theory" of his theory. Such a sub-theory might still have consciousness being as recent and superficial as Jaynes thinks it is, and might still have consciousness coming in because of social control by hallucinated divine voices was going out. But I cannot actually carve out such a sub-theory from Jaynes's theory: there are just too many connecting fibers in it, running in every direction, for me to be able to see where the surgery could begin with any hope of success.

I should add, however, that even if we had such a sub-theory, there would still be a good reason for being very suspicious of it. For any recognizable sub-theory of Jaynes's would still have, like its parent, the suspicious feature that it invites us to do something we are only too prone to do — I mean, to deny or doubt or minimize the inner life of others.

That dogs can even feel pain, let alone have beliefs or the like, was denied by Descartes and his followers. That women have souls was denied (or so at least I have often read) by certain Muslim philosophers. Mao's China, whatever we may have consciously thought of it, really *seemed* to be a society of human ants, did it not? During World War II we were encouraged, and needed little encouragement, to believe that Japanese soldiers and airmen were intelligent automata. (The Japanese are a hard case even now for us, apparently including Jaynes: on page 159 he actually hints that the Emperor Hirohito *was* bicameral.) In many cases, as children turn into adolescents, their parents seem to them to turn into mere livestock. If we come across an adult fellow-citizen who cannot read silently, we get a sudden twinge of doubt as to whether he has an inner life at all; and this despite the fact that reading silently is an accomplishment so recent, and so inessential to conscious life, that it is entirely unknown throughout classical antiquity.

Now, I ask you: when we know we are so prone to this mistake, even when we are in a position to avoid it, how can we trust ourselves to conclude, with the confidence that Jaynes does, that Hammurabi and Achilles had little or no inner life? How much do we know about Hammurabi or Achilles? It is true (and it is Jaynes's starting-point) that they make on us an impression of almost inexpressible foreignness. It is further true, and it is part of Jaynes's achievement to have shown, that their foreignness is in many respects uncannily like the foreignness of the schizophrenic or the deeply-hypnotized person. But it is impossible for us, situated as we are, to be rationally confident that we have here *knowledge of the absence* of inner life, and not just another humdrum case of the *absence of knowledge* of inner life.

It is an old observation (at least as old as Descartes) that if you look down from a tall building at people in the street, you get an illusion of looking at automata. No doubt this is connected with the unique importance of the face (cf. Jaynes's pp. 120–22). But distance in time, assisted as it nearly always is by ignorance, also tends to produce the same illusion. Everyone who has read a lot of history must have noticed this fact, and since Jaynes's theory *must* receive illicit help from this familiar source of error, he ought to have done a good deal to "discount" for it. But he does nothing at all.

Voices of the Dead

Jaynes's book — although I can neither accept his overall theory, nor separate out of it, as a sub-theory, his treatment of religion — throws more light on religion than everything else I have read on that subject. My position is therefore an unsatisfactory one, to put it mildly. Since I cannot see how to get out of it, I will try instead to draw others into it. That is, I will try to convey something of the extraordinary power of Jaynes's treatment of religion. He sees the problem, in all its scope and strangeness, and he never loses sight of it. Why *should* almost all human history be a tale of "the slow withdrawing tide of divine voices and presences," and of ever-renewed attempts, through prophets or poetry or peyote or whatever, to establish contact with "a lost ocean of authority" (p. 320)? This is the question of questions concerning our species.

Does it seem only a slight merit, to see this problem and never lose sight of it? It should not, because in fact it is an enormous merit, which scarcely anyone ever achieves. Of course it is only Enlightenment people who can see the problem of religion at all. But most of us, though we can see it, cannot keep it before our minds for more than a few minutes together, however hard we try. The fact of religion is so gigantic, and at the same time so incomprehensible, that it utterly daunts and depresses the Enlightenment mind. So we put it out of our thoughts.

If we are going to think at all, it will be about some smaller and less intractable mystery: of philosophy, or physics, or whatever it might be. So strong is the temptation to put religion out of our minds that no one can be blamed for surrendering to it. And yet to put aside religion is to put aside nine-tenths of human history. Jaynes is the only person I know of who, while not believing one word of religion — or one syllable, or letter — sees it in its true proportions, and steadily.

Jaynes is also completely devoid of Enlightenment superciliousness. Cicero says that, even in his time, it was impossible for
two augurs to meet without smiling: yet Jaynes expounds even
augury from the entrails of animals so seriously and sympatheti-
cally that both our ridicule and our disgust fade away. Jokes or
sneers at the expense of religion were the stock-in-trade, in differing degrees, to Bayle, Diderot, Voltaire, Hume, and even
Kant; still less can ordinary Enlightened people resist them. But
Jaynes is as free from levity as he is from credulity. This is an
inestimable merit. If it were objected that religion *is* ridiculous
and disgusting. Jaynes's reply would be, I suppose, that schizophrenics are too; but that jokes and sneers are not a way to understanding, or a sign of understanding, in the one case any more
than in the other.

Jaynes is more immune than any other thinker I know of to
the great temptation which besets the Enlightened when they
study religion. This is to let our disbelief and distaste affect the
very data of our study, so that we translate a certain crucial word,
or describe a certain religious practice or artifact, in some way
which subtly "rationalizes" religion: makes it appear less foreign
to our own minds than it really is.

He mentions many cases in which this has in fact happened,
especially in the translation of early writings. I will mention only
one of these examples, and even that one in a hypothetical case.
Suppose that we are studying a long-vanished society, and that
our excavations have turned up a large statue, and also thousands
of clay figurines of the same shape as the statue. We cannot
believe that this statute *is* the god So-and-So, and therefore
cannot imagine anyone else believing it either. Still less can we
believe, or even believe that these ancient people believed, that
each of the thousand figurines *is also* the god So-and-So. As a
result, although it may be quite clear from all the evidence that
the statue, and also each of the figurines, *was* the god So-and-So,
we are almost certain to describe them as a statue and figurines *of*

the god. In this way, by one tiny word, we launch an enormous error; and one which will only carry us further astray, the further we carry our researches. Yet we went wrong precisely because we were rational.

This ironic and even tragic propensity of the Enlightenment, to distort the very data of the history of religion, is so deep-rooted that there are limits to what anyone can do to guard against it. Between the religious frame of mind and the Enlightened one, there is a difference, which nothing can overcome, of perspective or dimension: like that between a boy of six and a man of sixty, or between beings of three spatial dimensions (like ourselves), and beings (supposing there were any) of two dimensions. Still, in many particular cases, something *can* be done to prevent this impassable gulf from being papered over by the rationalizing tendency: Jaynes has shown by example that it can. Most of the Enlightened, by contrast, are not even aware that the gulf exists; and they rationalize religion, and tend to rationalize everything else in human life too, by a kind of fatal instinct. This is probably the reason for the general disorientation of the extremely Enlightened: the fact that a Bertrand Russell or an H.G. Wells, say, never understands anything of the life going on around him, or at any rate precious little compared with other people who have far less intelligence and information, but more religion.

More than anyone else I have read, Jaynes has the ability to bring the religion-saturated past to life. No doubt this ability owes something to his freedom from superciliousness, and his immunity to rationalizing; but I cannot fully explain how he does it. It is certainly not by any marked literary gifts: as a writer, Jaynes is nothing special (though he obviously sometimes thinks he is).

The opposite defects, in most Enlightened writers on religion, are obvious: they are unhistorical, abstract, monotonous. They must be so, because they bring to the study of religion only a very few categories, and those categories severely intellectual ones:

theism-atheism, for example, or polytheism-monotheism. If that kind of thing is the only equipment you have, then almost all of the historical actualities of religion are bound to slip through your net and out of your sight.

But Jaynes loses sight of none of these actualities. I know of nowhere but in this book that you can meet, for example, not only with gods who are statues, or divination by sortilege, but with oracles, sibyls, and muses, all brought to startling life — yes, even muses. ... Here are the very distortions of face and limbs which the priestess of the oracle undergoes, as she pronounces the god's response. Jaynes, like a new Pygmalion, breathes life into religion, whereas the glare of the ordinary Enlightenment mind bleaches all life and sense out of it.

As to how he does it, I can say this much: it is partly by reminding us that religion formerly suffused *everything*. Take poetry, for example. We flee from it now, as from some dull and distressful relative. An announcement that a poetry-reading is about to take place will empty a room quicker than a water-cannon. Support for poets is a minor responsibility of the Minister for the Arts. Yet the professional reciters of Homeric poems were, to their contemporaries, precious vessels, in whom was preserved ancient knowledge of divine things. And Jaynes's theory has the beauty of implying that, in a sense, they really were so! So, in reading Jaynes, we undergo a *gestalt*-switch, and suddenly see once more, at least for awhile, that poetry might matter.

The book, however, is the very reverse of a junk-yard of religious actualities. It is systematic, and every historical exhibit is put in its proper historical place. Take demons, for example. Ignorant people of the Enlightenment often imagine that belief in demons is virtually coextensive with religion. The facts are that this belief was utterly unknown in early times, and that it reached its highest point only in the ripe civilization of the first two centuries A.D. — in the world of Lucian, Seneca, Petronius, and Apuleius. Jaynes's theory offers an explanation of both of these facts.

Or take the matter of prayer. We usually think of prayer as an inseparable part of religion. Jaynes argues very persuasively that it is, on the contrary, a late development: a result of receding gods, and dawning consciousness. The earliest accounts we can glean of the relation of men to gods seem positively to exclude the attitude — both the physical and the mental attitude — of prayer. And prayer is, after all, an attempt to elicit a response from gods who are silent and withdrawn, "in heaven." But the *first* gods, if Jaynes is right, were precisely not in heaven but with us; and always on the job, too. Hypnotized people do not pester the hypnotist with petitions, or with any expression of their will.

Jaynes has made a definite suggestion, where no one else had a single thing to offer. To explain what I mean, I quote some lines which I wrote a year before coming across his book:

Hegel held that animals have no religion, but as against that, Darwin (and others before him) said that, to a dog, its master is a god. If this is true, it is to the credit of canine intelligence, since the evidence for this theism is obvious and overwhelming. But where is the evidence for *our* belief that *we* are somebody's cattle? What is there, that could even have rationally first suggested this belief to our minds? Of course we might *be* somebody's cattle *and* have no evidence that we are; but that is only a trivial truth of logic. The question is, what on earth, or in the sky, or in the sea, could have given the cleverest species of animals on earth reason to believe that it is not the cleverest? That it ranks only third, or tenth (or whatever subordinate degree your religion assigns us to), in the order of intelligent beings. I have never met with a satisfactory answer to this question, or even with a promising answer. In that sense, religious belief is unintelligible to me.[1]

Hallucinated authoritative voices are at least *an* answer to the question I asked; whereas my previous reading and reflection had left me unable to suggest any answer whatever. Of course, I had been looking in all the wrong places — "on earth, or in the sky, or in the sea." In never occurred to me to look inwards, so to speak. Still, I do not now feel that I ought to have thought of Jaynes's answer myself. When Huxley first read *The Origin of Species* he exclaimed, "How extremely stupid not to have thought of that!"; and there was a good deal of justice in this self-reproach. But Jaynes's theory, though it may not be as good as Darwin's, is about ten times more original than Darwin was.

Jaynes has not only an answer, but a promising answer, to the question *why* there is religion. For a start: hallucinated authoritative voices are at least a *vera causa*. Does this seem not much? Yet it is enough on its own to put such voices miles ahead of most of the other candidates: gods themselves, visitors from outer space, "astral bodies," ghosts, Freudian god-knows-whats, and Jungian not-even-god-knows-whats? We *know* that such voices exist, and that they can control behavior. We also know that they sometimes have momentous consequences, both for the hearer of them and for those who are only told of them by the hearer: as for example in the case of Joan of Arc.

The burial-practices of early civilized men do seem to compel the conclusion that a lately-dead king was still heard, and heard as king. Nor were those practices confined to burials of rulers: they sometimes extended to other social superiors, and even to ordinary parents. All of these are people who, if they "spoke" at all after death, would speak with authority.

Moreover, there would be a kind of rationality in obeying such voices. Is there anything inherently irrational in carrying out the instructions of someone you know is dead? Not at all, unless our whole practice of making and respecting a "last will and testament" is irrational — a conclusion which some of the hardier spirits of the Enlightenment did not shrink from drawing. But even if they were right, it would seem to be still more irrational to disregard the instructions of an acknowledged authority, if you are in fact still "hearing" those instructions. Border collies make wonderfully clever sheep-dogs; but one which would obey all voice-instructions for a week, through (say) a tape-recorder fitted to his head, while the Shepard relaxed in town — would not this dog be a pearl beyond price, a Border collie far more rational than even the average of his breed?

Jaynes's theory of religion is already, I trust, appearing in the light of a promising one. But easily the most important point in its favor (though one not made by Jaynes) is this: that hallucinated sound is a cause of the very kind which is needed to explain religion. For consider: Religious beliefs are not arrived at by any complex intellectual process, or by anything which would ordinarily be recognized as reasoning. (If religion did require reasoning, most people would never arrive at it at all.) Quite the contrary: religious beliefs spring up spontaneously, and with irresistible force, almost everywhere in the soil of humanity. And yet, for the Enlightened, they are all false. What is required, then, in order to explain religion, is something which, first, is delusive, and second, has an immediate sensory quality, available and familiar to all.

Now, that is a very improbable combination. Immediate sensory experience, in any species, is for the most part *not* delusive. (The evolutionary reason is obvious: a species would have a poor chance of surviving if its sensory data were as likely as not to be delusive.) It is the improbability of this combination which makes it so very hard to think of *any* rational explanation of religion. But one thing which does exemplify the required combinations of delusiveness with sensory immediacy is *hallucinated sound*.

Surely this is a very striking circumstance? Of course, it would not count for much if we could easily think of half-a-dozen other things which combine immediacy with delusiveness, and which might have served to suggest our first idea of gods. But can we? I have not been able to think of even one other. If other people cannot think of any either, and if it is agreed that an immediate sensory base is required to explain religion, then Jaynes's theory is running in a one-horse race.

Even if Jaynes is altogether wrong about the voices of the dead, he seems to me to have picked out the right sense-modality for religion: hearing. Contact by touch with gods has hardly ever been so much as thought of. Visual contact with gods is seldom ever claimed, at any time, and even when such claims are made, nothing in religion, or at any rate curiously little, ever seems to depend on them. But any auditory contact with a god would be likely to be a very serious matter indeed. One reason for this is pointed out by Jaynes: that hearing is peculiarly "mandatory." You can do extremely little in the way of escaping sound, and certainly nothing which corresponds to turning your head away, or closing your eyes, in the case of vision. And hallucinated sound, of course, is mandatory absolutely: you cannot even turn the volume down. That is why such sound, even in the form of mere "ringing" and the like, constitutes a terrible affliction when it is loud and constant.

But there is an even more important reason, not adverted to by Jaynes, why auditory contact with a god would be likely to be momentous: namely, that such contact would furnish the only opportunity to learn what the god commands. *Authority* is (as Jaynes insists) of the essence of religion, yet, until the invention of writing, it is hearing alone which can receive imperative messages, or any normative message at all. If you want to inform someone of something, you can do it either through his vision or his hearing: show your guest where the toilet is, or tell him where it is. But if you want to get someone to *do* something, you *must* go through his sense of hearing. Imagine the command-system in an army where all the soldiers were deaf, or all the officers were dumb. Before the invention of writing, any scene, any visual display, is normatively impotent: it cannot tell you what is to be done, or even that anything at all is to be done. You simply cannot convey to the eye the idea of "to be done." Any picture of a man doing something might mean "Do as the man in this picture does," or "If you do as this man does I will kill you," or "Don't you think this would make a nice wallpaper pattern?", or any one of a million things.

For this reason, I think that Jaynes must be right, at least in thinking that social control originally depended on the sense of hearing. That religion is *the* medium of social control among early civilized men is certain. Together, these two facts give us a strong connection between religion and hearing. And then, out of earshot, social control *via* the sense of hearing could only be hallucinatory, unless or until it was exercised through moral beliefs and a sense of responsibility: two telltale marks, Jaynes would say, of conscious life.

Religion springs up spontaneously *almost* everywhere: not everywhere. Whether a society of atheists could subsist was a question debated often and urgently during the Enlightenment. By about 1880, it has been decided in the affirmative by the "anthropologists" (as they were then beginning to be called). But the question had also by then lost the political urgency which it had had for Europe in the 18th century; for it had turned out that religionless societies, though they exist all right, are all extremely primitive. Whether a *civilization* can subsist without religion would have been a better question; and it was, presumably, the one which was often really intended.

To *this* question, all the evidence points to a negative answer, and always has pointed that way. That a civilization has never *originated*, at least, without a religion, has long been known. That civilizations decay with the decay of religion, though not so certain, is well-confirmed. All this was acknowledged even by the Enlightenment's bitterest and deepest critic of religion, David Hume, who wrote: "Look for a people entirely devoid of religion. If you find them at all, be assured that they are but a few degrees removed from brutes."[2] This is true, but it comes very oddly from Hume. In particular, it ought to have moderated the satisfaction with which he looked forward to what he called "the downfall of some of the prevailing systems of superstition."[3] (But then Hume died in 1776, thirteen years before the balloon went up.) Anyway, if it is a fact that civilization arises, flourishes, and decays with religion, it is a fact for which Hume did not have the faintest glimmer of an explanation. But Jaynes does have an explanation: that hallucinated authoritative voices are the germ *both* of religion and of cities.

The Special Place

On religion, then, Jaynes's merits, all of them rare and some of them unique, are these. (1) He sees the problem and never loses sight of it. (2) He is entirely free from Enlightenment-superciliousness. (3) He is immune to the temptation to rationalize religion. (4) He brings the religious past to life. (5) He has a definite theory of the origin of religion. (6) His theory has much in its favor, and most importantly the fact that it postulates an *immediate sensory* origin for religion: a respect in which it seems to have no rival-theory. But the power of Jaynes's treatment of religion will, perhaps, be brought out better by the following two examples than by any list of its general merits.

Jonathan Sumption, in his valuable book *Pilgrimage*,[4] mentions that in the Middle Ages, pilgrimage sometimes became so popular, and hence so profitable to the favored places, that competition arose among the shrines — and, as a natural consequence, advertising. It has to be given out that *your* shrine delivered more or bigger miracles than its main competition, even if both of them should be, for example (a thing which could easily happen), shrines of Our Lady. A certain French monk who was attached to Coutances Cathedral published a book to prove that the Blessed Mary of Coutances was indeed superior to the Blessed Mary of Bayeux, and that to doubt this was not only weak-minded but dangerous:

> He points, for example, to the fate of Vitalis, a Norman who had come to the "insipid conclusion" that "the Blessed Mary of Bayeux and the Blessed Mary of Coutances were one and the same person, that is, the mother of God; and that consequently the Virgin of Coutances could not possibly be more merciful or more powerful than the Virgin of Bayeux." Vitalis accordingly refused to accompany his fellow-villagers on a mass pilgrimage to Coutances, for which the Virgin severely chastised him.

This is very good Enlightenment history, beautifully and amusingly done. But the aftertaste of it is extremely unpleasant, because it makes us despair more than ever of humankind. Vitalis, who was a monk of the 11th–12th centuries, had reasoned, for perhaps once in his life, like a rational being; and for this atrocious offense, the Virgin herself condescends to punish him! How *can* any Christian believe that the Blessed Mary of Coutances is superior to the Blessed Mary of Bayeux? But then, of course, this same mystery about identity runs through almost all religion. How can each of a thousand figurines *be* the god So-and-So? How can the Son and the Holy Ghost be distinct from one another, yet each identical with the Father? It is enough to make anyone despair; or else smile wearily and put the whole impossible business out of his mind.

But now see how one tiny touch of Jaynes loosens the logjam. Schizophrenics, it has been found (pp. 390–91), have an odd kind of tolerance, in that they do not object to their own identity being (so to speak) scattered. For example, one of them may be convinced, say, that he is Napoleon; but if he is introduced to another who is convinced that *he* is Napoleon, what happens is — complete agreement! Each of the two stands by his own identity-claim; but each also acknowledges, with perfect equanimity, that the other person is Napoleon.

Even so amazing a fact as this does not, of course, explain how a Christian can believe that Our Lady of Coutances is superior to Our Lady of Bayeux. Indeed, it does not explain anything. But it at least irresistibly suggests that there is a fault which is common to the religious and the schizophrenic, and where the fault lies. It seems to lie in their logical faculty, and more specifically in the logic-of-identity department.

There are various logical laws of identity. One of them is the symmetry law: that if x is identical with y, then y is identical with x. Another is the transitivity law: that if x is identical with y, and y is identical with z, then x is identical with z. A third law, which follows from those two, has no standard name, but might be called the no-scatter law: if x is identical with y, and z is identical with y, then x is identical with z. It is this law which seems peculiarly likely to fall into abeyance among both the religious and the schizophrenic. Could there be a particular cerebral locus on which compliance with this law depends, so that it is impaired if that part of the brain is imperfect, diseased, or damaged? The idea naturally suggests itself; although it does not sit very easily with the fact that any logical law must be something which is called into play everywhere, and all the time.[5]

Jaynes's theory (I hope it is unnecessary to say) is a variant of the madness theory of religion. Could it be that nearly every human being ever born has been mad? Some philosophers have, directly or by implication, ridiculed this suggestion as being logically impossible. I think that it is not only logically possible, but the actual truth; and Jaynes's theory implies no less. Of course, a word as simple and shocking as "madness" inspires all sorts of superficial objections. But once we start to assemble the telling details, such as a fault in identity-logic which is common to the religious and the schizophrenic, we can easily afford to give up that word, while having more reason than ever to think that we had been on the right track with it all along.

My second good example of Jaynes at work is his section (pp. 321–31) on the oracles of ancient Greece. In this case, as in every other case in the history of religion, the hardest thing to do is simply to see the facts steadily, and not be blinded by Enlightenment superciliousness or rationalism. This is especially difficult in the case of the oracles, because here we have 2,000 years of those obstacles to contend with. For the oracles gradually fell silent during the last century B.C. and the 1st century A.D. No one quite knows why, though many theories were canvassed at the time or soon after. (You can find some of these discussed by Plutarch, in his essay on the cessation of the oracles.)

The facts, or at any rate some of them, are these. For most of a thousand years, all Greece believed implicitly in the oracles, and, at least for the most part, accepted what the oracles said. Every question which a government found too hard, or which a group, or a private person, found too hard, was referred to an oracle, whether it was a question of fact or of policy, or a question of what was going to happen. The answer, at least in the period and at the places we know most of, was given *at once*, by a priest, or more often a priestess, who spoke for the god and was at the time "possessed" by the god: *plena deo*, "full of the god."

Cases of manipulation were not absolutely unknown, but only the most unteachable rationalist will suppose that they were typical. In the vast majority of cases, as in the very famous one which I shall mention, no one knew what the god was going to say. I cannot emphasize too strongly that *all* Greece believed in the oracles. Even at the height of the Greek Enlightenment, in the second half of the 5th century B.C., the oracles retained their full authority. With Socrates, and his many disciples and companions, the Homeric gods were very largely a joke — and, they considered, a disgraceful joke at that. But their skepticism did not extend to the oracles: quite the reverse. The Socrates who has meant so much to all later generations, and who changed the course of philosophy, was not the youthful Socrates: he was merely a student of mainstream Milesian science — physics, astronomy, biology. No, the Socrates who matters is the middle-aged and the old Socrates, who was an entirely different person. This was a man who haunted public places in search of knowledge, letting the air into democratic windbags, religious maniacs from the suburbs, professional immoralists, and the taxpayers generally. He spent his later life, as Sacco and Vanzetti said they spent their earlier life, "talking to scorning men on street corners"; and he met with the same fate as they did.

Now, what was it that transformed Socrates's life? Why, this: a friend of his took it upon himself to ask the Oracle at Delphi whether there was in Greece anyone wiser than Socrates, and received the reply that there was not. News of this hit Socrates like a thunderbolt. He knew himself to be ignorant, but then he also knew that the god could not lie or be mistaken. Therefore there *had* to be some unobvious sense in which the words of the god were to be understood. And finally, though only after a long and frustrating search, Socrates hit upon his famous and seminal interpretation: that many other people thought they knew something, but did not, while he alone knew that he knew nothing. So the god had spoken truly, after all!

These facts are as certain as anything in all antiquity: they are drawn from Socrates's speech when on trial for his life, as recounted by his disciple Plato shortly after the trial took place. Judge from them the depth of Socrates's trust in the Oracle of Apollo at Delphi: and, *a fortiori*, the authority which the oracles possessed among people who were not, as he was, at the forefront of the Enlightenment. And, from the insuperable difficulty which *we* have in taking these facts seriously, judge how disabling Enlightenment attitudes are. ...

In the 5th century, then, the oracles retained the position in Greek life which they possessed for the two preceding centuries. Their overall history, as Jaynes relates it, was in outline as follows.

At first there is just a certain *place*, usually distinguished by striking natural features, but with no people at all attached to it. Anyone who goes there can "hear" the god. (One of these "direct" oracles survived to a very late date.) Then there is a stage in which a priest or priestess is always present, but not "possessed" by the god: they are merely people who can "hear" the god when others cannot. Later again come the "classic" priests and priestesses, they of the distorted mouths and limbs, in some mental state characterized by extreme diminution of consciousness, and induced by elaborate preparations. Later still, a second class of persons appears: interpreters, not themselves possessed, but needed in order to explain the increasingly difficult utterances of the possessed. Then the answers gradually become impossible for anyone to make head or tail of; and finally no sound at all can be elicited, and the place becomes deserted.

It is, I think, only the first third of this sequence which might be seriously wrong: the second two-thirds of it seem to be pretty much agreed on by all authorities. Naturally, I do not know whether Jaynes is right about the first third. But if he is right, and even if he is right only about the very first stage — that is, if the oracles were all at first *direct* ones — then this theory of religion is powerfully confirmed.

For consider. Originally the god can be heard only at special places; then only by special people even there; then by even those people only when they are in a special and induced state; then only with the help of a second class of specialists to interpret what is said; and finally even all these piled-up specialisms are not enough. If this is indeed the history of the oracles, it scarcely admits of any other explanation than Jaynes's one: namely, that earlier still, *everyone* had been able to hear a divine voice *anywhere*, and that this capacity became progressively rarer, and progressively harder to exercise even by those who still possessed it.

Restoring the Oracles

Jaynes would have the whole of religion hang by the single slender thread of hallucinated voices. I do not believe that it can support so great a weight. The experience of hallucinating a voice seems, somehow, too special; and also too rare, even where, by the theory, it ought to be still rather common. Jaynes acknowledges that even those people who in childhood had an "invisible playmate" did not in general hallucinate the speech of the invisible one. Most people, as far as I know, never in their lives hallucinate a voice; certainly I never have. The nearest I have come to it is that once, for a few days after a beloved dog died, I "heard" around the place the familiar clinking of the metal parts of her collar.

There are whole huge parts or aspects of religion which do not figure at all in Jaynes's theory. One is what I do not shrink from calling the Velikovskian-astronomical part: for I am enough of an admirer of the late Immanuel Velikovsky to agree with him that the best explanation of the belief in planetary "wars in heaven," of the fear of comets, etc., is — wars in heaven. But here, of course, Jaynes would say in his own defense that planetary gods, being in heaven, must be a *late* religious development. And indeed it must be admitted that to mistake what we call Mars and Venus for gods would seem to presuppose a degree of scientific knowledge, or at least of disinterested curiosity, which is not easily ascribed to a very early stage of human history.

Then, even more importantly, there is nothing at all in

Jaynes's theory about the "Anaximandrian" or developmental aspect of religion. I have in mind Anaximander's justly famous observation, that the helplessness of the young is both more extreme and more prolonged in humans than in any other animal: a fact of which the implications are still unexhausted, despite 2,600 years since it was first pointed out. Surely this fact must have *something* rather important to do with religion; although, no doubt, not merely infantile life, but intra-uterine life, needs to be taken into account. If we absolutely had to choose between an historical or once-and-for-all explanation of religion, such as Jaynes's, and an explanation of it solely in terms of the biological development of every individual, Jaynes's way would be, in my opinion, the right way to go. But it is obvious enough that we do not have to make such a choice: there is nothing to stop a theory of religion being mainly historical but partly developmental. (In fairness I must add that, somewhere in this book, Jaynes refers to another book which he was then preparing, on the development of consciousness in children; but I do not know whether that book ever appeared.)

Those are two very large gaps in any theory of religion. But I must say that, looking over what I have written here, my strongest impression is, not how much Jaynes has left out, but of how little I have managed to convey of what he put in. If you think of Bach's *St. Matthew Passion* played on a tin whistle, and then think of it played and sung properly, you will have a fair idea of the difference between my account of Jaynes on religion, and Jaynes on religion.

The trouble is that nothing I could write would ever have more than ordinary Enlightenment merits of being sane, clear, and consequential. Jaynes, by contrast, though an Enlightenment man, has tapped such deep and long-forgotten sources, and given them such a flood of utterance, that, having done so, he is no longer an ordinary Enlightenment man like the rest of us.

He hardly could be. For he has, in a manner, restored the oracles after their long cessation: a work of Hercules, which could not possibly have been performed by the intellect alone, or be limited in its effects to the intellect alone.

NOTES TO CHAPTER 9

1. This quotation is from my essay "Idealism: A Victorian Horror-Story," published by Bradford Books/MIT Press, in my collection *Cole Porter and Karl Popper, and other Reputations Reconsidered.*
2. "The Natural History of Religion," in *David Hume, The Philosophical Works* (ed. Green and Grose, London, 1882), vol. 4, p. 361. Hume actually wrote, not "Look for," but "Look out for." But since the latter would now be apt to be misunderstood as "Beware," I have omitted the word "out."
3. These words are attributed to Hume by his best friend Adam Smith, in an account which he published of Hume's last days. See vol. 3, p. 9, of *David Hume, The Philosophical Works.*
4. Sumption, 1975.
5. I cannot forbear mentioning the following curious fact. I have elsewhere shown, in something which was written well before I had heard of Jaynes, that this very same law of identity is characteristically in abeyance among *another* class of persons: namely, those philosophers who are, in the technical sense of the word, idealists. Philosophical idealism has always, of course, been an offspring of religion, and has even been generally recognized as such.

PART V

Ancient Civilizations

CHAPTER 10

The Meaning of King Tut

JULIAN JAYNES

I THINK THAT THE treasures of Tutankhamun recently
exhibited throughout North America have been grossly
misunderstood. Our fallacy is to think that ancient peoples are
like ourselves. We assume that their minds worked the way our
minds do, that pharaohs had themselves mummied up in
fabulous pyramids out of a selfish yearning for immortality,
carved in effigy out of an elaborate pride, and consciously called
themselves divine out of peaking ambition. To think so is to drag
these objects through the mire of our own neurotic interiorizations.

Part of the reason for this misunderstanding was in the exhibit
itself. The particular items were presented to us like modern
pieces of art — separate, pedestaled, spot lit, emphasizing their
astonishing technology, making us wonder who did them, who
discovered them — and always in the busy midst of crowds, far
removed from the meant darkness of their hushed and difficult
context. We forget that these objects were not made to be viewed
by us, that the hieroglyphs were never intended to be read, that
the great gold mummy mask of the dead king, probably by now
the most famous such artifact from antiquity, was not meant to be
seen, being sealed away in nests of coffins and shrines within
shrines and then buried in rubble.

Of these facts we must think. What *are* these pieces if we are not meant to look at them?

The key to this exhibit was not in the exhibit at all. It was back in the Valley of the Kings on the north wall of the burial chamber (see Figure 1). Here, just along the left side of where the entombed mummy once lay, is a life-size mural. The head end of the mummy was to the left and the feet came opposite to the second figure from the right. This second figure from the right is a depiction of the mummy as if it had just been stood up erect from where it lay and dressed as Osiris, the god of gods that each king becomes at what we call death.

Facing him and beyond alignment with the coffin itself is Tutankhamun's successor, Ay, caped in the sacramental leopard skin usual in such succession scenes. In his hand is a wrench-like prying instrument called an adze; another lies on the table beneath (note the difficulty with perspective). Just how these instruments were used — and we find them in other Egyptian funerary scenes of the New Kingdom — is not presently known. But the result of what Ay is doing is well known and described in hieroglyphics that translate as "The Opening of the Mouth" of Tutankhamun's mummy.

A strange phrase. And this curious phrase and ceremony was used with statues as well as mummies all over ancient Egypt. But it is not so strange to anyone remembering the history of a thousand miles to the east and a few centuries earlier. In the great city-states along the Tigris and Euphrates, gods were wooden statues or idols, elaborately dressed, jeweled, and anointed, which from time to time underwent a ceremony called in cuneiform "The Washing of the Mouth." The idol was ritually carried to the river, where its wooden mouth was washed out with solutions of exotic ingredients as it was faced in various directions. And cuneiform texts state that such statues spoke and commanded their votaries what to do.

Figure 1. Life-size mural on the north wall of Tutankhamun's burial chamber in the Valley of the Kings (1325 B.C.).

Now all this is difficult if not impossible to understand if we think of these people as like ourselves. But there is another perspective. From a study of such events, as well as of the literature and remains of the various civilizations of that period, a group of psychologists is concluding that people in antiquity did not think introspectively or logically as we do, that instead they heard auditory hallucinations even as modern schizophrenics do (schizophrenia is a partial relapse to this earlier mentality). These hallucinations, particularly as they seemed to emanate from idols or statues, were the nature of gods, and these hallucinated gods were probably organized in the now silent speech centers of the brain's right hemisphere — the hemisphere associated with art and creativity. These civilizations had their pantheons of public gods, but each person also had his private personal god which told him what to do from his right hemisphere. In Mesopotamia the personal god was the *ili*, while in Egypt it was called a person's *ka*.

This different mentality, called the bicameral mind (since there is a god side and a man side), is thought to have organized all of the early civilizations from about 9000 B.C. up to shortly after the time of Tutankhamun. It is the secret explanation of Egyptian history. According to this theory, the function of the "Opening of the Mouth" of the mummy — like the "Washing of the Mouth" of idols in Mesopotamia — was to psychologically enable others to hallucinate authoritative voices more easily, to prime as it were the belief-prerequisites of hearing within the brain directives that seemed to come from idols or mummies, in this case that of Tutankhamun dressed as Osiris.

The theory also helps to explain the really crucial business of the mural: what is really going on at the left, up where the head end of the mummy with its golden mask once was. These three figures show Tutankhamun in the middle with his *ka* in tow. Note that the *ka* is wearing the Osirian beard — only the king's *ka* was an aspect of Osiris and could be so shown. The dead king is absorbing his *ka* and himself lovingly into the gently resisting figure of Osiris. This is what tradition with its absolute expectancies had decreed. And when it is said that each divine king in death becomes Osiris, this means according to the bicameral theory a merging of hallucinated voices into the bicameral mind of his successor. Hence the "Opening of the Mouth" by Ay of the Tutankhamun-Osiris mummy on the right of the mural.

To give us the feeling of all this, I suggest in a loose but not trivial sense that these three figures are similar to the Christian Trinity: God the Father as Osiris, the Son as Tutankhamun, and his *ka* as the Holy Ghost, separable in the world, but after the death of the Son, one God. The Golden Mask of Tutankhamun as Osiris in its glass case in the exhibit, which once covered the dried face of the mummy as it lay in its time-darkened linens, is what to us would be the very Face of God.

It is not a representation of the new combined deity, but the actual face. This is difficult for us. We are consciously logical and our minds insist on a single location for things. But bicameral mentalities guided through life by hallucinated voices had no such restrictions. Their lives and minds were permeated by what is called a paralogic compliance with verbally mediated reality. Since an auditory hallucination can happen anywhere, so the person or god from which it was thought to come had no single location.

Thus Tutankhamun-Osiris could at the same time *be* in his mummy clothes or *be* the great golden mask, or in the more than 400 figurines called shawabtis buried with him in his tomb, or even in his own internal organs removed during embalming and housed in the miniature canopic coffins in their golden goddess-guarded shrine. Or with Ra in the sun, as was traditional with a dead king. Or among the stars, as brought out by the central two figures of the mural where the dead king is being greeted by Nut, goddess of the sky.

Art in bicameral times is not the representation of reality. It is the creation of reality.

All of this, however, has a certain poignancy at this period. As we know from other evidence elsewhere, this earlier organization of the human mind was beginning to break down during these last centuries of the 2nd millennium B.C. The bicameral mind of hearing decisions as hallucinated gods is not efficient in complexities. The ceremonies of opening or washing the mouth of an idol or mummy are probably part of this; in earlier times such acts were unnecessary. So, too, the monotheism of Tutankhamun's probable father and predecessor, Akhenaton. As the bicameral mind breaks down, the gods are "heard" less and less. Akhenaton could "hear" only the disk god of the sun, Aton, who probably told him in hallucination something similar to what Moses just a century later heard from his god, Yahweh, that "Thou shall have no other gods before me," and so obediently put down the idols and rituals of other gods.

The young Tutankhamun heard differently inside his head. Probably at the command of his *ka* he had even renamed himself after his chief god: Tutankh-Amun means the living form of Amun. His brief reign is a nostalgic return to older classical bicameral ways of hearing many gods for the many situations and problems in which a king or country might find itself.

But only for a time.

Future kings will still wrap themselves in linen and gold and look to be hugged into eternity with Osiris. Yet increasingly they will be moving through parts of an ancient mind they less and less remember or understand. Increasingly they will become introspective and logical like ourselves. They and we with them will have gained immeasurably in putting aside this ancient mentality, gained a world of morality and logic and law and character and common sense.

But we will have lost, too. And an indication of that loss can be glimpsed in these unhurried epiphanies which we were never meant to see.

CHAPTER 11

Greek Zombies

On the Alleged Absurdity of
Substantially Unconscious Greek Minds

JAN SLEUTELS

> It was so quiet that I heard
> An ancient Greek zombie.
>
> It was so quiet that I heard
> My brain think in class.[1]

THIRTY YEARS AGO a study by the Princeton psychologist Julian Jaynes was published with the singular title, *The Origin of Consciousness in the Breakdown of the Bicameral Mind*. Jaynes claimed that consciousness is a fairly recent addition to the human mind that arrived only late in the 2nd millennium B.C. According to Jaynes, the Greeks in the *Iliad* as well as numerous other cultures of that and earlier periods were actually unconscious.

The work drew the attention of the general public, but its reception in academia has been proportionately dismissive. In academic circles Jaynes is generally seen as a maverick. In philosophy he is rarely mentioned and almost never taken seriously. The only notable exception is Daniel Dennett who appreciates

First published in *Philosophical Psychology*, 2006, 19, 2. © 2006 Taylor & Francis Ltd. (www.tandf.co.uk/journals). Reprinted with permission.

Jaynes as a fellow social constructivist with regard to consciousness. Most outspoken in his criticism is Ned Block, who rejects
Jaynes's claim as patently absurd.[2]

Though Jaynes's work is generally dismissed, it raises a very
serious question. I shall call this the question of Greek zombies,
even though it is neither specifically about Greeks nor specifically
about zombies, and certainly not about zombies in the popular
sense of the word. In the popular sense, zombies are dead bodies
re-animated and controlled like mindless puppets by a supernatural force. In this chapter, however, I use 'zombie' to refer to
living human beings endowed with a type of mind that is substantially different from our own; I assume that a structurally
unconscious mind of the sort described by Jaynes is an example
of such a radically different type of mind. Moreover, 'Greek'
brings out the fact that we are dealing with a fairly recent phenomenon in cultural history. The question of Greek zombies can
now be stated as follows:

(1) Is it conceivable that the human mind underwent a sub-
    stantial change in recent history?

Let me explain some of the concepts involved in the question.
'Conceivable' should not be taken here in the sense of being
merely logically possible. I shall take the idea of Greek zombies
to be conceivable if it is both empirically and conceptually possible, in the sense of being consistent with our present knowledge
of the actual world and its history.

Secondly, something undergoes 'substantial change' if its
nature or essence has been changed. In the strictest sense this
now seems to be a privilege of Roman Catholics ('transubstantia-
tion' of wine into blood and of bread into body), but I do not
intend to get involved in theology here. What a thing's essence is
may be a matter of deep metaphysical speculation. As a starting-
point, however, I am happy to take a thing's essence to be just

what our common conceptions say it is. Thus, I presume that consciousness is a constitutional aspect of the modern mind, in the sense that the notion of consciousness is an essential feature of our present common conception of the mind. Hence the switch from a constitutionally unconscious mind to a constitutionally conscious mind qualifies as a substantial change.

Finally, 'recent history' refers to historical rather than prehistoric times. In terms of thousands of years (ka), the period envisaged is the past 1–10 ka rather than the past 10–1000 ka, hence far removed from the outskirts of human phylogeny.

The name 'Greek zombies' I obviously borrow from Jaynes's suggestion that the Mycenaean Greeks were unconscious, which is also the focus of this chapter. That suggestion is only one particular instance of the broader question envisaged by (1). Hence, even if Jaynes should turn out to be wrong the question of Greek zombies would still be open. My strategy in this chapter will be to argue that Greek zombies are a real possibility because Jaynes's idea is not *obviously* wrong. Greek zombies of the sort envisaged by Jaynes, I argue, are consistent with our present knowledge of the actual world and its history. I will not try to establish that the claims made by Jaynes are *historically* correct, which would require a more detailed evaluation of the empirical data gathered by Jaynes than I am able to give here. For present purposes it suffices that the data make sense.

In the following sections I shall first say something about the importance of the question of Greek zombies, especially in the context of recent developments in psychology. Next, I give a summary of Jaynes's argument and that of his most outspoken critic, Ned Block. As will become clear, Block's main point against Jaynes is that it is patently absurd to believe that consciousness depends on culturally acquired concepts. In the remaining sections I discuss various aspects of this allegation, which brings me to the conclusion that Greek zombies are a very real possibility.

Fringe Minds

"I am thankful that I am not in the field of developmental psychology," Donald Davidson confessed in one of his last papers. Writing about the emergence of thought, Davidson noted that in the phylogeny of the human species as well as in the ontogeny of the individual, "there is a stage at which there is no thought followed after a lapse of time by a subsequent stage at which there is thought." According to Davidson, "What we lack is a satisfactory vocabulary for describing the intermediate steps."[3] Once there is thought and intentional action we can use our standard mentalistic vocabulary, and where we regard nature as mindless naturalistic vocabularies apply, but there is no vocabulary to describe the "half-formed minds" in between.

It is the conceptual embarrassment felt at the fringes of mind that made Davidson shrink from developmental psychology. This embarrassment is a serious problem not only for the study of the infant mind, but also for evolutionary psychology, cognitive archaeology and paleo-anthropology, as well as for disciplines such as animal psychology and cognitive ethology. The problem has become increasingly urgent in recent years due to a surge of interest in these disciplines. Particularly salient is the exposure of cognitive archaeology with groundbreaking work by authors such as Steven Mithen, Terrence Deacon, and Merlin Donald.[4]

The growing importance of the problem of fringe minds was recently brought out in a book-length study by José Bermúdez.[5] Bermúdez observes that the psychology of nonlinguistic creatures (infants, early hominids, animals) involves a widespread practice of ascribing to such creatures beliefs and desires, mental representations, as well as thinking and reasoning. These ascriptions are frequently treated in a metaphorical or merely instrumental way (from an 'intentional stance', to use Dennett's term), due to the lack of clarity about the nature of the fringe minds under examination. Bermúdez urges an extension of the mentalistic model to meet the conceptual requirements of these fields, and launches a conceptual framework that should allow nonlinguistic creatures within certain limits to be treated as "genuine thinkers."

The question of Greek zombies is closely related to the problem of fringe minds. In point of fact Greek zombies just *are* fringe minds, but alarmingly close to home. As long as we contemplate fringe minds that are conveniently distant from our own minds and correspondingly close to "mindless nature" (prenatal or very young infants, hominids well before 1000 ka, animals), the problem noted by Davidson may be deferred as not particularly urgent. It becomes much more urgent, however, when we turn to the fringe minds closer to home, for instance when considering prehistoric minds in the order of 100–10 ka ago. An illustration of this point is the controversy stirred by Nicholas Humphrey's paper on cave art.[6] Is the emergence of cave art in Europe about 30 ka ago proof that the humans of the Upper Paleolithic were among the first to have "essentially modern minds," as the received view has it, or should we follow Humphrey's diagnosis that the evidence actually suggests the very opposite conclusion, namely, that the cave artists were among the last to have "distinctly pre-modern minds"? Greek zombies call attention to an even more baffling possibility — that of minds substantially different from ours, yet belonging to human beings *very* much like us. So much like ourselves, in fact, that we find it almost impossible to believe that our ordinary mentalistic vocabulary of beliefs and desires should *not* apply to them as literally as it applies to us.

My strategy in this chapter is the exact opposite of Bermúdez. While Bermúdez lets the familiar model of the mind *reach out* to the fringes, I want to find out how far the fringe mind *reaches in*. An obvious advantage of my approach is that it is not in danger of inadvertently projecting onto fringe minds any biases of the mentalistic model. If there is such a thing as a specifically modern mind, we should beware of imputing its traits to babies and Neanderthals.[7]

Jaynes on Consciousness

What were Jaynes's reasons for making his extraordinary claim about Greek zombies? The bone of his argument consists of the historical evidence from Biblical and Homeric times, notably including inscriptions and other written sources from Egypt, Mesopotamia, and Greece, dating roughly between 3000 and 1000 B.C.[8] Jaynes argued that the reports of mental life overtly present or implied in this evidence make much more sense when taken as reports of minds that were *not* conscious in anything like the modern sense of the word, but instead were of a 'bicameral' nature, as Jaynes called it. In rough outline, the difference between the bicameral mind and the conscious mind is that the actions of bicameral persons are motivated by auditory and sometimes visual hallucinations such as hearing voices, seeing gods appear, obeying the voice of the god, and other divine apparitions and commands, whereas conscious persons experience a private, inner, mental space where individual deliberation takes place and where individual action is planned and motivated. In the bicameral mind an alien voice tells you what to do, in the conscious mind you plan and execute your actions yourself.

According to Jaynes, the two main features of the modern conscious mind are "mind-space" and the "analog I." Mind-space is the space in which mental contents are stored for introspection, while the analog I is the 'I' that does the introspecting. Both features are claimed to be absent in the bicameral mind, which quite literally has no room for introspection or deliberation, nor even for contents to be explicitly represented and grasped by an individual self. The bicameral mind is instead composed of voices from nowhere telling you what to do, or is better described as a 'blindness' (Greek *atè*, also meaning 'Fate') that comes upon people to guide their actions. In one of Jaynes's numerous examples,[9] we are told that Achilles will fight "when the *thumos* in his chest tells him to and a god rouses him." Similarly, Agamemnon, who robbed Achilles of his prize mistress, tells us, "Not I was the cause of this act, but Zeus and *moira*...."[10] Taking these and many similar passages as literal as possible, Jaynes argued that the ancient Greeks acted not for reasons represented and understood, but on blindly obeyed command.

Notice that when Jaynes denied that the ancient Greeks were conscious, he was not denying them everything that is commonly associated with consciousness. In the first chapter of his book, he tries to expel a number of alleged misunderstandings about the nature of consciousness. According to Jaynes, "consciousness is not what we generally think it is":

> It is not to be confused with reactivity. It is not involved in hosts of perceptual phenomena. It is not involved in the performance of skills and often hinders their execution. It need not be involved in speaking, writing, listening, or reading. It does not copy down experience, as most people think. Consciousness is not at all involved in signal learning, and need not be involved in the learning of skills or solutions, which can go on without any consciousness whatsoever. It is not necessary for making judgments or in simple thinking. It is not the seat of reason, and indeed some of the most difficult instances of creative reasoning go on without any attending consciousness. And it has no location except an imaginary one![11]

Jaynes's notion of consciousness clearly swerves from "what we generally think it is." Some of the suggestions made by Jaynes in this connection strike me as very insightful, about others I am skeptical. For the present argument it will not be necessary to take in these details, except for some points to be duly explained.

Jaynes's primary claim is that the minds of fairly recent cultures were substantially different from ours to the extent that they lacked consciousness. Jaynes also launched a number of secondary hypotheses as additional support for his primary claim. First, he discussed possible causes of the literal change of mind in ancient times. Secondly, he proposed a neurological basis for the differences between bicameral and conscious minds. Finally, in the last part of his book Jaynes dealt with vestiges of the bicameral mind in modern culture, discussing phenomena such as religious frenzy, hypnosis, and schizophrenia.

I will not be concerned here with either of these secondary hypotheses, nor even with any of the details of the primary hypothesis. What concerns me here is the conceptual thread of the arguments involved, both in Jaynes's defense of his primary hypothesis and in the response from his critics, to whom I now turn.

Block on Jaynes

In a review of Jaynes's book, Ned Block objected that its reasoning rests on a large-scale confusion of use and mention of 'consciousness'.[12] Even if everything Jaynes says about the historical events were correct, so Block argued, all he would have shown was that the concept of consciousness arrived around late in the 2nd millennium B.C., not that consciousness itself arrived then. According to Block, it is perfectly obvious that people were conscious long before they had the concept of consciousness, just like there was gravity long before Newton hit upon the concept of gravity.

In later work Block repeated his criticism in terms of a distinction between different kinds of consciousness serving different cognitive functions, which he claimed were conflated by social constructivists such as Dennett and Jaynes.[13] The two most prominent kinds of consciousness to be distinguished are P-consciousness and A-consciousness. P-consciousness is phenomenal awareness, such that for any P-conscious creature there is something it is like to be that creature. A-consciousness is characterized in terms of access to mental representations: "A state is access-conscious if, in virtue of one's having the state, a representation of its content is (a) inferentially promiscuous, i.e. freely available as a premise in reasoning, and (b) poised for rational control of action and (c) poised for rational control of speech."[14] Now, with these distinctions in place Block can say the following about the social constructivist's view of consciousness:

> *I hope it is obvious* that P-consciousness is not a cultural construction. ... The idea would be that there was a time at which people genetically like us ate, drank, and had sex, but there was nothing it was like for them to do these things. Further, each of us would have been like that if not for specific concepts we acquired from our culture in growing up. *Ridiculous!* ...
> What about A-consciousness? Could there have been a time when humans who are biologically the same as us never had the contents of their perceptions and thoughts poised for free use in reasoning or in rational control of action? Is this ability one that culture imparts to us as children? Could it be that until we acquired the concept of 'poised for free use in reasoning or in rational control of action', none of our perceptual contents were A-conscious? Again, *there is no reason to take such an idea seriously*. Very much lower animals are A-conscious, presumably without any such concept [my italics].[15]

What is most remarkable about Block's argument against the possibility of non-conscious human minds is its absence — the paucity of argument and the proportionate appeal to the reader's intuitions (highlighted by the italicized parts of the quotation). The same goes for the following passage from Block against Jaynes and Dennett. These writers, Block says:

> Allege that consciousness is a cultural construction —

Jaynes even gives its invention a date: between the events reported in the Oddysey [*sic*] and the Iliad. They seem to be talking about phenomenal consciousness, but if one accepts a notion of phenomenal consciousness as distinct from the cognitive and functional notions I have described, the idea that consciousness was invented by the Greeks is *ludicrous*. If there is such a thing as phenomenal consciousness as distinct from the cognitive and functional notions I have described, *surely* it is a basic biological feature of us. The same is true for access-consciousness …. *Obviously*, our ability to access information from our senses is genetically programmed. … The conflation is *especially silly* in Jaynes, where it is *obvious* that 'consciousness' in the sense in which it is supposed to have been invented by the Greeks is something like a theory of consciousness in roughly the phenomenal sense [my italics].[16]

It is evident that Block takes Greek zombies to be utterly absurd. It is equally evident, I think, that he has no real arguments for this claim, but only two sets of statements about P-consciousness and A-consciousness: they are not contingent on culturally acquired concepts (first quotation), and they are basic biological features (second quotation). These statements are motivated by intuitions: the first is *perfectly obvious* and to deny the second is *perfectly ludicrous*. In addition Block seems to make a tacit assumption (which presumably is also seen as obvious) that basic biological features cannot be contingent on culturally acquired concepts.[17]

For all the conceptual footwork involved in the distinction between kinds of consciousness, Block fails to make clear why Greek zombies should be ruled out as absurd. Neither conceptually nor empirically has this absurdity been established. The closest Block comes to offering an argument is when he observes in the first quotation that "very much lower animals are A-conscious, presumably without any such concept." I think this is mere handwaving, however.[18]

I grant everyone the right to share Block's intuitions, especially as they also happen to be mine. But I have learned to be wary of them. Uncritical rehearsal of intuitions is the shortest route to parochialism, as history has amply demonstrated. If we find it intuitively difficult to accept Greek zombies, this may just reflect our collective determination to reckon the Greeks among our peers rather than expose a salient feature of ontology.

In the following sections I take a closer look at the intuitions regarding Greek zombies. As appears from Block's discussion of the matter, the bone of contention is the question whether consciousness is a cultural construction (as Jaynes and Dennett believe it is) or a natural kind (as suggested by Block). My plan is as follows. First I consider the claim that consciousness is a cultural construction and examine whether this claim leads to patent absurdity. Next I consider the possibility that consciousness is a natural kind and examine whether this makes it "perfectly clear" that consciousness must be independent of its concept. I shall argue that neither route leads to the perfect clarity claimed by Block. Instead, each of the paths leads the way to taking Greek zombies much more seriously than was hitherto assumed.

Consciousness as a Social Construction

Suppose first that consciousness is a social construction, as claimed by Jaynes and Dennett and contested by Block.[19] All parties seem to agree that consciousness on this supposition must have a history that starts with the concept of consciousness, inasmuch as the empirical evidence for the reality of a social phenomenon is necessarily also evidence for the possession of the concept, although the reverse need not hold. You can have the concept of baseball without having the practice of baseball, but the reverse is impossible.[20] If this applies to consciousness, then consciousness cannot predate the concept of consciousness.[21]

Assuming that consciousness conceived as a social construction cannot predate the concept, it still remains to be seen whether Jaynes's evidence is strong enough to support the claim that the ancient Greeks actually lacked the concept. Although this point is not contested by Block, we should consider the question carefully. Empirical support is of necessity highly indirect here. Evidence for the claim that a person or a community in the past had a certain concept (or a set of concepts, beliefs, etc.) is always contingent on the behavioral repertoire of the person or community in question; evidence for the repertoire is in its turn contingent on the actual behavior displayed in the past; finally, evidence for the actual behavior is contingent on the marks left behind, notably including inscriptions and other written material. The inference from found marks to implicated concepts seems sound enough, even though it involves a relatively fragile chain of inferences to the best explanation. The inference from *absent* marks to *absent* concepts is much more dubious, however. Supposing that the best way to make sense of a mark M is to presume a behavior B from a repertoire R involving a concept C, then the *absence* of M is still perfectly compatible with the *presence* of either (B, R, C), (R, C), or even (C) alone. Maybe M was accidentally lost, maybe it will be found later, maybe B failed to produce M, maybe R failed to produce B, maybe C was mistaken by us to be involved in R while it was actually involved in some other R^*. The chances that all of these possibilities can be ruled out are very slim.

To support the claim that it was specifically C that was absent, we need to look for other arguments, which can indeed be found in Jaynes. The substance of his argument may be interpreted as taking the form of an inference from found M to absent C, or more precisely, an inference from M to a certain C^* different from C, with an additional argument to the effect that C^* precludes

C. C* is the concept of what Jaynes called the 'bicameral mind': the mind that is not an 'inner space' in which contents are presented to the 'I', but a mind featuring alien voices guiding people's actions. Jaynes's argument may now be put as follows: the best way to make sense of ancient reports of mental life is to assume that earlier cultures had a totally different conception of the mind that does not involve any of the features we now associate with consciousness.

Is this line of argument strong enough to support the conclusion that earlier cultures as envisaged by Jaynes had no concept of consciousness? Of course, much depends on how the details of the argument are filled in. A sufficient number of convincing examples of 'bicameral' descriptions of mind must be found, possible counterexamples must be located and adequately answered, and so on. Assuming that this works out in a satisfactory way, I think the answer to our question must be affirmative. Although there is still a *logical* possibility that earlier cultures may have had the concept of consciousness while failing to make use of it in their descriptions of mental life, the odds are heavily against it.

Concepts Reconsidered

The working hypothesis in the previous section was that consciousness is a cultural construction. On this assumption we found that it makes sense to claim that consciousness did not precede the concept of consciousness, and that the concept arrived late in the 2nd millennium B.C. This claim is consistent with the way we reason about the interpretation of evidence for cultural phenomena in the past, and both are consistent with the (tentatively accepted) empirical evidence gathered by Jaynes.

Yet, there is a twist here. One may wonder whether the rendering in the previous section does justice to Jaynes's argument. There is something awkward about the notion of concept in the argument. Although it makes sense to say that earlier minds lacked the concept of consciousness, it is much less clear whether it makes sense to say that they had an alternative bicameral conception of the mind. In point of fact it is unclear whether it makes sense to say that they had any conception of mind at all, or even, on a sufficiently strict construal of concepts, that they had any concepts at all. On most accounts, a conception of mind, in the sense of a more or less articulate theory of mind, requires an elaborate system of distinct and interrelated concepts figuring in a more or less articulate system of logically related propositional contents. This strikes me as precisely the sort of content, however, that in Jaynes's view requires a mind-space to be explicitly represented in for use by the analog I, or in Block's terms an A-consciousness of contents poised for free use in reasoning and for rational control of action and speech. Hence, if the reports of mental life given by earlier cultures are based on an alternative conception of mind, or an alternative theory of mind, that would imply that the authors of these reports must have been conscious — whether they had the concept of consciousness or not. If this is correct a dilemma ensues:

(2) Either cultures were conscious without having the concept of consciousness, or they were not conscious and could not possibly have had any theories at all.

Moreover, at least on some highly influential accounts involving inferential role semantics, similar considerations apply to concepts generally.[22] It may be argued that 'inferential promiscuity' in a sufficiently large network of concepts is a necessary feature of any concept. The idea is that the set of a concept's identity conditions, spelled out in terms of entailment and other logical relations, must be sufficiently rich before it makes sense to speak of a concept at all. Hence, concepts on this analysis require a sufficiently large, logically articulate system of clear and distinct concepts, or more precisely a system of inferential relations between belief contents of which the concepts are constituents. In philosophy of cognitive science, this requirement is often put in terms of a combinatorial semantics: mental contents must be compositionally structured according to an articulate system of combinatory rules and basic constituents, in terms of which their logico-semantic properties are fixed.

The sort of account of concepts just outlined is closely related to Block's notion of an 'A-conscious mental state', which critically involves logically articulate mental contents poised for use in reasoning. Following Block's analysis, I think it is safe to say that there can be no A-consciousness without concepts (strictly construed). More importantly, I think the reverse implication also holds: no concepts without A-consciousness. I fail to see how the strict construal of concepts could make sense without something like a 'virtual working space' in which these concepts can be put to work, so to speak — a virtual space with the functional properties attributed by Block to A-consciousness, and strongly reminiscent of mind-space à la Jaynes. Now, if this line of reasoning with regard to concepts is taken, dilemma (2) can be rephrased as follows:

(3) Either cultures were conscious without having the concept of consciousness, or they were not conscious and could not possibly have had any concepts at all.

Let me retrace the steps taken here. If consciousness is a cultural construction, then on the received view it must be based on a concept. To prove the absence of consciousness in earlier cultures, we therefore had to establish that the concept was absent. To make a case for the absence of the concept, we argued for the presence of a different concept that precludes the concept of consciousness. Yet, that different concept seems to imply that earlier cultures were conscious after all, which contradicts what we set out to establish. Moreover, on a sufficiently strict reading of concepts we must conclude that earlier cultures must have been conscious, lest they could not have had any concepts at all.

Summarizing the argument in general terms, if anything qualifying as a cultural construction is necessarily based on a corresponding concept, and if such concepts necessarily involve consciousness, then consciousness cannot be a cultural construction. Similarly, if anything qualifying as a culture is necessarily based on concepts, and if such concepts necessarily involve consciousness, then no culture can be unconscious.

On the face of it, we have reached a *reductio ad absurdum* of the claim that consciousness is a cultural construction. Although the argument as such was not given by Block, I think he would probably endorse it for its outcome. And who would want to deny that earlier cultures had theories or conceptions of the world, or indeed that they had concepts? The very same empirical material on which Jaynes based his claims (written records, inscriptions, etc.) seems evidence to the contrary. Surely all use of language involves concepts? Surely the descriptions of historical events as reported in the *Iliad* and other sources are based on a conception of world, of man, of gods, and of how they interact? To suppose otherwise goes against the grain of common sense.

A-Minds and B-Minds?

Before embracing the *reductio*, however, we should consider the alternatives more carefully. As far as I can see, there are three main alternatives for the conclusion that consciousness is not a cultural construction.

(4) First alternative: reject the claim that social constructions are necessarily based on a concept.

(5) Second alternative: reject the claim that concepts necessarily involve consciousness.

(6) Third alternative: accept that earlier cultures had neither consciousness nor concepts.

On the face of it, (6) entails (4), while being consistent with the rejection of (5). Moreover, (5) is consistent with the rejection of both (4) and (6). Finally, (4) is consistent with the rejection of both (5) and (6).

Are the options acceptable? It does not seem *obviously* absurd to embrace (4), provided one is prepared to give an alternative account of social constructions. If concepts are no longer available as founding factors, then other constructive elements need to be found to take their place. Option (6) is intuitively the most implausible alternative of the three, as pointed out above.

Jaynes's way out of the predicament was to opt for (5): he endorsed a different notion of concept such that consciousness is not necessary for having concepts.[23] This apparently also entails that one can have a 'theory' or conception of the world that is not articulated in deliberate, conscious reflection. In Block's terms, such concepts are clearly anything but "poised for free use" by the individual. Correspondingly, a bicameral person's behavior, including his speech behavior and other use of language, may witness his possession of particular concepts and conceptions, yet these are not items for the use of which he could meaningfully be held personally or rationally responsible. A bicameral person quite literally would not *know* what he is doing or saying, nor why he is doing or saying it, in the sense that his mind is constitutionally unable to explain, elaborate, question, doubt, or otherwise conduct articulate reasonings about its contents.[24]

The alternative notion of concept suggested by Jaynes puts the discussion in a new perspective, even if this notion was not worked out by Jaynes in sufficient detail. First, by embracing (5) Jaynes averted the looming *reductio*. Moreover, the notion of nonconscious concepts gives a new edge to options (4) and (6), which further strengthens the case against the *reductio*. Let me explain this by introducing a distinction between two different kinds of concepts which I shall call B-concepts ('B' for 'bicameral') and A-concepts ('A' for 'access', as in 'A-consciousness'). Although Jaynes did not explicitly draw any such distinction, I believe that it tallies with many of his points of contrast between the modern, conscious mind and the ancient, bicameral mind.

A-concepts are concepts in the relatively narrow sense indicated earlier. Their identity conditions are substantially determined by their place in an articulate and sufficiently large network of concepts, or more precisely, by their role in the system of inferential relations between mental contents (propositions) of which they are constituents. A-concepts presuppose A-consciousness, for the mental contents of which they are constituents are "poised for free use in reasoning." In point of fact, it is this possible use in reasoning that determines the identity conditions for A-concepts.

By contrast, the identity conditions for B-concepts are not in any way mentally articulated. Minds with B-concepts have no 'access' to anything like 'inferential relations' between B-concepts, for there is no such access and there are no such relations. Of course it is quite possible for us ('A-minds') to interpret the B-concepts of ancient minds ('B-minds') in terms of our own A-concepts, which is bound to happen whenever we interpret ancient texts. For instance, when we read an ancient report in which the expression for 'cow' occurs, we interpret this expression in terms of our familiar A-concept 'cow', laden with inferential relations to other concepts such as 'animal', 'non-human', and 'milk'. Actually, however, the expression should be taken to stand for a B-concept with no articulate inferential potentiality whatsoever. Following Jaynes, the identity conditions for the B-concept 'cow' should presumably be spelled out purely in terms of its "class of behaviorally equivalent things" (see note 24), which I take to consist of cows and all other entities (pictures of cows, stone figures, whatever) that elicit the same stock neural responses.

With this distinction between two kinds of concepts, (4) may be read as specifically denying that A-concepts are necessary for social constructions, while allowing for the possibility that B-concepts may take their place. Similarly, (6) may be read as denying that ancient cultures had consciousness and A-concepts, while allowing for the possibility that they had non-conscious B-concepts.

The distinction between A-concepts and B-concepts deserves to be explored more fully, I think, but that is beyond the scope of the present chapter. My point here is only to show that the claim that consciousness is a social construction is by no means obviously absurd, *pace* Block.

Let me sum up the results of the foregoing discussion. First, the distinction between A-concepts and B-concepts (or some functionally equivalent distinction) saves the claim that con-sciousness is a social construction from inconsistency. Secondly, the distinction seems to be able to make Greek zombies cohere with the overall conceptual structure of behavioral sciences, as well as with the empirical data on the minds of earlier cultures. Moreover, the idea of B-concepts ruled by identity conditions of a different order as compared to our familiar A-concepts, is arguably a welcome instrument when dealing with more remote fringe minds such as prelinguistic infants, early hominids, and animals.[25]

Finally, notice that my discussion leaves open the possibility that Greek zombies of the sort envisaged by Jaynes were actually P-conscious A-zombies with B-minds, that is to say: minds fed on B-concepts without A-consciousness, who may nonetheless have been P-conscious in Block's sense of the word. I am not particularly worried by this possibility, however, for two reasons. First, recall that my aim here is to establish the possibility of substantially different minds in recent history. In my book, P-conscious A-zombies with B-minds *are* substantially different sorts of minds. Secondly, I am quite skeptical about attributing

P-consciousness to beings that are *constitutionally* incapable of rational access to their alleged contents of consciousness. This strikes me as a merely gratuitous projection of our own self-image, for how could it ever be established that their alleged P-consciousness is more than a simple physiological reaction?[26]

Consciousness as a Natural Kind

What if consciousness is not a social construction but a natural kind, in the sense that it is a salient aspect of nature, presumably "a basic biological feature" as Block put it? Does this make it "perfectly obvious" that consciousness predated the concept of consciousness? If it does not, then this must be because it makes sense to think that some natural kinds may somehow be constituted by their corresponding concepts.

As a matter of fact, there is a well-known line of thought that allows for precisely this possibility, namely, idealism. The idealist holds our view of the world to be constituted by something like a conceptual scheme. Examples of this type of position include Kant's transcendental idealism, Kuhn's theory of paradigms, and Putnam's metaphysics of internal realism.[27] On the idealist view, we should distinguish the world as it is in itself (the noumenal world) from the world as it appears to us in experience (the phenomenal world). It is the phenomenal world, constituted in part by our concepts, that contains such phenomena as consciousness and gravity. Abstracting from that conceptual contribution, it makes no sense to speak of these phenomena. Hence, should there have been a time when the concept of consciousness (or gravity) was absent, or at least was not a constitutive part of the phenomenal world of our ancestors, it would not make sense to say that *at that time* and *for those beings* there was consciousness (or gravity). To insist nonetheless that there was consciousness (or gravity) at that time makes sense only with reference to our own present-day conceptual scheme that makes it impossible for us to see the world in any other way. We are then effectively projecting our own view of ourselves and of the world onto our ancestors: *we* experience ourselves as beings with consciousness, hence we assume that *they* experience themselves in the same way.

Although idealism makes the reality of natural kinds dependent on their corresponding concepts (or similarly constitutional features of experience), it does not necessarily follow that there could have been a phenomenal world without consciousness, as seems to be implied in Jaynes's work. It may be argued that consciousness is a necessary trait of all possible conceptual schemes, hence also a transcendental feature of any conceivable phenomenal world. No world-view without conceptual scheme, no conceptual scheme without consciousness. This is the line taken by Kant in his exposition of the transcendental unity of the apperception, expressed in the formula that for each mental content C it must be possible to add, 'I think C'.[28] In other words, thinking according to Kant transcendentally requires an individual consciousness to claim the thought as its own. This is quite obviously the exact opposite of what Jaynes claims about ancient minds.[13] Notice that Kant's view of consciousness as a transcendental feature of any mind capable of wielding mental representations is very close to the picture of A-consciousness using A-concepts as described in the previous section.

Even if Kant is right in his analysis of consciousness, this does not necessarily invalidate Jaynes's claims about the mental life of earlier cultures. It is far from inconceivable that earlier minds were not minds in the Kantian sense. As is well-known, Kant tied his account of the transcendental ego very closely to the historical conditions of Western science. Kant himself was fully aware of the fact that his view of the mind was specifically calibrated to meet the requirements of a number of scientific disciplines (specifically Aristotelian logic, Euclidean geometry, Arabian arithmetic, and Newtonian physics). Now, the Mycenaean Greeks and other putatively bicameral people were quite obviously strangers to that intellectual enterprise. That their minds may have been profoundly different from the minds shaped by Kant's needs is a very real possibility indeed.

That bicameral people were strangers to Kant's concerns is also strongly suggested by the descriptions related by Jaynes. In sharp contrast to modern descriptions of the mind (as exemplified by Descartes, Hume, and Kant), early accounts of inner life lacked all sense of 'content management', having neither room nor apparent need for anything like experiential unity, mental contents to claim as one's own, principles for the organization of experience, or a basis for construing experiential reality objectively. In view of this contrast, what Kant described as belonging to the rational mind may in fact better be seen as describing the mind of what the Enlightenment wanted man to be. Kant's view of consciousness as a transcendental prerequisite to experience may in fact have been determined by his own specifically modern frame of mind.

Realism and Consciousness

Idealism is not the only line to explore here. What can a realist make of the idea that natural kinds may be concept-dependent, and that consciousness may be such a natural kind? Realism is quite obviously the position endorsed by Block in his criticism of Jaynes. The drift of Block's argument seems to be that once we have conceptually identified such things as consciousness and gravity, it is perfectly clear that they must have been there all along waiting to be discovered, even though earlier thinkers failed to take notice of them. Now, if this is actually Block's point, then as stated it is certainly too strong, even for a realist. Considering that human knowledge is fallible, any realist must face the possibility that our current theories represent the world in the wrong way. This may be the case with gravity: Newton's idea of a force acting at a distance now seems to be a merely

metaphorical representation of the underlying space-time curva-
tures. Similarly, although we use the concept of consciousness to
describe our psychological reality, and in spite of the fact that our
best psychological theories are based on the assumption that consciousness is a real and *bona fide* phenomenon, we may be mistaken in this respect, as was pointed out by Paul Churchland in
his defense of eliminative materialism.[29] As a die-hard scientific
realist, Churchland argued that folk psychology has given us a
radically false picture of the mind. The mind as an inner space
where mental sentences are processed may serve as a useful
fiction in daily life, but its entire ontology is likely to be mistaken.
Churchland advised us instead to turn to neuroscience for a more
adequate understanding of the causes of human behavior.

    Applying this grim view to consciousness, we find that it may
be a *fake* natural kind instead of a real one. That would make
consciousness a social construct again: our routine descriptions
of mental life in terms of consciousness would turn out to be a
socially acquired (and misleading) way of describing ourselves as
human beings.

    To accommodate this possibility, Block's point about con-
sciousness may be rephrased along the following lines:

(7) Unless we are completely mistaken about its nature, con-
    sciousness as a natural kind predated its concept.

    The force of (7) derives from the fact that it is hard to believe
that we might be *completely mistaken* about the nature of consciousness. Of all things, nothing seems to be more intimately
known than one's own consciousness, this "introcosm that is
more myself than anything I can find in a mirror," as Jaynes put
it.[30] A well-known claim in epistemology is that the contents of
one's own consciousness are 'incorrigibly given'. Now, let us
assume for the sake of argument that this incorrigibility may be
extended to include not only the *contents* but also the *nature* of

consciousness itself, such that this nature is manifest to us in a way that we cannot possibly be mistaken about it. Even on this assumption, however, our incorrigibly intuitive knowledge of consciousness is necessarily restricted to present consciousness without revealing anything about the earlier history of the mind. Hence, the question of the history of consciousness cannot be answered by simply pointing to one's present intuitive certainty about its nature.

The importance of the historical dimension can be made explicit by putting the basic idea behind (7) in slightly cruder terms:

(8) If consciousness is real *now*, then it has *always* been real, while if it is not, then it never was.

As it is extremely hard to deny the reality of one's own present consciousness, P-consciousness as well as A-consciousness, one is much more prepared to affirm the antecedent of the first conditional in (8) than that of the second. Yet, both conditionals in (8) are almost certainly false, or dubious at best. I think it is reasonable to presume that consciousness has *not* always been real — surely there was a time in the past when there simply were no conscious creatures, even if there are now. Moreover, even if consciousness is not real *now*, this leaves open the question whether there happened to be conscious creatures at some time in the past (or will be in the future). To be sure, I am not saying that Block would endorse (8), nor that he would disagree with my explanation of why (8) is false. My point is only that Block failed to be sufficiently careful about the intuitions involved in considering the possibility of Greek zombies. The familiar intuitions about the *present* reality and nature of consciousness are really beside the point here.

In addition to the intuitions about consciousness, there are also intuitions about what makes something a natural kind, or more particularly "a basic biological feature." Consider once more the analogy between consciousness and gravity referred to earlier. Gravity as a natural kind (assuming we are not mistaken about its nature) has *always* been real, except maybe for a short time in the very early history of the universe, and it has been real *independent* of the conceptual apparatus of human inquiry. Biological natural kinds, by contrast, have *not* always been real, for they are subject to evolutionary processes, but like gravity, we naturally assume that their reality is *independent* of human concepts. For a large majority of biological phenomena this makes perfect sense. Obvious examples are sharks, lungs, meiosis, vertebrates, and photosynthesis (assuming that species as well as classes and processes may qualify as natural kinds). However, there are also many biological phenomena that should equally pass as natural kinds, yet for which the independence from human affairs is much less clear. Diseases such as AIDS, the plague, influenzas, and SARS are prime examples. Although the organisms (the bacteria and viruses) causally responsible for the disorders may in one sense be independent of human concepts, their recent evolutionary career has been contingent upon a vast complex of cultural factors, from sanitary conditions to international air traffic, and from dietary conditions to medical technology. What is more, the very nature (genetic identity) of the pathogenic organisms heavily depends on these cultural factors, which collaborate with the organisms' rapid growth and high mutation rates to mold the pathogens' genomes. In sum, both the disease and the organisms causing it presumably are "basic biological features" in Block's sense of the word, yet they are borne and shaped by culture, hence by concepts.

Can it be ruled out that consciousness is like a disease? Suffice it to note here that there is no *obvious* way to block this possibility in a non-*ad hoc* fashion, at least not as far as I can see. What is more, I think there is reason to believe that mental capacities in general are ontogenetically like diseases, consciousness included. The rapid growth and the high mutation rates of pathogen populations structurally resemble the extreme complexity and plasticity of neural structure, which shows itself both in the rapid growth of nervous tissue, in the sheer number of nerve cells and synaptic connections, in the ability of nerve cells to grow new synaptic connections, and in their ability to rapidly readjust existing connections. The ability of pathogen populations to rapidly adjust to culture-bound conditions and to settle in a new "onto-genetic niche,"[31] may compare to the ability of neural structure to adjust to culture-bound conditions. To continue the analogy, just like the pathogens' genetic identity is contingent on cultural conditions, so the mind's neural identity is, hence presumably *a fortiori* its very structure and capacities.

As a final objection, it may be pointed out that to allow cultural variation to influence substantial aspects of the mind, in the way envisaged by Greek zombies and exemplified by Jaynes, is at odds with a basic principle of metaphysics, namely, that we should make do with as few substantial natures as possible. The endorsement of this "Platonic impulse" in psychology[32] takes the form of a principle of psychological unity for all creatures belonging to a certain class, for instance all human beings. All creatures of the class are presumed to have substantially the same mind, that is, the same type of mental organization and capacities. Any large-scale differences in performance, for instance in historical or cultural perspective, should be construed as differences in accidental attributes, not in mental substance. Applying this principle to the alleged Greek zombies, so the objection goes, one can only conclude that they *must* have had substantially the same mind as we do, and that we have mistaken accidental changes for substantial changes.

The Platonic impulse is certainly a sound principle of methodology that can boost support from the principle of parsimony among others, but in the present context it is useless. This is so for two reasons. In the first place, how the principle is to be applied depends entirely on how the reference class is identified. Is the relevant class that of mammals, or primates, or hominids, or *homo sapiens*, or human beings, or human adults, or normal human adults, or maybe even something like normal, adult, literate, modern, Western human beings? Where is the boundary between peers and non-peers to be drawn?[33] The choice of reference class is obviously precisely what is at issue in discussing Greek zombies, hence it cannot serve as an independent argument.

Secondly, to insist on a substantial unity of mind where significant differences in performance are found may lead to a merely verbal dispute, for we simply do not know what the mind 'substantially' is. Taking consciousness as a substantial trait of the mind, are we obliged to say that a constitutionally unconscious creature has *no* mind, or that it has a substantially *different* mind? There is no clear-cut answer to this question. We may have a fairly clear conception of how *our* minds are supposed to work, yet we have no clear way of sifting accident from substance when projecting that conception into the past. Maybe the bicameral mind and the conscious mind (assuming that there are such things) should properly be seen as substantially the same type of mind, which would mean that consciousness is not an essential trait of mind. Maybe 'A-minds' and 'B-minds' (assuming that there are such things) are really instantiations of the same underlying mental substance, as yet unknown to us, which would mean that the processing of A-concepts is not an essential feature of mind. I am not sure whether it would take a discovery or a convention to decide these issues, but the effect of either would be the same, namely, to trade in a vast substantial difference for a *no less vast* accidental one plus a novel conception of mental substance. Until such a novel conception is in place, I am happy to take both consciousness and something like 'A-concepts' as substantial features, in the sense that they are entailed by our present established conception of the mind. Any mind that lacks them is a substantially different mind.

Conclusion

Greek zombies are supposed to have minds substantially different from ours while being very much like ourselves — so much like ourselves, in fact, that we find it difficult to believe that their minds could be substantially different. Are Greek zombies really possible? Our intuitions weigh heavily against that possibility. Upon closer examination, however, the intuitive absurdity of Greek zombies appears to be quite fragile. The discussion of Jaynes's example of bicameral Greeks, considered from different theoretical angles (social constructivism, idealism, eliminativism, realism), revealed that Greek zombies should be taken much more seriously than is commonly assumed, and this for three reasons. First, because the intuitions commonly appealed to in dismissing them do not stand up to scrutiny. Secondly, because the faults detected in the intuitions point the way toward a promising reconsideration of such notions as 'consciousness' and 'concept'. Finally, because a reconsideration of this sort is an important step toward a more unbiased view of fringe minds generally. In sum, Greek zombies are a possibility to be reckoned with. It may be hard to believe, but so are many facts.

NOTES TO CHAPTER 11

1.   From: "If You Had Super Ears," by John, pupil of Y3/4 at St. Bartholomew's Catholic Primary School (Rainhill, Merseyside UK). Posted on the Internet as part of the school's poetry project; see http://www.st-bartholomews.st-helens.sch.uk.

2.   See Dennett (1986, 1991); Block (1981, 1994, 1995). For an overview of Jaynes's work and its reception, see the Julian Jaynes Society website at www.julianjaynes.org. An exception to the unfavorable reception in philosophy, besides Dennett, is David Johnson, whose work explicitly aligns with Jaynes's; see e.g., Johnson (2003). Jaynes's established repute is now such that the merest association with his views causes suspicion. For instance, when Sarnecki and Sponheimer mention Jaynes in their review of Mithen (1996), the reader senses palpable implication. "It would be unfair, we think, to compare Mithen's work with Julian Jaynes's *Origins of consciousness* [*sic*],"

so the authors submit in a footnote, and they continue, "but it is worth noting that ...", which does little to improve Mithen's case (Sarnecki and Sponheimer, 2002, p. 184, n. 2).

3. Davidson, 1999, p. 11.
4. Mithen 1996, Deacon 1997, and Donald 2001.
5. Bermúdez, 2003.
6. Humphrey, 1998.
7. Notice that Bermúdez's proposal and mine are not necessarily in conflict. By extending the standard model of mind to cover fringe minds, Bermúdez also changes the overall framework in terms of which mind is conceived. In particular, in order to be able to describe the thought processes of nonlinguistic creatures, Bermúdez needs to avail himself of a notion of 'mental content' or 'concept' for such creatures, the identity conditions for which appear to be substantially less stringent than those for concepts as ordinarily understood. My converse approach will involve a similar reconsideration of the notion of mental content, as explained in the section "A-Minds and B-minds?"
8. Jaynes also discussed archaeological evidence for similar developments in America (Olmec and Maya cultures in Mexico, Incas and other Andean civilizations) and China.
9. *Iliad*, IX, 702f.
10. *Iliad*, XIX, 86–87.
11. Jaynes, 1976, pp. 46–47.
12. Block, 1981.
13. Block, 1994, 1995; Dennett, 1986, 1991.
14. Block, 1994, p. 214.
15. Block, 1995, p. 238.
16. Block, 1994, p. 217.
17. In my view, Block seriously misrepresents Jaynes when he says that "it is obvious that 'consciousness' in the sense in which it is supposed to have been invented by the Greeks is something like a theory of consciousness in roughly the phenomenal sense" (Block, 1994, p. 217). Although the matter is difficult to judge because of Jaynes's idiosyncratic view of ('generic') consciousness, I think it is much more apt to say that Jaynes was interested in the emergence of something like A-consciousness in roughly Block's sense of the word. Accordingly, my concern in this chapter will be mainly with A-consciousness and not with "a theory of consciousness in roughly the phenomenal sense," nor indeed with P-consciousness as such.
18. First, because it appears to be a matter of definition for Block. In his discussion of A-consciousness, Block explicitly says that he wants "to allow that nonlinguistic animals, for example chimps, have A-conscious states," and he adopts a definition to fit the purpose (Block, 1995, p. 231). Secondly, without independent motivation Block's claim about "much lower animals"

simply begs the question against Greek zombies. In addition, notice that the selective reactivity or 'simple thinking' of nonlinguistic animals that Block seems to envisage here is of the sort that Jaynes explicitly excludes from consciousness (Jaynes, 1976, Ch. 1).

Notice that the notion of consciousness as described by Jaynes (mind-space and the analog I) is in many respects a fair approximation of the notion of A-consciousness as described by Block. Mind-space is the space in which mental contents are explicitly presented for introspection, deliberation and planning of action by the analog I, or in Block's terms, where we find contents poised for use as a premise in reasoning and for rational control of action and speech.

19. The claim that consciousness is a social construction has also been made by other social constructivists such as George Herbert Mead (1934), Lev Vygotsky (1962) and Rom Harré (1986). For clarity and convenience I concentrate my discussion on Jaynes, however.

20. Would it be possible to play baseball *accidentally* without having the concept of baseball? It is certainly conceivable that a group of people would go through (at least some of) the motions of a baseball game, but I think they would not be playing baseball. Not, that is, until the moment when one of the group says, "Let's do *that* again," where *that* is followed by an articulate description of what makes something a game of baseball (presumably including at least part of the rules of the game). At that moment, we may say, the concept of baseball has been introduced and baseball is born.

21. Cf. Dennett, 1986.

22. Cf. Fodor & Lepore, 1992; Fodor, 1998.

23. Jaynes, 1976, pp. 30f.

24. Jaynes's approach to concepts is purely extensional. "Concepts are simply classes of behaviorally equivalent things," Jaynes said (1976, p. 31), which places them firmly outside the head. (More precisely, they are outside the head, but they are type-individuated in relational terms with reference to the user's behavioral repertoire.) According to Jaynes, our discriminative aptitude with regard to such classes is partly acquired in experiential development and partly based on innate neural structures. The neurally based aptitudes correspond to "root concepts" that are "prior to experience" and "allow behavior to occur at all" (*loc. cit.*). Jaynes's line on concepts is consistent with his treatment of 'reactivity', that is, the mind's aptitude to respond to the environment adequately and discriminatively. According to Jaynes, no consciousness is needed for this ability, nor indeed for the learning processes by which the aptitudes are acquired or modified. Moreover, a similarly 'automated' account is given of "simple thinking" and making judgments. As Jaynes put it, in many cases "one does one's thinking before one knows what one is to think about. The important part of the matter is the instruction

[in an experimental set-up], which allows the whole business to go off automatically" (*op. cit.*, p. 39).

25. As pointed out earlier, Bermúdez (2003) works with a notion of 'mental content' or 'concept' for prelinguistic creatures, the identity conditions for which appear to be substantially less stringent than those for concepts as ordinarily understood. This suggests at least a functional equivalent of the distinction between A-concepts and B-concepts, which merits further study. Notice that the line of reasoning proposed here also undermines the straightforward application of a 'language of thought' hypothesis to B-minds. Unless the standard notion of 'language' is reconsidered to match B-conceptual possibilities, it is not clear what a mental language in B-minds could be supposed to do. Interestingly, an analogous reconsideration of the notion of language has also been argued by David Olson (1994), based on work in developmental and cultural psychology. Olson's point is that our common conception of language (including our notions of intention, meaning, concept, and the like) is *literate* to the bone, which makes its application to other forms of communication such as pristine orality highly suspect. In accordance with this analysis, Olson urges a sharp contrast between the modern literate mind on the one hand, and on the other hand the minds of preliterate children and of preliterate cultures.

26. Block's functional distinction between A-consciousness and P-consciousness is targeted on explaining relatively isolated, abnormal phenomena such as blindsight (A-consciousness without P-consciousness), and brain damaged animals (P-consciousness without A-consciousness). Now, P-conscious Greek A-zombies would *structurally* and *normally* be like these brain damaged animals, or, to change the image, they would *structurally* and *normally* suffer from massive, pan-modal 'inverted blindsight' — we would be happy to think of them as having P-consciousness, yet they could not be said ever to have rational access to their conscious contents. This certainly strikes me as a type of mind substantially different from ours. Moreover, it makes me wonder whether the alleged possession of P-consciousness could ever be empirically demonstrated.

27. See Kant (1781/1787), Kuhn (1962), Putnam (1981).

28. Kant, 1781/1787, B131ff.

29. Churchland, 1979, 1989.

30. Jaynes, 1976, p. 1.

31. Tomasello, 1999.

32. Shweder, 1990.

33. As mentioned earlier, Jaynes explicitly denied that consciousness is necessary for thinking (1976, pp. 36ff). Moreover, in the Afterword added in the 1990 edition of his book, Jaynes suggested that what he has called the analog I is closely related to the Kantian transcendental ego.

34. For a devastating account of the cultural biases involved in attempts to draw the boundary, see Gould (1981).

REFERENCES

Bermúdez, J.L. 2003. *Thinking Without Words*. Oxford: Oxford University Press.

Block, N. 1981. "Review of Julian Jaynes's *The Origin of Consciousness in the Breakdown of the Bicameral Mind.*" *Cognition and Brain Theory*, 4, 81–83.

Block, N. 1994. "Consciousness." In S. Guttenplan (Ed.), *A Companion To The Philosophy of Mind* (pp. 210–219). Oxford: Basil Blackwell.

Block, N. 1995. "On a Confusion about a Function of Consciousness." *Behavioral and Brain Sciences*, 18, 227–247. Reprinted in N. Block et al. (eds.), *The Nature of Consciousness: Philosophical Debates* (pp. 375–415). Cambridge, MA: MIT Press, 1997.

Churchland, P.M. 1979. *Scientific Realism and the Plasticity of Mind*. Cambridge: Cambridge University Press.

Churchland, P.M. 1989. *A Neurocomputational Perspective: The Nature of Mind and the Structure of Science*. Cambridge, MA: MIT Press.

Davidson, D. 1999. "The Emergence of Thought." *Erkenntnis*, 51, 7–17.

Deacon, T.W. 1997. *The Symbolic Species. The Co-evolution of Language and the Brain*. New York: Norton & Co.

Dennett, D.C. 1986. "Julian Jaynes's Software Archeology." *Canadian Psychology*, 27, 2, 149–154. Reprinted in *Brainchildren: Essays on Designing Minds* (pp. 121–130). Cambridge, MA: MIT Press, 1998.

Dennett, D.C. 1991. *Consciousness Explained*. Boston: Little Brown.

Donald, M. 2001. *A Mind So Rare. The Evolution of Human Consciousness*. New York: Norton & Co.

Fodor, J. and E. LePore. 1992. *Holism. A Shopper's Guide*. Oxford: Basil Blackwell.

Fodor, J.A. 1998. *Concepts: Where Cognitive Science Went Wrong*. Oxford: Clarendon Press.

Gould, S.J. 1981. *The Mismeasure of Man*. New York: Norton & Co.

Harré, R. 1986. "Mind as a Social Formation." In J. Margolis, M. Krausz, and R.M. Burian, (eds.), *Rationality, Relativism and the Human Sciences* (pp. 91–106). Dordrecht: Martimus Nijhoff Publishers.

Humphrey, N. 1998. "Cave Art, Autism, and the Evolution of the Human Mind." *Cambridge Archaeological Journal*, 8, 2, 165–191. Reprinted in *The Mind Made Flesh. Frontiers of Psychology and Evolution* (pp. 132–161). Oxford: Oxford University Press, 2002.

Jaynes, J. 1976. *The Origin of Consciousness in the Breakdown of the Bicameral Mind*. Boston: Houghton-Mifflin. (With a new Afterword, 1990.)

Johnson, D.M. 2003. *How History Made The Mind: The Cultural Origins of Objective Thinking*. Chicago: Open Court.

Kant, I. 1781/1787. *Kritik der reinen Vernunft*. 1st ed. 1781 (A), 2nd ed. 1787 (B).

Kuhn, T.S. 1962. *The Structure of Scientific Revolutions*. Chicago: Chicago University Press.

Mead, G.H. 1934. *Mind, Self and Society*. Chicago: Chicago University Press.

Mithen, S. 1996. *The Prehistory of the Mind: The Cognitive Origins of Art and Science*. London: Thames & Hudson.

Olson, D.R. 1994. *The World on Paper: The Conceptual and Cognitive Implications of Writing and Reading*. Cambridge: Cambridge University Press.

Putnam, H. 1981. *Reason, Truth and History*. Cambridge: Cambridge University Press.

Sarnecki, J. and M. Sponheimer. 2002. "Why Neanderthals Hate Poetry: A Critical Notice of Steven Mithen's *The Prehistory of the Mind*." *Philosophical Psychology*, 15, 2, 173–184.

Shweder, R.A. 1990. "Cultural Psychology." In J.W. Stigler & R.A. Shweder (eds.), *Essays on Comparative Human Development*. Cambridge: Cambridge University Press.

Tomasello, M. 1999. *The Cultural Origins of Human Cognition*. Cambridge MA: Harvard University Press.

Vygotsky, L. 1962. *Thought and Language*. Cambridge, MA: MIT Press.

CHAPTER 12

Dragons of the Shang Dynasty

The Hidden Faces

JULIAN JAYNES

THE RECENTLY EXCAVATED vessels and images on loan for the first time at the Metropolitan Museum are no mere handicrafts of antique peoples whose attentions were on other things. They are much more. More even than we can understand. Some of them both represented and symbolized and so indeed "were" whole sections of China.

Twisting and writhing in bristling adamant surfaces, whose wild projections and intensities are controlled just short of confusion by a strictness of spacing, proportion, and symmetry, these vessels were the very centers of civilizing attention, objects that like the roods and grails of Christendom, the idols of Ur, the arks of tabernacles, or the Golden Enclosures of the Incas are the emanative cores of mystical power at the beginning of what has become the greatest assemblages of people ever known.

Axes That Beheaded

The most difficult mystery of these centers of sacrifice and authority is the dragon face that looks out from almost all the vessels of the Shang period. It stares fiercely out at us from vases and wine cups, from the sides, corners, and even legs of sacrificial food cauldrons, even from ceremonial drums and huge bells, wine buckets and jars, and from the axes that beheaded so many of a dead king's retinue to accompany him gruesomely into the earth.

Sometimes the face is more human, usually more animal, and always entoiled in swirling curls and volutes that to the uninstructed seem abstract, but with some practice (and imagination) are recognized as obsessive stylizations of what is more representational elsewhere, the horns, ears, mouths, claws, tails, fangs, and crests of dragons. Often the face as a whole is hidden in a visual *double entendre* where the frontal dragon face can secondarily be seen to be made up of side views of two dragons in head-to-head combat. It is the hiddenness and ambiguity of the face as a whole, relative to the stark frontality of the carefully sculptured eyes that is important.

A Different Mentality

Some hints as to the meaning of this can be found by looking at other early civilizations in which an emphasis on staring eyes at

Figures 1–2. Wine Vessel, 1500–1400 B.C.; detail of Wine Vessel.

the expense of other features was centrally important. In the drawings below, the first is a jar and lid from the Second City of Troy of about 2300 B.C. The second is a drum-idol of chalk from an early bronze-age burial mound at Folkton in England of perhaps 1600 B.C. And the third is one of many thousands of alabaster eye idols from Brak in Mesopotamia, dating about 3300 B.C. All three come from earlier civilizations that are regarded as being based on a different mentality than our own, a non-conscious mentality where people did not think as we do, but heard hallucinated voices called gods telling them what to do. Idols, including those shown, were the physical manifestations from which the divine voices seemed to emanate. The eyes are the focus of this phenomenon. Can we generalize from these earlier civilizations to the dragons' eyes of the Shang?

A Partial Diffusion

Let us become more historical. Chinese civilization had its beginnings in a long series of settlements beginning before 3000 B.C. in the upper valleys of the Yellow River where it rises in the

Figure 3. Line drawings, left to right: (1) Jar and lid from the Second City of Troy of about 2300 B.C. (2) Drum-idol from an early bronze-age burial mound at Folkton in England of perhaps 1600 B.C. (3) Alabaster eye idol from Brak in Mesopotamia, dating about 3300 B.C.

mountains and plateaus that fringe Tibet. Pottery designs here are so close to those of the same period from Turkestan and other western sites as to suggest a partial diffusion of agriculture and civilization itself from the older countries of the Near East. Earthenware idols from these sites suggest a bicameral mentality. By about 2000 B.C., these cultures had become the Xia civilization (once thought to be mythical) whose meager remains have been found further down the river at Erlitou. Then around 1600 B.C. the Shang Dynasty begins and spreads through a succession of phases and capitals to the 11th century B.C. when it is engulfed by the Zhou. Most of what we can surmise about the Xia and the Shang are consistent with the hypothesis that these were bicameral civilizations. The modern Marxian Chinese label for them as "slave societies" is extremely apt — strict hierarchies in which freedom could not be conceived or any individuality or indeed any humanity in our sense.

Nostalgic Remnant

Consistent with the bicameral hypothesis are the huge chariot burials of kings with slaughtered retinues, so similar to those in Mesopotamia, a nostalgic remnant of which occurs almost a millennium later with the army of terra-cotta soldiers buried with the great Emperor Qin, astonishing examples of which provide the more accessible parts of this exhibit.

Also consistent with other bicameral kingdoms is the slow transition of the Shang away from the bicameral mentality, until in its last phase at Anyang, it is reduced to communicating with its dragon god with oracle bones — even as Mesopotamia at approximately the same time was discovering their gods' decisions in animal entrails and stars. Indeed, I suggest that the reason the Zhou so easily engulfed the Shang is because the dragon-god was failing and easily replaced by the ancestor gods of the Zhou.

Coils of Ambiguity

But to return to the Shang dragon, we still do not understand why its face in these vessels is hidden in coils of ambiguity, unlike the eye-idols of earlier civilizations. A part of the answer may lie in considering the two sides of the cortex of the human brain. Discerning an imbedded figure is a strong left hemispheric function. Thus to see that there is a face at all in these bronzes engates the left or speech hemisphere. But facial recognition is a right hemispheric function, the side which we think in bicameral times was responsible for the verbal hallucinations called gods.

Staring at these Shang vessels, as one would in the sacrificial ceremonies in which they were lifted or poured or knelt before, the individual would be activating his two hemispheres in a unique way, the right for the speech of the dragon-god himself and the left for the individual's own acts of recognition of the god. Did this hiddenness of the dragon then enhance bicameral dialogue with it? And, to generalize, is this the neurological reason for the importance of ambiguity in all great conscious art today? An increase in the "dialogue" between the two sides of the brain?

This exhibit is one to see and ponder.

CHAPTER 13

The *Shi* 'Corpse/Personator' Ceremony in Early China

MICHAEL CARR

INTRODUCTION

IN ANCIENT CHINESE ancestral sacrifices, a participant called the *shi* 尸 'corpse, cadaver' ritually represented the spirit of a deceased ancestor. English translations of this ceremonial *shi* are commonly *personator* (used hereafter), *impersonator*, or *representative*, sometimes modified with a phrase like *of the dead/ancestor*. During a *shi* 'corpse' sacrifice, the ancestral spirit supposedly would enter the personator, preferably a grandchild of the deceased, who would eat and drink sacrificial offerings and convey messages for the departed. Scottish missionary and translator of the Chinese classics James Legge (1815–1897) described *shi* personation ceremonies as "grand family reunions where the dead and the living met, eating and drinking together, where the living worshipped the dead, and the dead blessed the living."[1]

This chapter reviews early Chinese linguistic and textual evidence about *shi* personation and relates it to the bicameral mind hypothesis of psychologist Julian Jaynes (1920–1997),[2] which may help to elucidate this little-understood ancient ritual. The role of *shi*

A version of a paper that first appeared in *Computational Analyses of Asian & African Languages*, 1985. Updated and revised for this volume by Michael Carr in 2005.

'corpse; personator' was an important part of early Chinese spiritual beliefs, and this remarkable practice of personating dead ancestors is an unsolved puzzle. No one has ever successfully explained why personation began and ended. Jaynes's hypotheses for the bicameral mind and the origin of consciousness can provide a means of putting together the pieces of this puzzle.[5]

The history of the *shi* ceremony also contributes new evidence to Jaynesian theory. Similar to the slow transition from bicamerality to rational consciousness that Jaynes documents in Egypt and Mesopotamia, this is significant corroboration from ancient China. The evidence concerning *shi* personation of the dead suggests that "consciousness" — subjective consciousness as outlined by Jaynes — did not become prevalent in China until the 1st millennium BCE, which coincides with Jaynes's bicameral chronology.[6]

The word *shi*'s semantic history goes from 'corpse, cadaver', to 'personator of the dead', to 'display; lay out' ("lay out a corpse"), to 'idle, inactive; motionless' ("corpse-like"), and to 'manage; direct'.[3] By analyzing the early occurrences of *shi* 尸, it is possible to trace significant changes in ancient Chinese attitudes concerning spiritual afterlife, ancestral sacrifice, and communication with the dead. Legends say the custom of *shi* personation began during the Xia 夏 Dynasty (ca. 2205–ca. 1766 BCE), although the oldest evidence comes from the Shang 商 Dynasty (ca. 1766–ca. 1122 BCE).[4] In particular, oracle records from the Later Shang or Yin 殷 Dynasty (ca. 1401–ca. 1122 BCE) include 𰼻 for *shi* 尸 'corpse; personator' among the earliest known Chinese characters. Classical texts and bronze inscriptions from the Zhou 周 Dynasty (ca. 1122–221 BCE) provide detailed information about changes in personation rituals. Western Zhou (ca. 1122–771 BCE) texts like the *Shijing* "Classic of Poetry" reverently describe ancestral spirits speaking through personators, but Eastern Zhou (770–221 BCE) texts began to criticize personation and extended *shi* into meanings like 'manage'. *Shi* personation ceremonies continued until the early Han 漢 Dynasty (206 BCE–220 CE).

This introduction presents four topics needed to discuss *shi* 'corpse; personator': Jaynes's hypothesis, early Chinese texts, some linguistic terminology, and the author's previous research.

The Bicameral Hypothesis

Jaynes proposes that consciousness — defined[7] in terms of spatialization, excerption, the analog 'I', the metaphor 'me', narratization, and conciliation — first developed sometime in the 2nd millennium BCE. Prior to that time, the preconscious human mind was *bicameral* ('two-chambered'). One hemisphere of the brain issued god-like voices and the other hemisphere intuitively followed their commands:

> Volition, planning, initiative is organized with no consciousness whatever and then 'told' to the individual in his familiar language, sometimes with the visual aura of a familiar friend or authority figure or 'god', or sometimes as a voice alone. The individual obeyed these hallucinated voices because he would not 'see' what to do by himself.[8]

In most situations, Jaynes believes that a bicameral person could unconsciously operate, react, and make judgments. However, in stressful situations, instead of conscious deliberation or reasoning, he/she would hear and obey a divine voice, perhaps as Agamemnon heard orders from Zeus in the *Iliad*.

This hypothesis can explain many historical aspects of early civilizations. In a "bicameral theocracy," people were controlled by the internalized voices of god-kings. Jaynes lists some common patterns: a dead king's tomb is replaced by a temple, his corpse is replaced by a statue or idol of a god, and in later bicameral theocracies that developed writing (e.g., Mesopotamian cuneiform, Egyptian hieroglyphics, and Chinese characters), the names of dead kings were often etymologically related to the words for 'god'.[9]

In the three decades since Jaynes proposed bicamerality, the hypothesis has negatively generated criticism, controversy, and occasional condemnation. Many questions remain unresolved. For instance, did the invention of writing affect bicamerality? Jaynes believes it was tremendously significant:

> Another cause [of subjective consciousness] is writing itself, because once something is written you can turn away from it and it has no more power over you, in contrast to an auditory hallucination which you cannot shut out.[10]

However, American educator and technology theorist Walter J. Ong (1912–2003) interprets a simple shift from orality to literacy instead of a momentous leap from bicamerality to consciousness:

> Whatever one makes of Jaynes's theories one cannot but be struck by the resemblance between the characteristics of the early "bicameral" psyche as Jaynes describes it — lack of introspectivity, of analytical prowess, of concern with the will as such, of a sense of difference between past and future — and the characteristics of the psyche in oral cultures not only in the past but even today. The effects of oral states of consciousness are bizarre to the literate mind, and they can invite elaborate explanations which may turn out to be needless. Bicamerality may mean simply orality. The question of orality and bicamerality perhaps needs further investigation.[11]

A cross-cultural pattern of the "living dead" was a common phase in many ancient civilizations (e.g., Egypt, Assyria, and China). The important dead were buried as if they were still living, and their graves contained not only personal belongings, but also food, drink, and weapons. Jaynes says:

Thus, from Mesopotamia to Peru, the great civilizations have at least gone through a stage characterized by a kind of burial as if the individual were still living. And where writing could record it, the dead were often called gods. At the very least, this is consistent with the hypothesis that their voices were still heard in hallucination.

But is this a necessary relationship? Could not grief itself promote such practices, a kind of refusal to accept the death of a loved one or a revered leader, calling dead persons gods as a kind of endearment? Possibly. This explanation, however, is not sufficient to account for the entire pattern of the evidence, the pervasion of references to the dead as gods in different regions of the world, the vastness of some of the enterprise as in the great pyramids, and even the contemporary vestiges in lore and literature of ghosts returning from their graves with messages for the living.[12]

For early China, this "entire pattern" includes much more than *shi* personation. Chinese archeological evidence seems generally consistent with bicamerality. Jaynes notes Neolithic Yangshao burials with "the corpse accompanied by pots of food and stone tools."[13] He mentions the extravagant Shang and Zhou royal tombs with sacrificial retinues, horses, and chariots, and asks, "Why all this? Unless the dead kings were thought to still live and need their chariots and servants because their speech was still heard?"[14] Jaynes states, "I have looked at the Chinese problem only in a cursory manner, enough to think that the Xia and Shang dynasties were bicameral, and then the Zhou becoming conscious."[15] If his conjecture is correct, then *contemporaneous* evidence — such as that found for *shi* personation — could exist from the period supposedly when the Shang lost bicamerality and the Zhou became conscious.

Pre-Han Texts

The dates of most early Chinese texts are historically uncertain,[16] largely owing to the infamous Qin Dynasty "burning of books and burying alive of officials" in 213 BCE. At the beginning of the Han era in 206 BCE, scholars started to collect, edit, and reconstruct the classics into their received forms. Han literati believed that Confucius 孔子 (551–479 BCE) compiled early Zhou texts into the *Wujing* 五經 "Five Classics."[17]

- The *Yijing* 易經 "Classic/Book of Changes" is a divination manual based on eight trigrams[18] and is the best known of these texts in the West.[19] The core section (called the *Zhouyi* 周易 "Zhou Changes") with 64 hexagrams and corresponding line statements possibly dates from the early Western Zhou (ca. 11th–10th centuries BCE), and the "Ten Wings" of philosophical commentary probably come from the late Western Zhou (ca. 9th–8th centuries BCE).

- The *Shijing* "Classic of Poetry" (or "Book of Songs/Odes") has four sections. Based on analysis of internal textual strata, University of Toronto sinologist W.A.C.H. Dobson tentatively dates the sections from the 11th to 7th centuries BCE.[20] The *Song* 頌 "Eulogies" are hymns praising the gods and ancestral spirits of the House of Zhou (ca. 11th–10th centuries BCE). The *Daya* 大雅 "Major Elegancies" are odes describing early mythology and Zhou military conquests (ca. 10th–9th centuries BCE). The *Xiaoya* 小雅 "Minor Elegancies" are miscellaneous odes, some of which complain against the ruling authorities (ca. 9th–8th centuries BCE). The *Feng* 風 "Airs" (or *Guofeng* 國風 "Airs of the States") are essentially folk songs (ca. 8th–7th centuries BCE, according to Dobson's provisional dating).

- The *Shujing* 書經 "Document Classic" ("Book of Documents/History") is a collection of writings and speeches attributed to rulers of the Later Shang period. Chinese scholars divide the canonical *Shujing* between the authentic "New Text" section (ca. 11th–6th centuries BCE) and the "Old Text," most of which was deliberately forged (early 4th century CE).

- The *Chunqiu* 春秋 "Spring and Autumn (Annals)" records the history of 12 dukes who reigned from 722 to 481 BCE in the state of Lu (home of Confucius). This tersely written text is augmented by three *zhuan* 傳 "commentaries" known by their authors. The shorter *Gongyangzhuan* 公羊傳 and *Guliangzhuan* 穀梁傳 commentaries are mostly in question-answer format, and the longer *Zuozhuan* 左傳 gives historical detail and background. All three probably date from the 5th to 4th centuries BCE.

- The *Lijing* 禮經 "Classic of Rites," which described ancient Chinese rituals, no longer exists, but portions of it went into the *Sanli* 三禮 "Three Ritual Compendia." Han officials edited extant fragments of ceremonial texts, sometimes with interchangeable names, into the following. The *Liji* 禮記 "Record of Rites" is an anthology of religious vocabulary, ceremonies, and social conventions. The *Zhouli* 周禮 "Zhou Rites" details the idealized duties for various ranks of government officials. The *Yili* 儀禮 "(Book of) Etiquette and Rites" describes formal procedures and aristocratic ceremonies. These three classics, redacted in the 2nd and 1st centuries BCE, contain assorted descriptions of ritual from approximately the 5th to 3rd centuries BCE.

A few other classics and dictionaries will be mentioned in reference to personation of the dead. Two primary Confucian texts are the *Lunyu* 論語 "Compiled/Arranged Words" (or "Confucian Analects") that disciples of Confucius put together circa the 5th century BCE; and the *Mengzi* 孟子 "(Book of) Master Meng," compiled around the 3rd century BCE by followers of Mencius

(372–289 BCE). The Daoist *Zhuangzi* 莊子 "(Book of) Master Zhuang" includes "Inner Chapters" attributed to Zhuang Zhou 莊周 (fl. 370–301 BCE) and other sections with pre-Han philosophical writings. The *Chuci* 楚辭 "Songs/Elegies of Chu" is an anthology of poetry and prose, primarily credited to Chu Yuan 屈原 (ca. 340–278 BCE) from the southern state of Chu. Lastly, citations will come from the two earliest extant Chinese dictionaries. The *Erya* 爾雅 "Approaching Elegancy/Correctness" is a compilation of early glosses to Zhou texts arranged (ca. 3rd century BCE) into semantic categories. The *Shuowen jiezi* 說文解字 "Commenting on Simple and Analyzing Complex Characters" dictionary was edited (ca. 100 CE) by Xu Shen 許慎.[21]

Chinese Linguistic Terminology

Some specialized terms are needed to discuss the character 尸 and the word *shi* 'corpse; personator'.

- *Characters* or *logographs* (viz., graphs that represent words) are the basis of written Chinese. In the West, these are widely misunderstood as "pictographs" or "ideographs," which are in fact minor subtypes of Chinese characters.[22]

- *Pictographs* or *pictograms* hieroglyphically depict material things, e.g., *kou* 口 'mouth', *mu* 目 'eye', or *mei* 眉 'eyebrow'. As exemplified by the historical changes in 'horse' characters below, many ancient pictographs have been graphically simplified beyond recognition.

- *Ideographs* or *ideograms* indicate abstract meanings. Some are universally transparent, like 一, 二, 三 '1, 2, 3'; other composite ideographs are more culture-specifically opaque, like *xin* 信 'trust' from *ren* 人 'person' and *yan* 言 'speech; speak'.

- *Semantic-phonetic* or *radical-phonetic characters* are the most common type of Chinese logographs. They have the following two elements:

- *Radicals, significs, classifiers,* or *semantic elements* are recurring graphic components like 水 'water', 竹 'bamboo', or 人 'person' that roughly indicate character meaning. Radicals hint at the semantic field for a word, and are the traditional basis for organizing Chinese character dictionaries. Most words written with the "horse radical" 馬 have 'equine' semantic associations (e.g., *ju* 駒 'colt', *qi* 騎 'ride (a horse, etc.); sit astride', or *tuo* 駝 'camel; hunchback'), but not all (e.g., *huan* 驩 'joy, rejoice' is a graphic variant of *huan* 歡 with the "lack/owe radical" 欠).

- *Phonetics* or *phonetic elements* are character components that roughly indicate pronunciation. For instance, *tong* 同 'same; together; harmony' is the phonetic in *tong* 銅 'copper' with the "metal radical," *tong* 侗 'immature; ignorant' with the "person radical," and *tong* 筒 'section of thick bamboo; tube' with the "bamboo radical." Owing to historical variations in phonology, characters sharing the same phonetic can be pronounced differently, compare *dong* 洞 'hole; cave' with the "water radical" or *dong* 恫 'fear, frighten' with the "heart radical."

- *Phonetic loan characters* or *loan-graphs* involve the rebus-like substitution of one homophonous character for another; e.g., borrowing *qi* 其 '(winnowing) basket' to write the pronoun *qi* 'he; she; it' that anciently did not have a logograph. In this case, a new character *ji* 箕 'basket' with the "bamboo radical" was created to disambiguate confusion over 其 denoting 'basket' or 'pronoun'.

While all languages change diachronically, Chinese, with a written record dating back over three millennia, can present a best-case study in linguistic change. The history of Chinese characters for *ma* 'horse' from pictographic 𢒈 to simplified 马 exemplifies the range of developments in written forms and writing materials.

- *Oracle* or *shell and bone characters* (甲骨文), which archeologists began discovering in early 20th century excavations, were anciently written on divination records from the Later Shang — 🐎 'horse' was a sideways pictograph of the head, mane, legs, and tail.

- *Bronze characters* (金文) primarily from the Zhou period were inscribed on sacrificial and ceremonial bronzes — 🐎 'horse' is still recognizable as a simpler pictograph. There were no accepted standards for oracle or bronze characters, and scribes wrote 'horse' in numerous variant forms, for instance, with or without hooves.

- *Small seal characters* (小篆) were enforced as the imperial standard during the Qin Dynasty (221–207 BCE) — 🐎 'horse' is a more angular pictograph.

- *Regular/Model characters* (楷書) have been the standard since the Later Han Dynasty (25–221 CE)[23] — 馬 'horse' has even less equine resemblance with four dots for legs.

- *Simplified characters* (简体字 [cf. 簡體字 in *regular*]) became the standard for the People's Republic of China in 1955–1964 reforms — 马 'horse' is written with a minimalist three strokes instead of the ten in 馬.

While some of this linguistic terminology admittedly sounds arcane, it will prove relevant to *shi* personation. For instance, the regular character 尸 for *shi* 'corpse; personator' hardly resembles the oracle pictograph 𠂆 of a corpse. Phonetic loan characters are especially germane because early texts used *shi* 尸 'corpse' (and *shi* 矢 'arrow') as a loan for 'lay out, display' (see pages 379–380).[24]

Previous Research

Lastly, I should introduce my interests with the bicameral hypothesis. When I first read *The Origin of Consciousness in the*

Breakdown of the Bicameral Mind in 1977, I was beginning a doctoral dissertation on the *Erya* dictionary. While looking up citations in classical texts, I sometimes saw what appeared to be descriptions of bicamerality, and later wrote five articles exploring bicameral possibilities in early China.[25] They sought to help answer a central Jaynesian question, "What mentality is reflected in the earliest writings?"[26]

"Sidelights on *Xin* 心 'Heart; Mind' in the *Shijing*"[27] surveyed mental vocabulary in the "Classic of Poetry."[28] Among the wide-ranging evidence Jaynes presents for his bicameral hypothesis, he interprets differences between the *Iliad* and the *Odyssey* as the first reliable linguistic verification for a leap from bicamerality to consciousness (ca. 8th century BCE in Greece). According to Jaynes, "we may regard the *Iliad* as standing at the great turning of the times, a window back into those unsubjective times"[29] of bicamerality. If this is true, then the *Shijing*, roughly contemporaneous with the *Iliad* and *Odyssey*, offers another window with a different view. Chinese, like Greek and many other languages, coined 'mind; mental; intellect' vocabulary from existing words with concrete bodily referents. The most common Chinese word for the seat of mental activity is *xin* 'heart; mind, intelligence; feeling, thinking', which the *Shijing* uses 168 times, much more frequently than any other body part (e.g., 47 occurrences of *huai* 懷 'bosom; cherish, dwell on; yearn; think longingly; mind'). The keyword for *xin* 'heart; mind' is *yu* 憂 'grief; sadness, sorrow; anxiety, concern': 37 percent of the *xin* usages co-occur with *yu*, and 76 percent of the *yu* are with *xin*. The *Shijing* has 103 characters written with the "heart radical" 心 (or 忄 on the side). Twice as many of these have semantically negative meanings like *nu* 怒 'anger, angry; rage; furious' as positive ones like *yi* 懌 'pleased, pleasure; happy'. Negative contexts generally predominate with mental vocabulary, e.g., "great Heaven is terrific, it does not ponder, it does not plan."[30] Within the *Shijing*'s lexical field for mental and emotional vocabulary, the largest subfield is 'grief; sadness; sorrow; pain; pity' containing about 60 words. There are about 30 in the 'think; thought' subfield (frequently written with graphic loan characters), with 16 meaning 'plan; ponder; inquire, consult', 11 'think broodingly, brood; worry', and only three words meaning 'know; understand; comprehend'. This linguistic evidence in the *Shijing* can support the hypothesis that during the early Zhou period, people were losing unsubjective bicamerality and gaining subjective consciousness.

"Personation of the Dead in Ancient China"[31] was the published version of a paper given to the 1984 Chinese Linguistics Seminar that Japanese linguist Mantarō J. Hashimoto 橋本萬太郎 (1932–1987) organized in honor of Chinese historical phonologist Zhou Zumo 周祖謨 (1914–1995). In contrast with that original article about *shi* personation, this chapter presumes no knowledge of the Chinese language or linguistic jargon and excludes some bicameral speculations about *zhaohun* 招魂 "recalling the soul," provisional and secondary burials, rich grave furnishings, and placing valuables in a corpse's mouth. This revised version includes sinological research published in the last two decades; for instance, the surrealistic bronze masks discovered in 1986 at Sanxingdui (e.g., Figures 1–3), which have been associated with *shi* personation.

"Big Heads in Old Chinese"[32] looked into early Chinese words meaning 'big/large head' and oracle characters depicting people with unusual heads. Cross-linguistic comparison finds that "big head" words are globally extended to mean 'important; influential person' (e.g., Japanese *ō-atama* 大頭 "big head" 'head, leader, boss') or 'headstrong; obstinate; arrogant' (e.g., Spanish *cabezón* "big head" 'bigheaded; obstinate, stubborn'). Here are four examples of oracle characters that show people marked by their heads. The graph 𡗗 for *tian* 天 'sky, heaven; nature; god; emperor' showed a 大 'great, big' person with a squared head (rounded in later bronze graphs), or occasionally a head depicted by two horizontal lines, like early graphs for *yuan* 元 'head;

principal, fundamental'. The oracle character 𝙭 for *xiong* 兄 'elder brother; elder; invocator, priest' depicted a kneeling (or sometimes standing) person with a □ 'mouth', which was taken figuratively to mean either 'head' or 'invocation'. To distinguish 'invocator' from 'elder (brother)', the "spirit/sacrifice radical" elucidates the character 𝙩 for *zhu* 祝 'invocator, prayer-master; priest; pray.'[33] The oracle graph 𝙮 for *dui* 兌 (or 兑) 'joy, happiness; penetrate, open a passage; opening' obscurely wrote two lines over a standing person with this same 'mouth/head'.[34] Commentators speculate that these two overhead strokes marked spirits/gods 'descending' in answer to prayers, prayers 'going through' the mouth of a invocator, or 'shedding' worry (cf. the same phonetic in *tui* 蛻 'molt; slough off') when a prayer is answered. A bicameral interpretation is that some ancient logographs represent preconscious states of mind, an alien mentality where "big head person" depicted 'heaven' or 'god'.

"The *ᵏ'ôg* 考 'To Dead Father' Hypothesis"[35] investigated why Chinese violates the linguistically universal avoidance of 'die; death' words and uses *kao* 考 'dead father' as a common word for 'examine, test; think'. The postulated answer is that *kao* < *ᵏ'ôg* (cf. Baxter's *ᵏhu*) anciently meant "to dead father," namely, 'to communicate with the spirit of one's dead father'. This hypothesis unifies *kao*'s different meanings of 'dead father/grandfather; father; old age; test; examine, investigate; think; thoughtful, clever; complete, achieve; strike; flaw; wail; personal name'. It also resolves several Chinese textual conundrums. For instance, commentators have interpreted *Kaopan* 考槃 "*kao* basin/tray," the ambiguous title of *Shijing* ode 56, as loan characters meaning 'complete/achieve joy', 'complete a hut', 'achieve withdrawal', 'beat the basin/table', or 'drum and dance'.[36] Evidence from early texts suggests that *ᵏ'ôg/ᵏhu* 考 was the name of an ancestral sacrifice associated with divination, 'striking' bells and drums to beckon spirits, 'completing' ancestral temples, drinking sacrificial wine, and spirit communication.

"Ritual Fasts and Spirit Visions in the *Liji*"[37] examined how the "Record of Rites" describes *zhai* 齋 'ritual fasting' that supposedly resulted in seeing and hearing the dead. This text describes preparations for an ancestral sacrifice that included divination for a suitable day, ablution, contemplation, and a fasting ritual with seven days of *sanzhai* 散齋 'relaxed fasting; vegetarian diet; abstinence (esp. from sex, meat, or wine)' followed by three days of *zhizhai* 致齋 'strict fasting; diet of grains (esp. gruel) and water'.

> Devoted fasting is inside; relaxed fasting is outside. During fast-days, one thinks about their [the ancestor's] lifestyle, their jokes, their aspirations, their pleasures, and their affections. [After] fasting three days, then one sees those [spirits] for whom one fasted. On the day of the sacrifice, when one enters the temple, apparently one must see them at the spirit-tablet. When one returns to go out the door [after making sacrifices], solemnly one must hear sounds of their appearance. When one goes out the door and listens, emotionally one must hear sounds of their sighing breath.[38]

This context unequivocally uses *biyou* 必有 'must be/have; necessarily/certainly have' to describe events within the ancestral temple; the faster 必有見 "must have sight of, must see" and 必有聞 "must have hearing of, must hear" the deceased parent. Did 10 days of ritual fasting and mournful meditation necessarily cause visions or hallucinations? Perhaps the explanation is extreme or total fasting, except that several *Liji* passages specifically warn against any excessive fasts that could harm the faster's health or sense perceptions.[39] Perhaps the explanation is inebriation from drinking sacrificial *jiu* 酒 '(millet) wine; alcohol' after a 10-day fast. Based on measurements of bronze vessels and another *Liji* passage describing a *shi* personator drinking nine cups of wine,[40] York University professor of religious studies Jordan

Paper calculates an alcohol equivalence of "between 5 and 8 bar shots of eighty-proof liquor."[41] On the other hand, perhaps the best explanation is the bicameral hypothesis, which provides a far wider-reaching rationale for Chinese ritual hallucinations and personation of the dead.

THE WORD *SHI*

In this section, *shi* 尸 is analyzed from the three linguistic standpoints of graphics, phonology, and semantics. The graphic information is the oldest, dating back to the Shang oracle bone inscriptions (from the late 2nd millennium BCE). The phonetic and semantic information concerning *shi* dates back to the Western Zhou Dynasty (1st millennium BCE).

The Character 尸

The modern Chinese logograph 尸 for *shi* 'corpse; personator; etc.' has been simplified beyond recognition from the original pictograph 𠂌 of a dead body. When the *Shuowen jiezi* notes that 尸 was initially "a pictograph of a prone body," the commentary of Duan Yucai 段玉裁 (1735–1815) elaborates that it "pictures the head hanging down and the back bent." Reviewing the early logographs for *shi* 尸 shown in Table 1, the oracle character 𠂌 pictures a person with bent legs; the bronze 𠂆 has a more bent back with dangling arms and legs; and the seal character 尸 is graphically reduced. These bent-over *shi* 'corpse' characters contrast with those for upright *ren* 人 'person' — the oracle 𠆢 has comparatively straighter legs, the bronze 𠂉 has straighter back and arms, and the seal 𠓜 is marginally pictographic.

Today, *shi* 尸 is more commonly used as a radical (see Chinese Linguistic Terminology on page 350) than to write the word *shi* 'corpse; etc.' Some characters written with this "corpse/body radical" involve the body, e.g., *wei* 尾 'tail' (with 毛 'hair'), *niao* 尿 'urine' (with 水 'water'), or *shi* 屎 'dung' (with 米 'rice').[42] Many other characters do not involve corporality, e.g., *wu* 屋 'house; room' (with 至 'go/come to') or *lu* 屢 'repeatedly; frequently' (with 婁 'a constellation'). The character 屍 for *shi* 'corpse, dead body', which dates back to the (ca. 3rd century BCE) seal graph 𢇼, combines *shi* 尸 'corpse; body' with *si* 死 'dead'. This semantically redundant *shi* 屍 'dead-corpse' graphically distinguishes the original 'corpse' meaning of *shi* 尸 from its various other meanings such as 'personator'.

Shang scribes used the oracle character 𓀒 interchangeably to write both *shi* 尸 'corpse' and *yi* 夷 '(eastern) barbarian, non-Chinese; peaceful, at ease; level'.[43] According to Chinese historical linguist Xu Zhongshu, this 𓀒 'corpse' with two bent legs resembles the "barbarian" (i.e., foreign) custom of sitting with one's legs stretched out instead of the Chinese custom of squatting/crouching on one's heels.[44] Note the bent-backed similarity between the bronze characters of 𓀒 for *shi* and 𓀒 for *yi*. Like the modern 夷 for *yi* 'barbarian; peaceful' written with 大 'big (person)' and 弓 'bow', the seal character 夷 is interpreted as 'big' and 'bow' (or perhaps some garment).[45]

Table 1 includes two sacrificial terms, *bi* 妣 'dead mother/grandmother; ancestress' and *kao* 考 'dead father; old (father); old age, longevity; examine; think'. *Bi* 妣 'dead mother' combines the "woman radical" 女 with a phonetic of *bi* 比 'compare; close; combine', which duplicates *bi* 匕 '(inverted) person; spoon'.[46] Scholars realized that 𓀒 was the primary form of *bi* 妣 from numerous oracles divining to (in modern characters) 妣甲 'Ancestress A'.[47] There are mirror images of a 'dead person' in the right-facing oracle *bi* 𓀒 and the left-facing *shi* 𓀒 'corpse' (which also had right-facing variants). Earlier forms of the "woman radical" appear in the bronze 𣎴 and the seal 𣎴 for *bi*, both of which have variants with double 比 instead of single 匕. *Kao* 考 'dead father; old (father);

Word	Oracle	Bronze	Seal	Modern
ren 'person'	〔graph〕	〔graph〕	〔graph〕	人
shi 'corpse'	〔graph〕	〔graph〕	〔graph〕	尸
yi 'barbarian'	〔graph〕	〔graph〕	〔graph〕	夷
bi 'dead mother'	〔graph〕	〔graph〕	〔graph〕	妣
kao 'dead father'	〔graph〕	〔graph〕	〔graph〕	考
zi 'first (of 12)'	〔graph〕	〔graph〕	〔graph〕	子
zi 'child'	〔graph〕	〔graph〕	〔graph〕	子

Table 1. Logographic Developments

examine, test; think' was cognate with *lao* 老 'old, be old; grow old'. The oracle 〔graph〕, bronze 〔graph〕, and seal 〔graph〕 characters for *kao* are traditionally taken to show an 'old' man with long hair (or a head-dress) leaning on a cane.

Personators may have been pictured in some early graphs for *zi* 子 that can mean either 'child; baby; young person' or 'first (of the 12 Earthly Branches), a cyclical/calendrical character'. Two complicated sets of early graphs differentiated these *zi* meanings. For 'child', the oracle 〔graph〕 is enigmatic (perhaps a simplified 〔graph〕 'first'[48]), while the similar bronze 〔graph〕 and seal 〔graph〕 characters clearly show the head and arms of an infant. For 'first (cyclical character)', the oracle 〔graph〕, bronze 〔graph〕, and seal 〔graph〕 show less resemblance to a child, and thus have various interpretations. The *Shuowen jiezi* says 〔graph〕 shows a table beneath a child depicted with hair, arms, and legs. Japanese sinologist Katō Jōken (1894–1978) sees an effigy with a ghost-mask and a body on a pole: representing either a personator or a spirit tablet.[49] Japanese sinologists Shirakawa Shizuka and Kobayashi Haku say the logographs picture a personator.[50] Xu Zhongshu believes these bronze and seal *zi* graphs depict a person holding up a baby who is serving as a personator.[51]

Pronunciations of Shi 尸

The Modern Standard Chinese (or "Mandarin") reading of 尸 is first-tone *shi*, and scholars have proposed earlier pronunciations. Comparative linguists reconstructed "Middle/Ancient Chinese" from rhyme tables in dictionaries like the *Qieyun* 切韻 "Cut Rhyme" (601 CE), and subsequently "Old/Archaic Chinese" (marked with *) from the rhymed parts of the *Shijing* "Classic of Poetry" (approximately one millennium earlier). Although this chapter regularly cites the reconstructions of University of Michigan linguist William Baxter,[52] for the sake of perspective, the second table compares how Swedish sinologist Bernhard Karlgren (1889–1978),[53] Chinese linguist Zhou Fagao (1915–1994),[54] and Wartburg College sinologist Axel Schuessler[55] reconstruct some key words.

The broadest phonological perspective for analyzing Chinese etymology is the Sino-Tibetan linguistic stock. Historical linguists generally believe that the Chinese, Karen, and Tibeto-Burman languages all derive from Proto-Sino-Tibetan. American linguist and psychiatrist Paul K. Benedict (1912–1997) proposes two Proto-Sino-Tibetan roots that may relate with *shi* 尸 'corpse': *(s-)raw* 'corpse; carcass' and *siy* 'die'.[56] Furthermore, he suggests that both *shi* 尸 'corpse' and *shi* 屎 'dung' had an Old Chinese pronunciation of *s-gljər*, coming from a hypothetical root of *s-kljəy* 'corpse; dung; refuse'.[57] Since "shit" is a common expletive in many languages, it makes sense that Old Chinese 'dung' and 'groan' were cognate. The *Shijing* (254, see fn. 102) uses *shi* < *hljijʔ* 屎 'dung' as a loan character for 'groan' when pronounced *xi* < *xʃij* 屎. This 'corpse' = 'excrement' etymology for *shi* is not only linguistically feasible, but also historically corroborated. Exposure burials were an ancient Chinese and Tibetan custom; a "corpse" was disposed of like "excrement." Burial was not widely practiced in China's early Stone Age. Skeletons from the Paleolithic and Mesolithic periods were often thrown away,

Modern Word	Karlgren 1957	Zhou 1970	Schuessler 1987	Baxter 1992
shī 尸 'corpse'	*śi* < **śjər*	*śiɪi* < **śt'jier*	*śi* < **hljəj*	*syij* < **hljij*
shǐ 屎 'dung'	*śi:* < **śjər*	*śiɪi* < **śt'jier*	*śi* < **hljəj*	*syijX* < **hljijʔ*
xī 屎 'groan'	*xji* < **Xjər*	*xiɪi* < **xjier*	*xji* < **hj-ʔ-əj*	*xjij* < **xĵij*
sǐ 死 'death'	*si:* < **sjər*	*siɪi* < **sjier*	*si* < **sjəjʔ*	*sijX* < **sjijʔ*
shǐ 矢 'arrow'	*śi:* < **śjər*	*śiɪi* < **śt'jier*	*śi* < **hljəjʔ*	*syijX* < **hljijʔ*
yí 夷 'barbarian'	*i* < **djər*	*iɪi* < **rier*	*ji* < **ljəj*	*yij* < **ljij*

Table 2. Middle and Old Chinese Reconstructions

sometimes with the skulls smashed. Early texts, for instance *Yijing*[58] and *Mengzi*,[59] mention ancient exposure burials.

Another perspective on the etymology of *shi* 尸 'corpse; personator' is word families — groups of cognate words underlying the lexical structure of Old Chinese. *Shi* has three proposed families. First, Karlgren, who pioneered word families, simply relates *si* < **sjər* 死 'die, dead' with *shi* < **sjər* 尸 'the dead, corpse'.[60] Second, Japanese sinologist Tōdō Akiyasu (1914–1985) reconstructs *shi* < **hljij* 尸 as Old Chinese **thier* and groups it among 24 words in a family with a root of **TER* 'straight; short; low'.[61] Several have already been discussed like **hljijʔ* 矢 'arrow', **hljij* 屍 'corpse', and **ljij* 夷 'barbarian; level'. Others include **kjijʔ* 指 'finger; point', **gjijʔ/s* 視 'look at; regard,' **tjijʔ* 低 'low; bent,' and **diʲijʔ* 弟 'younger brother'. He etymologizes *shi* 'corpse' from a body that had fallen down 'low',[62] and says personators anciently held a 'short straight' spirit tablet symbolizing the dead ancestor. Third, Japanese lexicographer Morohashi Tetsuji (1883–1982) reconstructs *shi* < **hljij* 尸 as **sjed*, and places it in a nine-member word family descending from a 'hurt; wounded; injured' etymological root.[63] Along with **hljijʔ* 'arrow', **hljij* 'corpse', and **ljij* 'barbarian', these include **dzjit* 疾 'sickness; illness', **ljiʲij* 痍 'wound', and **drjiʲijʔ* 雉 'pheasant.'

The Meanings of Shi

By the end of the Zhou Dynasty (3rd century BCE), the word *shi* 尸 had acquired several meanings: (1) 'corpse; body of a dead person', (2) 'personator of a dead ancestor', (3) 'motionless; inactive', (4) 'lay out; arrange; expose', (5) 'manage; direct', and (6) 'proper names (of a place, family, and bird)'. The basic meaning (1) 'corpse' was semantically extended into both (2) 'personator of a dead ancestor' (from "act on behalf of a corpse") and (3) 'motionless; inactive; doing nothing' (from "act like a corpse"). The fourth meaning of 'lay out, arrange; display' (i.e., *chen* 陳) came from generalizing "lay out a corpse." That of (5) 'manage; direct' (i.e., *zhu* 主) is probably derived from an older *shi* meaning of 'ancestral tablet,' which is symbolic of (2) 'personator'. Meaning (6) comes from the pronunciation of *shi* in proper names, and apparently lacks any semantic association.

EARLY TEXTUAL OCCURRENCES OF *SHI*

The Chinese classics use the word *shi* 尸 in all six of the above meanings. Their occurrences will be treated in that order, with emphasis placed on early information concerning personation of the dead. Finally, the overall pattern of *shi*'s occurrences will be discussed and summarized (see Table 3).

Meaning (1): Corpse

Ancient Chinese texts often use *shi* 尸 in its core meaning of 'corpse, dead body, cadaver', most frequently in contexts of war, death, and funerals. The *Yijing* "Classic/Book of Changes" probably has the earliest occurrence of *shi* meaning 'corpse'. In the sixth hexagram ䷆ *Shi* 師 "The Army," *shi* 尸 is used in two line statements:

Perchance the army carries corpses in the wagon.
Misfortune ... Let the eldest lead the army. The younger
transports corpses. Then perseverance brings misfortune.[64]

Both lines use *shi* with *yu* 輿 'palanquin; carriage; wagon' in the
compound *yushi* 輿尸 'carry corpses; corpse carrier, hearse'. The
exact meaning of this passage, like much of the language in the
Yijing, is unclear. German sinologist and *Yijing* translator
Richard Wilhelm (1873–1930) summarizes the predominant
commentaries that:

> Here we have a choice of two explanations. One points to
> defeat because someone other than the chosen leader in-
> terferes with the command; the other is similar in its
> general meaning, but the expression, "carries corpses in
> the wagon," is interpreted differently. At burials and at
> sacrifices to the dead it was customary in China for the
> deceased to whom the sacrifice was made to be repre-
> sented by a boy of the family, who sat in the dead man's
> place and was honored as his representative. On the basis
> of this custom the text is interpreted as meaning that a
> "corpse boy" is sitting in the wagon, or, in other words,
> that authority is not being exercised by the proper leaders
> but has been usurped by others. Perhaps the whole diffi-
> culty clears up if it is inferred that there has been an error
> in copying. The character *fan*, meaning "all," may have
> been misread as [*shi*], which means "corpse." Allowing
> for this error, the meaning would be that if the multitude
> assumes leadership of the army (rides in the wagon),
> misfortunes will ensue.[65]

It is possible that *shi* 尸 is a copyist's error for *fan* 凡 'all; every',
but improbable. In this context of "misfortune," the literal
'corpse' (of a soldier killed in battle) seems the most likely

meaning of *shi*. German sinologist Bruno Schindler (1882–1964) interprets this *shi* 'corpse' in the *Yijing* as meaning (5) 'ancestral tablet' and cites historical records of wooden spirit tablets being carried by armies at war.[66]

The *Zuozhuan* uses *shi* to mean 'corpse' in a syntactically unusual verbal sense of "to corpse," that is, 'to expose a corpse (esp. for public punishment)'. For example, after a 631 BCE battle, "Zuo's Commentary" says, "The people of [Cao] took their bodies, and exposed them on the top of the wall."[67] This sense of 'expose (a corpse)' is semantically similar to *shi* meaning (4) 'lay out (esp. a corpse)'. The "Three Ritual Compendia" frequently use *shi* 'corpse' in funereal contexts. Here is a typical *Liji* passage:

> As soon as death took place, the corpse was transferred to the couch, and covered with a large sheet. The clothes in which the deceased had died were removed. A servant plugged the mouth open with the spoon of horn; and to keep the feet from contracting, an easy stool was employed. These observances were the same for a ruler, a great officer, and an ordinary officer.[68]

Meaning (2): Personator

Shi 尸 meaning 'personator of a dead ancestor' is the topic of central interest. Obviously, rendering this into English is problematic because there is no Western analogy for the ceremonial *shi* 'corpse'. *Personator* is chosen as the nearest English translation. *Impersonator* would be possible, but this word implies falsehood, which was not originally associated with the *shi*. *Representative* is too general in meaning, and does not usually have a sense of spirituality, unless modified by *of the dead/ancestor*. Paper suggests *Incorporator of the Dead*,[69] which has a parallel 'one who embodies' etymology, but the derivate words *incorporate* and *incorporation* commonly have other meanings. *Medium* and *sha-*

man are similar with *shi* in meaning and are part of Chinese traditions; however, the descriptions of a dignified personator are unlike the spirit-possession of either. Another translational tactic would be to coin a nonce word, such as Waley's "the Dead One," Eberhard's "death boy," or Wilhelm's "corpse boy," but the sense of such a coinage is not always clear. Therefore, in the absence of a better English word, *personator* will translate this meaning of *shi*.

The *Shijing* "Classic of Poetry" has the earliest descriptions of the personation ceremony. There are fourteen occurrences of *shi* 'personator' in two pairs of consecutive poems (209–210 and 247–248). Karlgren's translation of the *Shijing* will be quoted;[70] but when there is uncertainty, Chinese commentaries as well as the translations of Legge[71] and British classicist Arthur Waley[72] (1889–1966) are quoted.

Odes 209 and 210 both mention using personators in ancestral sacrifices. In 209/1, there is an indirect reference to a personator, "we make (the representative of the dead) sit at ease, we (assist him =) encourage him to eat." The word translated "at ease" is *tuo* 妥 (ideographically with 爫 'hand' on 女 'woman') 'make comfortable; tranquil, relaxed; safe, secure; ready; satisfactory'. Legge notes that the personator:

> ...was necessarily inferior in rank to the principal sacrificer, yet for the time he was superior to him, occupying the place of his departed ancestor. This circumstance, it was supposed, would make him feel uncomfortable; and therefore as soon as he appeared in the temple, the sacrificer was instructed, by the director of the ceremonies, to ask him to be seated, and to place him at ease.[73]

In 209/5, there is a direct reference, "The august representative of the dead then rises, the drums and bells (by their sound) es-

cort away the representative." The following ode, 210/3, describes sacrificial oblations and how, "he presents them [wine
and food] to our representative of the dead and to our guests."[74]

Odes 247 and 248 praise the Zhou royal house. The former
describes a sacrificial feast for ancestral spirits, and the latter describes another feast (given on the following day, according to
commentaries) to reward the personator. Every occurrence in
both uses the term *gongshi* 公尸. This modifier *gong* 公 has many
meanings; in the *Shijing* alone, it can mean 'prince; duke; public;
official place, palace' or can be a loan character for *gong* 功 'effort;
achievement; result'.[75] Thus, *gong*-personator 公尸 could have
meant 'personator of the prince; duke; palace; effort; result; etc.'
Karlgren translates *gongshi* as "representative of the (dead)
princes." Translating "the personators of your ancestors," Legge
admits, "The expression 公尸, 'ducal personators', is somewhat
difficult to account for."[76] Waley translates *gongshi* as "ducal
dead" and "Dead One," and notes the "Impersonator of a former
Duke or ruler."[77]

A Jaynesian interpretation would be that *gongshi* 公尸 meant a
'bicameral personator' who hallucinated the spirits of dead
ancestors. There are three linguistic reasons to support this interpretation:

1. The graphic origins of *gong* 公: Shirakawa and Kobayashi
   say that the early 公 logographs combine 八 'open; reveal;
   release' with 口 'mouth', thus indicating 'to make one's
   words public/known (esp. in the ancestral temple).'[78]

2. With the above loan character relationship between *gong*
   公 and *gong* 功 'result' in the *Shijing*, *gongshi* could mean a
   'personator with achievements/results' in spirit communication.

3. The *Erya* (1A/28) defines *gong* 公 (and seven other words
   including *yi* 宜, see the *Shijing* on page 368) as *shi* 事
   'service; affair; performance; sacrifice; work', a word
   which other texts (e.g., the *Liji* on page 371) frequently

use to portray personators making contact with the spirits of the dead.

Shijing ode 247, describing another ancestral sacrifice, mentions, "the representative of the (dead) princes makes a happy announcement" (247/3, tr. Karlgren). Ode 248 "Wild Ducks" provides early details about the personation ceremony.

> The wild ducks are on the [Jing] (river); the representative of the (dead) princes comes and feasts and is at peace; your wine is clear, your viands are fragrant; the representative feasts and drinks; felicity and blessings come and (achieve, complete you =) make you perfect.

> The wild ducks are on the sands; the representative of the (dead) princes comes and feasts and (approves =) finds it good; your wine is plentiful, your viands are fine; the representative feasts and drinks; felicity and blessings come and (act for =) favor you.

> The wild ducks are on the island; the representative of the (dead) princes comes and feasts and reposes; your wine is strained, your viands are sliced; the representative feasts and drinks; felicity and blessings come and descend on you.

> The wild ducks are at the junction of the river; the representative of the (dead) princes comes and feasts and is (treated in temple-fashion =) revered; the feast is in the temple, that is where felicity and blessings descend; the representative feasts and drinks; felicity and blessings come and are piled up (heavily =) amply on you.

> The wild ducks are in the gorge; the representative of the (dead) princes comes and feasts and is befumed (by the spirits); the good wine makes you merry; the roast and broiled things are fragrant; the representative feasts and drinks; there will be no after trouble.

Each stanza has five rhymed lines: an allusion to wild ducks, 公尸來燕來X "the *gong*-personator comes, *yan* comes, [and] X," a description of sacrificial offerings, 公尸燕飲 "the *gong*-personator *yan* drinks," and a description of ancestral blessings.

The ambiguous keyword is *yan* 燕 'swallow; ease; feast, enjoy'. The *Shijing* uses *yan* both in its original avian meaning of 'swallow; swift' and as a graphic loan for 'rest; comfort; ease; calm, quiet; soothe; feast; beautiful; privacy'.[79] Karlgren translates "the representative feasts and drinks" for fourth-line "the *gong*-personator *yan* drinks" in every stanza. Compare "The personators of your ancestors feast and drink" (Legge) and "The Dead One quietly drinks" (Waley). Karlgren translates "the representative of the (dead) princes comes and feasts and …" for second-line "the *gong*-personator comes, *yan* comes, [and] X," where X is a different rhyme-word in the first four stanzas. Legge renders it as "The personators of your ancestors feast and …" and Waley as "The Dead One is calm and …." In 248/1, the X-word is *ning* 寧 'peace; tranquility; serenity; inquire about; preferable' — translated as "is at peace" (Karlgren and Waley) and "are happy" (Legge). In 248/2, it is *yi* 宜 'sacrifice; right; proper; approve; adjust' — "(approves =) finds it good" (Karlgren), "well disposed" (Waley), and "their appropriate tribute" (Legge).[80] In 248/3, the rhyming X-word is *chu* 處 'dwell; stay; keep still; a place' — "reposes" (Karlgren), "at rest" (Waley), and "enjoy themselves" (Legge). In 248/4 it is *zong* 宗 (written with 宀 'roof' over 示 'sacrificial altar; omen') 'ancestral temple; ancestry, ancestor; clan; to honor' — "is (treated in temple-fashion =) revered" (Karlgren), "is at ease" (Waley), and "are honored" (Legge). The final stanza, 248/5, varies the syntax with 公尸來止熏熏 "the *gong*-personator comes, stops/rests, [and] *xunxun*" — "the representative of the (dead) princes comes and feasts and is befumed (by the spirits)" (Karlgren), "The Dead One is resting, overcome" (Waley), and "The personators of your ancestors rest, full of complacency" (Legge).

This melodious compound *xunxun* < *ˣxjunxjun* reduplicates *xun* 熏 'to smoke (fish, etc.); fumigate'. The commentary of Mao Heng 毛亨 (2ⁿᵈ century BCE) glosses it as 和說 'harmonious speech/pleasure'; while the *Shuowen jiezi* writes it *xun* 醺 (with the "wine radical"), defined as 醉 'drunk, intoxicated; tipsy'. Karlgren says *xun* "fundamentally means 'smoke, steam, vapor, fumes' (common); here it means 'befumed, befuddled' (cf. Shakespeare: 'Keep his brain fuming')."[81]

Without using the word *shi*, *Shijing* ode 166 indirectly mentions a personator in a context about seasonal sacrifices made to 公先王 "princes [viz. the *gong* 公 in *gongshi* above] and former kings." "The (dead) lords say: 'We predict for you myriad years of life, without limit.'"[82] This context uses a word that specifies direct discourse, *yue* 曰 'say; speak; call, name', which indicates that the ancestral spirits are speaking, and the commentators agree that it must be through the personator.

In summary, the *Shijing's* descriptions of personation ceremonies have several themes. There is an abundance of sacrificial wine and food (odes 166, 209, 210, and 248) shared by both the ancestral spirits (through the personator) and their descendants. Drunkenness is frequently mentioned: 209/5 "The spirits [note: 'souls' not 'liquor'] are all drunk," 209/6 "all are happy; they are drunk," 247/1, 2 "We are drunk with wine," and 248/5 "the representative of the (dead) princes comes and feasts and is befumed (by the spirits); the good wine makes you merry."[83] Most significantly, the ancestral spirits speak directly through the intoxicated personators (166, 210, and 247), approve of the sacrificial offerings, and bless their descendants (166, 209, 210, 247, and 248).

The *Mengzi* "Book of Mencius" only has one *shi* occurrence, meaning 'personator', in this passage:

You should ask him, "Which do you respect most, — your uncle, or your younger brother?" He will answer,

"My uncle." Ask him again, "If your younger brother be personating a dead ancestor, to which do you show the greater respect, — to him or to your uncle?" He will say, "To my younger brother." You can go on, "But where is the respect due, as you said, to your uncle?" He will reply to this, "I show the respect to my younger brother because of the position which he occupies."[84]

Mencius makes the didactic point that personation was an exception to the usual social stratification. The younger brother, who is of lower status than his elders, was temporarily exalted above them during the time when he personated their dead ancestor. The *Liji* makes the same point about personation contradicting the established rules of hierarchy:

Thus it is that there are two among his subjects whom the ruler does not treat as subjects. When one is personating (his ancestor) he does not treat him as such, nor does he treat his master as such.[85]

The *Liji* repeatedly uses *shi* meaning 'personator' in detailed descriptions of the personation ceremony. Two remarkable passages record an ancient tradition about the history of personation. The first one describes how the Zhou changed certain rituals:

Under the [Zhou] dynasty the representatives of the dead sat. Their monitors and cup-suppliers observed no regular rules. The usages were the same (as those of Yin [Shang]), and the underlying principle was one. Under the [Xia] dynasty, the personators had stood till the sacrifice was ended (whereas) under the Yin [Shang] they sat. Under [Zhou], when the cup went round among all, there were six personators. [Zengzi] said, "The usages of [Zhou] might be compared to a subscription club."[86]

Commentaries to this passage describe personation with the word *shi* 事 'service (esp. to gods); sacrifice; blessing; performance; function; work'. In the *Zuozhuan* (624, 600, and 526 BCE), *shi* specifies 'sacrifice (in the ancestral temple)'. The *Liji* uses it in the line "to serve the spirits of the departed and God."[87] Another *Liji* passage enigmatically uses *shi* 事 to mean 'serve (the dead/living)': King [Wen], in sacrificing, served the dead as if he were serving the living. He thought of them dead as if he did not wish to live (any longer himself)."[88]

The second, and similar, *Liji* passage also uses *shi* 'serve, service':

> (When the representative of the departed) had made the libation with the [*jia*] cup, or the horn, (the sacrificer) was told (to bow to him) to put him at ease. Anciently, the representative stood when nothing was being done; when anything was being done, he sat. He personated the spirit.[89] The officer of prayer [*zhu* 'invocator'] was the medium of communication between him and the sacrificer.[90]

Legge translates *shi* 事 as "nothing/anything was being done" instead of "service (to the ancestral spirit)" and ignores the two conjunctions *ze* 則 'consequently; subsequently; thereupon; then' and *erhou* 而後 'and then; after that, afterwards'. A more literal translation of 古者尸無事則立有事而后坐也 is, "Anciently, a personator who had not served would consequently stand; one who had served would afterwards sit."

Other texts have similar descriptions. The *Gongyangzhuan* commentary by He Xiu 何休 (129–182 CE) says, "The Xia had standing personators, the Shang [Yin] had sitting personators, and the Zhou had six personators who would make serial toasts." The commentary by the prominent Neo-Confucianist Zhu Xi 朱熹 (1130–1200 CE) reiterates this, "In the ceremonies of the ancients, there was always a standing personator."

The above Chinese textual references to personation are not historical fact. However, they are evidence of an ancient tradition that the personation ceremony originated during the Xia Dynasty (ca. 22nd–18th centuries BCE) when the personator was not an inactive "corpse," but something like a medium who could make contact with the spirits of the dead before he/she would sit down to eat and drink. During the Shang Dynasty — or since the word used is Yin, the late Shang period (ca. 14th–11th centuries BCE) — the personator would sometimes sit down without having made contact with the spirits. However, during the Zhou Dynasty (ca. 11th–3rd centuries BCE), the personation ceremony degenerated into a drunken party with several personators repeatedly making toasts and drinking sacrificial wine.

The Han scholars who compiled the *Liji* venerated ancient rituals from China's "golden age." In light of this prejudice, these passages represent a strong criticism of changes in the personation ceremony. French sinologist Marcel Granet (1884–1940) mentions the above *Liji* context about Zhou personation parties:

It was not long before this archaic custom was criticized by the ritualists. When the sacrifices were offered simultaneously to several ancestors each of whom was represented, the ceremony was found indeed to assume a displeasing likeness to a picnic.[91]

In the late 2nd millennium BCE, personation supposedly was a sacred communion with ancestral spirits, but by the end of the 1st millennium BCE, the ritual had devolved into a drunken revelry.

The *Liji* has three passages in which the Confucian disciple, and exemplar of filial piety, Zengzi 曾子 (ca. 505–436 BCE, cf. the *Liji* on page 371) questions his teacher about the need for personators at ancestral rituals. For instance:

[Zengzi] asked, "Is it necessary that there should be a representative of the dead in sacrifices? Or may he be dispensed with as when the satisfying offerings [*yan* 厭 'enough food, satiated'] are made to the dead?"

Confucius said, "In sacrificing to a full-grown man for whom there have been the funeral rites, there must be such a representative, who should be a grandson; and if the grandson is too young, someone must be employed to carry him in his arms. If there be no grandson, some one of the same surname should be selected for the occasion. In sacrificing to the one who had died prematurely, there are (only) the satisfying offerings, for he was not full-grown. To sacrifice to a full-grown man, for whom there have been the funeral rites without a representative, would be to treat him as if he had died prematurely."[92]

This question attributed to Zengzi shows that people in the Zhou era were beginning to have doubts about personators. While staunch Confucianists were still carrying on the persona-tion tradition, they were dubious about spirit communication.

None of the early sources, like the *Shijing*, mention any rules about who should be a personator, but several later ones, like the *Liji* above, say that ideally, a personator should be a child of the same sex as the ancestor, and preferably either a legitimate grandson or his wife. The *Liji* explains the reason:

A rule of propriety says, "A superior man may carry his grandson in his arms, but not his son." This tells us that a grandson may be the personator of his deceased grandfather (at sacrifices), but a son cannot be so of his father.[93]

When a grandson personated the spirit of his grandfather, it created a reversal of the normal hierarchy within a family; the father would have to worship his own son. Why would a grand-child make the most suitable personator? Granet says the basic reason was a predominance of uterine over agnatic relationships; the grandfather is the closest of the uterine relatives, and thus closer to his grandson than the father is.[94] German sinologist Wolfram Eberhard (1909–1989) explains the Chinese belief that since a soul is small, it is best represented by a child.[95] Jaynes mentions a Greek parallel; the philosopher Iamblichus (ca. 250–ca. 325 CE) says "young and simple persons" make the most suit-able mediums.[96]

The *Yili* uses *shi* 342 times in the meaning (2) of 'personator', more than any other pre-Han text. It gives some highly detailed descriptions of personation ceremonies, for example:

> Then the host descends and washes a goblet. The per-sonator and the aide descend also, and the host, laying the cup in the basket, declines the honor. To this the personator makes a suitable reply. When the washing is finished, they salute one another, and the personator goes up, but not the aide.

> Then the host fills the goblet and pledges the persona-tor. Standing, facing north to the east of the eastern pillar, he sits down, laying down the cup, bows, the per-sonator, to the west of the western pillar, facing north, and bowing in return. Then the host sits, offers of the wine, and drinks. When he has finished off the cup, he bows, the personator bowing in return. He then de-scends and washes the goblet, the personator descend-ing and declining the honor. The host lays the cup in the basket, and making a suitable reply, finishes the washing and goes up, the personator going up also. Then the host fills the goblet, the personator bowing and receiving it. The host returns to his place and bows in reply. Then the personator faces north, sits, and lays

the goblet to the left of the relishes, the personator, aide, and host all going to their mats.[97]

One *Yili* passage specifically mentions female personators, "A man personates a dead man, and a woman a woman. In the latter case, a woman of a different surname is chosen, and as such not one of inferior standing."[98] This euphemistically means that for selecting a female personator, one should avoid the wife of a concubine's grandson. Legge translates *shi* as "personatrix" in a *Liji* description of a wife personating her husband's dead grandmother.[99]

Meaning (3): Corpse-like or Inactive

The next meaning of *shi* is 'corpse-like; stiff' or 'inactive; sedentary; motionless'. In most cases, the connotation of this usage is negative, and it means 'negligent; remiss (esp. in duties)'. This is evident in the literary Chinese expression *shiwei sucan* 尸位素餐 "personator seat/status and vegetarian meals" 'hold a sinecure; be an idler'. However, *shi* can have a positive meaning of 'calm; quiescent'. The *Zhuangzi*, which is full of wordplay, uses *shi* in both alternative connotations of 'corpse-like'. A positive meaning of 'quiet and motionless' is seen in the phrase, "sitting as still as a corpse he will look as majestic as a dragon."[100] In contrast, a negative one of 'negligence in duties' is seen in, "yet here I still am in the seat of honor."[101]

Perhaps the oldest textual occurrence in the 'corpse-like' sense is in a *Shijing* ode that complains, "the good men sit motionless and silent."[102] The exact meaning is ambiguous. Karlgren notes that literally it means,

'The good men act the corpse', play the part of a representative of the dead at a sacrifice, who sits still and silent during the whole ceremony; here then, remain inactive, do nothing to help.[103]

The semantic uncertainty is owing to an overlap between the meanings of *shi*, 'corpse-like' can mean 'personator-like' if it is assumed (against contexts like the *Shijing* above) that a personator is motionless and silent. From a Jaynesian perspective, the 'inactive; corpse-like' personator would be a conscious individual who could no longer hallucinate voices.

The *Lunyu* "Confucian Analects" has one occurrence of *shi* in describing the good traits of Confucius; "In bed, he did not lie like a corpse."[104] Commentators are divided over whether this means 'sleep with the arms and legs sprawled out' or 'sleep facing the north (the land of the dead).'

Shi means 'corpse-like' in two spurious sections of the *Shujing* "Document Classic." The first passage refers to a legendarily incompetent Xia emperor: "[Tai Kang 太康] occupied the throne like a personator of the dead."[105] Legge notes that although *shi* can mean *zhu* 主 'manage; preside over', i.e., meaning (5) below:

> Its proper signification, however, is 'a corpse', and it is often used for the personator of the dead in the funeral ceremonies of antiquity; — see the dict[ionary], which defines it in this application by 神象, 'the image of the spirit'. … [Tai Kang] was but a personator on the throne, no better than a sham sovereign.[106]

The second passage mentions another legendary ruler, sage Emperor Yao 堯 punishing Xi 羲 and Ho 和, two depraved court astronomers, for failure to predict an eclipse; "[Xi] and Ho, however, as if they were mere personators of the dead in their offices, (heard nothing and knew nothing)."[107]

In some early texts, there is vagueness as to whether *shi* means 'corpse-like' or 'personator-like'. Take for example, this *Liji* description of good posture, "If a man be sitting, let him do so as a personator of the deceased."[108]

Meaning (4): Lay Out

Shi's next meaning is defined as *chen* 陳 'lay out; set forth, array; display; arrange'. The semantic connection seems to be a generalization from 'lay out (a corpse)' to 'lay out (in general)'. Karlgren notes that early texts use both *shi* < *ʂjər* (Baxter's *ʰljij*) 尸 'corpse; etc.' and *shi* < *ʂjər* (*ʰljijʔ*) 矢 'arrow' for the meaning of *chen* < *dʒěn* (*drjin*) 陳 'set forth; display'.[109] Some scholars take them to be loan characters, which he rejects on phonological grounds. Karlgren instead postulates there was an Old Chinese word *ʂjər* (*ʰljij*) 'set forth; lay out' that was not represented by a character, and was written with either 尸 or 矢 graphic loans.

Liji commentators gloss *shi* to mean *chen* 'laid out' in two passages making a funereal distinction between 'corpse' terms, between *shi* 尸 'corpse on a couch' and *jiu* 柩 (the "wood radical" and a *jiu* 匛 'long; enduring' phonetic) 'corpse in a coffin'. "(The corpse) on the couch is called [*shi*] (the laid out); when it is put into the coffin, that is called [*jiu*] (being in the long home)."[110]

A *Shijing* ode lamenting that all the men have been called off to war says, "There are mothers who set forth the (sacrificial) dishes."[111] Clearly, this *shi* means neither 'corpse' nor 'personator', but the commentators and translators differ over what it should mean. Karlgren follows Mao's commentary that *shi* means *chen* 'lay out; set forth'. Waley follows *Shijing* commentator Ma Ruichen 馬瑞辰 (1777–1853) that *shi* 尸 means *shi* 失 'lose; lack' (*ʰljit*, not likely as a loan). Legge follows Zhu Xi's gloss that it means *zhu* 主 'manage' (see below), but from the wartime sacrificial context, it probably means 'lay out; set forth'.

The *Zuozhuan* verbally uses *shi* to mean 'lay out a corpse' in an account of executing disloyal ministers, "I have exposed the corpses of three ministers in one morning."[112] It also uses *shi* in the military sense of 'deploy/arrange (troops)'; "King [Wu] of [Chu] made new arrangements for marshalling the army."[113]

Meaning (5): Manage or Ancestral Tablet

The next meaning of *shi* is glossed as *zhu* 主 'manage, preside; spirit tablet, ancestral tablet'. The origins of this common logograph are unclear. The *Shuowen jiezi* gives a seal form of 坣 and says it is a pictograph of a 'wick' above a 'lamp'; thus taking *zhu* 主 to be the primary form of *zhu* 炷 'wick (of a lamp)'. This alleged semantic development was from 'wick' to 'wick-keeper; manager'. Karlgren rejects this etymology for historical reasons: *zhu* 主 'spirit tablet; manage' is attested as 𤕫 on Shang oracle bones, but *zhu* 炷 'wick' was only known from Han times onward. He suggests, "Possibly the graph is a drawing of an ancestral tablet on a stand."[114] Thus, the meaning of 'manage; manager' could have derived from the custom of a sacrificial 'manager; director' being responsible for holding an 'ancestral/spirit tablet'. There are several reasons that support this hypothesis. First, pre-Han texts like the *Zuozhuan*[115] and *Liji*[116] use *zhu* to mean 'ancestral/spirit tablet'. Second, there are early ritual terms such as *shenzhu* 神主 'spirit tablet' and *muzhu* 木主 'wooden spirit tablet'. Third, and most importantly, the *Chuci* uses *shi* 尸 in a parallel sense glossed as *zhu* 主 'ancestral tablet'.

The "Heavenly Questions" 天問 section of the *Chuci* queries twice about the first Zhou king, Wu 武 (r. ca. 1122–1115 BCE), who punished the remnants of the defeated Shang/Yin army. "When Wu set out to kill Yin, why was he so grieved? He went into the battle carrying the 'corpse'. Why was he in such haste?"[117] This usage of *shi* 'corpse' is unclear. The commentary of Wang Yi 王逸 (fl. 120 CE) says it means *zhu* 主, specifically *muzhu* 木主 'wooden spirit tablet', but Zhu Xi's commentary says it means *jiu* 'corpse in a coffin'. Oxford University emeritus fellow David Hawkes justifies his "corpse" translation above by explaining:

> According to some accounts it was the 'spirit tablet' of his dead father [King Wen] which King Wu carried in

his chariot to battle. But I think the poet understood him to have taken the actual corpse, and was surprised that he had not waited to bury it.[118]

Since the "Heavenly Questions" section contains many conundrums and riddles, it seems likely that this *shi* was an intentional *double entendre*, signifying both 'corpse' and/or 'spirit tablet'. A spirit tablet is a symbolic or metaphysical "corpse" because it is a resting place for a soul. Schindler says that, "Of course, it would have been impossible to take the corpse or even a living representative of it into the battle. There can only be a matter about a symbolic representative of the dead."[119]

The precise meaning of this *shi* 'corpse' = *zhu* 'spirit tablet' gloss in the *Chuci* was the subject of a disagreement between German sinologist Eduard Erkes (1891–1958) and Karlgren. Erkes proposed that the *zhu* was a wooden ancestral tablet shaped in the image of the deceased.[120] Karlgren differed with Erkes and argued that the *zhu* tablet was phallic shaped:

He seems to think that the substitution of [*muzhu*] 'wooden tablet' for the corpse (if really a corpse is intended; the word *shi* is ambiguous) proves the [*muzhu*] to have been an image of the corpse, and therefore he translates [*muzhu*] by 'wooden statue'. Nothing could be more arbitrary. The [*muzhu*], wooden ancestral tablet, was the resting place of the ancestor's spirit, once his body was dead and decomposed. In this sense it was a substitute for his body, his spiritual force had entered it, and therefore it was carried into battle, bringing this mental force of his into play on the side of his descendant. But this, of course, proves nothing at all about the shape of the [*muzhu*] or any similarity on its part to the "corpse." Erkes' argument falls to the ground, because the essential link in the chain is missing.[121]

Erkes countered Karlgren by citing other early texts that describe a human-shaped *muzhu*, which he aptly translated as "wooden lord," using the 'lord; master' sense of *zhu*. In particular, the (ca. 2nd–1st centuries BCE) *Shiji* 史記 "Record of History" repeats this same story about King Wu with the word *muzhu* 木主 "He (viz. Wu-Wang) made a wooden image of Wen-Wang and took it with [him] on his carriage into the battle."[122] Erkes suggested:

> … very probably the custom of carrying a [*muzhu*] into battle had developed from an earlier one of taking the body itself, and that therefore the [*muzhu*] was something representing the corpse, i.e., an image of the deceased.[123]

Finally, Erkes compared the use of human-shaped effigies in other Asian cultures, including Lolo, Mosso, and Annamese, "which somewhat recalls the *shi* of ancient China."[124]

The *Shijing* has one ode (or two[125]) in which *shi* is interpreted as *zhu* 'manage; direct'. In 15/3, a "reverent young woman" is preparing sacrificial offerings, and the ode asks, "Who sets them forth?"[126] Karlgren goes against both Mao's and Zhu's commentaries that gloss *shi* here as *zhu* 'manage; preside over (the sacrifice)', and he translates it as *chen* 'set forth (sacrificial dishes)', because the context describes mundane food preparation and not sacred ritual management, and owing to the poetic parallel: "She goes to deposit them" using *dian* 奠 'offer (libations), set forth (offerings)'.

The *Zuozhuan* unambiguously uses *shi* to mean 'manage; preside over'. "There is a saying of the ancients, that 'no one likes to preside at the slaying of an old ox.'"[127] Two early dictionaries try to reconcile *shi* meanings (4) *chen* 'lay out' and (5) *zhu* 'manage'. One *Erya* definition (1A/26) defines *shi* 尸 as *chen* 'lay out' and the next (1A/27) defines it as *zhu* 'manage'. The *Shuowen jiezi* (8/70a) defines *shi* as *chen* 'lay out'; and (8/72b) nebulously defines the graphic variant *shi* 屍 'corpse' as *zhongzhu* 終主 'end-manage'. It explains 屍 as an ideograph combining *shi* 尸 (meaning *zhu* 主 'manage') and *si* 死 'dead' (meaning *zhong* 終 'end; finish'), and folk-etymologizes that when someone 'dies' in a distant land, there is nobody to 'manage' their funeral. Linguistically, it seems more likely that *shi* had two separate but related meanings of 'lay out' and 'manage'.

Meaning (6): Other Senses

The remaining miscellaneous senses of *shi* are derived from its pronunciation and not its semantics. *Shi* is a place name (in Henan); a surname (notably of the Legalist philosopher Shizi 尸子, ca. 390–330 BCE); and a variant of *shi* 鳲 which is used in the names of birds (e.g., *shijiu* 鳲鳩 'cuckoo'). The only early textual occurrence is the *Zuozhuan* usage of *shi* as the toponym.[128]

Diachronic Summary

The word *shi* 尸 has a written history of over 3,000 years, and its usages have changed over time. The diachronic textual semantics of *shi* are important in understanding changes in the personation ceremony. In addition, this summary will show the importance of *shi* personation in corroborating Jaynes's estimate that subjective consciousness originated sometime around 1000 BCE.

The first recorded usages of *shi* are on Shang oracle bones and shells (ca. 14th–11th centuries BCE). Chinese historical linguist Li Xiaoding (1918–1997) states the oracle ⟨⟩ was used as a graphic loan for 'eastern barbarian; foreigner' (viz. *yi* 夷) before it was used to mean 'corpse' (viz. *shi* 尸).[129] Japanese sinologist Shima Kunio (1908–1977) compiled an invaluable concordance of oracle inscriptions, and it catalogs twenty *shi* ⟨⟩ occurrences in three miscellaneous contexts and five recurring phrasal compounds.[130] Three compounds refer to 'barbarians' (in modern characters, *fayi* 伐夷 'attack barbarians', *zhengyi* 征夷 'punish barbarians', and *yifang* 夷方 'barbarian regions'). One, in a context of sacrificing three bulls, seems ambiguous, *jianshi* 見尸 'see the corpse/personator'. The fifth compound 彳亍, which occurs on six inscriptions, likely refers to personators. This oracle graph 彳 is identified with two words, archaic *chan* 辿 'walk quietly; peaceful; name of a sacrifice' and *zhi* 祉 'good luck; blessings; happiness'. Either way, *chanshi* 'peaceful personator' or *zhishi* 'blessed personator',[131] these divinations are the historical terminus for *shi* meaning (1) 'personator of the dead'.

The third table summarizes the semantic occurrences of *shi* 尸 in classical texts, with the caveat of approximate dates for practically all pre-Han texts (as discussed on page 348).

Even within the admitted limitations of textual dating and occasionally ambiguous contexts, there is a general historical development among *shi* occurrences. The more basic meanings of (1) 'corpse', (2) 'personator', and (3) 'corpse-like; inactive' were used during the Western Zhou (ca. 1122–771 BCE). The derived meanings of (4) 'lay out' and (5) 'manage' became more common within Eastern Zhou (771–221 BCE) texts. Chinese classics use *shi* in all of its meanings, with 'personator' and 'corpse' being the most common. The senses of 'lay out' and 'manage' are infrequent, and only obscurely occur in three texts.

The *Shijing* is the most important early text for analyzing the diachronic development of *shi*'s meanings. In terms of Dobson's approximate dating for the *Shijing* sections (page 348), *shi* does not occur in the oldest section, the *Song* "Eulogies" (ca. 11th–10th centuries BCE). It means 'personator' 11 times and perhaps 'corpse-like' once in the *Daya* "Major Elegancies" (ca. 10th–9th centuries BCE). It means 'personator' three times and probably 'lay out' once in the *Xiaoya* "Minor Elegancies" (ca. 9th–8th centuries BCE). *Shi* may mean 'manage' once in the *Guofeng* "Airs of the States" (ca. 8th–7th centuries BCE).

TEXT	CIRCA (Cents. BCE)	OCCURRENCES IN THE MEANING OF:				
		'Corpse'	'Personator'	'Inactive'	'Lay Out'	'Manage'
Yijing	11th–8th	4				
Shijing	11th–7th		14	1	1	1
Shujing	11th–4th		2			
Lunyu	5th			1		
Zuozhuan	5th–3rd	40	1		. 3	5
Zhuangzi	4th–2nd	3	4	4		1
Mengzi	3rd		1			
Chuci	3rd	1				
Liji	4th–1st	26	66	1		
Zhouli	4th–1st	2	12			
Yili	4th–1st	17	342			
TOTALS		93	440	9	4	7

Table 3. Diachronic Textual Occurrences of *Shi* 尸

The differing topics of classical texts tend to skew the semantics of *shi* occurrences. Context generally establishes the meaning of *shi* — in a description of ancestral sacrifice; it would likely mean 'personator'. However, *shi* can be polysemous within a single passage. For instance, a *Zuozhuan* narrative about a double reburial uses *shi* in three meanings of 'personator', 'corpse' (twice), and 'manage'. In the 5th lunar month of 548 BCE, Duke Guang (heir of Duke Xiang "The Accomplisher," r. 572–542 BCE) was murdered by Cui Zhu and improperly buried. Soon afterwards, Cui was executed and buried.[132] Then in the 11th month of 544 BCE, despite being warned of an assassination plot at the autumnal sacrifice, Duke Xiang said:

"Who will dare (to make an attempt on me)?" and with this he went to the temple. Ma Ying was the [尸] personator of the dead [and killed when the conspirators attacked the Duke, who escaped] ... He sought for the [尸] body of [Cui Zhu], intending to take the head off, but could not find it [until he bribed a servant]. In the 12th month ... the people of [Qi] removed duke [Guang] from his grave, and put him in proper grave-clothes into a new coffin in the grand chamber, and in

the (old) coffin they exposed [Cui Zhu]'s [尸] body in
the market place. The people could all still recognize it,
and said, "This is [Cui Zhu]." … [Subsequently, one of
the duke's courtiers quotes *Shijing* (15/3) about sacrificial
offerings being] "placed in the ancestral temple, and
[尸] superintended by the young and elegant ladies."[133]

After hearing the original seminar version of this study, the
late Mantarō J. Hashimoto suggested that the only linguistically
reliable method of comparing changes in *shi* usages would be to
find a syntactic construction that recurs.[134] The closest thing to
such a recurring usage of *shi* involves the word *zai* 載 that either
means 'carry, convey; be loaded with' (cf. *yushi* 'corpse carrier' on
page 363) or is used as a grammatical particle meaning 'also;
and; as well as'. These words co-occur in three early contexts.
First, the *Shijing* (in a ca. 9th century BCE section) has "The good
men sit motionless and silent" and "The august representative of
the dead then rises"; *zai* is a conjunction in both cases while *shi*
means 'corpse-like' and 'personator'. Second, in the *Zuozhuan*
(written around the 5th–3rd centuries BCE, concerning 596 BCE),
"and took the body into the carriage"; *zai* means 'carry' and *shi*
'corpse'. Third, the *Chuci* (3rd century BCE) has "He went into
battle carrying the 'spirit tablet'"; *zai* means 'carry' and *shi*
probably means 'spirit tablet'. These usages are consistent with
the general pattern of semantic developments for *shi* from the
original 'corpse', to 'corpse-like' and 'personator', and then to the
derived meanings such as 'manage' and 'spirit tablet'.

BICAMERAL ASPECTS OF PERSONATION

The Introduction describes Chinese personation as an unsolved puzzle. A "puzzle" both literally, because it was a puzzling
custom, and figuratively, because its diverse pieces have never
been satisfactorily put together. This *shi* conundrum is over

3,000 years old; personation began in the 2nd millennium BCE and it continues symbolically with ancestral tablets in the present day.[135] The pieces in the personation puzzle can be reassembled with a radical hypothesis about the development of consciousness — the breakdown of the bicameral mind. The three parts of this final section will review opinions about how personation began, evaluate it in terms of Jaynes's hypothesis, and suggest some other bicameral possibilities.

Origins of the Personation Ceremony

The genesis of *shi* personation is a long-disputed controversy. French Jesuit scholar Henri Doré (1859–1931) summarizes the four principal opinions put forth by Chinese scholars, whose perspectives are worth quoting at length.[136]

The first opinion is that personation was a bygone superstition. Tang dynasty scholar Du You 杜佑 (735–812 CE) offers the following criticism:

> The ancients employed a personator. This rite deserves censure, and has been abolished by our great Worthies. One vied with the other in practicing it. Now that an era of progress has set in, and these silly customs have disappeared, it is important not to revive them; common sense bids to refrain from them. Some half-baked literati of our days would fain re-establish this ceremony of the personator. This is quite absurd.[137]

The second opinion is that the personator was not the agent of the departed, but merely its symbol. That is, 神象 "The image of the spirit."[138] The Han historian Ban Gu 班固 (32–92 CE) explains:

> The personator is found in the ceremony wherein sacrifice is offered to ancestors, because the soul emitting no perceptible sounds and having no visible form, the loving sentiment of filial piety finds no means of displaying itself, hence a personator has been chosen to whom meats are offered, after which he breaks the bowls, quite rejoiced, as if his own father had eaten plenty. The personator, drinking abundantly, imparts the illusion that it is the soul which is satiated.[139]

This passage sounds as though Ban had personally observed a personation ceremony.

Some Qing Dynasty (1644–1911 CE) scholars held a third opinion, namely, that the personator was the bearer of the ancestral tablet. Doré cites the *Jishuo quanzhen* 集說詮真 "Collected Sayings Explaining Truth," which says, "The filial son chooses a personator to carry the tablet, but not to be the resting place of the soul of the dead person. His intention is therefore manifest."[140] *Shi*'s meaning of 'manage' etymologically relates to 'ancestral tablet'. The *Yuzhou dayiyi* 宇宙大疑議 "Discussion of Universal Great Doubts" says:

> The personator is employed during sacrifices to the dead, in order to carry the ancestral tablet ... hence there is no need of having such a one immediately after death, as the tablet is not yet erected.[141]

In all three opinions, the writers condemn personators as mere representatives or tablet-holders for the dead.

The fourth opinion refutes the others and contends that a personator was temporarily the seat of a dead ancestor's soul, as the neo-Confucianist philosopher Cheng Yichuan 程伊川 (1033–1107 CE) writes:

The ancients, when sacrificing to the dead, employed the personator, because the soul and the vital force of the dead person after being separated from the body, seek an agent of the same nature. Now, men being all of the same kind, the father and the children being all of one family and of the same stock, the soul of the departed person is requested to come and establish its seat in one of them as in an agent.[142]

His eminent follower Zhu Xi 朱熹 concurs:

In ancient times all employed a personator when sacrificing to the dead. Since the descendants continue the life of their ancestors, the personator shares, therefore, in the life of the departed person, and the ancestor's soul descends undoubtedly upon his descendants, and reposes therein to enjoy the sacrifice offered.[143]

All four assumptions quoted by Doré are conceptually valid, but none of them fully explains either why personation began or why it ended.

Bicamerality and Personation

Two unanswered questions remain: Does the bicameral mind hypothesis explicate *shi* personation? and How well does personation fit within general Jaynesian paradigms?

The first question is whether bicamerality can explain Chinese personation of the dead. Several early sources give variations of the same chronicle about the *shi* ceremony. It began during the Xia Dynasty, when personators would communicate on behalf of the dead; continued during the Shang and Western Zhou Dynasties; but was criticized and discontinued after the Eastern Zhou Dynasty when personators were no longer able to speak for the dead. This coincides with Jaynes's 1st millennium BCE timeline for the breakdown of the bicameral mind in other parts of the world.

Based upon how pre-Han texts record changes in the personation ceremony and the semantics of *shi*, here are four hypothetical stages for interpreting *shi* personation as a bicameral practice. First, a bicameral person could have directly hallucinated voices from a *shi* 'corpse; dead body'. Jaynes states:

> According to the theory of the bicameral mind, hallucinations of a person in some authority could continue after death as an everyday matter. And hence the almost universal custom of feeding the corpses after death, and burying them with the appurtenances of life.[144]

Second, after a corpse had decayed, a bicameral individual might still have heard voices from a *shi* 'corpse; effigy' (perhaps a *muzhu* 'wooden spirit tablet'). Third, a borderline bicameral/ conscious person, who rarely or never hallucinated voices, could have relied upon a ceremonial *shi* 'corpse; personator' to transmit them.[145] Fourth, rational people would realize that ancestral spirits were not actually speaking through either personators or effigies. Increasing skepticism and criticism led to the rejection of both practices, which were replaced by wholly symbolic *shi* 'corpse; ancestral/spirit tablet', usually made of wood or stone. Thus, the answer is affirmative; bicamerality aptly explains personation of the dead.

The second question is how *shi* 'corpse' personation corresponds with the framework of bicamerality. It seems consistent with what Jaynes describes as the "General Bicameral Paradigm."

This paradigm has four aspects:

- the *collective cognitive imperative*, or belief system, a culturally agreed-on expectancy or prescription which defines the particular form of a phenomenon and the roles to be acted out with that form;

- an *induction* or formally ritualized procedure whose function is the narrowing of consciousness by focusing attention on a small range of preoccupations;

- the *trance* itself, a response to both the preceding, characterized by a lessening of consciousness or its loss, the diminishing of the analog 'I', or its loss, resulting in a role that is accepted, tolerated, or encouraged by the group; and

- the *archaic authorization* to which the trance is directed or related to, usually a god, but sometimes a person who is accepted by the individual and his culture as an authority over the individual, and who by the collective cognitive imperative is prescribed to be responsible for controlling the trance state.[146]

The *collective cognitive imperative* was the ancient Chinese belief that *shi* personators could ritually contact the dead. *Induction* would include the personation sacrifices and ceremonies. The personator's ensuing *trance* role allegedly resulted in spirit communication.[147] The *archaic authorization* was the deceased ancestor believed to speak through the personator. In ancient Chinese society, parents and grandparents were unquestionably authority figures.

Jaynes also proposes "six oracular terms" for Greece that are comparable to ancient Chinese customs.[148] (1) The "locality" oracle could be the *zong* 宗 'ancestral temple' where bicameral worshipers reportedly had visual and auditory hallucinations. If the *shi* personator, chosen because of ancestry, exemplifies the untrained (2) "prophet" oracle, then the specialized (3) "trained prophet" oracle would be the *zhu* 祝 'invocator; priest; sacrificial officer' or perhaps the *wu* 巫 'shaman, shamaness; spirit medium'.[149] UCLA professor of Chinese archeology and art history Lothar von Falkenhausen thinks the time-honored role of *shi* personators explains why the Chinese ritual texts rarely mention *wu* shamans:

> At ancestral sacrifices, the ancestral spirits descend into individuals designated from among their descendants, the "Impersonators" (*shi* 尸). Occupying their ritual rôle by virtue of their kinship position vis-à-vis the ancestor that is sacrificed to, the Impersonators are not trained religious specialists like the Spirit Mediums. Although it has been speculated that the actions of the *shi* may have originally involved trance and possession, the surviving source materials — none earlier than the Western Zhou period — show them as staid and passive, acting with the utmost demeanor and dignity.[150]

(4) The "possessed" oracle corresponds more with a frenzied *wu* shaman than a serene *shi* personator.[151] Several classical texts (e.g., see the *Shijing* on page 365) mention personators needing to be *tuo* 妥 'put at ease; made comfortable; relaxed', which implies something like anxiety. (5) The "interpreted possessed" oracle would be a *zhu* invocator overseeing a personator; as in the *Liji* (see page 371), "The officer of prayer [*zhu*] was the medium of communication between him [the personator] and the sacrificer."[152] (6) Failures of "erratic" oracles presumably resulted in the end of personation, sometime around the early Han period. Again, the answer is definitely affirmative; *shi* personation is congruous with the overall bicameral hypothesis.

Other Bicameral Possibilities

There are many potential applications of bicamerality for studies of early China. Here are three sinological illustrations — (A) a paleographic example of oracle characters, (B) a hermeneutic one about "two kinds of death," and (C) an archeological example of 12ᵗʰ century BCE bronze masks with enormous eyes.

(A) Several illustrations of possibly bicameral oracle and bronze characters are mentioned above. For instance, the oracle ideograph 秂 for *tian* 天 'sky, heaven; nature; god; emperor' showed a 大 'great, big' person with a divinely large head. The word *zi* 子 'child; first (of 12)' had two series of early characters, one had clear pictographs like 𐀤 and 𐀢 for 'child; infant', and the other had uncanny graphs like 𡿺, 𡿹, and 𡿼 for 'first', which are identified with *shi* personators.

Despite the great potentials for testing the bicameral hypothesis, using paleography in attempts to comprehend ancient mentalities is extremely speculative. Dutch scholar and diplomat Robert H. Van Gulik (1910–1967) says:

> Although the general purport of most bone inscriptions is now understood, the identification of many graphs and their exact connotations are still largely a matter of conjecture. The chief difficulty is that both the bone inscriptions and those found on sacrificial bronzes give by their very nature only a one-sided picture of Yin [Shang] culture. We find ourselves in approximately the same position as a man who in say the year 5000 would try to reconstruct our present Western civilization while having at his disposal only a collection of tombstones from a number of cemeteries now scattered over Europe.[153]

Even if "one-sided," Shang oracle inscriptions are invaluable direct evidence of divination three millennia ago. Archeologists have found more than 100,000 fragments of oracle shells and bones dating from the Later Shang period (ca. 1401– ca. 1122 BCE),[154] but only sporadic evidence of divination from earlier periods. Within the European tombstone parallel, this would correspond to an era when gravestones suddenly became commonplace after millennia of burials without them.

Perhaps the reason the Shang developed plastromancy (divination with turtle plastrons) and scapulimancy (divination with bovid scapulae) was because they stopped hearing their ancestral spirits or gods. Jaynes poses the question: "If hallucinated voices are no longer adequate to the escalating complexities of behavior, how can decisions be made?"[155] He answers: "But a more primitive solution, and one that antedates consciousness as well as paralleling it through history, is that complex of behaviors known as divination."[156]

Divinatory inscriptions can be interpreted as records of ancient Chinese thought. Shang oracle shells and bones reflect mentality on several levels. "Divination" is literally a means of communication with the divine. Keightley explains, "The king was a theocrat who presumably ruled in part by virtue of his extraordinary ability to communicate with the ultrahuman powers."[157] The frequencies and scope of oracle topics shows the Shang royalty had an almost irrational interest in ancestral opinions and interventions. The fact that the Chinese invented characters to document divinations indicates that writing itself had 'divine' associations. The Shang believed that the gods and spirits could read,[158] and reading or writing may have even had some hallucinatory function for the oracles.[159] Using bicamerality to reframe studies of oracle inscriptions could elucidate what the Shang people thought and believed 3,000 years ago.

(B) The Chinese language has two words meaning 'death', common *si* 死 'die, dead, death; rigid, inflexible; to the death, desperately' and euphemistic *wang* 亡 'perish, disappear; flee; lose; dead, deceased; the late … (for relatives and close friends)'.[160] They form the "synonym-compound" *siwang* 死亡 ("die and die") meaning 'die; death; dead' in general.[161] Erkes hypothesizes that the early Chinese believed in two different kinds of 'death', with *si* 'dead' meaning the deceased still had power to influence the living and *wang* 'perished' meaning the body had decayed and the power was gone.[162]

Erkes provides textual validation for his "two kinds of death" proposition. Since the *Zuozhuan* uses *siwang* as a compound meaning 'death', implying that the original distinction had been lost, he sought other texts. The *Daodejing* 道德經 "Classic of the Way and the Power/Virtue" has an obscure line 死而不亡者壽 that he translates "Who dies without perishing is long-lived."[163] *Daodejing* commentaries religiously interpret this line in reference to immortality of spirit, virtue, or words; Daoist life-prolonging practices; or meditations on death.[164] A *Zhouli* list of rituals for the royal ancestral temple includes 以喪禮哀死亡 "with the funerary ritual he mourns over the [*si*] and [*wang*]."[165] This context syntactically confirms that *si* and *wang* were different because of six phrasal repetitions "with X ritual he mourns over Y and Z" (e.g., *xiong* 凶 'bad crops; famines' and *zha* 札 'plagues; epidemics'). Zhu Xi's *Zhouli* commentary explains that *si* refers to a person who recently died and *wang* to a buried corpse. Erkes also cites a later (ca. 2nd century CE) text, the *Da Dai Liji* 大戴禮記 "Elder Dai's Record of Rites." A passage about the legendary Yellow Emperor 黃帝 says, "When he died, the people feared his spirit for a hundred years, when he was buried, they used his instructions for a hundred years." Erkes concludes:

> From this passage it becomes clear that the [*si*] was regarded as being still alive and thereby able to influence the living, whereas the *wang* was completely gone and only remembered by his life and teachings. From this it appears that the distinction between [*si*] and *wang* seems to have been caused by the belief in two souls which the Chinese share with most peoples. In death, the *hun* 魂 'spiritual soul' left the body, whereas the *po* 魄 'bodily soul' remained until the body had dissolved. So the [*si*] seems to mean a dead man who is still in

possession of his enlivening principle and thereby able to act and to exert a certain influence on the living, a "living corpse," whereas the *wang* is one whose body has dissolved together with his *po*. He therefore leads no longer a concrete existence and is regarded as powerless and negligible.[166]

These two Chinese 'soul' words are *hun* 魂 'spiritual/ethereal soul; finer spirit' and *po* 魄 'bodily/corporeal/sentient soul; baser spirit', respectively combining the "ghost radical" 鬼 with *yun* 云 'cloudy; dark' and *bai* 白 'white' phonetics. In Yin-Yang theory, the *po* soul comes at conception and after death remains on earth as a ghost until the corpse decomposes, while the *hun* soul comes at birth and goes to heaven after death.[167] The *siwang* 死亡 ("die and die") 'death' synonym-compound has a parallel in *hunpo* 魂魄 ("soul and soul") meaning 'soul; spirit; psyche; life force' in general. Eberhard explains the Chinese belief that the soul/spirit remains in the body after death:

> It is evident from all we have said so far about the dead that he is not really dead after his death. He is a so-called revenant, a living corpse. The belief in the revenant is alive still today among the simple people, and this is not necessarily a survival of an ancient "pre-animistic" belief. … Thus, until his final death, i.e., some time after physical death, he can have a family life: when an unmarried young man died, he was posthumously married to a girl who also had recently died before.[168]

American sinologist Homer H. Dubs (1892–1969) denounces Erkes's proposal that *si* and *wang* originally referred to two different kinds of "death."[169] He quotes the *Shuowen jiezi* definition of *wang* as *dao* 逃 'flee; disappear', and cites several texts, including a similar phrase in the *Zuozhuan*, 死而不朽

"They died but suffered no decay."[170] He argues that since the *Zuozhuan* is an older text than the *Daodejing* (which is not certain), then *siwang* must have meant 'dead and gone'. However, Erkes rejects Dubs's criticism based on "the widely accepted but entirely erroneous assumption that, the older a text is, the older also are the notions contained in it." He concludes that the dates of the *Zuozhuan* and *Daodejing* are irrelevant because, "What counts is not the age of a text but the age of an idea."[171]

This "two kinds of death" idea can also explain a baffling *Liji* passage about symbolic grave furnishings. Discussing the living and the dead, it quotes Confucius to obscurely distinguish between *zhi* 至 'go to; come to, arrive at; reach to' and *zhi* 致 (with the "strike radical") 'cause, cause to become; bring, bring about, effect; send'.[172] 至死而致死之不仁 "Going to the dead and causing the dead [to come/go], that is not humane":

> In dealing with the dead, if we treat them as if they were entirely dead, that would show a want of affection, and should not be done; or, if we treat them as if they were entirely alive, that would show a want of wisdom, and should not be done.[173]

Karlgren quotes the Han commentary of Zheng Xuan 鄭玄 (127–200 CE) that the first verb *zhi* 至 means *wang* 往 'go to; towards', and believes the second causative *zhi* 致 means 'cause to come, bring to', which he translates verbatim, "(going to:) approaching the dead and (bring them to the dead:) assign them to the dead, only that would be a lack of affection."[174] In a lengthy footnote, Legge cites the commentators' explanations, e.g., "In the offerings put down immediately after death, there is an approach to treating the deceased as if he were still a (living) man," and complains:

We should like to have something still more definite. Evidently the subject was difficult to those editors, versed in all Chinese lore, and not distracted by views from foreign habits and ways of thinking. How much more difficult must it be for a foreigner to place himself 'en rapport' with the thoughts and ways of men, so far removed from him in time and mental training![175]

Compare that to Jaynes:

As soon as we go back to the first written records of man to seek evidence for the presence or absence of a subjective conscious mind, we are immediately beset with innumerable technical problems. The most profound is that of translating writings that may have issued from a mentality utterly different from our own.[176]

If the ancient Chinese mentality dichotomized death between present *si* 'dead' and absent *wang* 'perished', it would explain this enigmatic *Liji* passage and more.

The bicameral hypothesis supports the idea that *si* originally meant the 'recently dead (whose voice was still audible)' as opposed to *wang* 'long dead (whose voice was inaudible)'. Concerning bicamerality among the Incas, Jaynes comments:

... when it was reported by the Conquistadors that these people declared that it is only a long time after death that the individual 'dies', I suggest that the proper interpretation is that it takes this time for the hallucinated voice to fade away.[177]

Similarly, Jaynes mentions attending a lecture by University of California at Berkeley professor emeritus David Keightley on Chinese archaeological findings from the Neolithic period:

The talk was extremely interesting, particularly in his emphasis on double burials, that is, some time after a first burial with pots and other grave goods, etc., the bones were dug up and placed elsewhere without any ceremony. This was fascinating to me, because it is similar to what we know of other cultures, such as in South America, and on the basis of bicameral theory, would mean that the second burial is when the voice of the deceased was no longer heard.[178]

The belief in two kinds of 'death' and 'soul' is culturally widespread. The Hawaiians, for example, contrast metaphysical *'uhane* 'spirit; soul; ghost' and physical *'unihipili* 'spirit of a dead person, believed to remain in bones or hair of the deceased' (cf. *'uhinipili* 'thin; grasshopper-like; flexed position in traditional burials, with bound arm and leg bones').

(C) Chinese archeology will be significant in proving or disproving the bicameral hypothesis. For instance, burial practices during the Eastern Zhou period went against many centuries of tradition and substituted symbolic grave goods (e.g., swords without edges) for actual ones and representative figurines (e.g., terra-cotta servants) for sacrificial victims. Chinese burial customs have been relatively slow to change, and in the absence of external factors, such as the introduction of Buddhism and cremation, rapid modification is remarkable. Although the Eastern Zhou people still believed in an afterlife where ancestral spirits needed food and companionship, they reasoned that a spirit would not resent substituting a straw dog for a real one.[179]

Regarding the archeologically important question of bicameral hallucinatory effigies, Jaynes believes:

A third feature[180] of primitive civilization that I take to be indicative of bicamerality is the enormous numbers and kinds of human effigies and their obvious centrality to ancient life. The first effigies in history were of course the propped-up corpses of chiefs, or the remodeled skulls we have referred to earlier. But thereafter they have an astonishing development. It is difficult to understand their obvious importance to the cultures involved with them apart from the supposition that they were aids in hallucinating voices. But this is far from a simple matter, and quite different principles may be intertwined in the full explanation.[181]

He describes effigial figurines and idols, many with large eyes and open mouths ("eye idols") that he believes helped bicamerals to hear voices.

Large eyes were also a characteristic motif on early Chinese sacrificial bronze vessels. Oxford University professor of Chinese art and archeology Jessica Rawson summarizes the historical changes in Shang bronze styles:

Cumulatively the effect was to develop the patterns from relatively abstract embellishment, in which the principal focus of attention was either a pair of eyes or a single eye, to motifs that were specific and differentiated.[182]

Some Shang sacrificial bronzes with enlarged eyes, perhaps like spirit effigies/tablets, could have originally functioned as bicameral hallucinatory aids.[183]

Figures 1–3 show masked bronze faces with eerily enormous eyes, excavated in 1986 at Sanxingdui 三星堆 ("Three star mounds") in Sichuan.[184] Archeologists found more than 1,000 artifacts of gold, bronze, jade, ivory, and pottery, which radiocarbon dated circa 12th to 11th centuries BCE. These treasures had been ritually disfigured, burned, and buried in two carefully arranged pits (a custom called "fire burial"). This previously unknown bronze culture in southeast China, which was in the kingdom of Shu 蜀 during the Shang Dynasty, had advanced casting technology; for instance, the world's oldest bronze life-size standing human statue (overall height 260 cm.).

Archeologists excavated around 40 bronze heads. At least six originally had attached gold foil masks, and the head in Figure 1 was in the best condition. Its disproportionately large eyes and eyebrows had traces of black paint. Many Sanxingdui masks and heads had paint smears — black on the eyes, pupils, and eyebrows; and vermillion on the lips, nostrils, and ear holes. Jay Xu, Seattle Art Museum curator of Chinese art, suggests this vermillion paint had a ritual function:

> … judging from the points it was applied to, this might not be coloring but something ritually offered for the head to taste, smell, and hear (or something that gave it the power to breathe, hear, and speak).[185]

Figure 1. Sanxingdui Head, Bronze with gold foil, H. 42.5 cm.

These pierced ears, seen on all the heads and masks, presumably held earrings or decorations. Owing to the pointed, cylindrical necks of bronze heads like Figure 1; archeologists suppose they were mounted on pottery or wooden supports, perhaps dressed in clothing.

Figure 2 exemplifies the 20 bronze masks with comparatively human features. Many had openings cut or drilled into the bronze — which was technically more difficult than casting holes. This mask has four square holes on the sides (note the right cheek); the one in Figure 3 has three openings, one on the forehead (probably for a decoration) and two on the sides. Archeologists believe that the bronze masks were adapted with side-holes for a novel method of mounting on a pole or a wooden body. One explanation is that the people at Sanxingdui imported the masks and adapted them for local purposes. Another explanation is that these haunting masks were initially held by personators and later affixed to effigies or spirit tablets.

Figure 3 shows the largest of three zoomorphic masks that combine animal or mythical forms with the angular human features and exaggerated almond-shaped eyes common to the other masks. In the description of Xu:

> Its size and the monstrous pupils of its eyes make this one of the most weirdly supernatural of all the Sanxingdui sculptures. Pointed ears raised alertly may mean the creature's hearing is as acute as its sight.[186]

The motif of large eyes was extremely significant to the ancient culture of Sanxingdui. Pit #2 contained around 100 unattached bronze eyes and eye parts. About 30 were bulb or cylinder fittings that resemble the bulbous eyeballs in Figure 3 (16.5 cm. long, with a middle band). About 70 were one-piece "diamond-shaped fittings" or two- or four-piece "triangular appliqués," with raised centers (some painted with double-circle black eyes and pupils) and small mounting holes. Archeologists suggest these bronze eyes and eyeballs were attached to huge wooden statues, effigies, or perhaps temple architecture.

In terms of the bicameral mind hypothesis, it is feasible that these bulging-eyed, big-eared bronze heads and masks were "eye-idols" designed to induce hallucinations. They made a stunning impression upon the Sanxingdui dig supervisor Chen De'an 陳德安:

> Even the archeologists were taken by surprise. Chen recalls his first reaction to the artifacts in pit #2: "I couldn't believe the way the eyes on that one mask popped out so far from the sockets. The feeling that they were staring at me kind of addled my brain. I had no idea what we were looking at."[187]

Figure 2. Sanxingdui Mask, Bronze, H. 26.6 cm.

Figure 3. Sanxingdui Mask with Protruding Pupils, Bronze, H. 66 cm.

In the original Chinese,[188] this "addled" is *hunhun* 昏昏 'murky, unclear; mentally confused/clouded, semiconscious; absorbed; entranced', which is a word with preconscious resonance.

Liu Yang, curator of Chinese art at the Art Gallery of New South Wales, characterizes these phantasmagoric bronze masks as something that *shi* personators may have worn:

> The ritual origin of masks is an almost world wide phenomenon with varied ritual practices in different cultures and societies. In general, two important classes of masks may be distinguished: those worn by the living and masks of the dead. Although we have no evidence that Sanxingdui masks were made for the deceased, there is little doubt that masks were worn in ritual ceremonies. The dozens of individual heads and several figures in various postures from the two pits provide vivid examples of how the masks worked. Undoubtedly, masked ritual played a vital role in community life of the ancient Sanxingdui inhabitants.
>
> The use of a mask was intended to identify the wearer with the figure he represented. Early Western Zhou ritual texts such as *Liji* recorded an old tradition of using the representative of the deceased (called *shi* 尸, corpse) in a ceremony dedicated to ancestors. The *shi* was generally a close, young relative who wore a costume (possibly including a mask) reproducing the features of the dead person. The *shi* was an impersonator, that is, a person serving as a reminder of the ancestor to whom sacrifice was being offered. During such a ceremony, the impersonator was much more than an actor in a drama. Although the exact meaning may have been different, the group of Sanxingdui masked figures in bronze all have the character of an impersonator. It is likely the masks were used to impersonate and identify

with certain supernatural beings in order to effect some communal good.[189]

It is possible but unverified that Chinese personators wore these hypnotic bronze masks, recursively representing the spirit of a dead ancestor with a mask that represents a face disguised by a mask.

CONCLUSION

This study assembles a variety of data about the word *shi* 尸 'corpse; personator; etc.', personating the dead, and thanatological practices in ancient China. All of them are consistent with the hypothesis of bicamerality, and none contradicts it. Personation does not prove the hypothesis, but it strengthens the possibility that the Xia and Shang Chinese were bicameral, and the Zhou made the transition to rational consciousness.

Critics can argue that Jaynes's bicameral mind is an unprovable or unnecessary conjecture. There are already various non-bicameral explanations for *shi* personation and all of the other Chinese death beliefs and customs. However, without the bicameral hypothesis, at least one explanation has to be proposed for each of them. Proposing many different reasons for corresponding traditions across cultures ignores what Jaynes calls "the entire pattern of the evidence."[190] For example, Dutch sinologist J.J.M. De Groot (1854–1921) notes an interesting parallel between Roman *imagines majorum* 'wax masks of ancestors' and Chinese representations of the dead.[191] The bicameral mind is the simplest explanation with the widest applicability.

Jaynes's bicameral hypothesis is a revolutionary model for the development of consciousness, one that remains open to rectifications. Ancient China will be particularly important in proving or disproving preconscious bicamerality because of the abundance of evidence dating from the very period in which consciousness supposedly began. Jaynes largely based bicamerality on evidence from the Near and Middle East, thus it needs testing against the Far East and elsewhere. His hypothesis opens new potential avenues of research concerning ancient China.[192]

Over many generations, Chinese scholars have failed to comprehend fully mysteries like *shi* personation because they assumed that ancient consciousness was more or less the same as their own, which Jaynes calls the "presentist fallacy."[193] The bicameral mind hypothesis offers a coherent and powerful explanation for many aspects of ancient Chinese culture. Sinologists cannot afford to ignore bicamerality, nor can bicameralists overlook China.

NOTES TO CHAPTER 13

1. Tr. Legge, 1895d, p. 135.
2. I am grateful to Marcel Kuijsten for proposing that I rewrite my 1985 paper on *shi* personation as a contribution for this book honoring Prof. Jaynes. Thanks go to Matthew Hanley and Brian McVeigh for their suggestions and comments. This is dedicated to Terry's and my late parents, James H. Reardon, Jr., Jimmie E. Reardon, Edward R. Carr, and Ruth L. Carr.
3. English translations of Chinese texts are cited from customary versions; all other translations are by the author. Romanization of Chinese is standardized to the toneless Pinyin system, indicated with square brackets in quotations, e.g., substituting "[Zhou]" for "Chou." Chinese characters are given for the first occurrence of a term, or when necessary to distinguish homonyms like *shi* 尸 'corpse' and *shi* 屍 'corpse'. N.B., besides the standard usage of single ' and double " quotation marks to punctuate quoted material, this chapter follows the linguistic convention of using double quotation marks to signify literal meanings and single marks to signify semantic meanings, for instance "from the horse's mouth" means 'on the best authority, from a reliable source' (cf. Chinese *makoutie* 馬口鐵 "horse mouth iron" 'tin plate').
4. For the sake of consistency, "traditional" Chinese dynastic dates are given. The traditional dating for the Zhou defeat of the Shang was 1122 BCE, but as David Keightley says, "At least twenty different dates have now been

proposed for the conquest, ranging from 1122 to 1018 BCE" (Keightley, 1978, p. 171). Recent scholarship dates this dynastic change at around 1054 BCE.

5. Jaynes, 1976.

6. Jaynes (ibid., p. 313) says, "Chinese literature jumps into subjectivity in the teaching of Confucius with little before it."

7. Ibid., pp. 48–66.

8. Ibid., p. 75.

9. Proposals for the origin of the Shang word *di* 帝 'god; divine king; deceased king; sovereign' include the name of an early Shang ruler, the collective name for ancestors, or the name of a sacrifice (viz. *di* 禘 with the "spirit/sacrifice radical").

10. Jaynes, 1986, p. 136.

11. Ong, 1982, p. 30.

12. Jaynes, 1976, p. 165.

13. Ibid., p. 162.

14. Ibid., p. 163.

15. Personal communication dated December 20, 1982.

16. University of Cambridge sinologist Michael Loewe (1993) wrote an excellent introduction to this subject.

17. A lost companion sixth text, the *Yuejing* 樂經 "Music Classic" was unrecoverable.

18. *Yijing* divination is a type of sortilege based upon permutations of three broken/unbroken lines into eight *trigrams* (e.g., ☷ *Kun* 'Earth', ☶ *Gen* 'Mountain', ☵ *Kan* 'Water'), which combine into 64 *hexagrams* with six lines (e.g., 'Earth' over 'Water' forms ䷆ *Shi* 'The Army').

19. Jaynes (1976, p. 242) discusses sortilege. He also describes *Yijing* divination as "a direct heritage from the period just after the breakdown [of the bicameral mind] in China" (p. 440).

20. Dobson, 1968.

21. Unlike all the above Chinese texts that are only approximately datable, the *Shuowen jiezi* is dated with certitude: Xu Shen completed his dictionary in 100 CE, and waited (for political reasons) until September 19, 121 before presenting it to Han Emperor An 安.

22. I highly recommend the readable erudition of John DeFrancis (1984).

23. *Regular characters* were based on the Qin *clerical characters* (隸書), which were developed for calligraphic brush writing.

24. *Shi* 矢 'arrow' in the *Shijing* "Classic of Poetry" illustrates the interpretive difficulties with loans. Besides using *shi* literally meaning 'arrow' (e.g., 220/1); this text also uses 矢 as a loan character for *shi* 誓 'swear; vow; oath' (56/1) and for *shi* 施 'spread out, set forth; extend' (262/6).

25. Electronic copies are available through the Julian Jaynes Society:

www.julianjaynes.org. I will always be grateful to Prof. Jaynes for his counsel and encouragement on my research.

26. Jaynes (1976, p. 68) asks, "[W]hat is the mentality of the earliest writings of mankind?"
27. Carr, 1983.
28. Jaynes (1976, p. 361) claims, "The first poets were gods. Poetry began with the bicameral mind."
29. Ibid., p. 83.
30. 194/1, tr. Karlgren, 1950, p. 140.
31. Carr, 1985a.
32. Carr, 1985b.
33. Early graphs for 示 are taken to depict either a 'sacrificial altar/table' or 'divination stalks'. On oracle inscriptions, *zhu* 'invocator' frequently had a verbal sense of 'to carry out invocations'; see Childs-Johnson, 1995.
34. In the *Yijing*, ☱ *Dui* 兌 "The Joyous/Lake" is one of the eight trigrams, and when doubled forms the hexagram ䷹ *Dui* 兌 "The Joyous/Lake" (58).
35. Carr, 1989.
36. The *Zhouli* (5/31, listing official duties of the *Bingren* 冰人 'iceman') refers to a mortuary ice-basin called the *shipan* 尸槃 'corpse tray' that was only used when an emperor died. Since there is no full English translation of the *Zhouli*, the French version by Edouard Biot (1803–1850) is cited: Biot, tr. 1851, vol. 1, p. 106.
37. Carr, 1996.
38. 47/2a–2b, tr. auth. Compare the translation of Legge, 1885, vol. 27, pp. 210–211.
39. E.g., 3/2a, tr. Legge, 1885, vol. 27, p. 87.
40. This context is about types of ritual goblets. 25/15, tr. Legge, 1885, vol. 28, p. 246.
41. Paper, 1995, pp. 112–114.
42. Writing *shi* 屎 'dung' with *mi* 米 'rice; food' is euphemistic; compare the pictographic oracle *shi*  without rice. Another oryzi-scatological character, *fen* 糞 'dung, excrement; manure; fertilizer' ideographically denotes that which is *yi* 異 'different; separate' from 米 'rice'.
43. A second oracle character 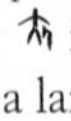 identified with *yi* 'barbarian' shows a smaller person kneeling alongside a larger one with outstretched arms.
44. Xu, 1988, p. 942.
45. Another bronze logograph identified with *yi* 'barbarian; level' is , showing something wrapped around an arrow (or person).
46. Compare the character for *bei* 北 'north; turn ones back' that shows two people back-to-back.
47. Because *jia* 甲 is the first cyclical character in the Ten Heavenly Stems, this amounts to addressing divinations to "Ancestress A," in a cycle of ten divinations.

48. Since many oracle inscriptions are dated, cyclical and calendrical characters have relatively high frequencies of usage. The preeminent Chinese scholar of oracle inscriptions Dong Zuobin 董作賓 (1895–1963) analyzed the epigraphic evolution of cyclical characters across his "Five Periods" of the Later Shang kings (ca. 1401 BCE–ca. 1122 BCE), and found *zi* 子 was written 𠙘 in Periods I–IV and 㞢 in Periods IV–V. See Keightley, 1978, p. 200.

49. Katō, 1970, pp. 944–945.

50. Shirakawa and Kobayashi, 1982, p. 556. Both these Japanese interpretations gloss Chinese *shi* 尸 'personator' with the Japanese word *katashiro* 形代 "shape represent" 'ritual representative of a dead person's spirit; a paper doll in Shinto purification rites'.

51. Xu, 1988, p. 1571.

52. Baxter, 1992.

53. Karlgren, 1957.

54. Zhou, 1970. Note that standard IPA *j* replaces the "yod" *j̯* consonant used by Karlgren and Zhou.

55. Schuessler, 1987.

56. Benedict, 1972.

57. Personal communication dated August 4, 1984.

58. Tr. Wilhelm, 1967, p. 525.

59. Tr. Legge, 1895b, p. 259.

60. Karlgren, 1934. These only differ in aspiration. Compare Baxter's *sjij?* 死 and *hljij* 尸 reconstructions.

61. Tōdō, 1965, pp. 749–753.

62. Compare English *cadaver* < Latin *cadere* 'fall; die' and Greek *ptoma* 'fall; corpse'.

63. Morohashi, 1982, vol. 2, p. 1346.

64. Tr. Wilhelm, 1967, pp. 34–35.

65. Op cit, p. 34.

66. Schindler, 1923.

67. Tr. Legge, 1895e, p. 208. Note that *Zuozhuan* citations are given by the Western calendar rather than Chinese reign title years; thus 631 BCE rather than 28th year of Duke Xi 僖公.

68. 22/21, tr. Legge, 1885, vol. 28, p. 181. Cf. "easy stool" in fn. 79.

69. Paper, 1995, p. 112.

70. Tr. Karlgren, 1950. Since *Shijing* citations are by ode/stanza, translation pages are omitted for the sake of brevity.

71. Tr. Legge, 1895d.

72. Tr. Waley, 1937.

73. Tr. Legge, 1895d, p. 369.

74. All tr. Karlgren, 1950.

75. Karlgren, 1964, no. 1042.
76. Tr. Legge, 1895d, p. 447.
77. Tr. Waley, 1937, p. 215
78. Shirakawa and Kobayashi, 1982, p. 339. Cf. *dui* 兌 'penetrate' as a hexagram in fn. 34.
79. Karglren, 1964, no. 120. *Yanji* 燕几 "easy stool" was the name of a stool used to prop up the feet of a corpse (*Liji* 22/21, tr. Legge, 1885, vol. 28, p. 181, see page 366, cf. fn. 68).
80. The Mao commentary says this *yi* 宜 means 'to be good at one's *shi* 事 'business; sacrifice; service' (cf. *Erya* 1A/28 on page 369).
81. Karlgren, 1964, no. 894.
82. 166/4, tr. Karlgren, 1964.
83. All tr. Karlgren, 1964.
84. 6/1/15, tr. Legge, 1895d, p. 400.
85. 18/14, tr. Legge, 1885, vol. 28, p. 88.
86. 10/25, tr. Legge, 1885, vol. 27, pp. 405–406. This context uses the word *ju* 醵 'pool money (for a feast, etc.)'.
87. 7/9, tr. Legge, 1885, vol. 27, pp. 369–370.
88. 24/6, tr. Legge, 1885, vol. 27, p. 212. Compare what the *Liji* 2/3 says about serving the living and the dead (see page 397). Cf. fn. 173.
89. While Legge translates *shi* as "representative," the verb in 神象也 "He personated the spirit" is *xiang* 象 'delineate; depict; outline; represent; symbolize'. For the *Shujing* (see page 378), Legge more literally translates this phrase as "The image of the spirit." Cf. fns. 106 and 138.
90. 11/69, tr. Legge, 1885, vol. 27, p. 446.
91. Granet, 1930, p. 337.
92. 7/39, tr. Legge, 1885, vol. 27, pp. 337–338.
93. 1/73, tr. Legge, 1885, vol. 27, p. 87.
94. Granet, 1930, pp. 316, 337–338.
95. Eberhard, 1968, p. 338.
96. Jaynes, 1976, pp. 344–345.
97. John Clendinning Steele (1868–?) translated the *Yili* into English. 17/12b-13a. Steele, tr. 1917, pp. 195–196.
98. 14/9b, tr. Steele, tr. 1917, p. 119.
99. 15/26, tr. Legge, 1885, vol. 28, p. 75.
100. 11/15, 14/63. This quotes the translation by English sinologist Angus C. Graham (1919–1991). Tr. Graham, 1981, pp. 212, 214.
101. 1/24, tr. Graham, 1981, p. 45.
102. 254/5, tr. Karlgren, 1950. The following line uses *shi* 屎 'dung' as a loan character for *xi* 'groan', see Table 2.
103. Op cit., p. 214.
104. 10/16, tr. Legge, 1895a, p. 235.

105. 8/1/1, tr. Legge, 1895c, p. 156.
106. Tr. Legge, 1895c, p. 157. Cf. fns. 89 and 138.
107. 9/4/1. Tr. Legge, 1895c, pp. 165–166.
108. 13/50. Tr. Legge 1885, vol. 28, p. 25.
109. Karlgren, 1967, no. 1511.
110. 2/47 and 35/2, tr. Legge 1885, vol. 27, p. 117 and vol. 28, p. 374.
111. 185/3, tr. Karlgren, 1950.
112. 573 BCE, tr. Legge, 1895e, p. 405.
113. 689 BCE, tr. Legge, 1895e, p. 77.
114. Karlgren, 1957, no. 129a.
115. 624 BCE, tr. Legge, 1895e, p. 233.
116. 9/23, tr. Legge, 1885, vol. 27, p. 247.
117. Tr. Hawkes (1959, p. 55). Hawkes (1959) wrote the preeminent English translation of the *Chuci*.
118. Ibid.
119. Schindler, 1923, p. 320.
120. Erkes, 1928.
121. Karlgren, 1930.
122. 4/2b. Tr. Schindler, 1923, p. 320.
123. Erkes, 1931.
124. Ibid.
125. Some commentators take *Shijing* ode 185 (see page 379, cf. fn. 111) to use *shi* meaning *zhu* 'manage; preside over', but it is more likely in the sense of *chen* 'lay out'.
126. Tr. Karlgren, 1950. Cf. the *Zuozhuan* quote on page 384.
127. 573 BCE, tr. Legge, 1895e, p. 405.
128. 515 BCE, tr. Legge, 1895e, p. 717.
129. Li, 1965, p. 2745.
130. Shima, 1971, p. 5.
131. This could grammatically read as a verb-object, 'to calm/bless the personator'.
132. Tr. Legge, 1895e, pp. 514–515.
133. Tr. Legge, 1895e, pp. 542–543. Cf. fn. 126.
134. I am grateful to Hashimoto Sensei's encouragement and suggestions on my first *shi* personation paper presented in Tokyo on June 21, 1984.
135. As a modern indication of how strongly the Chinese believe in ancestral/spirit tablets, the Red Guards systematically destroyed them as part of the "Four Olds" (old ideology, culture, customs, and habits). Internet shoppers can purchase ancestral tablets online. To see what is available, suggested search terms are Chinese *paiwei* 牌位 or *shenzhu* 神主 and Japanese *ihai* 位牌.
136. Doré, 1914, vol. 1, pp. 99–102.

137. Op cit., p. 99.
138. Cf. fns. 89 and 106.
139. Doré, 1914, vol. 1, p. 100.
140. Op cit., p. 101.
141. Ibid.
142. Op cit., pp. 101–102.
143. Op cit., p. 102.
144. Jaynes, 1976, p. 290.
145. The frequent references to inebriation suggest a period when personators could only marginally hear voices, namely, drinking "spirits" to contact 'spirits'.
146. Jaynes, 1976, p. 324.
147. Although we cannot know how personators perceived their speaking in voices of ancestral spirits, Jaynes (1976, p. 91) describes a schizophrenic patient admitting, "They are not at all real voices but merely reproductions of the voices of dead relatives."
148. Jaynes, 1976, pp. 329–330.
149. The difference between (2) "prophet" and (3) "trained prophet" oracles may be graphically fossilized in *xiong* 兄 'elder (brother); invocator' and *zhu* 祝 (with the "spirit/sacrifice radical") 'invocator; priest'.
150. Von Falkenhausen, 1995.
151. There is a dictionary distinction between *wu* 巫 'shamaness' and the rare word *xi* 覡 'shaman'.
152. 11/69, cf. fn. 90.
153. Van Gulik, 1961, p. 4.
154. In analyzing the uneven chronological distribution of divination inscriptions, Keightley (1978, pp. 139–140) notes that "approximately 55 percent of all fragments come from period I" (ca. 1240–ca. 1181 BCE). This could be owing to "an accident of discovery" or other factors, but it remains uncertain "whether divination was indeed more frequent in period I than in all the other periods combined."
155. Jaynes, 1976, p. 236.
156. Ibid. Chinese methods of divining were diverse. The *Shijing*, for example, mentions divination with dreams (e.g., 189, 190, 192), tortoise shells alone (50, 166, 209, 244), shells and milfoil stalks [i.e., *Yijing* sortilege] (58, 169), and grain (196).
157. Keightley, 1978, p. 136.
158. University of Chicago professor and curator emeritus Tsien Tsuen-hsuin (1962, p. 3) wrote an excellent introduction to the history of Chinese writing.
159. Jaynes mentions the right hemisphere as the possible location of bicameral hallucinations, and it apparently has a special role in processing Chinese

characters. See Tzeng, et al. 1978. Recent research suggests both hemispheres are used in reading Chinese.

160. To digress briefly, the early written forms of Chinese *si* 死 'die; death' and *wang* 亡 'lost; gone' are illustrative. The modern character 死 for *si* 'death' combines two uncommon radicals: *e* 歹 'bone fragment; skeletal remains' (also read *dai* 歹 'bad; evil') and *bi* 匕 'person; spoon' (primary form of *bi* 妣 'deceased mother', see Table 1). This same depiction of *si* 'death' is evident in the seal 𣦵 and bronze 𣦶, which show people with bone fragments, perhaps denoting provisional or secondary burial. However, the oracle graph 𣦵 for *si* pictures a corpse in a box/coffin, which may have distinguished interment from exposure burial. The modern character 亡 (or graphic variant 込) for *wang* 'perish; die' derives from enigmatic oracle 𠤎, bronze 𠃊, and seal 亾 graphs. Most scholars take these to show the bent body of a dead 人 'person', placed in something.

161. Chinese has an exceptional category of coordinate compounds involving synonyms, for instance, *genben* 根本 "root and root" 'basic; essential' or *huodong* 活動 "lively and moving" 'active; movable'. See DeFrancis, 1984. pp. 182–183.

162. Erkes, 1952.

163. Erkes, 1952, p. 156.

164. *Daodejing* commentaries, which Erkes mentions, and the Han-era text excavated in 1978 at Mawangdui give a graphic variant of *wang* 忘 (with the "heart radical") 'forget' for *wang* 亡 'perish'. University of Pennsylvania professor of Chinese language and literature Victor H. Mair (1990, p. 100) has a different interpretation: "To die but not be forgotten is longevity." He mentions that the received text has *wang* 'perish' instead of *wang* 'forget', and says, "Here is a good example of the imposition of a religious interpretation on the [*Daodejing*] that was not present in the original. Few commentators have questioned the absurdity and illogicality that result from the unwarranted emendation 'He who dies but does not perish has longevity'" (p. 118).

165. 5/12b, tr. Erkes, 1952, p. 156. Cf. Biot 1851, vol. 1, p. 423.

166. Erkes, 1952, p. 158.

167. For a detailed study, see Brashier, 1996.

168. Eberhard, 1968, p. 337.

169. Dubs, 1952.

170. 548 BCE, tr. Legge, 1895e, p. 507.

171. Erkes, 1954.

172. Compare the modern words *zhisi* 至死 'unto/until death' and *zhisi* 致死 'cause death; lethal, deadly'.

173. 2/3, tr. Legge, 1885, vol. 27, p. 148. Ancient Chinese philosophers debated the proper balance of frugality and extravagance for burials. Riegel (1995,

p. 318) mentions a popular late Zhou saying (cf. fn. 88), "Serve the dead [*si*] as you serve the living, serve those gone [*wang*] as you serve those here."

174. Karlgren, 1971, no. 115.
175. Legge, 1885, vol. 27, p. 148.
176. Jaynes, 1976, p. 68.
177. Op. cit., p. 163.
178. Personal communication dated March 23, 1984.
179. People in China have buried dogs with the dead (frequently in "waist-pits") since Neolithic times. Eberhard (1968, pp. 461–463) discusses reasons dogs accompanied the dead: companionship, protection from demons, and food [*sic*].
180. The first two features are temples as "the houses of the gods" and "the living dead."
181. Jaynes, 1976, p. 165.
182. Rawson, 1980.
183. Early cultures in China had regional differences in constructing spirit tablets. Chinese archeologist and anthropologist Kwang-chih Chang (1931–2001) says archeological evidence shows, "In the north these images were made of clay, and, occasionally, of lead: wooden ones prevailed in the south" (Chang, 1977, p. 366).
184. These pictures come from "Treasures from a Lost Civilization: Ancient Chinese Art from Sichuan," www.seattleartmuseum.org/sichuan/, where they can be seen in color.
185. Xu, 2001, p. 96.
186. Ibid., p. 108.
187. Tsai, 1995.
188. See www.sinorama.com.tw/ch/show_issue.php3?id=199958805104C.TXT &page=1.
189. Liu, 2000.
190. Jaynes, 1976, p. 165. See the quote on page 347.
191. De Groot, 1892–1910, pp. 114, 173.
192. In commenting on the first version of this study, Alexis Rygaloff, professor of sinology at the École des Hautes Études en Sciences Sociales (EHESS) in Paris, noted that in order to test the bicameral hypothesis it will be necessary to use information from all specializations. For example, several early texts (e.g., *Liji* 12/34 and 30/20) say the dead were buried with their heads to the north, associated with Yin and the land of the dead. In fact, many excavated Shang and Zhou graves are oriented to the north, but not all, other orientations are also found.
193. Jaynes, 1986, p. 143.

REFERENCES

Baxter, W.H. 1992. *A Handbook of Old Chinese Phonology*. Berlin: Mouton de Gruyter.

Benedict, P.K. 1972. *Sino-Tibetan: A Conspectus*. J.A. Matisoff (ed.). Cambridge: Cambridge University Press.

Biot, E., tr. 1851. *Le Tcheou-Li: ou Rites des Tcheou*. 3 Vols. Paris: Benjamin Duprat.

Brashier, K.E. 1996. "Han Thanatology and the Division of 'Souls'," *Early China*, 21, 125–158.

Carr, M. 1983. "Sidelights on *Xin* 心 'Heart; Mind' in the *Shijing*." [Abstract in the] *Proceedings of the 31st International Congress of Human Sciences in Asia and North Africa, Tokyo and Kyoto, Aug. 31–Sept. 7, 1983*, 824–825.

Carr, M. 1985a. "Personation of the Dead in Ancient China," *Computational Analyses of Asian and African Languages*, 24, 1–107.

Carr, M. 1985b. "Big Heads in Old Chinese." 18th International Conference on Sino-Tibetan Languages and Linguistics, Bangkok, August 27–29, 1985. [Unpublished]

Carr, M. 1989. "The *ʾKʾôg* 考 'To Dead Father' Hypothesis." *Review of Liberal Arts* (人文研究), 77, 51–117.

Carr, M. 1996. "Ritual Fasts and Spirit Visions in the *Liji*." *Review of Liberal Arts* (人文研究), 91, 99–126.

Chang, K.C. 1977. *The Archeology of Ancient China*. 3rd ed: New Haven: Yale University Press.

Childs-Johnson, E. 1995. "The Ghost Head Mask and Metamorphic Shang Imagery." *Early China*, 20, 79–92.

DeFrancis, J. 1984. *The Chinese Language: Fact and Fantasy*. Honolulu: University of Hawai'i Press.

De Groot, J.J.M. 1892–1910. *The Religious System of China*. 6 Vols. Leiden: E.J. Brill.

Dobson, W.A.C.H. 1968. *The Language of the Book of Songs*. Toronto: Toronto University Press.

Doré, H. 1914. *Researches into Chinese Superstitions*. 15 Vols., Tr. M. Kennelly. Shanghai: Tusewei.

Dubs, H.H. 1952. "A Note to Erkes' Paper." *Asia Major*, 3, 159–161.

Eberhard, W. 1968. *The Local Cultures of South and East China*. Tr. A. Eberhard. Leiden: E.J. Brill.

Erkes, E. 1928. "Idols in Pre-Buddhistic China." *Artibus Asiae*, 5–12.

Erkes, E. 1931. "Some Remarks on Karlgren's 'Fecundity symbols in Ancient China.'" *Bulletin of the Museum of Far Eastern Antiquities*, 3, 63–68.

Erkes, E. 1952. "[*Si er bu wang*] 死而不亡." *Asia Major*, 3, 156–159.

Erkes, E. 1954. "A Note on Dubs's Note in A.M. III, 2." *Asia Major* 4, 149–150.

Graham, A.C., tr. 1981. *Chuang-tzu*. London: George Allen and Unwin.

Granet, M. 1930. *Chinese Civilization*. Oxford: Routledge and Kegan Paul.

Hawkes, D., tr. 1959. *Ch'u Tz'u: The Songs of the South*. Oxford: Clarendon.

Jaynes, J. 1976. *The Origin of Consciousness in the Breakdown of the Bicameral Mind*. Boston: Houghton Mifflin.

Jaynes, J. 1986. "Consciousness and the Voices of the Mind." *Canadian Psychology*, 27, 128–148.

Karlgren, B. 1930 "Some Fecundity Symbols in Ancient China." *Bulletin of the Museum of Far Eastern Antiquities*, 2, 1–67.

Karlgren, B. 1934. "Word Families in Chinese." *Bulletin of the Museum of Far Eastern Antiquities*, 5, 9–120.

Karlgren, B., tr. 1950. *The Book of Odes*. Stockholm: Museum of Far Eastern Antiquities.

Karlgren, B. 1957. *Grammata Serica Recensa*. Stockholm: Museum of Far Eastern Antiquities.

Karlgren, B. 1964. *Glosses on the Book of Odes*. Stockholm: Museum of Far Eastern Antiquities.

Karlgren, B. 1967. *Loan Characters in Pre-Han Texts*. Stockholm: Museum of Far Eastern Antiquities.

Karlgren, B. 1971. *Glosses on the Li Ki*. Stockholm: Museum of Far Eastern Antiquities.

Katō, J. 加藤常賢. 1970. *Kanji no kigen* 漢字の起源 [The Origins of Chinese Characters]. Tokyo: Kadokawa.

Keightley, D. 1978. *The Sources of Shang History*. Berkeley: University of California Press.

Legge, J., tr. 1885. *The Li chi*. 2 Vols. Reprinted in the *Sacred Books of the East*. 1897. Vols. 27–28. Oxford: Oxford University Press.

Legge, J, tr. 1895a. *The Chinese Classics, Vol. I: The Confucian Analects, the Great Learning, and the Doctrine of the Mean*. Oxford: Oxford University Press.

Legge, J, tr. 1895b. *The Chinese Classics, Vol. II: The Works of Mencius*. Oxford: Oxford University Press.

Legge, J, tr. 1895c. *The Chinese Classics, Vol. III: The Shu Ching*. Oxford: Oxford University Press.

Legge, J., tr. 1895d. *The Chinese Classics, Vol. IV: The She King or the Book of Poetry*. Oxford: Oxford University Press.

Legge, J, tr. 1895e. *The Chinese Classics, Vol. V: The Ch'un Ts'eu with the Tso Chuan*. Oxford: Oxford University Press.

Li, X. 李孝定. 1965. *Jiagu wenzi zhishi* 甲骨文字集釋 [Collected Explanations of Shell and Bone Characters]. 8 Vols. Taipei: The Institute of History and Philology.

Liu, Y. 2000. "Behind the Masks: Sanxingdui Bronzes and the Culture of the Ancient Shu." In Y. Liu and E. Capon (eds.). *Masks of Mystery: Ancient*

Chinese Bronzes from Sanxingdui. Sydney: Art Gallery of New South Wales, 23–48.

Loewe, M. 1993. *Early Chinese Texts: A Bibliographical Guide*. Berkeley: The Society for the Study of Early China.

Mair, V.H., tr. 1990. *Tao Te Ching, the Classic Book of Integrity and the Way*. New York: Bantam.

Morohashi, T. 諸橋轍次, et al., (eds.). 1982. *Kōkanwa jiten* 広漢和辞典 [Expanded Chinese-Japanese Dictionary]. 4 vols. Tokyo: Taishukan.

Ong, W. 1982. *Orality and Literacy: The Technologizing of the Word*. London: Methuen.

Paper, J. 1995. *The Spirits are Drunk: Comparative Approaches to Chinese Religion*. Albany: State University of New York Press.

Rawson, J. 1980. *Ancient China: Art and Archeology*. San Francisco: Harper and Row.

Riegel, J. 1995. "Do Not Serve the Dead as You Serve the Living: The *Lüshi chunqiu* Treatises on Moderation in Burial." *Early China*, 20, 301–330.

Schindler, B. 1923. "The Development of the Chinese Conceptions of Supreme Beings." *Asia Major*, 1, 298–352.

Schuessler, A. 1987. *A Dictionary of Early Zhou Chinese*. Honolulu: University of Hawai'i Press.

Shima, K. 島邦男. 1971. *Inkyo bokuji sōrui* 殷墟卜辞綜類 [Concordance of Oracle Writings from the Ruins of Yin], 2nd rev. ed. Tokyo: Hoyu.

Shirakawa, S. 白川静 and H. Kobayashi. 小林博. 1982. *Kanji ruihen* 漢字類偏 [Categorized Chinese Characters]. Tokyo: Mokuji.

Steele, J., tr. 1917. *The I-Li, or Book of Etiquette and Ceremonial*. London: Probsthain.

Tōdō, A. 藤堂明保. 1965. *Kanji gogen jiten* 漢字語源辞典 [Etymological Dictionary of Chinese Characters]. Tokyo: Gakutosha.

Tsai, W.T. 1995. "Riddle from the Ancient Past: The Mysteries of Sanxingdui." *Sinorama Magazine*. Tr. D. Mayer. www.sinorama.com.tw/en/print_issue.php3 ?id=199958805104E.TXT &mag=past.

Tsien, T.H. 1962. *Written on Bamboo and Silk: The Beginnings of Chinese Books and Inscriptions*. Chicago: University of Chicago Press.

Tzeng, O., D. Hung, and L. Garro. 1978. "Reading the Chinese Character: An Information Processing View." *Journal of Chinese Linguistics*, 6, 288–305.

Van Gulik, R.H. 1961. *Sexual Life in Ancient China*. Leiden: E.J. Brill.

Von Falkenhausen, L. 1995. "Reflections on the Political Role of Spirit Mediums in Early China: The *Wu* Officials in the *Zhou li*." *Early China*, 20, 297–300.

Waley, A., tr. 1937. *The Book of Songs*. New York: Random House.

Wilhelm, H., tr. 1967. *The I Ching or Book of Changes*. Tr. C.F. Baynes. Princeton: Princeton University Press.

Xu, J. 2001. "Bronze at Sanxingdui." In R. Bagley (ed.). *Ancient Sichuan: Treasures from a Lost Civilization*. Princeton, NJ: Seattle Art Museum and Princeton University Press. 59–152.

Xu, Z. 徐中舒. (ed.). 1988. *Jiaguwen zidian* 甲骨文字典 [Shell and Bone (i.e., Oracle) Character Dictionary]. Chengdu: Sichuan Cishu.

Zhou, F. 周法高. 1970. "Lun Shanggu yin he *Qieyun* yin 論上古音和切韻音" [On the phonology of Old and Middle Chinese]. *Journal of the Institute of Chinese Studies of the Chinese University of Hong Kong*, 3, 321–457.

INDEX

INDEX

Hope College, 37
Hull, Clark, 25
Hume, David, 286, 294, 324
Humphrey, Nicholas, 108, 307
Hunter College, 37
Husserl, Edmund, 260
Huxley, Aldous, 282
hypergraphia, 124
hypnosis, 5, 7, 34, 53, 196, 205,
    212, 221–224, 229–230, 269,
    272, 310

Iamblichus, 374
idols, 7, 34, 40, 44, 89–91, 131,
    298–301, 337, 339–341, 345,
    398, 401
ili, 90
Iliad, 38–39, 87–88, 90–91, 107,
    114–116, 186, 242, 269–270,
    303, 312, 318, 345, 353
imaginary playmates. *See*
    hallucinations in children
Incas, 40, 331, 337, 396
India, 21, 39, 89, 331
International Society for the
    History of the Behavioral
    Sciences. *See* Cheiron Society
Interpretation of Dreams, The, 8, 55
introspection, vii, 4, 99, 111,
    131–132, 181, 192, 194, 196,
    198, 210, 234, 243, 308, 332
intuition, 111, 113–114,
    163–165, 313, 326, 330

James, William, 53–54, 173, 181,
    195–196, 236
Jaynes, Clara, 15–16, 20, 22
Jaynes, Helen, 15, 19–20, 22–23
Jaynes, Julian, v, vi, xi–xii, xv,
    1–9, 71, 75, 95–96, 98–109,
    111–112, 115–120, 123–125,
    127–132, 141–142, 160–161,

163, 165, 169–174, 176,
180–194, 203–205, 210,
212–213, 215, 221, 233–259,
267–289, 291–293, 297,
303–305, 308–325, 328, 330,
337, 343–347, 353, 366, 374,
381, 385, 388–390, 392,
396–398, 403–404
    actor and playwright, 26, 27
    and Aristotle, 246–258
    childhood influences, 15–18,
        240
    college years, 18–20, 240
    course on consciousness,
        52–56
    graduate school, 24–25
    New England ancestry, 14–15
    prison life, 21–24
Jaynes, Mildred, 22
Jaynes, Rev. Julian Clifford,
    14–17
Jaynes, Robert, 15, 22–23
Jenks, Nina, 14
Jesus. *See* Bible, Jesus
Joan of Arc, 282
Johns Hopkins University, 37
Johnson, David M., 10, 330
Johnson, Marcia, xi
Joly, Henri, 33
Jonestown, 132
Joseph (deaf boy), 99
Julian Jaynes Collection, 236–237
Julian Jaynes Conference on
    Consciousness, v, 4–5, 8
Julian Jaynes Society, xi–xii, 9,
    330
Jung, Carl, 127, 282

ka, 90, 299–301
Kahler, Erich, 55
Kant, Immanuel, 240, 278,
    322–324, 333